Practical Sailor

GUIDE TO

Sailing Gear

GUIDE TO
Sailing
Gear

Take the Guesswork
Out of Gear Buying

edited by Dan Dickison
and the Editors of *Practical Sailor*

THE LYONS PRESS
Guilford, Connecticut
An Imprint of The Globe Pequot Press

The content of this book has been distilled from articles published in *Practical Sailor*. In many cases, the testing methodology and other details have been omitted or condensed to concentrate on the results and recommendations. A more in-depth treatment on most of these topics can be found in the original articles published in the magazine.   —Dan Dickison

A disclaimer about prices: Prices noted in text were accurate at the time the original articles were published in *Practical Sailor* and are provided in this book to convey price ranges as well as relative prives. All prices are subject to change without notice by manufacturers and retailers.

To buy books in quantity for corporate use or incentives, call (800) 962-0973, ext. 4551, or e-mail premiums@GlobePequot.com.

The Lyons Press is an imprint of The Globe Pequot Press.

10 9 8 7 6 5 4 3 2 1

Printed in the United States of America

Project Editor: Jennifer Taber
Designed by Diane Gleba Hall

ISBN-13: 978-1-59228-080-3
ISBN-10: 1-59228-080-3

Library of Congress Cataloging-in-Publication Data is available on file.

Contents

FOREWORD vii
    By Timothy H. Cole

1. SAIL-HANDLING EQUIPMENT AND
DECK HARDWARE I
    Blocks 1
        Snatch Blocks 3
        Ratchet Blocks 5
    Cleats and Clutches 6
        Cam Cleats 6
        Rope Clutches 8
    Shackles 12
    Rigid Boom Vangs 14
    Mainsheet Travelers 16
    Winches 18
        Winch Handles 21
    Backstay Adjusters 24
        Hydraulic Backstay Adjusters 24
    Mainsail Control Systems 24
    Furling Units 27
        Small-Boat Furling Units 27
        Roller-Furling Units—
            What the Experts Say 29
        In-Boom Furling 31
    Running Rigging—An Overview 33
        High-Tech Line 37
        High-Tech Line Shackles 40
    Spinnaker Snuffers 42
    Gear Lifts 44

2. SAILS AND RIGGING 47
    Working Sails—A Comparative Primer 47
        North Sails 48
        Quantum Sailmakers 50
        UK Halsey Sailmakers 51
        Hood Sailmakers 54
        Neil Pryde Sails 55
        Doyle Sails 56
    Discount Sail Options 59
    Turnbuckles 67
    Shroud Terminals, Swaged or Mechanical? 69

3. ONBOARD PLUMBING 71
    Bilge Pumps 71
        Manual Bilge Pumps 71
        Electric Bilge Pumps 72
        Bilge Pump Switches 74
    Marine Toilets 77
        Simple, Portable Heads 79
        Composting Toilets 80

4. ELECTRICAL SYSTEMS 83
    Batteries 83
        12-Volt Wet-Cells 83
        Deep-Cycle AGM Batteries 85
    Battery Chargers 88
    Battery Selector Switches 91
    Battery Boxes and Trays 93
    Electrical Distribution Panels 95

12-Volt Power Boosters 98
Power Inverters 99
Solar Panels 102
Portable Gas Generators 103

5. NAVIGATION AND ELECTRONICS 107

Compasses 107
    Hand-Bearing Compasses 107
    Steering Compasses 110
Barometers 113
Handheld GPS Units 114
Big-Screen Chartplotters 116
Marine Radar Units 118
Marine Radios 121
    Fixed-Mount VHF Radios 121
    Handheld VHF Radios 124
Stand-Alone Depthsounders 125
Nautical Charts 126
    Electronic Charts 126

6. STEERING AND PROPULSION 129

Diesel Mechanics' Forum 129
Picking a Prop 132
Sail-Drive Pros and Cons 134
Shaft Seals 136
Soundproofing Materials 139
Four-Stroke Outboards 142
Trolling Motors 144
Tiller Autopilots 145
Tiller Extensions 147

7. ANCHORING AND DOCKING 151

Anchor Chain 151
Anchors 154
Anchor Rode Kellets 159
Anchor Rodes 161
Chafing Gear 162
Power Windlasses 165
Boat Poles 169

8. SAFETY AND SURVIVAL 171

Jacklines 171
Harness Tethers 172
Safety Harnesses 173
Lifelines 174
Personal Flotation Devices 176
    Type IV Throwable PFDs 176
    Belt-Style Inflatable PFDs 178
    Vest-Style Inflatable PFDs 179
PFDs for Kids 182

Personal Strobe Lights 185
Fire Extinguishers 186
406-MHz EPIRBs 189
Personal Locator Beacons 191
Life Rafts 192
Sea Anchors 201
Onboard Medical Kits 203

9. ONBOARD MAINTENANCE 205

Tool Locker 205
    Marine Tool Kits 205
    Multitools 208
    Sailor's Knives 209
Specialized Tools 211
    Digital Multimeters 211
    Portable Oil Changers 215
Cleaners 216
    Gelcoat Restorers 216
    Nonskid Cleaners 217
    Rust Removers 219
    Bilge Absorbers 221
    Bilge Cleaners 222
Bottom Paint Strippers 225
Paints and Varnishes 227
    Bottom Paints 227
    Topside Paints 231
    Varnishes 233
Nonskid Compounds 236
Teak Treatments 238
Waxes 240
Caulks and Sealants 242
Self-Bonding Tape 246
Corrosion Inhibitors 246

10. CREATURE COMFORTS 251

Deck Gear 251
    Pedestal-Mount Cockpit Tables 251
    Cockpit Seats 254
Galley Amenities 256
    Barbecue Grills 256
    Single-Burner Stoves 258
    Coolers 260
Cabin Comfort 263
    Marine Air-Conditioning 263
    Cabin Fans 269
    Cabin Lights 270

APPENDIX: Contacts and Useful Websites 279
INDEX 287

Foreword

For more than three decades, *Practical Sailor* magazine has illuminated the often murky world of sailboat commissioning, equipping, and general fitting out. This modest color periodical has helped cruising sailors around the world avoid needless expense, and its editors have taken special pride in fostering safety at sea through in-depth articles—from lifeline stanchions to life rafts. *Practical Sailor*'s policy of accepting no commercial advertising has freed its editors and writers from outside influence so they can focus exclusively on the needs of the reader. The editors of *Practical Sailor* have been careful not to abuse this special trust in everything they cover, from bottom paints to cabin fans, marine heads to galley stoves, storm sails to boom vangs indeed every imaginable appurtenance for a cruising sailboat, whether for coastal cruising or offshore passagemaking.

For the first time, *Practical Sailor*'s editors are bringing this wealth of information and expertise to an audience outside its normal subscribership—amalgamating previous content into one volume that covers a remarkable breadth of sailing gear and equipment. In so doing, the editors of *Practical Sailor* are bringing to cruising sailors everywhere their opinionated and unfettered analysis so that sailors can acquire the best available equipment.

Practical Sailor has managed to sustain its remarkable track record of bringing quality information to the sailing public through the extraordinary work and keen interest of a select group of sailors, technicians, writers, editors, and a vast network of cruising sailors around the globe who contribute real-world experiences through the magazine's famous "Mailport" section. Editor Dan Dickison has compiled this body of work into a compact volume that is sure to assist sailors of all experience levels as they confront the often arduous task of equipping a cruising sailboat for both safety and comfort. We wish to thank *Practical Sailor*'s writers and editors for their many years of contributions, and we would also like to thank Lyons Press for collaborating with us in bringing this important information to sailors everywhere.

TIMOTHY H. COLE
Executive Vice President
Belvoir Media Group
Sarasota, Florida
September 2006

P.S. For readers of this book who are interested in learning more about *Practical Sailor,* visit www.practical-sailor.com or call 1-800-424-7887.

CHAPTER 1

Sail-Handling Equipment and Deck Hardware

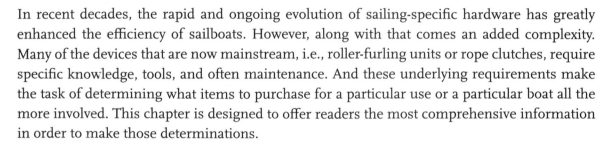

In recent decades, the rapid and ongoing evolution of sailing-specific hardware has greatly enhanced the efficiency of sailboats. However, along with that comes an added complexity. Many of the devices that are now mainstream, i.e., roller-furling units or rope clutches, require specific knowledge, tools, and often maintenance. And these underlying requirements make the task of determining what items to purchase for a particular use or a particular boat all the more involved. This chapter is designed to offer readers the most comprehensive information in order to make those determinations.

When possible, it has always been *Practical Sailor*'s outlook to favor simple, functional products, preferably those with built-in longevity. That's being practical, right? This is because we know firsthand that everything an owner might install aboard her or his boat will regularly be put to the test, so product reliability cannot be overemphasized. Of course, ensuring the best product liability and functionality doesn't always mean spending more money, but often that is the case. When it comes to sail handling, we find that the old adage of "having the proper tool for the job" applies in spades. What follows is a compendium pertaining to some of the most important elements of deck hardware and sail-handling gear.

Blocks

The most universally found piece of mechanical gear on boats is the block. It's what a landlubber calls a pulley, but the seagoing world is so jargon-bound that most marine dictionaries can't stand even to list the word "pulley."

That fascinating 1885 maritime classic, *Paasch's Illustrated Marine Dictionary*, published in Antwerp by Capt. Henry Paasch, lists 58 kinds of blocks. Another reference, *The Visual Encyclopedia of Nautical Terms Under Sail*, assembled in 1978 by a big-name British committee (including Alan Villiers, no less, and G. P. B. Nash, who at the time ran that time-zero place in Greenwich, England), shows—besides garden varieties like fiddle and snatch—cat blocks, cheek blocks, hook blocks, jack blocks, jewel blocks, made blocks, monkey blocks, and ninepin blocks, and that's only halfway through the alphabet.

Essentially, blocks are used to change the direction of a line, or in a tackle (a.k.a. "handy billy"), which is pronounced "tay-kul" by purists, if you please. The tackle can be a single whip, butt, double whip, gun

Small blocks like these are the jacks-of-all-trades on deck and aloft. When compared one to one, the efficiency differences are negligible, but when those differences are multiplied by the number of sheaves in a system, inefficiencies can mount up. If you're only using one or two blocks like this, price should be as much a determinant as efficiency.

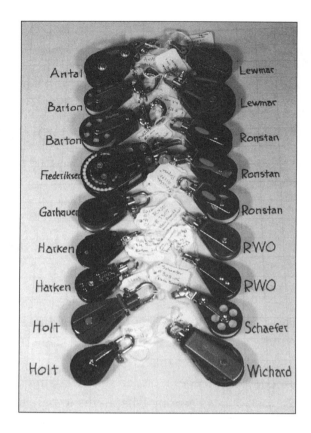

tackle, luff tackle, burton (Spanish or plain), tail jigger, garnet, etc. Blocks, of course, evolved from deadeyes, which are the round or oval disks of hardwood, grooved, with holes for the rig tensioning lines. (Deadeyes were also the precursors of turnbuckles.)

In the early 1990s, a major change in block technology occurred with the development of what *Practical Sailor* called "hollow" blocks. In response to a 1992 *America*'s Cup syndicate request for a high-load, low-weight block with less friction (meaning that smaller, lighter winches could be used), engineers at Harken Yacht Equipment put their computers to work, using finite elemental analysis, and developed the custom *America*'s Cup blocks. Soon smaller versions of these blocks were offered to the rest of us. Harken dubbed these products "Airblocks." Frederiksen responded with "Orbit" blocks, Lewmar used the term "Ocean" blocks, and Garhauer Marine eventually offered "Light" blocks. By substituting a big hub (often part of the cheeks, which eliminates the straps) with lots of bearings for a conventional small axle, and a bushing or a couple of races of plastic or stainless steel ball bearings, the hollow blocks greatly expand the bearing surface, make the block lighter, stronger, more durable, and much cheaper to make. For non-Keynesian progress, how can you beat that? And, a bonus of the hollow block is that the large hole in the middle makes it possible to use webbing (or a lashing) to affix the block in almost any manner.

Another engineering advance in recent years has been the universal head, allowing the block to swivel and automatically align the line, or be fixed. For the manufacturer, the adjustable head cuts down on the number of models, and for the consumer makes it less likely that the block won't work.

Most of the companies catering to the yacht market offer a full range of blocks for pleasure boats of any size. To assess modern blocks, *Practical Sailor* gathered up 40-millimeter blocks (or the nearest equivalents) for close examination and a "loss-to-friction" experiment. The 40-millimeter size was selected because they're small enough, with moderate working loads, to make possible bench testing by hand. The blocks were gathered from the major manufacturers, including (in alphabetical order): Antal Marine of Italy; Barton of England; Frederiksen from Denmark (now part of Ronstan); Garhauer Marine and Harken Yacht Equipment, of the U.S.; Holt Allen and Lewmar, both from the U.K.; Ronstan, the Australian manufacturer; RWO from the U.K. (specializing in small boat blocks); Schaefer Marine, from the U.S.; and the French firm Wichard.

No block is friction-free. The nearest you might come to that would be a finely made block with a line running through it at a very slight angle. That would place very little load on the block. Even then, if you put 10 pounds on the pulling end, you'd get slightly less than 10 pounds at the working end. As the bending angle increases, it's more and more important that the block be as friction-free as possible. The heat that can affect blocks is created not by the sheave but by the line, which must move considerably as the large arc (fibers on the outside curve) travels at a different rate than the small arc (the compressed inner curve).

For light loads, it's generally held that blocks with ball or needle bearings are best. A light load generally would be defined as a load well below the stated safe working load (SWL) of any size of block, big or small. When the load reaches toward the upper limits of any block's SWL, most block manufacturers prefer a solid axle bearing, perhaps with a self-lubricating bushing of some special material mentioned earlier. Fred Cook, the chief executive officer of Schaefer, told us: "The safe working load is what's important. Keep in mind that that is the load at which damage begins . . . material starts to flow. Then comes bending of the cheeks or axle, deformation of the ball bearings, stretching of the shackle, and so forth. Worse, any deformation encourages corrosion. . . . Breaking strength is a useless specification. Don't even think about it. That's why we don't state the breaking strength of our blocks."

So, in our test, we steered clear of even the SWL and sought instead to measure and compare, at loads well below safe working loads, how friction-free each sample might be under typical day-to-day loads. On the test bench, a horizontal four-part tackle was set up, with the fall leading finally through an overhead single block (the block being tested). The 4:1 tackle expanded the output and made it more measurable. The rig might be said to resemble a mainsheet tackle or vang system. At the output or load end, a big Chatillon Iron Clad Model 140 spring scale (which has a 200-pound limit) was interposed between the 4:1 tackle and a heavy shock cord arrangement to dampen the loads. At the pulling (or fall) end, a smaller Chatillon Model IN-50MRP (which has a maximum needle) was attached to the fall. All blocks used had swivel heads to assure fair leads (any side loads severely affect a block's SWL).

Each block was rigged, then "pulled" multiple times. Between all pulls, slack was removed from the tackle, and the scales zeroed. The "pull" numbers for each block were recorded and averaged; the "AVG"

numbers can be regarded as an "efficiency rating." They're simply a ratio of effort expended to work produced. In other words, if the fall were to be pulled to a limit of 30 pounds on the small scale, and a result of 90 pounds were recorded on the big scale, the rating would be 3.00.

▷ **The Bottom Line** For most sailors the differences between these blocks would hardly be noticeable when considered one block at a time, but when you multiply an inefficiency (or an efficiency) by several identical blocks that might be in a system together, the differences would be more pronounced, especially for racing sailors. Even then, however, we suspect that at these loads, no difference would be so significant that it couldn't be negated by a half-hour of trimming practice.

On the question of ball bearings versus plain axles, the 12 blocks with ball and/or needle bearings had a relative efficiency average of 2.47. With the seven plain axle blocks, the average was 2.41. With a 50-pound pull, that would mean loads of 123.5 pounds for the fancy blocks and 120.5 pounds for the plain axle blocks. Perhaps the only observed peculiarity in the ball-bearing/plain-bearing matter was that Lewmar's new "Syncro" plain-bearing block did better than its much-admired block with many bearings. Lewmar may be on to something with this new block.

Our low-pressure efficiency ratings put the Frederiksen block at the top, followed closely by Garhauer and Schaefer, tied for second. Given the negligible differences between all these blocks, if we were in the market, we'd weigh price at least as heavily as efficiency. In that case we'd consider Garhauer a Best Buy, but would also look at the 11 other blocks selling for $20 or under, and decide which would fit best with other deck hardware and systems.

SNATCH BLOCKS

If blocks are the most universally found hardware on sailboats, no item is as ubiquitous as a snatch block. True, these devices can be expensive, and they're not the strongest piece of gear one can use for running rigging, but they can be moved around the boat and used almost anywhere they're needed, which means that they're very versatile. Keep in mind, however, that many manufacturers of snatch blocks recommend against using them for applications in which the line turns more acutely than 135 degrees. Most snatch blocks are not built to withstand the increased loads associated with such applications.

Snatch blocks get fastened with snapshackles, "D" shackles, strops, webbing, bridles, or lashings—to anything that's in a position to facilitate the odd hauling job at hand. Most typically, snatch blocks are attached to the toerail or a padeye to route spinnaker sheets or guys, or to lead a preventer or an alternative sheet for the headsail. When the air is light, they can make a terrible racket banging on the deck. So, they often have rubber, PVC, or urethane covers on the cheeks or, even better, have beckets or simple eyes for attaching strops (led up to a lifeline) to keep them from driving the off-watch berserk.

There are myriad snatch blocks available for multiple applications. *PS* reviewers ultimately favored the models from Garhauer and Antal for their user-friendly and reliable characteristics. Those blocks appear at 4:00 and 5:00 o'clock in this photo.

Attached to the boom bail or a saddle, they can hoist aboard a human or a dinghy. Snatch blocks also can serve in anchoring situations, sometimes positioned to prevent chafe. And, of course, they can change line leads on almost anything.

If the snapshackle used for attachment is a good one, the swinging arm will open easily and have a proper chamfer to actuate the spring-loaded pin and then permit it to lock home. The snapshackle works in concert with a swivel post to keep all leads fair. It works even better with what somebody chose to call a "trunnion," which means that the shackle pin itself is a hinge. (A real trunnion is actually the arrangement of pins on either side of an old-fashioned cannon that permit it to tilt up and down.) The shackle trunnion, combined with a swivel post, becomes a universal joint, precluding the snatch block from

getting caught with its knickers in a twist. It doesn't like loads improperly applied and if abused can fail suddenly and dangerously.

The great appeal of the snatch block is, of course, that it can be put in place, opened to place a bight of line in what is called the "swallow" (the space through which the line runs), and closed. Even a line under some load can be forced into the swallow. There's no need to chase down and reeve the bitter end. But keep in mind that snatch blocks are not generally made to be as strong as regular blocks. There are more moving parts. If you want a snatch block to do a heavyweight job, use a big one. Just always be aware of their safe working loads, as specified by the manufacturer.

Among their other less endearing features is that both the block and the shackle can be difficult or impossible to open when under a load. Even worse, they have been known (usually when shaken, as in violent slatting) to open inadvertently. Also, a snatch block often is said to like only line that makes obtuse angles (more than 90 degrees, less than 180 degrees). However, they often are used as turning blocks or in a block and tackle. If large enough, there's no problem.

Just over five years before this book was published, *PS* tested 11 different snatch block products from (in alphabetical order) Antal, Barton, Garhauer, Harken, Holt-Allen, Lewmar, Nicro, Ronstan, Schaefer, Suncor, and Wichard. Some are light duty; others are rugged. To operate, some require two hands (and strong ones to boot); some are one-handed child's play. Some are cranky, some smooth as silk. To make this evaluation more manageable, we've divided the group into those that are traditional and those that are modern.

▷ **The Bottom Line** All of the old-style snatch blocks—the Bartons, the Lewmars, Nicros, Schaefers—are much more difficult to operate than any of the newer designs. There's nothing wrong with them; it's just that the new ones are better. And among the newer designs, the push-button Harkens, which have been an industry standard for years ago, now seem somewhat complicated, though they're still easy to operate.

The Ronstan Cam Locks are fairly inexpensive and have the virtue of a positive lock, but, in our view, they deserve reworking to clean up a good design. The Barton one-design blocks rate a Best Buy for a very small cruising boat, but check the working loads and keep in mind that they lack beckets. You might need a couple of thump pads. Good-looking and the smoothest of all, the Wichard snatch blocks would be a good choice for a small to medium-sized boat.

Leaving the biggest and best for last, the Garhauers and Antals, both designed with one cheek pivoting on the axle, are outstanding. They are strong, clean designs. Due to their more affordable price and 10-year guarantee, Garhauer's snatch blocks remain our Best Buy. The very refined Antals shine in every other category, but carry glaringly high prices.

RATCHET BLOCKS

Cruising sailors might well ask, why spend any time in this book discussing ratchet blocks, those devices are strictly for racing sailors, right? Wrong. Dan Rondeau, an engineer in charge of technical service and new products at Harken Yacht Equipment, contends that drag-inducing blocks like ratchet blocks offer an important advantage for sail and line handling. "With a ratchet block, when you uncleat a line, you can easily play the line out in full control or haul it in, and that can come in handy, say when you're tailing a heavily loaded control line on a furling drum."

The 75 mm version of Harken's new ratcheting Carbo Blocks. The block in the top of this photograph has a switchable ratchet (the switch is recessed), and the block at the bottom is what Harken calls a Ratchamatic. Its ratcheting mechanism switches on automatically when the load on the line rove over the sheave reaches a predetermined but adjustable limit.

Ratchet blocks would seem to make sense in a number of other applications, particularly for flying spinnakers or gennakers, and for mainsails. When eased through a ratchet block at low load, these lines will run freely, and when hauled in, the ratchet element will require less strength on the part of the user to resist the tension on the line. Shorthanded crews, take note!

Most of the major sailing hardware manufacturers build ratchet blocks, and most claim some proprietary technology. *PS* has yet to conduct a comprehensive test of these products, though we have closely examined those from several manufacturers. Here is a quick review:

Ronstan-Frederiksen's Ultimate Ratchet Blocks are made in 60-, 75-, and 100-millimeter sizes. The cheeks are machined from anodized aluminum and held together with stainless machine screws. The on-off switch, which can be operated under load, is low-profile and sits at the center of the cheek. These blocks carry twin races with Delrin ball bearings. For smaller applications, the company also makes the Smart Ratchet block, which can be adjusted to have the ratchet function engage at various settings. These blocks, which are advertised as the "world's smartest block," have stainless straps reinforcing composite cheeks.

Harken manufactures three different lines of ratchet blocks, beginning with its Hexaratchet blocks, which have eight-sided, solid aluminum sheaves and Delrin bearings. These come in three sizes and

varying configurations (single, double, fiddle, with or without beckets, and with or without cams). More recently, the company introduced its lines of Ratchet and Ratchamatic blocks. The Ratchets have on-off switches and the Ratchamatics have ratchet functions that automatically engage when the line rove around the sheave comes under load. These blocks come in either Harken's patented Carbo construction (fiber-reinforced nylon resin) or hard-coat anodized aluminum bodies and are built in several sizes and configurations. The sheaves on both models are made of eight-sided, hard-coat anodized aluminum.

Both Lewmar's Synchro blocks and its Racing line of blocks are available with ratchet functions. The Snychro blocks are built using composite cheeks, and the anodized aluminum sheaves turn over dual races of Delrin ball bearings. The ratchet switch is recessed in the cheek. The Racing ratchet blocks are similarly constructed; however, the cheeks are fashioned from aluminum. Both models are built in several sizes and configurations.

For smaller boats, Holt Allen builds a line it calls Carbon Auto Ratchets. The concept here is similar to Harken's Ratchamatic and Ronstan's Smart Ratchet. Holt-Allen uses stainless side straps to bear the load with composite cheeks and sheaves.

And finally there's Oxen's self-cleating block, which isn't actually a ratchet, but it can serve a similar function as it allows the user to adjust the line under load. These blocks, which are mostly for smaller boat applications (they aren't built for line larger than $^3/_8$ inch), have perforated stainless cheeks, and these blocks aren't truly ratchets, but they do allow the user to adjust the line and leave it.

Cleats and Clutches

CAM CLEATS

In Ye Olden Days, the belaying was done on square or round pinrails (a.k.a. fife rails) at the base of a mast or at a rail, in which were inserted a flock of belaying pins made of iron, bronze, or wood like teak or lignum vitae. Lines, in very precise patterns, were affixed to the belaying pins, which had only to be withdrawn to free a line. It took some muscle if the line was heavily loaded, less if the pin was properly tallowed.

No one knows when bitts appeared. They probably first came in pairs, until somebody ran an athwartships pin through one.

Horn cleats came along a little later, and an offshoot was the jam cleat. But the most enduring of all the modern line-holding devices is the cam cleat. The cam cleat has persisted because it's a marvelously simple gift from the field of mechanical engineering. We know not who invented the cam, which facilitated eccentric circular movement, but it enjoys an almost perfect application in the cam cleat. And cam cleats are useful in many applications—halyards, sheets, guys, lifts, travelers, vangs—almost any place where a control line must be frequently adjusted.

The cam cleat made its debut about halfway through the last century. Used primarily in those early days on one-design racing boats like Thistles, Lightnings, Flying Scots, Snipes, and all of the ever-changing Olympic-class boats, the early versions frequently slipped and the too-sharp cam teeth chewed voraciously on any line. Improvements followed steadily. Today, cruising boat owners, shorthanded or fully crewed, use them for all sorts of purposes, and of course they're standard for a myriad of small control lines on racing boats.

The field of cam cleats is somewhat dominated by Harken, Ronstan, and Schaefer, but also in the race are Barton, Holt-Allen, and RWO. Lewmar makes

The cam cleat, top row center, occupies a significant position in the evolutionary progression of line-holding devices.

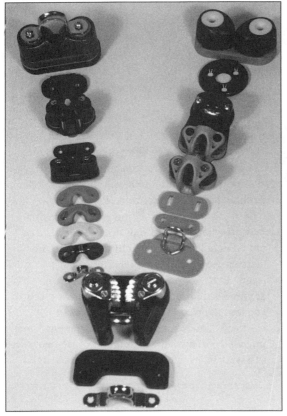

Cam cleats are manufactured from a variety of materials in various sizes and can be coupled with numerous optional components like angular mounting pads, fairleads, and eye straps.

At its simplest, the cam cleat (like this early Barton model) uses two spring-loaded discs with teeth molded on their exteriors to restrict the movement of line.

a limited range. The Servo, a clever German cleat, is not often seen in the U.S.; a Servo cleat called a "Spring" is used on some of the new Wichard sailing hardware.

In an early (1992) test of 16 cam cleats, *PS* learned that there's no point in testing the breaking strength of these devices. In that test, we discovered that the best cleats easily withstood a 1,000-pound linear pull, without slipping. That's far beyond what will happen on your boat—or what ought to happen, unless you're harboring a fearless and housebroken gorilla. An important part of our more recent tests include observations regarding the ease of operation—both securing and freeing the line.

The cam cleats that worked toward the top of the test procedures (those that held 1,000 pounds and were easiest to operate) were the Harken Cam-Matic 150, a big Holt-Allen, Ronstan's RF 5010, a big stainless steel Schaefer, and the Nash Trigger Cleat. Ronstan's then-new C-Cleats earned Best Buy desig-

nations. Other makers represented were Nicro, Servo, Nashmarine, Barton, RWO, Saylor, and Tuphblox.

With the explosion of line-holding devices—cams, clams, lance cleats, stoppers, V-cleats, rope clutches, etc.—*PS*, using its famed Doomsday Chafing Machine, undertook in 1997 to test them all for line abrasion. Obtained for that test were new samples of 11 cam cleats from the 1992 tests. The line used was New England Rope's popular Sta-Set.

The 1,000-cycle test indicated that the British-made Clamcleats and Ronstan's then-new V-Cleat created less line wear than cam cleats. The best cam cleats were Harken's then-new Carbo-Cam and Ronstan's C-Cleat.

Since those tests, cam cleats are now offered not only in metal versions, but also made from powerful plastics. The relatively new horses in the race include Barton, Holt-Allen, RWO, and Spinlock. The latter gave up cam cleats in 1999 and introduced its PX Powercleat. The PX can be released under heavy tension by lifting up on the line. Harken's Trigger Cleat is similar, but it releases with a downward pull.

▷ **The Bottom Line** Our tests indicated that the differences between most of these products are not of a magnitude that should deter anyone from selecting any cleat that suits their purpose, space, and wallet. However, the latest round of 1,000-cycle tests give the highest marks, for the least abrasion, to Harken's Carbo-Cam, Ronstan's C-Cleat, Spinlock's

SCHAEFER'S UNIVERSAL DECK MOUNT CLEAT

Among sailing hardware manufacturers, Harken's products may be the most innovative. Antal's may be more elegant. Garhauer's may be the most robust. And Lewmar and Ronstan may be quicker to take advantage of composite materials. But Schaefer Marine has a sound blend of all such qualities—and it shows in the company's "Universal Deck Mount Cleat."

The most interesting facet of this new product is the basic deck fitting, which is a low-profile, stainless steel casting. It requires in the deck a 1¾-inch (45 mm) hole, which must be clear of any obstructions underneath (to permit the installation of the ⅛-inch-thick backing plate). The fitting should be, of course, positioned only where it can withstand the loads that may be applied. After proper bedding, the fitting is intended to be secured with four ⁵⁄₁₆-inch machine screws, flat or oval head, which are not supplied because their length will be determined by the particular deck thickness where they're mounted.

The deck fitting is a somewhat complicated casting. The receptacle hole is threaded at the bottom; the upper portion of the hole has a four-dog twist lock. Once in place, this deck fitting accepts the following:

1. A sturdy cleat (with a four-dog base) that can be mounted quickly and easily by placing it in the hole, matching up the dogs, and, after lifting two small levers that raise two spring-loaded detent pins, applying a quarter turn, which locks it in place and engages the pins.
2. A Schaefer Series 8 stand-up block that mounts in the threaded portion of the deck fitting. (An O-ring serves as a washer.)

PX Powercleat, and RWO's new Carbocleat, with its shallow cams and "progressive" teeth.

So far, there's nothing quite so handy as a cam cleat for tweaking a moderately loaded line with minimum effort. But remember—just as the old-time sailor's feet were at risk when he pulled the belaying pin, one's fingers can be in danger when snapping a taut line out of a cam cleat, especially one that has an integral fairlead. Match the cleat to the anticipated load, and make sure you have a mechanical means to relieve that load when it goes over your muscular threshold.

ROPE CLUTCHES

A book could be written about the ways sailors have struggled with the bitter end of a rope. Many are the devices seamen have cobbled together to control and belay the ends of the lines on board. Over the years, that struggle has evolved from basic bollards to belaying pins to cleats and now rope clutches.

These devices, introduced only a couple of decades ago, represent an interesting development. A clutch not only belays the bitter end of the line and makes it easy to trim or ease; by being rove semi-permanently, it keeps the line accessible with hardly the need to look at it. However, because it's somewhat difficult to thread a line through most of these clutches, you'll not want to do it often, meaning that when you're rigged for sailing, the lines will remain in their assigned clutches.

Aboard a boat, there are almost as many uses for clutches as there are control lines. In our most recent test of rope clutches (early 2006), we selected five of the most popular clutches from four makers. For easy assimilation of the results, small models for ⁵⁄₁₆-inch (8 mm) line were chosen. Using strength as the only consideration and ignoring the fact that ½-inch (12.5 mm) line is much easier on the hands, the ⁵⁄₁₆-inch line probably covers most cruising sailor's needs.

When choosing a clutch for a given task, it's best to select a unit with an upper rope range the size of

3. A deck eye (a.k.a. screw eye) that threads into place. It has an O-ring, as well.

If the deck plate is to be left idle, a threaded nylon plug (furnished, but you might want to buy some spares) will protect the threads in the cavity. Despite the nylon plug, one suspects that the fitting's cavity will need to be cleaned occasionally to avoid damage.

We checked around, and the only similar products we could locate are from Harken Yacht Equipment and Antal Marine Equipment. Both Harken's custom Removable Padeye Base and Antal's Screwed Eyebolt can have either a padeye or a stand-up block screwed into them. The base from Harken is novel in that the padeye is designed to swivel so

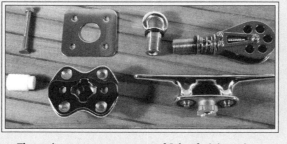

The various component parts of Schaefer's ingenious Universal Deck Mount enable this device to serve as a mounting base for either a cleat, a block, or a padeye. None of the parts are inexpensive, but collectively it is a versatile product.

that it lines up with the greatest load. Both are similar to Schaefer's Universal Deck Mount, but neither company has yet fashioned their product to accept a cleat.

It's important to note that both Harken and Antal have resolved the problem of moisture or dirt collecting in the threaded recess in their bases by way of permanent nylon inserts that screw further into the threaded recess when whichever fixture is screwed in above them, but also back out to be nearly flush with the top of the base when that item is removed. This is a clever solution that isn't present on the Schaefer product, but the Universal Deck Mount still rules this domain due to its inclusion of a cleat.

the line to be belayed. That provides the least slippage and best holding, even though it might not be the best for line abrasion. Within a maker's line of clutches, there usually are several different designs. Testing them all would have been a complicated endeavor, so we took the easy way out and kept our selections limited.

This *PS* test aimed to evaluate three factors: slippage, ease of bleeding, and line abrasion. Most of the rope clutches in our test are built around a cam, one of the engineering world's most amazing tools. These simple, powerful gadgets can be shaped to do all sorts of intricate tricks. In a rope clutch, a cam is rotated against a base plate to squeeze and hold a line. In the course of rope clutch development, the cam was given teeth, and that was the problem with the early ones. They abraded line very badly. Then followed nearly endless tinkering with the cam teeth. The base plates on which the cams squashed the line evolved, too, from just smooth, to scored, knurled, or serrated (more teeth

and more abrasion), then shaped, all in an effort to increase holding power and reduce abrasion. Along the way, a few makers eschewed the cam and tried two plates, forced together by wedges, but that approach got rather complicated. Spinlock worked it out best and still uses it on its monster clutches. For small clutches, all but one maker—Lewmar—stuck with the simple cam. We tested four cam-type clutches—all made outside the U.S.—and one non-cam clutch.

Two of the tested cam clutches are by Antal Marine. One Antal clutch is the new Cam 611, which has a steel-reinforced resin case, an aluminum base, a simple bronze cam mechanism, and stainless, self-aligning bushings. The Cam 611 is said to cover a rope range of 1/4 to 7/16 inches (6 to 11 mm), a slightly unusual stretch for any clutch. The other Antal, the V-Grip 12, has a rope range of 3/8 to 1/2 inches (10 to 14 mm). It was included in the testing field not only to have one of the company's V-Grips (which has a toothed cam cast in a "V" shape), but to deliberately

SPINLOCK PX POWER CLEAT

Perhaps nothing on boats has developed as steadily and soundly as line-holding devices—cams, clams, jams, clutches, stoppers, and plain old horned cleats. Back in early 2000, Spinlock changed tacks and introduced an innovative product for line retention—the PX Power Cleat.

Spinlock makes this product largely of carbon fiber, with two stainless axles, three springs, and two ring-like inserts to reduce wear from rope abrasion. Using a single serrated cam against a curved serrated base (which gives it a large gripping surface), the PX has slanted ridges on the movable, hinged housing that, when lifted up by the line, act to move small wheels on the ends of the cam axle and swivel the cam up and away from the line. When the line is lowered, the spring forces the cam back down to grasp the line. Spinlock calls the cam mechanism "Rolacam" and has applied for patents. It is ingenious engineering utilizing some interesting geometry.

How well does it work? We mounted one of each size and

The PX Powercleat from Spinlock is a simple but effective device that is sold in two sizes (for 3 to 8 millimeter line and for 8 to 12 millimeter line).

jerked them around unmercifully over several weeks, but could not induce a malfunction of any kind. As stated by the warning on the package (which doubles as a drilling template), you don't want to have your fingers close to the PX when you lift up. This is true of any device holding a line under considerable tension.

The PX comes in two sizes—for 4–6-millimeter ($^5\!/_{32}$ to ¼ inch) line and 6–11-millimeter (¼ to $^7\!/_{16}$ inch) line. The small version has a safe working load of 140 kilograms (about 300 pounds) and a breaking strength of 280 kilograms (about 600 pounds). The large version goes 200 kilograms/440 pounds and 400 kilograms/880 pounds. The strengths are roughly equal to Harken cams and Ronstan C-Cleats, and the products are attractively priced. The PX Power Cleats are available in singles and doubles, with optional wedges, adapters for block arrangements, and, for those who like color-coding, have easily installed inserts in red, yellow, and blue. The cam, if it wears, can be replaced easily.

check on the slippage and holding of $^5\!/_{16}$-inch line in a clutch really meant for larger line.

The third cam clutch we tested is made by Easylock, a Swedish company whose clutches are marketed by Scanvik in the U.S. Easylock once dominated the clutch business. It still claims, "Easylocks have been used by more yachtsmen than any other rope clutch." The first-ever model—the Easylock I—is still in production. Its larger models, recently tweaked to better deal with modern lines, are the

Mini, Midi, and Maxi. For the tests, *PS* selected the Midi.

And the fourth cam clutch is by Spinlock, the 30-year-old British company that boasts unabashedly of its leadership in "rope control." Spinlock makes a horde of cleats, jammers, and what it calls "line parkers," big and small, upside-down, and sideways. A favorite with racing sailors, Spinlock clutches can be repaired quickly and easily. The problem is that even though called they're "clutches," Spinlocks cannot be

Rope clutches like Spinlock's XAS represent the most advanced form of line-holding device. This particular model exhibited the tightest grip in recent *Practical Sailor* tests, but it must be used in concert with a winch for easing the line gradually.

eased under load. The company warns that you must take a turn or two on a winch before you release the clutch handle. Despite failing to meet our exact definition of a clutch, Spinlock's XAS, which has an amazing rope range of ⁵⁄₃₂ to ½ inch (3.9 to 12.5 mm), is included here.

We omitted any clutches from Garhauer Marine, because the company is currently developing a new product. Both Ronstan and a French company called Francespar also make rope clutches, but each declined having their products tested against more recent designs.

The only non-cam clutch we tested was the Lewmar Superlock D1, which was invented in 1991. The D1 we tested this time around had a rope range of ¼ inch to ⁵⁄₁₆ inch (6 to 8 mm). The Superlock is Lewmar's solution to the vexing problem of finding a way to release a line under load without putting the line on a winch to relieve the strain on the cam.

Lewmar's Superlock tore up the pea patch with a new idea for a rope clutch. Like nothing else in the engineers' arsenal, the non-cam clutch has a series of in-line, parallel rings hinged at the base (see the accompanying picture). A line is run through the rings and then the rings are tilted with a single lever connecting them. When tilted, the rings force the line to snake through them, creating friction to hold the line securely. When the rings are allowed to resume

their former configuration, the line straightens and can be eased, which can be done without alarm if the lever is released gradually. Because the rings are smooth, there's little abrasion. Lewmar makes two models—the D1 (small) and D2 (large), which was re-engineered last year.

▷ **The Bottom Line** Equal to its company's claims, the clutch with best holding power with all four types of line employed in this test was the Spinlock. If it's a deadly grip you need, Spinlock is the ticket. However, like the Antal and Easylock, it cannot be eased under load. As mentioned earlier, you must take up the load on a winch before releasing or adjusting the line. Peculiarly, the small Antal, the Cam 611, eases line well, but only with the Warpspeed line. It was no surprise that the cam-type clutches did more damage to the ropes than did the Lewmar. The wear produced by the 25 "passes" used in this test were not substantial enough to show photographically. However, we noted in the cycle when broken filaments first appeared. At the end, differences were easily detected.

Which is the best overall clutch? It's like picking the best-ever guitar player. Was it Django Reinhardt, Barney Kessel, Andres Segovia, or Chet Atkins? Reinhardt was a maimed-hand phenomenon. For jazz, Kessel has no peer. The classicist Segovia sounded like there were three expert players going at it. But

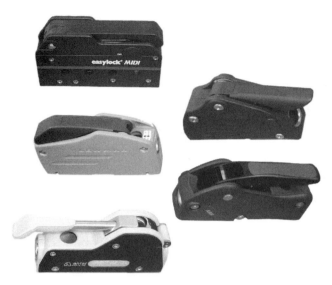

Five different styles of line clutch. They are (clockwise from bottom left) Antal's Grip 12, Lewmar's Superlock D1, Easylock's Midi, Antal's Cam 611, and Spinlock's XAS. The Lewmar product is the only non-cam clutch in this group. It relies on a series of in-line parallel rings to restrict the line. These cause little abrasion without sacrificing holding power.

the one who could do the best with most of it was Atkins, who unfortunately is remembered primarily as a country music player. Because it combined good holding, can be eased gradually, and showed no wear on any line (even under a magnifying glass), the Lewmar is *PS*'s Best Choice—and in a rare convergence of price and performance, it is also the least expensive.

Shackles

The basic "D" shackle hasn't changed much in the last century. It now comes in dozens of varieties, including the bow shackle, which is just a "D" with a bloated head radius to accept anchoring gear. Of course, the clevis pin now has threads on it that fit into those tapped into one end of the shackle, and many shackles feature captivated clevis pins so they can't unthread themselves. But perhaps the most noteworthy innovation has been the snapshackle,

which may have been invented because skippers grew weary of watching shackles (or their pins) bounce off the deck and over the side. And now, there are at least a half dozen varieties of snapshackles available.

We gathered up a lot of shackles in various sizes for this report. All are metal, except for the British-made, molded Delrin "Nab Shackles." These are made in two sizes, for $^3/_{16}$-inch or $^5/_{16}$-inch line. They're for low-load applications like attaching light-air spinnaker sheets to the sail's clews.

For the metal shackles, *PS* did no testing to verify the manufacturers' claims about strength. Even though modern line often is far more powerful than the hardware to which it is conjoined, shackles don't often break, even the extremely light stamped shackles. They'll usually bend and distort first. All the shackles we tested were closely examined for fit and finish, ease of use, susceptibility to accidental opening, as well as price and weight. (Due to the vagaries of time, prices have been left out of this book.)

In the U.S., the big-money players in regular shackles are Schaefer Marine, Wichard, Ronstan, and Suncor. Seen less often are shackles offered by, among others, RWO, Lewmar, and Barton (all English companies), Plastimo (a French manufacturer with global reach), and Harken, as well as the "Anja" shackles (distributed in the U.S. by Euro Marine Trading) and others imported from the Far East (like the Sea-Dog Line). Very light duty shackles (for one-design sailors) are a specialty of another U.S. company called Race-Lite.

Ordinary shackles are not expensive, and comparing prices by characteristics is a bit difficult. Consider, for instance, the matter of strength, which is the most important selection factor. Schaefer uses "safe working load." Suncor uses "working load limit," and Wichard and Ronstan use "breaking strength." We prefer the way Schaefer and Suncor set their limits, but in any case we have no reason to doubt the engineering statements of any of these manufacturers. No manufacturer wants to face the loss of reputation and, quite possibly, litigation that might follow a failure. Thus, shackles tend to be overengineered across the board.

For snapshackles, Gibb (British), Ronstan (Australia), Sparcraft and Wichard (both French), and Schaefer and Tylaska (representing the U.S.) are the heavies in the game. In the smaller sizes, Ronstan has a good and very reasonably priced line of standard snapshackles, plus its uniquely articulated trunnion shackles, which tend necessarily to be on the heavy side. However, the very strong Wichard shackles and the very soundly made Schaefers seem to dominate.

For big-boat applications, the snapshackle roost was ruled for years by Sparcraft and Gibb, both in the medium-sized pin-lock versions (Sparcraft's Presslock was "it") and in the big trigger-release models. Sparcraft and Gibb were the best on the market . . . and they're still very serviceable. However, both makes tend to appear indifferently made, especially when compared with the well-engineered shackles being produced by Wichard and Tylaska.

Introduced several years ago, Wichard's "Quick Release," which opens with a tug on a lanyard, is outstanding. Wichard also offers the only forged trigger-operated shackle. Made in three sizes, it appears to be—size for size—the strongest trigger-release snapshackle made.

But most big-boat owners will profess that Tylaska shackles are the ultimate. Tylaska J-Locks are sleek, beautifully made, easy to use, but also expensive.

They have keyway-fitted double-locking pins (another patent) that are guaranteed not to flog open. They're made in three sizes.

All Tylaska's snapshackles are trigger-operated, and come in five sizes, with standard or large bails. To get the precise shape needed, Tylaska uses castings, which generally are inferior in either strength or precision to forgings or machined parts. So, because it's always possible to get a flaw in a casting, every piece is proof-tested to half of its rated breaking strength before going out the door.

▷ **The Bottom Line** Selecting "D" shackles is like voting in Florida—confusing enough to dimple your chad. There's a clear choice between manufacturers like Schaefer, Wichard, Ronstan, and Suncor, but it's often a strength-versus-price decision. (Hayn Marine of Rocky Hill, Connecticut, also manufactures several styles of shackle, but this company doesn't sell directly to individual boat owners.) Suncor is making some fine hardware at prices that come close to matching those of Ronstan. And Schaefer's shackles are good examples of this old company's very reliable products. However, in the final run-through, the strength and fine corrosion-fighting finish on Wichard's forged shackles, plus their smooth, snag-free captive

There are literally too many kinds of shackles manufactured to list in any one location. The basic D-shackle hasn't changed much in the past century, but innovations have occurred elsewhere, particularly in snap shackles, like those seen in the center of the photo.

Manufacturer	Model	Price*	Type	Weight	Instructions	Lines & Blocks
Forespar 800/266-8820 www.forespar.com	Yacht Rod (Medium) ✔	$873	Spring	11 lbs.	Good	Yes (w/cam cleat)
Garhauer 909/985-9993 www.garhauermarine.com	RV20-1-SL $ RV20-1 AL ✔	$374 $429	Spring	12 lbs.	Fair	Yes
Hall 401/253-4858 www.hallspars.com	QuikVang (B 18) ✔	$1180	Spring	11 lbs.	Excellent	Yes (w/cam cleat)
Marine Products Engineering 800/833-0008	Vang Master (M4) ★	$1100	Pneumatic Piston	7 lbs.	Excellent	Yes (w/cam cleat)
Selden 843/760-6278 www.seldenmast.com	Rodkicker 20	$685 (without tackle)	Gas Piston	10 lbs.	Good	Yes (w/cam cleat)
Seoladair 800/437-7654 www.boomkicker.com	Boomkicker	$482	Rods	4.5 lbs.	Excellent	Yes
Sparcraft 704/597-1502 www.sparcraft.com	Ocean Vang	$362	Springs	10.5 lbs.	Poor	Yes

$ Budget Buy   ✔ Recommended   ★ Best Choice   *As installed, prices will vary by as much as 20 percent depending on installation.

pins, make them worth the higher cost. Ronstan and Schaefer are our Best Buys. For snapshackles, there's no question. For their excellent strength/weight ratio, Wichard and Schaefer are the Best Buys, while Tylaska's J-Locks and trigger snapshackles are the downright ultimate.

Rigid Boom Vangs

A rigid boom vang can be one of the best gear investments for a sailboat owner. Often lightweight, these products not only serve to support the boom (along with a topping lift), but they're vital for sailors who value efficient sail trim. In evaluations over the years, *Practical Sailor*'s editors have preached that determining the appropriate rigid vang for your boat and your style of sailing is not a one-size-fits-all affair. The process is fraught with conditional answers that only a boat owner can supply.

First, you have to determine if you want a rigid vang primarily for supporting your boom. If that's

the case, then the performance of the vang may be less important to you than the cost and the product's purported longevity. If you want a vang that will allow you to make fairly precise refinements to your mainsail trim as well as support your boom, you'll be looking more closely at how easy it is to adjust and its range of adjustability. Then, you have different types. Do you favor a spring-loaded, gas-cylinder, pneumatic, or rod vang? Our most recent evaluation (early 2006) included all four types.

It's important to note that you shouldn't install a rigid vang on a boom that rotates, as this will compromise the gooseneck fittings on the vang or the boom itself. Also, standard, off-the-shelf rigid vangs like the ones evaluated here are not suitable for use with in-boom furling. For those applications, you'll want heavier-duty equipment.

For this test, *PS* amassed a group of eight rigid vangs from seven manufacturers. We asked each company to send a vang that would be suitable for a 36-foot sloop with a 13-foot boom. We told them that

Warranty	Conclusions	Return Force	Stroke
3 yrs.	smooth operation, adjusts in 4" increments	600 lbs.	7 in.
10 yrs.	seems bulletproof, smooth operation, limited adjustability	650 lbs.	8 to 12 in.
3 yrs.	smooth operation, adjusts in 1" increments	600 lbs.	6 in.
4 yrs.	smooth operation, best range of adjustment	500 lbs.	16 to 18 in.
3 yrs.	requires some assembly, worked well	876 lbs.	7 in.
5 yrs.	just a boom support, tackle needs to be added	600 lbs.	16 in.
1 yr.	squeaky and binding before *PS* lubricated it	300 lbs.	15.7 in.

Rigid boom vangs like Forespar's Yacht Rod, shown here, can be a boon to performance aboard most boats. The four holes shown in this vang allow you to adjust the range of the vang after installation, a feature not seen on all rigid boom vangs.

we were upgrading from a 4:1-purchase soft vang, that our objectives were convenience and safety, and stipulated that there were no suitable fittings on the mast or boom for attaching the new vang. We also mentioned that the mainsail on this boat weighed 50 pounds, and we described the spars as having rectangular grooves for the attachment fittings. All of the vangs were mounted to a mast-and-boom display unit so that our testers could evaluate not only functionality, but the complexity of the installation as well. We looked closely at the vangs as well as the mounting fittings, which can vary according to the type of spar you have. We operated each vang multiple times, examined the construction quality, and noted the stroke range, the maximum return force, as well as the ease of use, and overall weight.

We looked at vangs from the following manufacturers: Marine Products Engineering (the Vang Master, the only pneumatic vang tested); Garhauer Marine (two vangs, the RV20-1SL with a stainless outer tube, and the deluxe RV20-1AL, with a 6061

T aluminum outer tube); Forespar (Yacht Rod); Hall Spars & Rigging (QuikVang); Seoladair (Boom-kicker, a simple set of fiberglass rods held captive at either end with anodized aluminum collars meant to be used with an existing tackle); Selden Mast (Rod-kicker, which uses gas pistons for resistance); and Sparcraft (Ocean Vang).

▷ **The Bottom Line** For cruising sailors, it's most important that a rigid vang works to support the boom and secondarily to trim the mainsail. If simple support is what you're after, almost all of these products are suitable. Factor in ease of operation, and you can whittle that group down by excluding the Sparcraft's Ocean Vang. This product didn't return the boom reliably to its initial position when released, and it squeaked far more than we would have expected. (Representatives from Sparcraft told us afterward that the company has put hundreds of these products on boats and has never experienced those problems.)

If post-installation adjustment is the next criterion, you can overlook the vangs from Selden and Seoladair, which worked perfectly well in all other aspects. So, you're left with our selection of vangs from Garhauer, Forespar, Hall, and Marine Products Engineering (the Vang Master). The Garhauers offer limited adjustment pre-installation, the Yacht Rod adjusts in 4-inch increments, the QuikVang in 1-inch increments, and the Vang Master's range is virtually unlimited.

If you want a basic rigid boom vang that is well built and functions smoothly for the least dollar outlay, Garhauer is the clear choice. Astoundingly, these rugged vangs are about half the price of those from the other builders, and with a 10-year warranty, they are hands-down the most economical option.

If you are interested in a smoothly operating vang that you can use to reliably control your mainsail, those from Forespar or Hall definitely fit the bill, and we recommend them. But of all the vangs, the Vang Master from Marine Products Engineering has the best adjustability, the smoothest operation, the longest stroke range, and the longest warranty of these three, and thus, even with its high price tag, it is our top choice overall.

Mainsheet Travelers

Over the years, *Practical Sailor* has reported numerous times on mainsheet traveler systems. We try to keep up with developments in this area due to the vital role such systems play on board sailboats, but we admit that it's difficult to keep pace with equipment evolution. A case in point: After our most recent test went to print, Harken Yacht Equipment introduced a new pivoting traveler system for use on board *America's* Cup boats. No doubt this ingenious application will trickle its way down to more common craft in a few years' time.

Properly installed and functioning mainsheet travelers are versatile devices, offering sailors a number of key advantages over simple mainsheet rigs traditionally used aboard sailing craft. These newer systems permit you to sheet to windward in light air to enhance your vessel's pointing ability; they allow you to depower the sail in puffy conditions without touching the mainsheet; and they enable the mainsheet to be substituted for a vang when sailing upwind. They also enable you to easily move the boom off centerline when at anchor, which can be convenient aboard some boats.

Contemporary mainsheet traveler systems have evolved so that almost every product on the market offers appealing features, including almost frictionless cars, modular system components that let you lead the mainsheet and control lines in virtually any configuration, installation so simple even a child can do it, and very reasonable prices.

To evaluate products currently available, *PS* gathered products from five of the six companies most recognized for making or selling travelers for mid-sized boats in the U.S.—Antal Marine (represented in the U.S. by Euro Marine Trading), Harken Yacht Equipment, Lewmar, Ronstan, and Schaefer Marine. The sixth, Garhauer Marine, sent us a traveler after the fact because the company was in the process of introducing a new system that wasn't available in time for our test. Two other companies were considered—Frederiksen (now part Ronstan), which did send a car and track for a smaller-sized boat; and

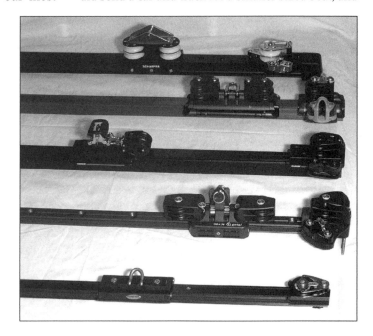

To evaluate mainsheet travelers for mid-sized sailboats, *Practical Sailor* gathered models from the most active manufacturers of these devices. The models tested are (from top to bottom): Schaefer Marine, Lewmar, Harken, Antal, and Ronstan. Not shown is Garhauer Marine's new MBT.

Rutgerson, of Sweden, which wasn't able to provide products in time for our test.

From each company we requested a 4-foot section of track, a car appropriate for that track on a sailboat 34 to 36 feet LOA, and equipment for a 4:1 control line. The track, we told them, would have to span a 28-inch opening (as in a cockpit footwell or companionway application), unsupported. We will note here that those travelers set forward for mid-boom or three-quarter-boom mainsheet arrangements are thought to be subjected to greater loads than those set up for boom-end sheeting. Each of the manufacturers whose products we tested offer guidelines for various applications, including working load limits, and buyers should take care to purchase a system rated for their intended application.

Schaefer Marine's mainsheet traveler car and track form a system that is nearly bulletproof. The car itself weighs 2.5 pounds and the track is an inch and half high and equally as wide. That bulk is needed because this system has the highest center of effort among the traveler cars and tracks that PS tested, which means it would have the least resistance to torsional loading.

Instead of installing our specimens on an actual boat, we built a jig to evaluate several parameters. We examined ease of installation, functionality, electrical isolation, sliding smoothness, track strength, flexibility of mounting, car control, mainsheet block attachment and support, center of effort angle, instructions, form and fit, and cost.

▷ **The Bottom Line** All of the products we evaluated appear to be well engineered and suited to the task of controlling the mainsheet orientation on a mid-sized sailboat. We found their overall functionality and load capacities to be more than acceptable, and didn't discover any flaws in concept or workmanship. That said, several of the products stood out from the others due to their engineering. Schaefer Marine's wheel-bearing car appears to take the old-school approach, eschewing ball bearings in horizontal races and beefing up the car material. At its narrowest, the aluminum car is nearly a third of an inch thick (0.323 inch), and on the sides, where the wheels are affixed, it's almost a half inch (0.414 inch). From a visual perspective, its engineering seems almost crude alongside its competitors, but there's a lot to be said for the reliability of a stout, simple device when you're well offshore in big winds and waves. And Schaefer likes to point out that Torlon bearings do degrade over time, whereas stainless ones last much longer.

Each of the other cars and tracks appear to be the products of more complex engineering. In the case of Antal Marine's car, this is evident in the use of two races of ball bearings. This car took top honors in our two car smoothness tests. With Harken's car, advanced engineering has resulted in captive ball bearings and the lowest car center-of-effort angle in this test. (The COE angle is defined by lines drawn from the point on the track where the car's bearings touch it to the pivot point of the car's toggle or shackle that attaches the mainsheet purchase system. This angle is an indicator of the car's torsional loading; a lower angle means potentially less torsional loading.) Lewmar's car is also highly engineered and thoughtfully assembled. And Ronstan's car has achieved its minimal profile—it is the smallest one we tested—through improved engineering. However, we felt that Ronstan's decision to have the installer drill his or her own holes in this track was more a drawback than an advantage. These holes must be precision drilled, and once they're done, the track's anodized surface is compromised.

Overall, we like the advanced engineering of Harken's car, and we applaud the company for including fully diagramed instructions with its traveler. The bullet-proof fabrication of Schaefer's system is also appealing, but we cannot overlook that it has the highest car center-of-effort angle in our test, no buffer to withstand impact between car and end fitting, and the highest price.

	Antal Marine	Harken	Lewmar
Price*	$1,430	$933.90	$644
Car Smoothness (vertical)	1 (tie)	1 (tie)	4
Car Smoothness (45°)	1	2	3
Electrolysis Isolation	Yes	No	No
Track Deflection (inches)	.289"	.073"	.082"
Car COE Angle	65°	52°	64°
Car Safe Working Load	2,200 lbs.	2,300 lbs.	2,090 lbs.
Car Controls	roller bearing sheaves	roller bearing sheaves	sheaves on bushings
Instructions	no instructions provided	diagramed instructions	no instructions provided
Track Mounting	pre-drilled 4" O.C. for 8 mm countersunk machine screws	hex-head bolts slide inside track; rectangular washers provided	hex-head bolts slide inside track bottom, no rectangular washers provided
Form-Fit-Function	Ergonomic design, stand up block, smooth operating car with dual races of ball bearings, takes torsional load with minimal friction; track must be supported throughout its length.	Substantial track, lowest COE angle minimizing torsion; smooth operating car with captive, recirculating bearings; T-bolts on track provide installation flexibility	Substantial track, T-bolts provide installation flexibility, 1⅛" diameter blocks with bushings for car control. Car ball bearings can be changed without removing car from track, but not as easily as Antal's.

*includes all components

Due to its superb engineering—this is the only car in our test that utilizes two races of ball bearings—Antal's system would be our No. 1 choice save for its steep price. For those sailors who want elegant engineering, a fractionally smoother car, and better corrosion resistance—and don't mind paying a premium for all that—this is the choice. Harken's would rank second. For the rest of us, it's hard to resist Lewmar's more accessible price. Lewmar builds a car that is also elegantly engineered, though it is quite long, which lessens the amount of distance it can move the mainsheet. Still, at over $200 less than Antal's system, we think we can live with a little less efficiency.

Winches

Anyone who has been on the bitter end of the sheet when a big genoa starts to fill—whipping and shaking with terrifying violence—knows how important it is to have a winch to convert that flailing energy into forward propulsion. Winches are to sailboats what the inclined plane was to the Egyptians. They make the difficult easy and essentially place the impossible within human reach. The equivalent of a dozen or more men who were needed in olden times to heave on a square-rigger's halyard or brace is represented on a modern sailboat by a small, precision-made, cylindrical machine packed with levers and gears.

The refinement of gearing and the development of smooth-operating self-tailers has promoted modern winches from two-man to one-man workhorses with amazing power. Their only drawback is weight, and their proclivity to induce fidgety idlers to rotate them mindlessly, just to hear the pawls ratchet.

Practical Sailor selected two-speed, self-tailing winches in the very popular No. 30 size for this evaluation. The size designation generally refers to the lowest (most powerful) power ratio. The seven winches selected for this test are the Andersen (Danish), Antal (Italian); Arco-Hutton (Australian), Harken (which manufactures in both Italy and the

Ronstan	Schaefer
$675	$1,010.65
5	3
4	5
No	No
.240"	.087"
55°	76°
1,935 lbs.	3,750 lbs.
roller bearing sheaves	roller bearing sheaves
no instructions provided	no instructions provided
installer drills the holes in this track and chooses hardware.	pre-drilled 4" O.C. for ¼" countersunk machine screws
Simple light-duty track and car; track must be drilled by installer, and must be supported throughout its length; very low-profile car with single layer of ball bearings.	Strong, high-profile track, SS ball bearings inside SS wheels provide bulletproof car design; considerable torsion introduced with lower sheet angles, 1¾" diameter blocks with Delrin sheaves and Torton bearings.

U.S.), the Lewmar (British), and two Dutch winches, the LVJ and the Meissner, one of the biggest winch makers in the world.

Although racing sailors often want the lightest possible equipment and black anodized winch drums have been popular for years, the weight difference between aluminum and chromed-bronze models is only about 25 percent; that's because under the drum they're mostly all bronze and hardened steel—except for the Andersens, which have stainless axles and other internal parts. Anodized aluminum gets shabby looking more quickly and does not wear as well as chrome (which will wear away in time, too). Neither is as good as stainless. Bronze is long lasting, but if you want it to look good, you should buy stock in a metal polish company.

The finish on the portion of the drum that engages the line differs, too. Andersen's ribs and Harken's smooth aluminum drums are the easiest on the line; Arco-Hutton's needle peening is probably the toughest on line.

These winches all are first-class gear that tend to defy comparison or judgment. They're just different. With a minimum of cleaning and lubricating, all of them will last virtually forever. Besides closely examining these seven winches (especially the self-tailing mechanism), and using them for many hours, our test procedure was designed to determine which winches deliver best on their promised power ratios. Another way to put it is: How much of its power ratio does each winch lose in useless friction?

In our test, instead of using a standard 10-inch winch handle, we substituted a Sears Craftsman ⅜-inch-drive torque wrench with a ⅝-inch adaptor fitting that just happens to fit the internationally accepted star socket on winches. Using some stout shock cord and StaySet line, we assembled our test apparatus to simulate headsail loads. With each winch, three turns (the minimum recommended by any winch maker) were taken on the drum before being seated in the self-tailing groove.

We made arithmetic adjustments in our calculations because of the long torque wrench handle. (The handle is 13½ inches from the center of the socket to a pin in the wobble handle. This seemingly slight increase in the length of the torque wrench over a standard handle provides more than 33 percent more power.) Finally, the loads achieved and recorded with each winch were converted to a percentage of the manufacturers' stated claims. It was not expected that the stated claims, which are theoretical, would be "proved" because any winch loses much of its advantage to friction. The loss with these seven winches was about 50 percent, except for the very efficient Andersen.

The results of our efficiency calculations indicate that the Harken winch ranked first in high gear because, with 10 pounds on the torque wrench, it delivered a 140-pound load, 63 percent of the 220 pounds it theoretically should have. The Andersen winch was close behind. In low gear, the Andersen delivered 300 pounds, 90 percent of the 333 pounds it theoretically should deliver. The Arco-Hutton finished second best in low gear.

After the 10-pound tests were completed, some additional higher load tests were done to introduce high-output figures to include in PS's considerations. The high-load testing produced no surprises.

The gleaming, efficient Andersen (bottom left) was *PS*'s best choice among this group, which includes (clockwise from top left): Harken's B32.2STA, Lewmar's 30C-ST, Meissner's 21STB32, LVJ's 31S, Arco-Hutton's 30ST, Antal's W 30.2, and Andersen's 28ST. (The numerical designations indicate power-ratios.)

Because this was not (and could not) be a precision procedure, the test findings can be said only to indicate which winch provided the greatest advantages, in both high and low gears, and which were easiest to use.

Our considerations regarding ease of use pertained mostly to how easy it was to place three wraps on the drum, catch the self-tailing guide, and sock the bitter end home in the self-tailing groove. That, along with how easy it was to disengage the line from the self-tailing groove for easing were our criteria. We confirmed that winches with self-tailing arms that protrude as little as possible and that have big fixed grooves are easier than those with protruding arms and small spring-loaded self-tailing grooves. For instance, on those winches with big, fixed grooves—the Andersen, LVJ, and Meissner—it's easy to guide the line into place, so easy you can do it with one hand. With the Antal, Harken, and Lewmar winches, which have small guide arms and small spring-loaded slots, it often takes two hands.

Serviceability was also considered. Those winches that open up via simple threads (Andersen, Harken, Lewmar, LVJ, and Meissner), are preferable to those (Antal and Arco) that still depend on the very difficult to manage—but easy to lose—retainer rings.

▷ **The Bottom Line** When selecting winches for your boat, the important considerations are what kind of sailing you do, in what weather, and how quickly you change sails to comfortably match the winds. If you're a racing sailor who presses hard, winches need to have ample power to handle loads that would not be imposed by a conservative cruising sailor who changes or reefs sails to avoid unnecessary strains on sails or rigging.

There are great differences in the gear ratios of these seven winches. The Andersen and Antal winches have high-gear ratios that would quickly bring in a jib sheet. With the Harken and Meissner winches, the high-gear ratio might mean that you would want to overhand the slack before resorting to the winch handle. On the other hand, for final trimming in strong winds, the low gear power of the LVJ (42:1) and Harken (32:1) would make life somewhat more comfortable than the Andersen's 26.5:1 ratio. (As tested, the Andersen's efficiency makes up for much of that disadvantage.)

This is why that the Andersen, made mostly of stainless steel, is *Practical Sailor*'s choice as the best of these seven. Its ribbed drum is famously gentle on lines, it's easy to operate and service, and its long-lasting metal is the easiest to keep looking good. As an aside, this winch's larger sibling, Andersen's No. 40, was our top choice in an earlier test for similar reasons.

For low-gear power, the standouts are Harken (famous for good bearings) and the massive LVJ and Meissner. In between, the Lewmar (which is very nicely engineered) and the Antal (which is beautifully machined and polished) are fine examples of their makers' products.

Make	Andersen ★	Antal	Arco-Hutton	Harken $	Lewmar	LVJ ✔	Meissner
Model	28ST	W 30.2	30ST	B32.2STA	30C-ST	31S	21STB32
Price	$720	$895	$620	$575	$780	$845	$995
Warranty	3 yrs.	3 yrs.	"If you can break it, we'll replace it."	3 yrs.	3 yrs.	1 yr.	3 yrs.
Drum Diameter	2¾"	3"	2⁵⁄₁₆"	2¹⁵⁄₁₆"	2¹⁵⁄₁₆"	3"	3"
Drum Finish	Ribbed	Small ridges	Needle peened	Smooth	Knurled rough	Knurled fine	Fine peened
Top Fastener	3 Allen screws	Retainer ring	2 retainer rings	Threaded bolt	Threaded top	Threaded top	Threaded top
Line Size Range	⅜"–½"	⁵⁄₁₆"–½"	⁵⁄₁₆"–⁹⁄₁₆"	⁵⁄₁₆"–½"	⁵⁄₁₆"–½"	⅜"–⁹⁄₁₆"	⁵⁄₁₆"–¹⁵⁄₃₂"
Weight	9 lbs.	9.5 lbs.	20 lbs.	9.3 lbs.	12.3 lbs.	18.75 lbs.	15.1 lbs.
High Gear Ratio	1.3:1	1:1	2.3:1	2.4:1	2:1	2.4:1	2.5:1
Low Gear Ratio	3.7:1	4.4:1	5.2:1	4.7:1	4.2:1	4.5:1	4.8:1
High Power Ratio	9.5:1	6.8:1	14.2:1	16:1	13.8:1	14.7:1	16.7:1
Low Power Ratio	26.5:1	28:1	31:1	32:1	29.2:1	42:1	32:1
Efficiency Rank High/Low	2/1	7/4	5/2	1/3	4/7	3/6	6/5
Serviceability	Excellent	Fair	Poor	Good	Good	Good	Excellent
User Friendly Rank	3	6	7	5	4	2	1

★ Best Choice ✔ Recommended $ Budget Buy

Last but surely not least, if you want a brute of a winch, the Arco-Hutton from Australia won't disappoint you, other than the fact that it's difficult to service, and this is primarily because you must cope with not one but two difficult retainer rings.

WINCH HANDLES

It's not uncommon to encounter racing sailors who travel with their own personal 8-inch winch handles. These folks usually claim that short handles make for faster trimming and therefore more efficient maneuvers on board. That's true, of course, provided you have the speedy beef to take advantage of the handle's smaller radius. Otherwise, the only reason you should buy a short winch handle is that you can't swing a standard 10-inch handle in the available space. (The usual problem here is a retrofitted dodger, bimini, or some other piece of on-deck gear.)

Practical Sailor's research revealed that most manufacturers offer both 8-inch and 10-inch versions of their line of winch handles. Almost all of these come in locking or non-locking versions. But there's a tremendous range in price and quality among the 28 handles that we collected for our evaluation. At the low end, there's a $24.50 plastic Bernard (now sold by Beckson) handle that would produce hardly any tears if it hopped overboard. On the top stock end is a carbon-fiber Titan Viper, for $189.90. (These are prices from early 2004, so adjust accordingly.) At the custom-order end of the spectrum, there's a polished bronze model from Antal with a teak handle. It's truly a thing of beauty, which Antal will engrave with your boat's name. Drop one of these beauties in the drink, and your skipper is likely to luff up and say, "Fetch."

Except for the handles needed for the classic bronze Murray winches (they are gorgeous), virtually all handles now have ¹¹⁄₁₆-inch (17.5 mm) octagonal star studs, and most have, with square locking plates operated with thumb-operated, spring-loaded levers.

And yet another great improvement in recent years was the development of better hand grips. The move toward more ergonomic (and two-handed) grips was pioneered by Harken and a company called Titan. An Australian named Geoff Cropley invented the Titan handles, which are remarkably lighter (half the weight and half the price of existing metal handles) because they're rendered from composite materials. The Titan handles became so popular that Lewmar bought the company. And, in late 2005, Schaefer Marine jumped into the winch handle game, offering 10-inch forged aluminum handles (locking and non-locking) for a very reasonable price. Those weren't included in this report as it was originally published before that date.

Most of these handles come in both lock-in and non-locking versions. *Practical Sailor's* testers got a good workout using the handles in a two-speed winch. All were run up to 200 pounds, at least three times, to see if we could note differences in smoothness, grip comfort, and effort required. Viewed in informal price groups, the differences were not remarkable. As would be expected, the Holt, Bernard, and

Sea-Dog handles did not feel as smooth or comfortable (especially as the load reached the upper limits) as the more expensive handles (Andersens, Antals, Harkens, and Lewmars). For discussion purposes, these 28 handles will be divided into three categories—the lightweight but well-proven plastic models, the medium-weight aluminum versions, and finally, the stainless and plated bronze heavyweights.

▷ **The Bottom Line** For a small boats or small winches, a Titan Primary 8-inch lock-in is rivaled perhaps by the Sea-Dog 10-inch fiberglass-reinforced nylon handle. Racers who regard weight as the essence of evil and money as no object could choose Titan's Viper Carbon.

Among the higher-quality handles, it really is difficult to choose, and certainly not possible to judge by finish and function alone. Price must be factored in, and we suspect that on a given day any of the handles from Harken, Antal, and Andersen could come out ahead of the pack.

For everyday cranking, it's hard to beat single handles with knobs on top like Lewmar's Maxi Grip, and it's nice if the knob can rotate independently of the vertical handle. If we were going out today to buy a handle, it would be the Harken 10-inch single handle with SpeedGrip (model B10CSG) or the 8-inch model (B8ASG) if there were space restrictions. (*PS* Editor-at-Large Nick Nicholson had this to say about his Harken winch handles after sailing his cruising boat halfway around the world: "The only parts of any Harken hardware showing significant wear are the studs on our Speed Grip winch handles. These have begun to corrode significantly because they

The most common material used in winch handles is aluminum. These handles are but a sampling of the products available in 8-inch, 10-inch, non-locking, and locking, single-handled and double-handled winch handles. Beginning from the far left are two handles from Holt, four from Antal Marine, five from Harken Yacht Equipment, two from Lewmar, the gaudy, rubber-coated translucent Condor made by Titan, and a simple model from Sea-Dog. *PS* deemed Harken and Antals handles the best among those made of aluminum. Subsequent to when this photo was taken, Schaefer Marine joined the ranks of winch handle manufacturers and now markets 8- and 10-inch handles in stainless steel.

Make & Model	Price	Type	Size	Grip	Handle Bearings	Lock-In	Comments
Andersen 507197	$57	Lock-In	8"	Single Plastic	No	1-Way	Well-made, good in hand
Andersen 507198	$103	Lock-In	10"	Single Plastic	No	2-Way	Excellent finish; will last forever
Andersen 507320	$159	Lock-In	10"	Double Plastic	No	1-Way	Well-made, but heavy on price
Antal 2031	$120	Lock-In	10"	Single Teak	No	2-Way	Excellent workmanship; best chrome
Antal 2011	$67	Lock-In	8"	Single Rubber	Yes	2-Way	Good rubber grip; excellently made
Antal 2021	$95	Non-Lock	10"	Single Rubber	Yes	N.A.	Excellent workmanship, but pricey
Antal 2022	$112	Lock-In	10"	Single w/Ball Grip	Yes	2-Way	Ditto above
Antal 2023	$132	Lock-In	10"	Double Rubber	Yes	2-Way	Ditto above
Bernard WH1000	$35	Non-Lock	10"	Single Plastic	No	N.A.	Light aluminum; light duty only
Bernard WH800	$24	Non-Lock	8"	Single Plastic	No	N.A.	Same as above
Harken B10ADL	$129	Lock-In	10"	Double Plastic	Yes	2-Way	Excellent workmanship; good grips
Harken B10AL	$81	Lock-In	10"	Single Plastic	Yes	2-Way	High quality and a good buy
Harken B10CSG	$95	Lock-In	10"	Single w/SpeedGrip	Yes	2-Way	A popular favorite; very well made
Harken B8AP	$50	Non-Lock	8"	Single Plastic	Yes	N.A.	Good, versatile shorty, well made
Harken B8ASG	$81	Lock-In	8"	Single w/SpeedGrip	Yes	2-Way	Terrific all-around handle; well-made
Harken B8ASGLP	$75	Lock-In	8"	Low Profile SpeedGrip	Yes	2-Way	Well-made; no vertical handle
Holt 1221 L	$38	Lock-In	8"	Single Plastic	No	2-Way	Gets the job done; fair workmanship
Holt 1331	$38	Non-Lock	10"	Single Plastic	No	N.A.	Same as above
Lewmar/29140121	$90	Lock-In	10"	Single w/PowerGrip	Yes	2-Way	Decently finished; trigger bound in test
Lewmar/29140081	$70	Lock-In	8"	Single w/PowerGrip	Yes	2-Way	Good, but outdone by competition
Lewmar/29141112	$120	Lock-In	10"	Double Plastic	Yes	2-Way	Same as above
Sea-Dog/604200-3	$20	Lock-In	8"	Single Plastic	No	1-Way	Mediocre workmanship, but good buy
Sea-Dog/604100	$29	Lock-In	10"	Single Plastic	Yes	2-Way	Again, good buy, and it does float
Sea-Dog/604300	$48	Lock-In	8"	Single Plastic	No	2-Way	Scratchy trigger on test handle
Titan/Condor	$60	Lock-In	10"	Single w/Maxi-Grip	Yes	2-Way	Gaudy, but pretty well-made
Titan/Maxi Magnum	$40	Lock-In	10"	Single w/Maxi-Grip	Yes	2-Way	Workhorse, decently made
Titan/Primary	$37	Lock-In	8"	Single Plastic	No	2-Way	Decently made shorty at a good price
Titan/Viper Carbon	$190	Lock-In	10"	Double Plastic	Yes	2-Way	Well-made; flashy, techy, tough

are always left in the winches when we're sailing. An aluminum stud sitting in a stainless steel or chrome-plated bronze socket full of salt water is going to corrode no matter what.

"You can now buy these handles in chrome-plated bronze, with bronze studs. We prefer the light weight of the aluminum handles, but would rather have the more rugged chrome-plated bronze stud. Essentially, we haven't worried about a single piece of Harken gear, and we haven't needed to. It was the perfect choice five years ago, and it would be the right decision today.") Enough said. However, if we needed to save a few dollars, we'd have no trouble buying a roughly equivalant Lewmar or Titan single-handle-with-ball offering, either of which would get the job done in style enough.

Backstay Adjusters

HYDRAULIC BACKSTAY ADJUSTERS

When it comes to specialty gear for sailboats, often there are but a few players in a particular market. In the case of hydraulic backstay adjusters, there are only two, Navtec and Sailtec, which serve the U.S. market. Navtec, under the Umbrella of Vector Marine, has created a budding monopoly on a global scale. However, Bob Brehm's Sailtec, up in Oshkosh, Wisconsin, is keeping Navtec honest. In fact, in the last several years, it sometimes seems like Sailtec, a little five-person company, has not only been keeping Navtec honest, it's been keeping them up all night.

Navtec ruled this domain for a long while. But, competitively speaking, Bob Brehm found not one but two Achilles' heels. By using the hydraulic cylinder as the case and by placing the return line and gauge on the outside, his Sailtec adjusters could be made less expensively and could have longer strokes—the latter very important because of the trend toward bendy rigs, some with split backstays that require considerable "take-up." "The exposed return line is not pretty," Brehm told *PS*. "I wish I had theirs, but that good-looking case is very costly."

A minor advantage of the exposed return line is that it permits easy conversion to a remote panel and pump, if later desired. (That way, the same gear can be used to power a boom vang.)

Navtec's models, which are made in three basic sizes, had strokes of 7, 8, and 8.5 inches. Sailtec offered roughly the same nominal sizes in both standard sizes (with strokes greater by 2 inches) and long versions (with strokes almost twice as great). Sailtec also gained ground by shaving Navtec's prices. The price difference for an individual buyer is not great, but it's important to a cost-conscious boatbuilder. (And for the keen racing sailor, the Sailtecs also are somewhat lighter in weight.)

When Navtec decided to respond to Sailtec's pressure, it didn't flinch. It redesigned its entire line, engineering from the ground up, and testing continually. After that period, Navtec kindly loaned *Practical Sailor* a prototype of its new line. It looks remarkably like a Sailtec, mostly because of the exposed return line, but we didn't say that to the rep when he dropped off the prototype. He told us that the biggest improvements were the increase in stroke and moving the gauge from the bottom to the top of the tube for easier reading.

When we checked back with Brehm about Navtec's new exterior return line, he issued this comment: "I'm flattered." Then he explained that although he has over the last five years or so made 17 "running changes" (as engineers call improvements to existing equipment), Sailtec had underway a "design sweep" (which was what Navtec just finished doing).

"To begin with," said Brehm, "you know where the gauge is going."

▷ **The Bottom Line** Navtec and Sailtec backstay adjusters are both almost foolproof; each is designed to fail in the safe position. This means that an adjustable pressure-relief valve prevents a careless user from overtensioning a boat's rig or breaking something. The aircraft aluminum cylinders—gun drilled, honed, and polished—never wear out. Nor does the powerful piston and rod, usually made of stainless running in bronze bearings. The seals and valves rarely fail—all because everything that moves is bathed in fine hydraulic oil. When something fails, it's usually the pump. A complete rebuild typically costs $300 to $400, about a quarter of the original cost.

Navtec and Sailtec peck away at each other, arguing about needle versus ball valves, who has the beefier piston rod, whose takes the fewest strokes, which can stand a side load, etc. But they openly admire each other's equipment. When considering functionality or reliability, it's not possible to pick one over the other. But factor in price, and Sailtec has had the edge. One thing is for certain: This is as good an example as one will ever find of the value to the consumer of a spirited, appreciative competition between two good companies—one large, one small—determined to outdo each other.

Mainsail Control Systems

The three S's of mainsail handling get a lot of attention, and rightfully so, too. Whether it's a small

Steve and Linda Dashew's 78-foot Beowolf utilized full-battened sails on its main and mizzen. The couple favors simple but reliable means of attaching the sail to the sail track.

family sloop or a flat-out ocean racer, there are few troubles for a sailor worse than having difficulty setting, shortening, and striking the mainsail. To make it four S's, you might also throw in stowing.

On a modern sailboat, handling the mainsail quickly and surely is equally important, both as a safety measure and as a matter of convenience. Thanks to a lot of thoughtful engineering—beginning with the replacement of laminated, steam-bent, copper-riveted oak hoops (they also came with brass machine screws to dismantle and slip on an already stepped mast) or iron rings with parrels—with good mast hardware, it's less complicated, too.

Sail-handling efficiency took a step forward from the external bronze or stainless steel track when the boltrope luff and slotted mast system came into the mainstream some years ago. This system presents a nice shape to the wind and eliminates the gap between sail and mast. It remains the current choice

for conventional raceboats, but is not much favored by club racers and cruising sailors. A boltrope sail can be difficult to hoist, a mess to lower and, in a mounting breeze, requires at least two crewmen to reef.

An attempt to overcome the boltrope sail's shortcomings arrived with nylon slugs—plastic extrusions, lashed or webbed to the sail—that fit in a circular mast groove. Like metal slides on a metal track, the slugs stay in the groove and pile up when the sail is struck or reefed. In early versions, the slugs were too weak. When one broke, the load on its neighbors quadrupled, and soon the luff went like the buttons on a fat man's vest. Today's best slides are made of UHMW (ultra high molecular weight) plastic, which is tough, hard, and slippery—ideal properties for sail slides.

As the metals industry became more and more adept at squirting liquids out of precision-made dies, the next development was an extruded aluminum

THE DUTCHMAN VERSUS LAZY JACKS

Want to see the sparks fly? Simply bring up the topic of mainsail containment systems in your local cruisers' watering hole, and then profess that one is superior to another. That should get the fracas going.

In responding to a reader's query in mid-2000, which ran along the lines of "Why is The Dutchman better than simple lazy jacks?" *PS* wrote the following: "The main advantages of The Dutchman [the proprietary system of mainsail containment that uses monofilament lines woven through the sail] are that the monofilament is lightweight, does not bang against the mast or sail (chafe considerations), has less windage than most lazy jacks, and is almost invisible. While it works best with stiffer sails that will take a fold, it will work with any sail, at least in keeping the sail on top of the boom and not letting it fall onto the deck.

"Lazy jacks are a more robust system and would be the right choice for heavy full-battened sails, as one sees on multihulls. They require a bit more work than The Dutchman, which stays in place and requires no adjustment or fiddling when raising and lowering the sail. Lazy jacks that can be led forward once the sail is hoisted are preferable (like the EZ Jax and Schaefer systems), but that requires you to perform that operation, at the mast. And when raising, you have to be head-to-wind so that the

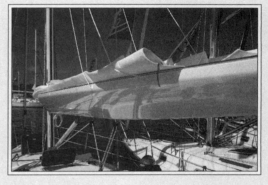

Lazy jacks, like those rigged aboard this Tartan 3400, afford a simple means of containing the mainsail. The Dutchman system is slightly more involved because holes must be perforated in the sail.

roach of the sail, especially at the battens, doesn't come up inside one of the lazy jacks.

"Price aside, we like The Dutchman for its simplicity and would choose it for most boats, unless we had a traditional boat, maybe with a gaff rig, or a full-battened sail like a Freedom or multihull. Then we'd choose lazy jacks.

"The bottom line is that both work to keep the mainsail on top of the boom, and that's the whole point. By the way, Harken and other companies sell lazy jacks, both in kit form and by individual components."

mainsail track with an internal shape needed to accept plastic or metal slides. This facilitated a host of refinements. A sail being lowered tends to fold on both sides of the boom, which twists and racks the slides, and tends to bind or break them. Aluminum slides, hardened by anodizing, are excellent, but here again the UHMW plastics are tending to prevail.

There have been extensive and successful efforts to improve slides (and slugs).

Then battens came along to complicate the issue. You can now get battens in almost any size and most shapes. Bainbridge—one of the main suppliers to sailmakers of sailcloth and mast hardware—offers 15 batten shapes in its latest catalog.

There's also an ever-growing need for specialized kinds of track. Some hardware makers now have proprietary track for use only with their hardware. Harken offers over a dozen different track types. Working in the other direction, which seems equally if not more sound, Antal Marine introduced track that can be easily and securely mounted in any spar's existing round luff groove. It uses a half-round slug and a clever fastener. With this approach, there's no need to drill and tap holes in the mast, but Antal's track can only be used with the company's own hardware—low-friction plastic slides mounted inside an aluminum car. Because a boat owner who wants a new sail-handling system often cannot afford to buy a new mast, other manufacturers have also tooled up to make other adapter tracks in a similar fashion, like Dutchman, Facnor, and Selden.

Ultimately, there are full-battened mainsails and the track systems developed to support them. These systems have to stand up to the forward pressure exerted by the batten on the mast, and these forces have taxed some very inventive minds to come up with better slides and cars (with ball bearings, wheels, or special inserts). Because of the growing popularity of full-battened mains, the competition has been intense.

PS has reviewed Fredericken's expensive yet versatile Ballslide track system, Harken's much-admired Battcar approach, the Tides Marine Strong system, Schaefer's Battslide, Martin van Breems' Dutchman, and Antal's HS system. We've also looked at those from Facnor, Rutgerson, Sailman, Schaefer, and Selden. Such low-friction systems designed and built to handle the loads generated by full battens under pressure fall into two basic categories: those that use a dedicated track attached to the mast, and those that utilize a slide or car fitted for the existing groove in the spar.

Not long ago, Schaefer Marine and North Sails collaborated to create a new batten box they're calling the Parco Batten Box. The principal advantage of this product is that it allows battens to be loaded from the luff end of the pocket, thus enabling the sailmaker to permanently close the batten pockets on the leech end. The Parco Batten Box has a sliding cover that opens with just one fastener and offers a range of adjustment up to 50 millimeters, longer than any other comparable batten box on the market. (*PS* has yet to test this new device.)

Of course there are other systems, like in-boom and in-mast furling. In the earliest versions of boom furling/reefing (inside or around), the sails often unwound themselves when wind pressure was applied, which made a frightful noise. They've gotten better, and they offer unmatched convenience, but they remain expensive. And the same can be said, in general, for in-mast furling systems. Evolution among these systems has come a long way since the mid-1970s when Ted Hood introduced the Stoway mast. Several sparmakers now offer in-mast furling systems; in fact, the folks at Selden Mast say these units represent the fastest-growing sector of their business. Still, such systems are complicated, expensive, and somewhat heavy. At *PS*, we feel that such systems are still more appropriate for larger boats, 40 feet and longer. However, we're encouraged by recent developments with vertical battens and articulating battens that enable these furling systems to support mainsails with positive roach.

Furling Units

SMALL-BOAT FURLING UNITS

The development of reliable headsail furling ranks high on any list of devices that have significantly changed the way boats are sailed in the past several decades. Hanked-on sails, while having certain advantages, are steadily disappearing in favor of roller-furling jibs and genoas, particularly aboard cruising vessels. Furlers essentially keep the crew off the bow and reduce the time spent handling sails. And thanks to improved designs, the sight of a tattered furling genoa flogging itself to death also is disappearing. Jams, once the bane of furlers, are much less frequent.

Practical Sailor has tracked the evolution of headsail furling systems for many years. In 1988 we undertook a comprehensive evaluation of available models and followed that in mid-1995 with an evaluation backed by a reader survey, which showed marked improvement in performance, reliability, and customer satisfaction. At that time, 77 percent of all survey respondents said they would buy the same furler again, led by Cruising Design Inc. (CDI) and Famet (an older system) at 100 percent, followed by Profurl, Schaefer, Harken, and Furlex. Two years later, we updated the group, highlighting the new Hood SeaFurl 5 and redesigned Furlex. Then, in April 2000, we published a comprehensive article about furling units for small boats, and in the summer of 2004 we published a survey taken of professional riggers, sounding them out on their furling preferences.

The advantages of a plastic luff in a furling unit are several. First, unlike rigid aluminum luff extrusions, which are shipped in lengths of about 6 feet and must be connected with splices or link plates and fasteners, pliable plastic extrusions normally come as one piece and require no assembly. Secondly, the PVC can take a fair amount of abuse and is not as easily dented as rigid aluminum extrusions, an important consideration for any owner when stepping and unstepping the mast. Thirdly, cost is less, making furling more affordable for owners of small boats. Plastic won't corrode, of course, but is subject to ultraviolet attack. Nevertheless, the addition of UV inhibitors should give these products adequate life spans. So we set out to test these kinds of systems.

PS obtained furler kit packages for smaller boats (up to 24 feet) only from CDI, Hood Yacht Systems (Sea Flex), and Schaefer (SnapFurl). Ease of furling is affected most by the bearing surfaces, but also by the ratio of the foil diameter to the drum diameter; after all, the difference in the two is what gives you a mechanical advantage; the higher the ratio, the more advantage. We measured all three and developed these approximate ratios: Schaefer 2.14, Hood 1.65, and CDI 1.45.

All three systems are fairly simple to assemble, with few pieces. The average do-it-yourselfer should be able to install his or her own with basic tools. The one critical job is cutting the luff extrusion to the right length. All manuals give explicit instructions. And compared to larger-boat furlers, these—especially the CDI and Sea Flex—are simpler and lack such features as integral adjusters.

▷ **The Bottom Line** Between the two least expensive—Hood and CDI—the latter has a bushing bearing at the bottom, with optional ball bearings. Hood does not. In addition, CDI's internal halyard reduces friction. While we like Hood's clever design, the CDI is a bit less money and has a long track record of customer satisfaction. At least until more experience is gained with the Sea Flex, we'd go with CDI.

Schaefer's SnapFurl isn't much more expensive than either of the other two. It has just about everything top-end furlers for larger boats do—ball bearings top and bottom, many stainless parts, and what appears to be a good two-part luff extrusion—at a much lower price. It rates a Best Buy, hands down. Harken also makes furling units for smaller boats, but the luff sections are aluminum extrusions. (The company did once make a product called the Heli-Foil, which had a plastic luff section, but it's not produced any longer.)

This photograph exhibits the upper and lower units of various furling systems available for smaller boats. These products are, from left: CDI, Hood Yacht Systems, and two models from Schaefer.

Roller-Furling Units— What the Experts Say

By almost any measure, roller-furling units have evolved to become nearly ubiquitous in our pastime. That evolution has rendered many of these products superbly functional. To wit, an overwhelming majority of respondents to a recent reader survey gave these products high ratings for reliability and functionality. Our experience concurs with that. (We have installed furling units on two of our test boats in the past.) It seems that these systems are generally earning their keep, but that's an outlook which needs to be further qualified.

To do that, we felt it would be instructive to field the comments of those who install and repair roller-furling units on a regular basis, so we tracked down professional riggers around the country. Some of these individuals were involved in furler developments early on, and all of them have hands-on experience dissecting frozen set-screws, replacing damaged extrusions and worn bearings, or simply puzzling though the machinations of differing installations. They often view headsail furling units in a harsher light than the rest of us, so we asked about the most common issues encountered, as well as their experience with particular products. Here's what they said, followed by responses from the manufacturers:

"Most of the problems with roller furlers stem from improper installation," said Svendsen's Boat Works' Doug Fredebaugh from the San Francisco Bay Area, a rigging veteran with over 20 years of experience. "Anything from having the foil the wrong height to having the halyard restrainer in the wrong position, to bad rig tune—an often overlooked culprit—can lead to poor roller-furling performance. If you have lots of time and are very careful, roller-furling units are easy to install. However, there are always going to be places where you can misinterpret instructions and end up doing something irreparable like cutting the foil to the wrong length."

"Owner installation is a double-edged sword, because there are owners with different levels of mechanical abilities," explained Annapolis Rigging's Collin Linehan, who has been a rigger for nine years and a sailmaker for six prior to that. "It's something owners can do, but often a customer comes into it with these grand ideas and then they run into problems.

"It's when you stop paying attention—say, furling the sail without looking up—that you risk running into problems. Old halyard wraps, improperly located halyard restrainers, and user error are the most typical problems we see. The most important thing that all of these furler producers could put in their operating instructions would be a line that says: 'If you think there's a problem, stop and look around.' You should never need a winch to turn a furler, these units are meant to be operated by hand."

"Of course I have a vested interest in saying that people shouldn't put units together themselves," admitted Keys Rigging's Gary Shotwell, a 30-year rigging veteran, "but from a purely benevolent standpoint, I really think it is a fairly complicated process. We've had a few dismastings due to halyard wraps. The other thing to be on the lookout for is what some boatyards will do to a roller-furling unit in the process of taking the mast down. Often the people doing the job don't understand the mechanics of the unit. And reassembly by yard personnel almost always leaves the potential for some kind of trouble."

"The cause of most problems is poor or improper installation and not the furler," agreed Sound Rigging and Yacht Service's Todd Rickard in Seattle, basing his remarks on 12 years as a rigger. "There aren't that many problems with today's furlers. The fact that most boats in the 1970s and '80s had hank-on sails led to something of a roller furler binge in the '90s. Roller furlers have been standard on new boats for the last three to five years. Buying a furler requires the same philosophy as buying winches: the benefits of oversizing make life easier. I just saw a 44-footer with a Schaefer 2100 on it. The unit fit, but the owner is going to be disappointed in its performance in high winds because it's not properly matched to the vessel's size."

"Some of the biggest problems we see," opined Fritz Richardson of San Diego's Pacific Offshore Rigging, "are owners not setting the sail up with the right length tack pennant. But typically, furlers don't break now as they did in the earlier stages."

"I'd say most of the problems start at the top end of the swivel unit," offered Alan Veenstra of the Chicago Sailing Club, basing that on his 40 years

Professional riggers have spent much of their careers messing with roller-furling systems like the Pro-Furl unit shown here. Due to that close interaction, these folks have gleaned valuable lessons that we can all benefit from.

of experience. "The length of the pennant is often incorrect, as is the angle. If the furler is too low, the halyard will wrap. If there's a deficiency, it's that the top swivel is paid less attention than the drum. It's hard to know from deck level if the jib is the right height. If the sail is too long, it'll jump off the furler and jam; if it's too short, you risk a halyard wrap."

"It's not a very intricate thing to put together," countered Eddie Brown, who is involved in installing about 60 furling units a year while he commissions new Bénéteaus for St. Barts Yachts in Charleston, South Carolina. "If you are replacing one with the same brand, there's no problem, you can put it right together, but if you've got to go and figure out measurements and mess with toggles and link plates and whatever you've got to hook up there; then it can be a little tricky doing pin-to-pin measurements."

"The biggest challenge for an owner installation is changing over to a mechanical wire end fitting," said John Fretwell of Rig Works in San Diego. "That, and going aloft. Mechanical fittings are more expensive than a swaged fitting, and though you might end up coming out ahead eventually in terms of rerigging, few people are going to own a boat long enough to worry about rerigging it two or three times. Problems will vary by manufacturer, but in a general sense, corrosion between stainless and aluminum causes most of the problems we see, especially if the unit lives in an anchor well, which is now becoming popular."

▷ **The Bottom Line** The functionality of modern roller-furling units depends first and foremost on proper installation. Predictably, the riggers we spoke to favor professional installations, partially because they've witnessed the downside of owner installations, and, of course, because they too need to put food on the table. And many of them cautioned against the temptation to purchase undersized units as a means of saving money. As with anchors and winches, oversizing has its advantages, but our riggers made it clear that this is only necessary if your brand of sailing warrants it.

These professionals also counseled that prospective buyers consider the aftermarket prices for things like set-screws, foils, and bearings, as most units eventually require replacement parts or some servicing, and higher-end units will likely have higher aftermarket part prices. They also said that though maintenance on headsail furling units is now quite minimal (the sealed bearings of Profurl are virtually maintenance free, while other units require little more than a periodic rinse with fresh water), it's a good idea to check the foil connections once a season. Set-screws can work loose, and you should also check for signs of corrosion between stainless steel fasteners and aluminum foil sections.

Even with the proper installation, maintenance, and inspections, things can go wrong. Spinnaker halyards or other headsail halyards kept on the bow could inadvertently get wrapped in the upper swivel, and an overzealous or inattentive crew might damage the unit by not noticing this. Headsail halyard tension, several riggers told us, should also be eased when the boat is at rest for long periods to retain sail shape.

They also emphasized that there are other important considerations for those in the market for a new furling system. You need to consider your use of the product. Will it be for racing, occasional offshore cruising, or just daysailing? And how do you feel about swaged end fittings versus mechanical terminals? What about foil shapes? Do you want rounded extrusions? And will you be able to keep up with the minimum maintenance requirements, or are you hoping that "maintenance-free" means just that? All of these are important considerations.

So who comes out on top? Our unofficial winner in this highly subjective survey is the one product none of these riggers faulted; one that was invariably used as a standard for excellence: "I'm not sure I want this in print," said an unnamed rigger who was referred to us by another manufacturer's distributor, "but I highly recommend Schaefer. They're reliable. I like the bearings, they require very little maintenance, they are robust, the installation is easy, and they are quite conducive to disassembly." Harken's furlers garnered high praise, though they seemed to be more complicated to install and disassemble, and Selden's Furlex and Profurl both won emphatic support among many of our riggers. All told, the bar has been pushed to an extremely high level by these four product lines, and collectively they represent solid investments.

IN-BOOM FURLING

Practical Sailor readily acknowledges that with each passing year, sail-handling systems get more and more refined and efficient. Even so, the mainsail remains a challenge. Stacking systems, lazy jacks, The Dutchman, in-mast furlers—all of these contribute their share of convenience and control, but none has proven to be the ultimate answer for all manner of vessel. Stowing, furling, and reefing the main is still a sizable chore, especially as the size of your boat increases. And, as always, when we attempt to conquer the considerable forces of wind and wave by mechanical means, we tread a fine line between convenience and chaos.

In the late 1980s, Hood Yacht Systems introduced the Stoboom, and rolling the sail inside the boom became an option. More affordable and less risky than furling the main inside the mast, these boom furlers were a big hit. However, the newly engineered hardware proved to be more complicated and ultimately less convenient than it looked. It was, according to one owner who sailed a Hunter 42, "the costliest consumer mistake I ever made."

Hood eventually pulled that product off the market. But the advantages of in-boom furling that prompted Hood's "noble experiment" have not disappeared with the Stoboom. Compared with in-mast furling, the boom-based systems weigh less and keep that weight lower. Probably the most significant selling point of a sail that lives in the boom, however, is its shape. Up until recently, in-mast furlers generally meant roachless, high-aspect triangles, thus with reduced mainsail area, distorted shape, and less draft control.

We've talked with sailmakers, and most peg the overall performance loss that you'll pay for the convenience of in-mast furling at 20 percent or worse. With in-boom furling systems, you can assure yourself of a powerful modern sail plan with plenty of roach, with full-length battens helping to control sail shape and reduce flogging.

There are other pluses—freedom from reefing-line clutter, variable sizing potential, automatic sail-covering, and the ability to retain your original mast, to name a few—but to us the most telling difference is safety: If an in-mast furler jams, it's probable that someone will need to go aloft to free it. Until then, you'll be stuck with a hoisted mainsail in what may be exactly the wrong conditions. A jam in the boom can be addressed from on deck. If all else fails, just drop the sail as you would a normal main and furl it on top of the boom instead of inside.

Today there are five in-boom systems on the market. We've sailed them all, noting design, construction, and performance. We did our best to see how each delivers on the promise of boom furling, and at what price. One overall conclusion is that these systems really work. We put the gear through paces that occasionally created problems, but those snags never kept us from executing our set/reef/reset/douse evolution. The products we reviewed are from Schaefer Marine, John Mast, ProFurl, Leisure Furl, and Furlboom.

Though they share the same basic idea, the five systems are significantly different. So are the companies that produce them. Leisure Furl has been around since the early 1990s, and its track record and testimonials are impressive. Schaefer Marine, a well-established hardware company, on the other hand, offers a new system born of three years of design and development, but without much time in service. ProFurl engaged in extensive aerodynamic testing and material analysis before introducing a boom furler in the late '90s. That big French company with dealers in 52 countries has since been energetic in promoting boom furling to both the general public and among sailmakers.

Furlboom ("designed and built in Australia by Aussie yachtsmen to suit our rugged sailing conditions") has had a varied career and is now built and sold by the recently formed Yachting Systems of America in Costa Mesa, California. Like Leisure Furl, the company has concentrated efforts on centralizing manufacture and now offers a system that is entirely American-made.

▷ **The Bottom Line** In-boom furling units are intimidating due to the mass of controls, prohibitions, and caveats that go with them. However, we like the amount of research and development that these devices have attracted. Chart the progress from Stoboom to the present, and you have a record of innovation and clever design that makes the marine industry look pretty smart.

It's difficult to assign ratings to systems we've only evaluated short-term, and not in truly demanding conditions. But here are some basic assessments: The John Mast reefer is an older design, and the company has yet to establish an aggressive sales presence in North America. Its unit for a maximum P (mainsail hoist) of 42 feet listed (in 2001) for

In-boom furling systems, like the Leisure Furl on board this Catalina 470, have evolved to become much simpler and more reliable, but they remain expensive.

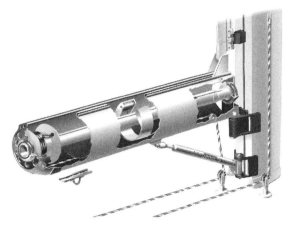

Schaefer Marine's in-boom furling system (shown in the illustration here) is somewhat simpler than those of its competitors and should be appropriate for small to medium-sized sailboats.

$6,850. This includes a boom vang, but not a sail. ProFurl gets high marks for convenience and quality. The product is built in five sizes. A 42-foot P unit retailed (in 2001) for $7,920, including a solid vang and boom brake. Schaefer's promising unit looks like it will fill the need for a simpler system that people with small to mid-sized boats can use and afford. A reefer to accommodate up to a 44-foot P retailed (in 2001) for $7,500, but the boom vang was not included. We think that Furlboom is an excellent value at $7,250 (2001 price) for a mainsail with a 42.6-foot P dimension, despite the fact that the boom vang is not included.

However, Leisure Furl still strikes us as the most-rugged, best-proven unit. To match up to a 50-foot luff length, you will need to pay $9,300 (in 2001). Installation (*PS* recommends professional installation), boom vang, and a new sail will boost that price a lot. If you're willing to pay the freight, that reefer will render good service and excellent convenience, but our feeling is that Leisure Furl's competitors have closed the gap and make attractive alternatives.

Running Rigging—An Overview

Do you occasionally contemplate replacing the frayed, stiff, dirty running rigging on your boat with some of the beautiful new stuff that hangs in reels on the wall of your chandlery? Unlike having the luxury to replace all the furniture in your house at one time, which few of us ever can afford to do, replacing running rigging is within the realm of most nautical wallets.

As a guide to how close you can come to reality, our market scan takes a look at cheap, medium-priced, and expensive approaches to fitting out a 32-foot sloop. For a different boat size, you can ratchet the figures up or down proportionally and still get close to the actual cost to do that glorious renewal of the lines that hoist, trim, lower, or control the sails aboard your boat.

Whether nylon or Dacron, any of this traditional "twisted" rope is easiest to splice. Olefin, a family that includes polypropylene and its near cousin polyethylene, was once rather scorned for marine usage, but is increasingly being worked into very high-tech line. Despite the fact that it's lousy for some applications (it's slippery, difficult to knot or splice, and deteriorates in sunlight), its light weight pleases the dedicated racers. Polypropylene is the lighter and more buoyant cousin, used mainly for water-skier towropes and as rescue lines on some throwable devices.

Finally—and that's a poor choice of a word in this magic new world of manhandling the atoms—there are high-performance fibers, lots of them, a new one every year or so. Their generic names have fancy handles like HM (high modulus), polyester-polyarylate, para-aramid, PBO, or UHMW-PE (ultra-high-molecular-weight polyethylene). They're more commonly known by trade names like Kevlar, Technora, Spectra, Dyneema, Twaron, Vectran, and Zylon, which get used in rope with proprietary names like Vizzion, Z-Tech, Crystalyne, V-12, Tech-12, Aracom, Spectron 12, Ultra-Tech, T-900, Spectron 12 Plus, Vectrus, SM Ultra-Lite, Warpspeed, Spectrum, HRC, Marstron. For some reason, it's popular right now to include "12" in a trademarked name. Hyphens are hot, too.

Rope prices vary radically. For example, for ¼-inch line you can pay as little as 8 cents a foot for stranded polypropylene, or 20 times as much, well past $1.50 a foot, for the exotic stuff. For general comparison purposes, here are some basic, easy-to-remember

Even the most modest chandlery will offer a plethora of line for running rigging applications. These come in a variety of sizes and are made from a surprisingly large number of varying source materials.

figures: For 1/2-inch line, the best three-strand nylon is about a half a buck a foot. Good Dacron double-braid is about twice as much—75 cents to $1 a foot. The exotic stuff can be five times as much as Dacron, right up around $5 a foot. Whatever line you like, *Practical Sailor* long has considered 1/2-inch or 7/16-inch a good all-around size for bare hands. When some pulling is called for, the smaller the line diameter, the tougher it is on the hands. A piece of 1/4-inch Yale Vectrus Single Braid ($1.60 a foot) has a breaking strength of 8,000 pounds, but bare hands couldn't tolerate a hundredth of that load.

In the rope industry, there's an international move underway to clarify what "breaking strength" means. In the U.S., it means "spliced breaking strength." Rope is tested with the ends fixed with eyesplices. In other countries breaking strength is a calculated figure based on individual yarn strength times the number of yarns; it yields a good comparative figure, but it doesn't hold up when a line is clamped, knotted, or spliced. Use of the "spliced breaking strength" figure would deflate somewhat the foreign manufacturers' claims.

The exotic lines, in those sizes that make it easy to handle, present different problems. They're far stronger than is usually needed for sheets and hal-

yards. With a 1/2-inch piece of really fancy line, something like New England Ropes' Z-Tech PBO Zylon ($10.50 a foot), you could pick up your whole 32-footer—plus the one next to it. (If you have a curious chemical bent, you might like to know that PBO is poly-paraphenylene-2 6 benzobisoxazole fiber, made by polymerizing diaminoresorcinol dichloride and trephthalic acid in polyphosphoric acid. With this chemical stuff, maybe it's better not to ask.)

The fancy lines made from these fibers have made a big difference to hardware manufacturers. Gear like blocks, padeyes, sheaves, cam cleats, track, and clutches rarely used to fail—and then usually only when hit with a huge shock load. More often, excessive loads resulted in parted lines. Now, with such strong line, it's the hardware that's at risk. Blocks with nylon ball bearings are now found with ground-up remnants. Far more expensive Torlon balls are better. And solid metal bushings are occasionally needed.

Because some new fibers don't like to go around sharp bends (Kevlar, in fact, is so bad at it that most ropemakers have given up using it), sheaves have tended to become larger. To get long service from these lines, one must heed the sheave size recommendations. Most of this powerful, modern line is made as braid. The braids first appeared as "double-braids," which were a loosely braided core contained in a more tightly woven cover. They could be hard or soft, stiff or pliable, fuzzy or shiny. They could rely completely on their cores for strength, or share the loads between core and cover. Such characteristics were controlled in the manufacturing process. Nowadays, braid comes as not only double-braid (sometimes the core isn't braided but is laid in "parallel" strands); it can be single-braid, a.k.a. plait, multi-plait, eight-plait, sixteen-plait, or even (and we consider this one a misnomer) plait with a three-strand core. It could be called "strand/plait," but try saying that fast three times. By the way, if you're of a curious mind, don't ever pass up a chance to see ropemaking machines in action. It all happens in the open, right before your very eyes, but the high-speed machines are perhaps the most perplexing and noisiest devices known to man.

How are the high-tech braids to splice? From "not easy" to "very difficult." Some are almost impossible to cut. A hot knife is useless. The common approach used by riggers is to use an old knife, sharpen it, hack away at the line, then sharpen the knife again. Because most of the really exotic braids do not take kindly to ordinarily reliable knots (see the following section for some eye-opening figures), it's best to learn to make eyesplices.

Samson Ropes was the bellwether in this technology, and for a couple of decades had most of the yacht business. As part of something called The American Group, it still is the biggest ropemaker in the Western Hemisphere. Other big manufacturers are Columbian (which used to give Samson some competition) and Wellington. In the halcyon days in the 1970s and '80s, when pleasure boating ballooned, two smaller companies—New England Ropes and Yale—appeared and worked their way to the head of the parade. They were aided by Samson, which for some reason, decided to downplay its recreational line and concentrate on industrial business. Several years ago, Samson decided to get back in the recreational fray. Good line also is made in Germany by Gleistein, in France by Lancelin, and in Britain by Marlow and Bridon, and in Italy by Maffioli. However, the most conspicuous suppliers of rope for pleasure boaters in the U.S. currently are New England Ropes, Yale, and Samson.

Ropemaking has become intensely technical, with many different sorts of material and many designed-in characteristics. It can be made hard (meaning tight and dense), soft (meaning flexible and easy on the hands), or stiff (a cowboy's lariat is difficult to bend). The design can concentrate on straight-line strength, flexibility, durability, or abrasion resistance—and, of course, the so-far impossible dream is to make a single line that is tops in all categories.

Again, there are problems attendant upon any such specialization—bending around sheaves and

There has been an astounding explosion in ropemaking technology. Here are three relatively new products and one that's been around for at least a decade; from top to bottom: Warpspeed from Samson Ropes, V-12 from New England Ropes, Sta-Set (the old standby) also from New England Ropes, and Vizzion, from Yale Cordage. Warpspeed is made of Dyneema, V-12 is made of Vectran, and Vizzion has a Vectran olefin core.

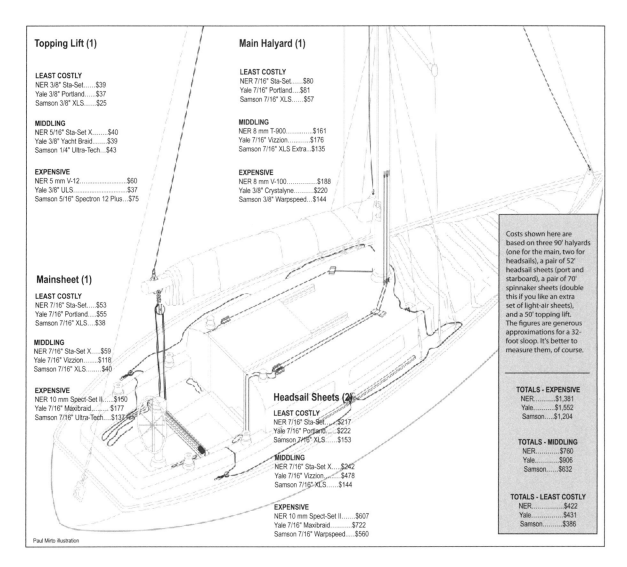

Topping Lift (1)

LEAST COSTLY
NER 3/8" Sta-Set......$39
Yale 3/8" Portland......$37
Samson 3/8" XLS......$25

MIDDLING
NER 5/16" Sta-Set X........$40
Yale 3/8" Yacht Braid.......$39
Samson 1/4" Ultra-Tech...$43

EXPENSIVE
NER 5 mm V-12.........................$60
Yale 3/8" ULS............................$37
Samson 5/16" Spectron 12 Plus...$75

Main Halyard (1)

LEAST COSTLY
NER 7/16" Sta-Set......$80
Yale 7/16" Portland....$81
Samson 7/16" XLS......$57

MIDDLING
NER 8 mm T-900.............$161
Yale 7/16" Vizzion...........$176
Samson 7/16" XLS Extra...$135

EXPENSIVE
NER 8 mm V-100..............$188
Yale 3/8" Crystalyne.........$220
Samson 3/8" Warpspeed...$144

Mainsheet (1)

LEAST COSTLY
NER 7/16" Sta-Set.....$53
Yale 7/16" Portland....$55
Samson 7/16" XLS....$38

MIDDLING
NER 7/16" Sta-Set X.....$59
Yale 7/16" Vizzion.......$118
Samson 7/16" XLS........$40

EXPENSIVE
NER 10 mm Spect-Set II.....$150
Yale 7/16" Maxibraid......... $177
Samson 7/16" Ultra-Tech....$137

Headsail Sheets (2)

LEAST COSTLY
NER 7/16" Sta-Set......$217
Yale 7/16" Portland.....$222
Samson 7/16" XLS......$153

MIDDLING
NER 7/16" Sta-Set X.....$242
Yale 7/16" Vizzion........$478
Samson 7/16" XLS......$144

EXPENSIVE
NER 10 mm Spect-Set II.......$607
Yale 7/16" Maxibraid..........$722
Samson 7/16" Warpspeed.....$560

Paul Mirto illustration

Costs shown here are based on three 90' halyards (one for the main, two for headsails), a pair of 52' headsail sheets (port and starboard), a pair of 70' spinnaker sheets (double this if you like an extra set of light-air sheets), and a 50' topping lift. The figures are generous approximations for a 32-foot sloop. It's better to measure them, of course.

TOTALS - EXPENSIVE
NER..........$1,381
Yale..........$1,552
Samson.....$1,204

TOTALS - MIDDLING
NER...........$760
Yale...........$906
Samson......$632

TOTALS - LEAST COSTLY
NER..............$422
Yale..............$431
Samson.........$386

resisting the degradations of sunlight, to name two. As we found in our rope tests, not only are some of the high-tech ropes devilishly slippery, but they weaken considerably when knotted. And, as mentioned earlier, some line is almost impossible to cut with a knife, hot knife, hacksaw, or anything else, and so would not be a good choice for a life harness or life raft tether.

Now, let's return to the original proposition, which was a complete replacement—on three different cost levels—of basic running rigging for a 32-foot sloop. Included are halyards, mainsheet, headsail sheets, and topping lift. Not included are an anchor rode (a

subject all in itself) and short lines used as outhauls, downhauls, barber haulers, reef pendants, cunninghams, preventers, vangs, etc.

For the three-level estimates, only the three major manufacturers of recreational marine line will be used. They are New England Ropes (NER), Yale, and Samson. They are the ropemakers favored, respectively in the order listed, in the discount catalogs of West Marine, BOAT/U.S., and Defender. And what's involved here is more than 600 feet of line. That's a heap of expensive spaghetti. To make price comparisons reasonable, lines from each manufacturer were chosen according to the makers' recommendations or the lines' rated breaking strengths. In some cases, the strength match-up was about 10 percent off. Many of these lines come in a choice of white with a bit of color-coding or solid colors; for pricing purposes the lower-priced white always was selected.

Even with only three manufacturers, the choices, although logical, must be considered quite arbitrary; the lines were chosen primarily to illustrate three cost levels available to a boat owner interested in renewing running rigging. The totaled figures for New England Ropes, Yale, and Samson are intended only to show the price range.

If you wanted to keep things very simple, you could, for $343 (55 cents a foot), rig the whole boat with the original Samson double-braid. Once called Parallay, it's now called LS. Twenty years ago, many racing and cruising sailors were delighted to be rigged with Parallay (or perhaps Columbian's Intrepid). Because you need 624 feet of line, you might even get a special price on a 600-foot reel.

As shown on the sailboat diagram, the price to replace the running rigging with some good-to-beautiful line can be as little as $299 or as much as $1,552—a five-fold difference. Every rope manufacturer listed here can supply printed material describing its offerings, and most have excellent websites; some of these have rigging guides showing what kinds and sizes of line they suggest for various purposes.

HIGH-TECH LINE

Most experienced sailors know that any line or rope, when knotted or even rove over a bend (like a sheave in a block), undergoes some stress that detracts from the strength that its maker claims. So, the part of a line most likely to come close to the rated breaking strength is the straight middle of that line. Unless abraded in some unusual fashion, line almost never breaks here. The parts of a line that ordinarily fail are the secured ends.

A generalization on which you can rely almost universally is that the strongest end treatment on any line is a splice. A neatly done splice, with a properly sized thimble, cuts the breaking strength of a line only about 10 percent, depending upon the kind of line it is. However, when knotted, the deterioration

in a line's breaking strength is much more severe.

Brion Toss, one of the world's most respected riggers, contends that knotting any rope made of what he calls "HM fibers" (high modulus) causes a "60, 70, or 80 percent" reduction in the line's strength. As an example, he said a piece of $^3/_8$-inch line made of Spectra, with a breaking strength of about 8,500 pounds, would, when formed into a bowline, have a breaking strength of but 2,000 to 2,500 pounds. He said that with some HM line subjected to heavy loads near their breaking strength, the core would snake out of a bowline. That's downright alarming.

His observations (including "... there simply is no way to tie a knot in an appropriately sized HM line and still have any factor of safety...") sent a lot of eyebrows skyward around *PS*'s offices. Toss suggested that sailors go back to splicing or, if they wish to tie knots in high-tech line, they accept that the line must be "massively oversized, in which case it is far bigger, heavier, and more expensive than necessary; or it is the right size and probably on the edge of breaking."

To investigate Toss's claims, we mounted a *Practical Sailor* bench test. The goal of this test was to see for ourselves just how much knots really do rob high-tech lines of their breaking strength. *Practical Sailor* engaged the facilities and expertise of Aramid Rigging (which at the time was located in Portsmouth, Rhode Island). The company, owned then by Alex Wadson, does all kinds of rigging—from conventional to very high-tech approaches for large yachts and racing boats. As implied by the company name, Wadson and his crew know much about the advantages and limitations of man-made fibers. After extensive discussions with Wadson, we decided to use line of four different categories.

To serve as a sort of baseline, we chose New England Ropes' Sta-Set, a double-braid (Dacron cover and Dacron core). It was expected that our various end treatments (knots) would fare best with this "traditional" line. As a example of moderately high-tech line, the choice was Yale's Aracom-T, which has a Technora core and a Dacron cover. If there were problems with knots, it might be with line of this type. Moving up the line, the next choice was another popular line, Yale's Maxi-Braid Plus. It has a braided Spectra core and a smooth Dacron cover.

For a very exotic line, Yale Light was chosen; it has a composite polyethylene-Spectra core and a cover of braided polyethylene. It seemed most likely that Yale Light would be trouble. Finally, to test a specific splice recommended by Toss, a piece of Samson's most expensive line was chosen. It is Spectron 12 Plus, a 12-strand single-braid made of coated Spectra. We'll note emphatically that this was not a test of one company's line against another. New England Ropes, Yale, and Samson (and other companies, too) all market line that would fit in each of the three categories.

The size of the lines, six in each category, eighteen in all, seemed not very important. The sizes were chosen for approximately equal breaking strength—with no consideration for cost. In 2001 prices, the $7/16$-inch Sta-Set (89 cents a foot) has a listed break strength of 6,600 pounds. Yale rates its $5/16$-inch Aracom T ($1.44 a foot) at 9,700 pounds. Yale's $5/16$-inch Maxi-Braid Plus ($1.70) has a break strength of 5,700 pounds. The $3/8$-inch Yale Light ($1.26 a foot), the largest size made, is rated at 5,000 pounds. Samson's $1/4$-inch Spectron 12 Plus has a breaking strength of 9,200 pounds.

Next, we decided to pull-test most of these lines with five kinds of terminations. They are a bowline with a double turn, an anchor bend, a clove hitch with one half hitch, a constrictor knot (also known as an Ashley's hitch, and said by Toss to be the best of the knots), a plain eyesplice, and, for the one piece of single-braid, a Wadson adaptation of the multiple Brummel. With one exception, one end of each of these pieces of line had conventional splices, as specified by each line's manufacturer. And in some cases, some extra line samples were pulled to destruction with knots in both ends.

We mounted each piece of line in Aramid Rigging's giant stretching machine, which runs 88 feet long. Basically, the machine is two 5-inch I-beams, with trolley cars (secured by huge pins) and a pneumatic ram mechanism in the box-shaped space created by the beams. It applies the load very gradually. The assorted rope splices and knots were tied over or slipped on smooth 2-inch pins, to minimize the damage done by severe bending. (Our first couple of tests used a section of 3-inch steel pipe around the shackle pin, but this quickly deformed and we discarded it.)

No thimbles were used on the splices, because it was the knots that were expected to fail. And everything in this linear lineup was firmly anchored. Along with intermittent snaps, cracks, and groans as knots and splices draw tight, the testing gets noisy (like rifle shots) when a good piece of line lets go.

Coupled to a computer read-out, the machine permits on-the-spot observation and also records data about properties like strength, elongation, creep, snap-back, hysteresis failure, extensibility, residual strength, and whether Michelle Pfeiffer is more beautiful than Deborah Kerr. So, besides being observed visually, each of the pull-to-destruction segments produced a graph paper chart clearly showing at what poundage the breakage occurred—as well as a broken piece of rope to examine and photograph.

The data did not fall in patterns as neat as one might prefer. Nonetheless, our test results certainly support the position of Brion Toss, which is that these HM lines lose a great deal of their strength when knotted. However, the figures don't do much to lend credence to his position that the Brummel splice solves the problems. The Brummel splice is a difficult splice, not known to many sailors and not even shown in most books on ropework. The test data showed that splices are better than any knot—except that in very slippery line (like Yale Light) splices tend to pull out.

It's tempting to shout, "Don't tie knots in exotic line!" However, that would be both an exaggeration and oversimplification. If you like generalities, here are several: The more expensive the rope, the more strength is lost when knotted, and the more likely a knot can be expected to slip. Mind you, all of this fancy rope is freely recommended, by the makers and in marine catalogs, for use in situations where knots are commonly used by most sailors. These include halyards; main, jib, and spinnaker sheets; vangs; topping lifts; guys; and travelers. They're often called "ideal" for winches and stoppers. If you use these ultra-strong (and ultra-expensive) varieties of line for such purposes, there's a way out of the dilemma that is created: It'll take you to a black hole—the one in the most remote reaches of your wallet.

It's fine to say that all rope terminations should be splices. Amateurs who do their own marlinespike work learned with the introduction several decades ago of three-strand nylon that a couple of extra tucks were called for—to counter nylon's slipperiness. The appearance of Dacron double-braid called for even more skill—and usually a diagram to keep track of the fid-length markings and the points at which the cover goes in the core and the core goes in the cover. At first, it all seemed very mysterious, but plenty of dedicated sailors set themselves to the task and overcame the problems.

The sailor faced with the occasional need to attach a shackle to a halyard or attach a pair of sheets to a self-tailing jib, can stop by the rigger's shop and pay to get it done. The rigger will even select the proper line—subtracting from its rated strength the weakness (which he should know) induced by the splice. An alternative is to buy oversized line and tie knots in it. Although severely weakened even by knots like the bowline, oversizing will take care of the problem. With this approach, the already-high cost could double.

As Brion Toss observed, you wind up with line that is "far bigger, heavier, and more expensive than necessary." And you still have slipperiness to worry about. So what's the final alternative? Unless you are a fierce racer and intend to banish at any cost any excuse for losing, equip the entire boat (except for that nylon anchor rode) with any of the excellent varieties of Dacron double-braid.

▷ The Bottom Line

- In virtually all cases when a knot held, the rope broke at the very front of the knot, at the first turn compressed by an overlay. If you have an important connection made with a knot of any kind, retie it occasionally in a slightly different place.
- Although rigger Brion Toss said he has seen the core crawl clean out of the cover of a line subjected to heavy loads, the *PS* tests turned up no similar instance.
- The only test made of the Brummel splice was on a piece of Samson's Spectron 12 Plus. It's an all-Spectra single-braid with a rated breaking strength of 9,200 pounds. With splices in both ends, it broke at 7,078 pounds—77 percent of its rating.
- In defining a rope's strength, manufacturers and catalogs currently tend to use "breaking strength"

instead of "safe working load," as they used to do. Breaking strength defines the load that produces a break or rupture. Long before a rope breaks, it undergoes severe and permanent damage. A better term from the user's viewpoint is "safe working load" or simply "working load limit," which is the load that can be endured repeatedly without doing damage. Unfortunately, the preferable term gets so complicated by things like "design factors," dynamic loading, age, wear, UV attack, etc., that manufacturers no longer routinely specify the SWL.

- In the slippery lines (especially Yale Light), the splice occasionally pulled out before the knot broke. The splices failed when the cover broke, which released the splice enough to free the core.
- When synthetic line undergoes heavy stress, it heats up—sometimes dramatically—and creates a small welded mass of plastic. You can perhaps tell if a knot is getting near its breaking point by feeling it.
- The double turns over the pin used on the bowlines were useless, as they probably would be with any knot. Unless there is abrasion, the turn is not where the break occurs.
- Unless it's used on a surface with some friction, like a rough piling or mooring bitt, the clove hitch shouldn't be considered a reliable knot, even without an added half hitch. Early in the testing, *PS* took to adding a buntline hitch to get it to hold. That made it a different ball game. The lines so secured then broke (at fairly respectable loads) at the buntline hitch.
- The most unusual result was with a piece of Yale's Maxi-Braid Plus. With splices in both ends, the line broke the core (but not the cover) in the middle of the piece. Rated at 5,700 pounds, the break came with a load of 9,030 pounds. Why, we do not know.
- When using slippery line, it's strange and unpleasant to watch a well-made knot like an anchor bend slowly but surely snake its way free when a load is applied.

Practical Sailor's seat-of-the-pants reaction to all of these readouts is simple: High-modulus fiber already has an accepted place in the standing rigging of high-performance boats, where all terminations are professionally made. It can and most likely will have a place in shackle-ended running rigging (mainsail and headsail halyards, topping lifts, maybe heavy-air spinnaker sheets) aboard a lot of weekend handicap racers, where 20 pounds of weight saved aloft can add several seconds per mile on the course. It can make a difference in the same way to performance-minded cruising sailors. But until the ropemakers figure out a way for this stuff to face up to The Knot without sacrificing The Wallet, it just can't be a trusted mate on deck. Brion Toss, not surprisingly, is absolutely right.

HIGH-TECH LINE SHACKLES

For some time, it has been our view that, as a stand-in for a standard 10-inch steel I-beam 50 feet long and weighing 1,720 pounds, there will be, sooner than you think, a piece of rigid foamed plastic that you can pick up with one hand. And the plastic beam will never corrode or fatigue, which means that you could pair it with glass (the world's other wonder material) and build something to last forever. A bellwether for this world-of-tomorrow view is rope, which has progressed rapidly from manila to nylon to Dacron and now to some of the most amazing stuff ever conjured.

PS has published a fair amount of material about UHMW-PEs (ultra-high-molecular-weight polyethylenes), as the new chemically engineered ropes are designated. Still, it sets our jaw agape that Yale Cordage is making a new line out of Zylon that, in the 1/8-inch size, has a breaking strength of 5,000 pounds. (The newest "hot line" is made in Italy by Gottifredi Maffioli. Maffioli makes Dyneema single- and double-braid in 6–14 millimeters and a small-boat line, 3–9 millimeters, called Swiftcord, with a fuzzy cover.) These high-tech ropes are bald-facedly challenging steel wire in virtually every application—a not only for boats but in architecture, industry, utilities, and telecommunications.

High-tech line seems extremely well suited to applications like halyards, running backstays, and lifelines, where it can be terminated by a splice or a custom metal or composite fitting. And, as we'll see, high-tech line is beginning to replace metal fittings themselves.

There are a number of companies and individuals working on ways to capitalize on the almost unbelievable strength of these new fibers. Again, the emphasis is on not only running rigging, but standing rigging, too. The goal is to replace wire, rod, and metal fittings with much lighter line. It's mostly to save weight aloft, which is vital on a racing boat, but is also of concern on any boat. Unless it's a keel, wrecking ball, or offensive lineman in football, any engineer will take "light and strong" over "heavy and strong."

It was probably inevitable that devices like metal shackles be replaced by high-tech line. The movement to make stainless steel shackles obsolete was started, in part, by Harken Yacht Equipment. Because it caters to serious racing sailors, Harken started offering webbing attachments for its blocks some time ago. Webbing is, by any measure, much stronger than conventional Dacron rope and much lighter than steel.

The strength of the new UHMW-PE line (it's stronger than Dacron webbing) stimulated Harken to bring out (in 1999) a line of versatile blocks called Ti-Lites, which utilize a lacing of three turns of 1/8-inch Spectra. The line used is Yale's "Pulse," which has a Spectra fiber core and a Dacron cover. In the 1/8-inch size it has a breaking strength of 800 pounds. With a six-part lacing, the strength of the "shackle" jumps to 2,380 pounds. Because the lashing eliminates not only the shackle, but also the head post and swivel, the weight savings is impressive—3.1 ounces for the conventional block versus 2.4 ounces for the Ti-Lite. In any endeavor, a weight saving of that magnitude (without sacrificing strength) is big news.

The next development was already in the works. It doesn't matter much who came first with the idea of using just a loop (or ring) of UHMW-PE line in lieu of a stainless shackle. In essence, they're not much different than old-fashioned manila grommets, which were often used as strops.

Yale Cordage in Biddeford, Maine, announced in 2002 that it was bringing to the marketplace a device to replace a metal shackle. Called a Yale "Loup," its basic purpose is to reduce weight. On the 110-foot catamaran *Team Adventure*, which sailed in The Race, 30 Yale Loups replaced metal shackles and attachment points, with a weight saving of more than 200 pounds. "After the race," said Yale vice president Dick Hildebrand, "some of the Loups tested better than when they left the factory. They didn't look like they've been around the world."

The Loup was a joint creation of Yale CEO Tom Yale and rigger Brian Fisher, of Aramid Rigging. Fisher said he and Yale spent eight months developing the product, which is basically a ring of Dyneema with a Spectra cover. He good-naturedly declined to say how the ends of the Dyneema are joined. "That's a secret," he smiled. But Fisher did explain that to add about 15 to 20 percent more strength, the Loup is annealed, meaning that the ring is pulled under a heavy load and hit with live steam.

Depending on how it's rigged, the safe working load of the Yale Loup, which is made of 9- to 21-millimeter line in stretched-out lengths from 4 to 24 inches, ranges from 3,604 to 44,100 pounds. Yet they weigh from a half ounce to 4 ounces, about a third of the weight of stainless shackles of equivalent strengths, and that doesn't count the weight saving from eliminating the posts on the blocks. The Yale Loup is, of course, a closed ring. To affix one to a block, the block must be dismantled. For padeyes and other applications, the Loups must rove around themselves.

A Loup can be rigged vertically (just stretched out), as a "basket" (doubled), as a "choker" (looped back on itself), or "boned," which means with a pin. Yale Loups, simple but labor-intensive, range in price from about $25 for a little half-ounce 9-millimeter version, 4 inches long, with a basket safe working load of 7,208 pounds, to $45 for a 21-millimeter, 10-inch-long model with a basket SWL (safe working load) of 44,100 pounds. Pretty stunning, no?

About the same time Fisher was scheming up his Loup, on the other side of this little sphere on whose surface we swarm, a professional engineer named Don Curchod was also noodling. He got thinking

about using what he calls the "super-braids" to "overcome the weight and cost problems in metal boat hardware." After a year or two of prototypes, he came up with what he now calls "EquipLites," which, until you see one, is difficult to explain.

An EquipLite is a loop of exotic line with the ends cold-fused, one end of which is inserted and secured in an aluminum double-spool (or bobbin, as Curchod calls it), one groove of which engages the other end of the loop, with the other groove for splicing to a halyard, sheet, etc. Right?

EquipLites can be substituted for shackles and swivels, and offer a weight savings of 65 to 90 percent. Curchod distributes these in the U.S. via Hall Spars & Rigging in Bristol, Rhode Island. Although priced at near the cost of equivalent stainless hardware, EquipLites are not cheap. They go for $65 for a small one (0.2 ounce) with a breaking strength of 5,000 pounds, and $279 for a biggie (5.6 ounces) that'll take 55,000 pounds.

Curchod makes other versions, including a two-block arrangement, a swivel version, etc. The EquipLites initially had some developmental problems because the flanges on the bobbins tended to bend out of shape.

Aramid Rigging introduced a near duplicate, which it calls a LoopIt—a ring of Dyneema with a Spectra sleeve and an aluminum spool with two

Doubled (or basketed) Yale Loups are shown here restraining the blocks for running backstays on board a modern racing boat. These blocks have to be disassembled to accept the Loups, and if the Loups were to be used with a padeye, they would have to be made in place.

grooves. So far, the LoopIt comes in but one size—a 20,000-pounder for about $100. Aramid uses a beefier flange made from a superior grade of aluminum to avoid the bending problem and uses a cylindrical metal pin in the spool to keep it in place.

These weight-saving gadgets are fast popping up on big racing boats. If you watch the run-up events to the *America*'s Cup on television, you'll occasionally catch a glimpse of such devices aboard the IACC boats. They're a bit strange to look at, but eminently utilitarian. Price aside (and they should come down in time), it's the light weight that is alluring. Almost as sure as the rising sun, they'll soon begin appearing on stock cruising boats. And they are further testaments to the eventual fate of steel I-beams, H-beams, girders, trusses.

Spinnaker Snuffers

In decades past, many sailmakers manufactured their own spinnaker sleeve or snuffer—the tubular devices often favored by shorthanded crews for facilitating the setting and dousing of spinnakers. Materials and designs varied considerably in these products, and the results were mixed. Today, spinnaker sleeve manufacturers have more or less settled upon a common design solution. Moreover, except for North Sails, all major sailmakers in North America have ceased producing spinnaker sleeves, opting instead to resell sleeves from companies specializing in them.

We found two such makers in the U.S.: ATN, Inc., builders of the ATN Spinnaker Sleeve; and the V. F. Shaw Co., producers of the Chutescoop. Local sailmakers do occasionally take on the job of building custom spinnaker sleeves because the fundamentals of the design are well known and not patented by anyone.

ATN, based in Hollywood, Florida, sees itself as the innovator in spinnaker sleeve design, having introduced many of the design features that are now considered standard. The company claims to have built more than 17,000 sleeves to date. V. F. Shaw Co., based in Bowie, Maryland, first introduced the Chutescoop in 1979 and takes a minimalist approach to spinnaker sleeve design, eschewing the elaborate systems found in competing products. The SnufferPlus spinnaker sleeve by North Sails is strikingly similar to that of ATN, but with a more streamlined design and simpler materials. We tested the three spinnaker sleeves on the water. But first, we had a good look at them on the dock.

The basic elements of a spinnaker sleeve are fairly simple: a tapered fabric sleeve attached to a rigid opening at the bottom, with control lines rigged for raising and lowering the sleeve over the sail. Additional design features—now nearly universally adopted by the designs we tested—include:

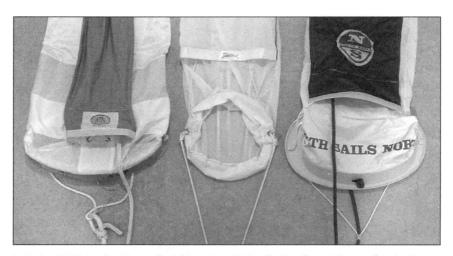

Both the ATN Spinnaker Sleeve (far left) and North's SnufferPlus (far right) come fitted with rigid, bell-like mouths to gather the spinnaker as the sleeve is pulled downward while dousing. (Those mouths are facing downward in this photo.) The Chutescoop (center) relies upon a stainless steel hoop sewn into the sleeve for that purpose (facing upward in the photo). Note that the secondary sleeve (where the control lines are run) on both the ATN and North products are fashioned from a distinctly different color to readily indicate if there is a twist in the sleeve. On the Chutescoop, this feature is a 1/4-inch strip of green nylon barely visible on the right side of the product.

Product	ATN Spinnaker Sleeve	Chutescoop	North SnufferPlus
Sleeve Material	Knitted polyester	1.5 oz nylon	200 denier nylon
Bell Material	Fiberglass-Kevlar	N/A	Gelcoated fiberglass
Total Weight	14 lbs.	8⅜ lbs.	9¼ lbs.
Control Line	Braided polyester/nylon	Braided nylon	Braided polypropylene
Price	$470	$264.15	$399.50
Ease of Operation	Excellent	Good	Excellent
Construction Quality	Excellent	Fair	Excellent
Warranty	30 days	1 year	No written policy*
Comments	works well, ruggedly built, heaviest one tested	works fine, lightly built, lots of line that could get tangled	works well, well built, best bell opening of the three

*will refund money to any unsatisfied customers

- a separate sleeve for the control line, sewn externally to the main sleeve, to keep the control line from fouling the sail;
- a pendant between the uppermost attachment point of the sleeve and the shackle for the head of the sail, to allow room for the sleeve to gather when raised;
- upward- and downward-facing bridles on the rigid opening of the sleeve, to ensure a fair pull;
- a swiveling shackle within the sleeve for the head of the sail;
- a low-friction block over which the control line runs, to raise and lower the spinnaker sleeve;
- a stripe of contrasting color, to help indicate if the sleeve is twisted.

Low weight is also an important consideration—both at the top of the rig, and on deck as one maneuvers the sail and sleeve in and out of the cabin or locker. An important engineering consideration is the fabric of the sleeve. It should be smooth enough so it doesn't create excessive friction between itself and the fabric of the sail. The fabric of the sleeve must also be chosen so that it does not bleed color onto the spinnaker when wet. Finally, it is important to keep the control line block firmly anchored in its downward position at the top of the sleeve. We have seen firsthand the damage to a sleeve's stitching and fabric that can occur when the control line does not have a fair lead. Two out of the three spinnaker sleeve manufacturers in our test have taken steps to address this issue—North and ATN.

In our tests, the ATN spinnaker sleeve set and doused with ease. We did notice, however, that the thin portion of the tapered control line came into our hands near full-hoist. On douses, the leech tapes of the spinnaker followed the acute corners of the diamond opening of the ATN bell exactly as intended.

The Chutescoop did its job smoothly as well, with just as little friction on sets and douses as the other products tested. The circular hoop functioned well, collapsing the chute in the windiest of our tests. The circular hoop showed no tendency to twist around the sleeve. However, it did tilt up on edge because the downward bridle attaches only at two points on opposite sides of the hoop. We are concerned that the metal hoop of the Chutescoop is too hard an edge for the sail to pass over, and we foresee the potential for wear on the sail's stitching over time, particularly on the luff and leech tapes. One must also be careful when attaching the halyard to the top of the Chutescoop to make sure that the twin control lines are on the same side of the halyard. If not, one of the two control lines could take a half turn around the sleeve relative to the other, which will lead to unnecessary friction and wear.

Our testers felt that North's SnufferPlus required slightly more effort to raise than the ATN sleeve, though this may have resulted from the textured surface of the braided control line rubbing over the lip of the bell on the way down to the deck. We also feel that the SnufferPlus could benefit from a swivel shackle within its head. In one of our four sets, the sail was twisted a half turn relative to the sleeve. Asymmetric spinnakers, with distinct luff and leech tapes, can easily develop a half-twist depending on which tack the sail is set on and to which side of the sail the control line is facing. The webbing pendant did absorb this twist, but when twisted, the pendant presents a potential source of friction for the control line.

ATN sells its sleeves by the foot—$10 per foot for sleeves up to 55 feet in length, or $470 for the one we tested. In lengths between 55 and 100 feet, ATN sleeves cost $12 per foot, and the cost ascends accordingly. In the upper sizes, ATN appears to be in sole possession of the market (except for custom-built products), with nine bell sizes up to 9 feet in circumference to accommodate the world's largest megayachts. As for its warranty, ATN will fully refund the purchase price within 30 days, but the company says no customer has ever requested that.

The V. F. Shaw Company offers nine standard sizes for the Chutescoop, from 20 feet up to 50 feet in sleeve length. The cost of a Chutescoop is a function of the sleeve length and hoop diameter. Per foot, the pricing for the Chutescoop works out to fall within a range from roughly $5 per foot for smaller sleeve sizes to approximately $6 per foot for the largest sleeve size. The price of the Chutescoop sleeve we tested was $264.15. The maker of the Chutescoop offers a one-year warranty on the product.

North produces sleeves up to 70 feet in length. Below 55 feet in length, North's pricing works out to be $8.50 per foot; at 55 feet and above, the SnufferPlus is $12 per foot. The price of the SnufferPlus we tested was $399.50. North Sails does not have a written warranty policy on snuffers, but the company will accept and refund the return of a product that does not meet the customer's satisfaction.

▷ **The Bottom Line** The ATN Spinnaker Sleeve is the most rugged of the three we tested, but at the cost of greater weight. It has a lot of design features, which is a sign that the manufacturer has put much thought into product improvement. But the increased labor costs of its assembly make it the priciest of our group.

The Chutescoop is an economy product, perhaps best suited for casual use on smaller boats in coastal settings. We liked its low weight and low price, but some features were questionable, and we have concerns about how the Chutescoop (and the spinnaker used with it) will stand up to wear and tear in the long run.

Our winner—North's SnufferPlus—is significantly lighter than the comparable ATN Spinnaker Sleeve, which is an advantage, and is more competitively priced for boats under 45 feet.

Gear Lifts

There was a time when you could unclamp the 70-pound outboard from the transom of the inflatable, stand braced like Atlas in the cosmos, press the engine overhead, and settle it onto its mount on the rail. Those jerry jugs full of fuel and water, those bags of groceries, those duffels that the country cousins brought with them, full of hard-soled shoes and fancy French water and hair dryers—all those things, back in the day, popped over the toerail and onto the deck with a blithe effort on your part.

There comes a time, however, when the joy of wrestling heavy pieces of gear on and off the boat begins to fade. Losing an engine overboard, or nearly losing it while barking your shins and knuckles, stubbing your toe, and ripping your shorts, makes you yearn for an easier way. And, of course, gear hoists (a.k.a. gear lifts, motor hoists, lifting davits) are the way.

In the late 1990s, *Practical Sailor* reviewed five hoists—from Forespar, Garhauer, St. Croix Marine, Atkins & Hoyle, and Marshall Design. Marshall Design at that time made the Nova Lift, which was distinguished from the others by the fact that it relies on a cockpit winch for hoisting power, rather than using a block-and-tackle arrangement at the end of its hoisting crane. We found that they all performed as specified, with only a few minor disturbances, and we noted that all hoists were easy enough to set up, take down, and stow.

At the end of the first round of tests we liked the Nova Lift for its clean, clever design, and its effective use of existing winch power. Best Buy honors, however, went to the Garhauer Lifting Davit, which worked like a charm for a lot less money than the competition. A year later, we covered the Kato Lift, from Kato Marine. Like the Nova Lift, it's an attractive design made of a single piece of stainless steel tubing with appropriate bends. Unlike the Nova, it uses a block-and-tackle for hoisting. We liked it as much as the Nova Lift, and it cost less, so it was easy to recommend. More recently, we revisited this realm, and compared a then-new product with the Lifting Davit from Garhauer. The newcomer is from Island Marine Products, a Florida company.

Both products functioned well, but there is a difference in how the lines are controlled and belayed. The Island Marine hoist has a thin-horned cleat welded to the top of the crane section; with a heavy load to lower, the hoister can take a turn around the base of the cleat for better control. The Garhauer hoist has a cam cleat mounted on the back of the crane section which controls the line on the hoist. When a load is lowered, the line must be kept clear of the cam cleat. Essentially, the Island Marine hoist offers better control on the way down, and the Garhauer better control on the way up.

Gear lifts come in three basic forms, or design styles. First is the fold-down crane style, represented by the Forespar and Garhauer hoists. Second is the removable-crane style, represented by the St. Croix Marine, Island Marine, and Atkins & Hoyle lifts. Third is the one-piece bent-pipe style, represented by the Nova Lift and the Kato Lift. The Tops-in-Quality Hoist-A-Weigh models are a variation of this, but with permanently welded bracing systems.

Given the typical chores assigned to these lifts, we can see no overwhelming advantage to any of them. It seems to be more a matter of style, stowage convenience, and type and frequency of use. If we were lifting a 100-pound outboard on and off a dinghy transom several times a week, we'd probably leave the hoist rigged and ready anyway, whether we could detach the crane arm or not.

Granted, aesthetics are important, and some of these hoists, if left rigged, will certainly look out of place on some boats. To our eye, the least obtrusive hoists are the Nova Lift, now marketed by Forespar Marine, and the Kato Lift. Both of these are simple bent-pipe designs that rely on the wall thickness of the stainless tube for strength. The original Nova Lift was designed to work with a cockpit winch for mechanical advantage, but Forespar now makes a version that integrates their Marelon winch on the lower part of the upright. The Kato Lift, rated for slightly more weight, is still more attractively priced

By hoisting this 180-pound editor, *PS* verified the versatility of gear and motor lifts. This unit, from Island Marine Products, features a demountable crane section for ease of stowing.

than either Nova Lift version. We'd opt for a 4:1 or 6:1 tackle, rather than the supplied 3:1 version, which would bring the price in line with the original tackle-less Nova Lift.

▷ **The Bottom Line** The new Island Marine lift is an excellent piece of workmanship for a decent price. (So is the St. Croix Marine hoist that seems to have inspired it.) We'd be glad to own either one, but think of them more as permanently mounted hardware on bigger boats, or even on docks. (There's a nice situation—a hoist on board the boat, and a matching hoist on your private deep-water dock, tended by a cadre of Olympic synchronized swimmers . . . but we digress.)

Among the single-piece, bent-pipe-style hoists, we still like the Kato Lift. It's well built, priced right, and enthusiastically supported by its makers in Annapolis. When we spoke with them, they were busy custom-making a set of extended davit supports for an owner who had clearance problems.

Again, there are always issues of stowage, looks, hoisting habits, and mounting options to consider, but when you weigh everything together, the Garhauer lift is still difficult to beat. It's a superb design, excellently built, for a price that sets it well apart from the competition. *PS* reader Neil Walters of Dunedin, Florida, wrote: "I purchased a Garhauer lifting davit. It is built like a fine precision watch, easy to install and remove each time I use it. They are also the cheapest-priced davit on the market by far. The quality is unbeatable. With a lifting harness, it makes it a snap to lift the outboard to the dock or back to the boat." We think Neil has it right.

The Garhauer Lifting Davit is an excellent design, and it's very reasonably priced. Here, it handles a routine lifting chore, suspending a 48-pound jug of water by way of its purchase system and cam cleat.

CHAPTER 2

Sails and Rigging

Sailboat owners generally pay so much attention to deck hardware, electronics, and other gadgets that they often overlook the most integral equipment on board their boats—the sails. Perhaps that's due in part to the nearly overwhelming complexities of sail shape and the explosive evolution of materials and sailmaking technology. Admittedly, this is a realm where even the professionals find it challenging to keep pace with all the developments. We've made no attempt in this chapter to do that, but instead offer what we hope will give readers some firm groundwork for making sail purchases and considering rigging components.

Working Sails— A Comparative Primer

The companies that make and market sails usually segment their consumers (and thus their products) into two general realms, racing and cruising, with the former normally garnering the lion's share of R&D resources as well as the marketing muscle. This situation, however, appears to be in flux. Most sailmakers now acknowledge the existence of a vital market among cruising, or less racing-oriented, sailboat owners. That's great news for the non-racing sailor, as these companies attempt to arrive at innovative approaches for sails that hold their shape longer and offer good performance along with a broad range of adjustability.

What's important about good sail shape? As one sailmaker likes to explain it, using poorly shaped or blown-out sails is like driving on bald tires. You're pretty sure your car will take you from A to B, but you won't be able to turn well or stop promptly, so your enjoyment of driving will be diminished, and perhaps your safety as well.

Before wading into these complex waters, it's good to know some essential terminology and understand a few basic concepts involved in sailmaking, so here's a quick primer.

Upwind sails are characteristically built in two ways, either by crosscut or composite construction (often referred to as laminated sails). Crosscut sails are essentially built of woven polyester fabric (most often known by DuPont's trademarked name, Dacron) where the panels of cloth run from the luff of the sail to the leech. Composite construction can be achieved in several ways, but the objective is to align the load-bearing fibers of the main structural material (often referred to as the scrim) with the primary load paths of the sail. Doing this requires layering different materials, since mere woven polyester, with its strength primarily in the fill (or short axis) direction of the weave, won't suffice for more than modest loads and thus isn't sufficient in composite construction for sails that will be hoisted on boats over 20 feet.

Regardless of the sail or sails you consider, don't just nod when a salesperson tells you what's best for your boat—get them to tell you why it is that he or she is specifying a particular material or construction method, and you'll ultimately have a greater sense of satisfaction regarding the product you end up purchasing.

PS interviewed principals from six major sailmaking labels to assess their product lines and to get their take on what approach might work best for a new suit of sails. We also asked them to offer us a quote on a mainsail and a 150-percent headsail for a hypothetical boat. We told them that the boat is a 10-year-old, 14,000-pound, single-spreader sloop, which we keep in New England in the summer and take to Florida in the winter. We rarely race the boat, but go offshore about four times a year, and often sail in the evenings with the family. We told them that sail shape and performance were important considerations. Here is a company-by-company rundown of product options. (All quotes were rendered in late 2003, so adjust prices accordingly.)

NORTH SAILS

Often seen as the industry's 800-pound gorilla, North Sails offers an extensive range of products and services through its franchise system, with a network of 40 loft facilities in Canada, the U.S., and the Caribbean alone. This company markets no fewer than seven products targeted at recreational and cruising-oriented sailors, ranging from the proprietary NorDac 4800 series of mainsails and genoas to the high-tech Marathon 3DL laminated sails.

According to longtime sailmaker Dan Neri, who spent several years managing North's cruising sail development in Portsmouth, Rhode Island, and now runs the company's 3DL facility in Minden, Nevada, in-house research has brought about some important advances. "It used to be that the least expensive sails were more durable, but not equal in performance to the more expensive sails," he said. "Now almost all sailcloth products essentially give you equal durability, but they don't give you equal shape-holding ability, and that's the big difference." In general terms, says Neri, the more you spend now, the better shape-holding you're going to get.

North builds its least costly sails out of NorDac 4800, a material woven from Dacron fibers that the company buys from several sources and then sends to a mill, specifying the parameters of the weave to create a proprietary product. NorDac 4800—available in weights from 4 to 9 ounces (per square yard)—is used to build mainsails and headsails. Though it's advertised as "tightly woven cloth," the weave isn't as tight as that in the company's next step up, Premium NorDac. The latter is woven from "high-tenacity" Dacron, which means it will stretch less than the fibers used for NorDac 4800. This ultimately translates into longer shape retention.

Neri explained that the polyester fabric used to make most cruising sails these days is impregnated with resin. With a more tightly woven fabric you don't have to use as much resin. A less expensive cloth gets most of its bias strength (resistance to stretch on a diagonal) from the resin, whereas the more expensive cloth derives more of its strength from the weave.

The next step up is a laminated fabric the company calls Soft NorLam, which is assembled with a Mylar film in the middle of two woven Dacron layers. This is where the oriented construction begins within North's product line. For larger boats the company offers a range of fabrics using woven Spectra layers laminated on both sides of the Mylar film. (Spectra is a polyethylene fiber produced by Allied-Signal. It has tremendous initial resistance to stretch, but does elongate over time with constant stress.) For roller-furling headsails, North markets a Soft NorLam sail it calls the RF2, which it says is especially suited to this application because stronger fabric is concentrated in the leech and the foot areas, using panels of varying weights.

The lightest NorLam cloth uses 5-ounce Dacron laminated to Mylar; the heaviest uses 10-ounce woven Spectra or Spectra and carbon for mega-yacht applications. According to Neri, NorLam has a big advantage over Dacron panels because it stays

Working sails, like the reefed mainsail and 110-percent headsail shown here, are ordinarily built with either crosscut or laminated methodologies. These two are laminated sails, built by North Sails under the Marathon 3DL product name.

relatively stable on the bias until it ultimately yields, while Dacron used without any additional structure will distort gradually over time.

"Longevity in sails is totally dependent upon how the boat is used and where," he explained. "We've found that customers who really work their sails get about four years out of laminated sails, and at the end of that period the sails are essentially shot. If the same customer had Dacron crosscut sails, he could milk those sails for roughly seven years. The big difference is that at the end of three or four months with the Dacron sails, you'll have the same shape that the Norlam sails will have at the end of about three years. That's essentially why sailboat owners who make the move to composite sails just don't go back to Dacron."

The higher-end headsails and mainsails offered by North—specifically for long-distance cruising sailors who value sail shape and performance—include the company's trademarked Spectra/Dyneema material, used when light weight and low stretch are the prime considerations, and Marathon 3DL, North's marquee product for high-end cruising inventories.

Many sailors are familiar with North's 3DL process, in which laminated sails are built on a large mold with yarns laid out and sandwiched in between layers of film to carry the primary loads. Neri said that a Marathon 3DL sail is basically a 3DL sail sand-wiched between Dacron covers on each side. The sails are protected, he explained, by their oversize yarns. "Even if the sun breaks down all the UV inhibitors and blockers we use, and cooks the outside of the yarn, the core of the yarn retains its strength." For the strength in its 3DL sails, North primarily uses Vectran yarn, which Neri admitted doesn't have the best resistance to UV degradation, but holds up because of its size.

The outer layers of Marathon 3DL sails are made of a proprietary product North calls TF, which is a customized 1.7-ounce NorLam taffeta/film developed expressly for this application. According to North, the TF film not only protects the internal fiber matrix of the sail from chafe, puncture, and UV degradation, but combats off-axis stretch and contains double the usual amount of titanium dioxide UV screening agents, plus a fungicide to discourage mildew growth.

Neri admitted that the Marathon 3DL sails are more expensive, perhaps by 30 percent, but he offers the following perspective on that issue: "It seems like misplaced economy to save whatever the difference is by buying a Dacron sail and having what turns out to be a poorly shaped airfoil for most of the sail's life. When you weigh that gain against the total amount of money you spend to enjoy your boat, you might as well have a sail that retains its shape and consequently makes the boat faster, makes it not heel over as much, and is easier to hoist, reef, and douse."

THE QUOTE Neri wasn't convinced that our hypothetical boat represented a realistic consumer. "The customer doesn't sound like a real boat owner, or if he is one, he needs some help figuring out what he wants to do with the boat. Few boats cruise from New England to Florida. A 35-foot boat like this would maybe go to Maine once a summer, or to the Elizabeth Islands or Block Island a few times, and the owner would not use its racing sail for those trips. So it is unrealistic to say you are buying a sail for some racing and mostly cruising. Also, you wouldn't want a 150-percent genoa for offshore trips. If I got this inquiry, I would call the guy and work him through to a more honest assessment of what he needs before offering a price or recommending any products."

After explaining why this customer should opt for a high-clewed headsail and a main with two full battens, Neri supplied the following quotes: a mainsail of 8-ounce Dacron with two full-length battens and two reefs for $2,105; and a 140-percent genoa of 7-ounce Dacron, with UV leech and foot, and a rope-luff reefing pad with reefing patches for $2,852.

QUANTUM SAILMAKERS

Quantum is a relatively young firm whose salesmen like to distinguish their company as a custom sailmaker. According to Dave Flynn, a Quantum salesman and consultant, "Quantum builds sails for a very broad spectrum of clients. We build engineering-intensive products that are high quality, and we tend to attract customers who are a little more demanding due to custom issues." He said that roughly 50 to 60 percent of the sails this company builds are crosscut Dacron, which is still a relatively cost-effective way to fabricate sails. But Quantum's specialty is composite-built sails.

"Performance is really important for cruisers," explained Flynn, "because it's about good sail shapes that offer better control of the boat. For Quantum, that's where better materials and stronger, less stretchy sail construction comes in." Flynn said that both composite and crosscut construction will produce sails that last long, roughly 3,500 hours, "but composite sails have a longer life as a critical

airfoil . . . in rough terms you gain probably two to three times in the shape life of a sail by going with composite construction."

According to Flynn, all composite sails are made using the same basic structure—large oriented fibers that do most of the work and a piece of Mylar film sandwiched between two woven layers of cloth. "Many cruising boat owners have a hard time accepting Mylar, but Mylar is nothing more than polyester extruded in a sheet. The reason to use it is that it is equally strong in all directions. When you take this film and stick it in a composite laminate, you achieve bias stability." What really differentiates one product from another in the market, said Flynn, is the structure inside the laminate.

For its cruising customers, Quantum offers three choices of structural yarns in the composite sails it builds: Polyester, Spectra, and Vectran. The lower end in terms of cost begins with Dacron fibers, which Flynn says can be used in composite applications to render sails that are slightly lighter than a comparable crosscut sail. These sails have the same flex and UV resistance as their crosscut cousins, but hold their shape much longer. Another polyester option

These two illustrations of mainsails from Quantum Sailmakers indicate the difference in panel layout from a crosscut sail (left) to a laminated sail (right).

is Fentex, a high-modulus yarn that has no greater flex, UV resistance, or durability than Dacron, but stretches two to three times less. According to Flynn, Dacron works well for smaller, lighter-weight boats, Pentex yarns work well in sails on boats up to 45 feet, and after that customers are encouraged to buy sails built with Spectra, Vectran, or even carbon yarns.

Spectra is what Quantum recommends for high-load applications where performance and durability are required and cost is less of a concern. Spectra, however, is quite expensive, said Flynn, particularly in scrim form, and it does have two other drawbacks: it is subject to creep (it elongates under constant load), and laminates built with this fiber are particularly susceptible to mildew.

Vectran—a polyester-based liquid crystal fiber manufactured by Hoechst-Celanese—is heavier than Spectra, yet offers five times the stretch resistance of polyester. It also has great flex characteristics, but is more expensive and more prone to UV degradation than Spectra. It is also slightly heavier, so Quantum recommends Vectran in applications where weight is less of a concern.

Flynn said that Quantum will specify varying weights of the woven Dacron taffeta—the bread in the composite construction sandwich—depending upon the application (mainsail, headsail, etc.). Because any laminated sail is susceptible to moisture penetration, these layers are usually treated with a fungicide to combat mildew. Quantum obtains this cloth from a variety of suppliers. "We do our own testing and analysis of sailcloth," explained Flynn, "and we buy accordingly." He said the company customarily purchases Dacron from Challenge Sailcloth, Bainbridge International, and Contender. "The reality in this industry is that cruising sailors are the ones who more often than not get stuck with the low end of any product line, because the perception is that they don't know any better. And it's almost impossible to tell the difference between a good-, a mediocre-, or a poor-quality fabric unless you test it. So we differ from other sailmakers in that we only use the best materials. We don't use any of the low-end fabrics." This policy, Flynn admitted, means Quantum's products often carry a higher price tag.

THE QUOTE Flynn offered two possible constructions for mainsail and headsail—woven polyester, or polyester composite using oriented construction. "Your ultimate choice would be based on the emphasis of sail shape versus budget. I would probably steer you toward a woven polyester mainsail, but a polyester composite headsail," he said. "I would also recommend that you think hard about making the headsail smaller than 150 percent, particularly if this is to be the all-purpose roller-furling sail for offshore use."

For a mainsail, Option 1 would be a 317-square-foot sail made from 7.62-ounce Challenge HA woven polyester (including luff and foot hardware, pultruded fiberglass battens, leech cord with cleat, telltales, sail ties, and a sailbag); the base cost would be $2,203. Reefs would be optional, with two costing an additional $132. Option 2 would be 317-square-foot sail with tri-radial construction using Dimension's CX7T, including hand-sewn luff and foot hardware, pultruded battens, leech cord with cleat, telltales, sail ties, and a sailbag. The base cost would be $2,748, but add two reefs ($164) and it would be $2,913.

For a headsail, Option 1 would be a 450-square-foot RF genoa, made with 6.62-ounce Challenge HA woven polyester, including luff attachment hardware, leech cord with cleat, telltales, and sailbag. The base cost would be $1,786, but add a UV acrylic cover ($377) and foam luff ($197), and the overall price would be $2,360. Option 2 would be a 450-square-foot RF genoa made using tri-radial construction and Dimension's CX6T, including luff attachment hardware, leech cord and cleat, telltales, and a sailbag. The price here, including UV acrylic cover and foam luff, was $3,439.

UK HALSEY SAILMAKERS

In business for almost 50 years, UK Sailmakers merged with Halsey Lidgard Sailmakers, another enduring firm, in mid-2005. Now operating as UK Halsey, the company offers sails for nearly every facet of the sailboat market, but general manager Adam Loory hastens to point out that the company prides itself on its custom sailmaking. "All our sails are custom-designed and custom-made for each customer. We don't have off-the-shelf products, and we use our own proprietary design program to complement that service."

Sailmakers can build long-lasting shapes from modern materials, and these shapes can be fine-tuned with a myriad of sail and rig controls. The challenge today is for cruising sailors to understand and operate these advanced sails.

The company does have a franchise arrangement with a loft in Hong Kong that builds custom and OEM sails, said Loory, "but you can't compare the OEM sails to the custom sails they or any other UK loft builds." For the non-OEM sails, he explains, every prospective customer is asked nine essential questions about his boat and the kind of sailing he or she does. "Then you have to measure the boat so that whatever you design fits all the specifics of that particular boat. Sails really can't be stock items. They have to be custom."

UK Halsey's worldwide group comprises 43 lofts and sales offices, more than half of which are in the U.S. Every loft can build woven Dacron crosscut sails, but they can also create sails using a patented construction process that UK Halsey markets under the name Tape-Drive.

"This is essentially a two-part construction process," explained Loory, "where the skin that defines the sail shape is a separate element from the part of the sail that gives it strength and shape-holding ability." He offers an analogy from the construction industry where "a traditional sail is sort of like a masonry construction process in which the walls define the shape and hold up the building. With Tape-Drive, it's more like a modern office building where the structure is derived from a steel skeleton and the shape is provided by the glass curtain of walls.

"The idea behind the tapes is to have them oriented so that they run continuously between the three corners of the sail to handle the primary loads. On a 30- to 40-foot sailboat you'll have anywhere from 30 to 60 tapes on a leech of the sail, which is a lot of structure. And most of the tapes we use have a breaking strength of around 1,000 pounds.

"The huge advantage for the cruising sailor," continued Loory, "is that the Tape-Drive grid keeps any damage localized. If you get a minor problem with your sail while you're out sailing—like a spreader tip poking through it—you can keep sailing without fear of the sail ripping.

"We can match the materials to the budget and performance demands of a customer. We can make a Tape-Drive sail with a polyester laminate or a Kevlar laminate, both of which are less expensive than Spectra. And the tapes can be reinforced with Kevlar, carbon, Pentex, or fiberglass yarns."

According to Loory, the company buys its laminate materials and Dacron from Dimension Polyant, Bainbridge International, and Challenge Sailcloth. Some of the tapes it uses are actually fabricated at UK lofts.

To cater to the cruising market, UK Halsey produces what it calls a Passagemaker genoa in two different constructions—Dacron and Tape-Drive. Each incorporates roller-furling with a UV cover, foam luff, reefing reinforcements on the foot and leech, and each is fitted with marks aft of the tack so that the user can achieve the proper settings when furled. "For roller-furling sails we make our UV covers sacrificial. They're put on last, and they even cover the webbing for the rings. This makes the cover easier to service and replace once it wears out."

UK Halsey's mainsails for the cruising market are also designed and built in either crosscut or Tape-Drive configurations with full-length battens, which

Loory said offers three important advantages: the sail holds its shape more easily, it lasts longer, and it's easier for the user to handle. He also points out that full-battened mainsails tend not to slat when a boat rolls in light air and large waves, and they offer better projected area downwind by supporting the leech of the sail. The company also builds roller-furling mainsails.

UK Halsey's most advanced cruising sails are made of a Spectra laminate with Kevlar or carbon fiber tapes in the Tape-Drive configuration.

THE QUOTE For a mainsail, Loory recommended a full-battened sail made of Dacron. He cautioned that full-length battens are a little difficult to race with because they lock in one shape that most adjustments can't vary. "It is also more difficult to tell when a full-batten main is luffing," he cautioned.

Determining the size of the genoa, said Loory, is contingent on where the boat will spend the majority of its sailing time. "In traditionally light-air areas like Long Island Sound and the Chesapeake Bay, you want the biggest sail possible without taking a rating penalty (155 percent of LP is best). If the boat sails mostly in Buzzards Bay or San Francisco Bay, a smaller sail would be appropriate (125 to 135 percent of LP)."

Regardless of its size, Loory based his quote on a roller-furling sail (in this case 140 percent of LP) and offered quotes for both a Spectra laminate and a Pentex laminate, each reinforced with the patented Tape-Drive construction system. "The biggest difference the customer will notice is that the Spectra laminate is white, while the Pentex laminate will have a gray-green color because of the UV protection in the laminate. The Spectra Tape-Drive sail will last up to eight years with proper care, while the Pentex laminate sail will last half that time." Loory said that he wouldn't quote on a Dacron headsail due to the "owner's" plans to occasionally race the boat.

"Given what this owner wants to do, the inventory really needs an additional sail," said Loory. "Any boat going offshore needs a working jib to use in heavy weather. A roller-furling genoa can handle most sailing conditions and points of sail during coastal sailing, but if you're offshore and need to go to windward for long distances in a breeze, a rolled-up genoa is not going to cut it. The aerodynamic shape of a rolled-up sail is too inefficient. Coastal sailors can deal with the inefficiency since a quiet harbor is usually no more than a few hours away—an extra hour bashing to windward because of poor sail shape is inconvenient, but survivable. If you're well offshore with the wrong jib, it can lead to life-threatening circumstances."

For a mainsail, he'd use 7.0-ounce Dacron, with full battens, two reefs, racing number, draft stripes, and a sailbag, and charge $3,061. For a headsail, he offered two options: Option 1 would be a Tape-Drive Spectra genoa, including foam luff, UV leech and foot covers, reefing reinforcements, racing numbers, draft stripes, and a sailbag, for $4,895; Option 2 would be a Tape-Drive Pentex genoa, including

Sailmakers face a continual challenge keeping up with demands for convenience. Headsail roller-furling is a done deal. Today, the issue is mainsail control and containment. Here, an Ericson 35 charges upwind with a surprisingly contemporary suit of sails from UK Halsey.

foam luff, UV leech and foot covers, reefing rein-forcements, racing numbers, draft stripes, and a sailbag, for $4,420. As for a working jib, Loory speci-fied 8.3-ounce high-modulus Dacron with 95 percent LP, including UV leech and foot covers, draft stripes, and a sailbag, for $2,841.

(At the time this article was prepared—2003—Halsey Lidgard Sailmakers also offered quotes, but that information has been removed since the com-pany thereafter merged with UK Sailmakers.)

HOOD SAILMAKERS

If there's one company among the larger sailmaking firms that's truly invested in the non-racing realm, it's Hood Sailmakers. Headquartered in Middletown, Rhode Island, Hood is distinguished in a number of important ways. First, this is the only company that has eschewed laminated sail construction, and it is one of the few companies that creates its own sail-cloth, which it has since the early 1960s.

According to Tim Woodhouse, president of Hood Sails, the main focus of the company's R&D resides in two areas—woven polyester and Vectran. "As other sailmakers began moving into laminates sev-eral years ago, we went the other way," he explained. "We found that we couldn't offer customers anything approaching a three-year warranty with laminated products, no matter what adhesive we used—and we're talking about a sail that would be roller-reefed. To me, that's just unacceptable."

Woodhouse told us that the company's cloth manufacturing division—Hood Textiles, located in Cork, Ireland—creates a fairly narrow range of fabric intended for use in durable, longer-lasting cruising sails. "Our facility manufactures a full line of woven, high-tenacity polyester sailcloth, which we only sell within our franchise system."

Woodhouse claimed that many sail-buying customers don't realize that there are three qualities of polyester fiber available for weaving sailcloth—low-, medium-, and high-tenacity. "Consumers and a lot of experienced sailors don't know this," he said, "but there is a substantial difference in the quality, dura-bility, and stretch resistance of the fabric, depend-ing upon what level of fiber it's been made of." He claimed that the vast majority of polyester fibers on

the market today are low-tenacity, and said that Hood only makes products from high-tenacity polyester. "We also make a proprietary product that incorpo-rates Vectran, which we call Vektron—it's essentially Vectran yarns commingled with the polyester."

Woodhouse labeled Vektron a successful alterna-tive to laminates. "It has significantly longer life than a laminate. It has the same longevity as a Dacron, but it is lighter and lower-stretch than Dacron." One key advantage of incorporating Vectran, he said, comes from the material's high resistance to heat, which keeps it from distorting when the polyester into which it's woven is heated in the finishing process that almost all sailcloth is subjected to.

Saving weight and maintaining durability is Vektron's chief advantage, said Woodhouse, particu-larly when it comes to sails built for larger vessels. In 2003, Hood built a new Vektron mainsail for the 130-foot J-Class yacht *Endeavour*. It ended up almost 50 percent lighter than the boat's previous mainsail. "For a more common boat, say one that displaces 15,000 to 20,000 pounds, we'd probably specify 9-ounce Dacron for sails, but in Vektron we would use a 7.7-ounce material. Of course this would be for a guy who wants to go world cruising, and he'd get about 30,000 to 40,000 miles out of either sail with routine maintenance in stitching and seams."

Woodhouse claimed the original Vektron sails that Hood built back in 1992 are still being used. "We've had no instances of the fabric failing. Very few people have put in that number of hours on lami-nated sails and are still using them." He did allow that a Vektron sail is roughly 15 percent more expen-sive than the Dacron alternative that his company would build. Nevertheless, Vektron products make up half the sails Hood now builds.

Some lofts in the Hood franchise system have a greater percentage of racing clients, so they work with laminates in the dinghy and one-design areas, said Woodhouse. Those lofts are free to purchase sailcloth through the four main industry suppliers (Bainbridge International, Dimension Polyant, Chal-lenger Sailcloth, and Contender), a factor Woodhouse believes offers them flexibility in the marketplace. Nonetheless, his opinion remains the same: "When you start asking customers what their expectations are for the longevity of a sail, some of them haven't thought about it. Racing customers in particular have become accustomed to diminished expectations in this regard. They speak in terms of hours, not days. Unfortunately, the longevity of racing sails has gone down, not up, with new laminate technology. Our products are addressing through R&D what the average sailor out there wants and needs, and to me that's better-performing, more durable sailcloth. I just don't think we can get there with laminates."

THE QUOTE Hood's quote began with two fabric options for a mainsail: either 7.5-ounce woven Dacron or 6.0-ounce woven Vektron. Woodhouse explained: "I would recommend the Vektron for the mainsail for performance, durability, and ease of handling, as well as a so-called softer hand." Option 1 would be 303-square-foot mainsail made of 7.5-ounce woven Dacron with four standard E-glass and epoxy RBS battens; batten pockets fabricated in a separate step and completely closed to separate the batten from the body of the sail; two rows of five-step stitching; slug slides or boltrope on the luff and foot as desired; leech line operable at the clew and at each reefpoint; a Hood patented press ring in the clew; standard aluminum headboard, telltales, four sail ties, and a sailbag, for $2,337. Other options include two reefs, a cunningham cringle, foot shelf, sail numbers, draft stripes, and insignia for an additional $633. Option 2 would be a 303-square-foot mainsail made of 6.0-ounce woven Vektron (everything else the same) for $2,420.

Full battens are indeed an option, but Hood didn't deem them necessary. The additional cost would be $470. "If the spar has an internal round slug track section, this does not lend itself easily to low-friction operation with the additional compression generated by full battens," said Woodhouse. "You may also then have to look at proprietary batten receptacles and so on, so the price goes up—but we're not convinced the value goes up with it."

For a headsail, Woodhouse told us: "We're of the opinion that 150 percent is too big for this boat and its stated use. We would really recommend the customer consider a sail closer to the 135 percent size. We also wouldn't recommend a roller-furling genoa for the stated purpose. It is too light, and though all sorts of characters have sailed all over the place with only one headsail on a furler, we consider that prac-

tice extremely poor seamanship. So we'd specify a 135-percent roller-reefing headsail (484 square feet) designed slightly flatter for greater utility as the sole headsail." Woodhouse said he'd specify either 8.0-ounce woven Dacron or 6.0-ounce woven Vektron. The sail would have a luff tape, telltales, UV sunshield, foam luff pad, reinforcing at the head and tack to accommodate reefing strains, reef memory marks on the foot, leech, and foot lines, Spectra webbing in head and tack, Hood press ring in the clew, and a sailbag. The Dacron version would cost $3,523; and the Vektron one $4,104.

NEIL PRYDE SAILS

The name Neil Pryde might draw more recognition as a maker of windsurfing sails and an OEM supplier, but the company is also a strong player in the custom cruising and recreational sailboat market. According to Managing Director Tim Yourieff, who operates out of the U.S. corporate headquarters in Milford, Connecticut, "most of our sails are built for cruising boats. Our true niche is really performance cruising."

Neil Pryde Sails offers four distinct lines of product: Performance Cruise, Cruise Plus, and Cruise, as well as sails designed and built expressly for less demanding, recreational boats, called Inshore sails. The majority of Neil Pryde sails are cut and assembled at its massive facility in China, which company literature touts as "the largest centralized sail loft in the world." Yourieff explained that this helps his company maintain the highest construction standards possible. "We're able to put a lot of detail in the sails because we manufacture them in a central facility."

Yourieff said that all design work is done in the U.S., and all materials originate here as well. To interact with and service its customers, Neil Pryde Sails has a system of 30 lofts worldwide, all of which are sales centers and some of which are service lofts.

The company's entry-level product—the Inshore line—is for weekenders or daysailors, but essentially not for boats over 25 feet. These sails are ordinarily single-ply, crosscut Dacron sails of up to 6.5-ounce cloth, with plastic headboards, a single row of stitching, and no frills. "We get our Dacron from Challenge

Sailcloth and from Contender," Yourieff explained, "and we don't cut corners on the fabric—it's all high-tenacity Dacron."

The next step up for cruising or non-racing customers is the Cruise line, which also means crosscut Dacron sails (built of either Challenge's High Modulus or Contender's Super Cruise fabrics) that the company advertises as "inshore cruising sails designed to handle additional offshore use as well." These sails are single-ply panels reinforced in the highest load areas with "block" patches (not radial). They also have heavy-gauge aluminum headboards with stainless steel liners and hand-sewn slugs.

Then, by opting for what the company calls its Tradewinds specifications, customers can get what charter boat clients get—heavy reinforcements on almost every aspect of the cloth, stitching, and hardware. Yourieff labeled these "truly the best-value cruising sails on the market today. . . . We've had guys do circumnavigations with the Cruise-level sails. I wouldn't recommend that specifically, but they're good sails."

After that comes the Cruise Plus line, which are also crosscut Dacron sails. "The biggest difference here," explained Yourieff, "is that we two-ply the leech and the head, and all the reinforcements are radial. And the sail numbers and insignias are included in the price." These sails, he said, are really intended for the bluewater sailor. Though the Cruise Plus sails have many standard features, the roller-furling headsails in this line don't come standard with foam luffs or UV-resistant sail covers. Like all the company's sail products, these carry a two-year warranty for work and materials.

Neil Pryde's top-of-the-line sails for cruising customers are built as Performance Cruise sails. These are laminated, tri-radial sails, and it's in this realm where the customer choices are the broadest. These sails are generally sandwiched inside a Dacron taffeta, though occasionally the taffeta is just on one side. This is intended to protect the scrim fibers and the film from abrasion and UV degradation. Yourieff pointed out that customers have a number of choices regarding the fabric—polyester, Pentex, or Spectra.

THE QUOTE For our hypothetical customer, Yourieff recommended Neil Pryde's Cruise Plus range of sails. "This construction standard is specifically designed for sails that will see blue-water, offshore sailing, which you will encounter between New England and Florida. For the mainsail, I would recommend a full-battened sail, as this tends to greatly reduce sail flogging and therefore increases the sail's life span. For offshore sailing I would recommend three rows of reefs, or two rows and a storm trysail." Yourieff continued by adding, "you should definitely cover the sail while it's not in use, especially in Florida. You may wish to consider our Lazy Bag cover for this." A 317-square-foot Cruise Plus mainsail made of 8.3-ounce Challenge High Modulus Dacron would run $1,951.48. Add one reef, and the cost jumps up $146.35. Add four full battens for another $194.97, and a Lazy Bag sail cover $611.68, and the total cost is $2,904.

"For the genoa," said Yourieff, "in addition to an Acrylic UV suncover, I would strongly suggest fitting the sail with our Multi-Track foam luff system. This option helps to reduce sail draft when the sail is partially furled in order to maintain a reasonable shape when reefed in strong winds." Yourieff specified a 150-percent Cruise Plus (545.69 square foot) furling genoa with two-ply head and clew made out of 6.9-ounce Contender Dacron for $2,622.16. Adding a UV Suncover would bump that price up $298.02, and a Multi-Track Foam Luff would add $195.58, making the total price $3,115. (Should we want to consider Yourieff's suggestion of a storm trysail, one made of 9-ounce orange cloth would run $685.)

DOYLE SAILS

Like many sailmakers, Doyle Sails offers several product lines identified by marketing trade names. Bluewater Sails, DuraSails, 2+2 mainsails, and QuickSilver Genoas comprise Doyle's lexicon of labels for the cruising customer. But these labels are simply a point of departure, said Mark Ploch, a franchisee and proprietor of Doyle Ploch Sailmakers in New York and Clearwater, Florida.

"We're a custom sail loft, and every sail, just like every owner, has a unique set of needs," explained Ploch. "If a guy owns a Catalina 30 on Lake Lanier, he's not going to need a Bluewater-style sail. We'd probably lean in the direction of a DuraSail for that customer, but we'd make some important alterations, like not building as much roach into his mainsail as we would for the same boat in southern California. And the clews on any headsail, whether we specified a QuickSilver genoa or a sail built with Doyle Vectran, would automatically be raised for better visibility. After that, if the client didn't have specific preferences, we'd build the sail along the lines of our normal DuraSail standards."

Doyle Sails, which has been in existence for almost 40 years, has 20 lofts around the U.S. The company's basic non-racing product is its line of DuraSails. These are crosscut Dacron products—both mainsails and headsails—without any of the costly frills included in the company's other products. This, claimed Ploch, results in a good sail value for small- to medium-sized boats. DuraSails are offered with a three-year warranty.

Doyle's next line is called Bluewater Sails. These are essentially crosscut Dacron sails with a finish and details that step them up from DuraSails. For instance, these sails are built with the reinforcement needed for ocean passages, including larger patches that are usually triple-stitched, heavier taped edges, Spectra webbing, and lower-stretch leech lines. Depending upon the usual factors—the kind of sailing a customer does, his or her sailing locale, and that person's expectations regarding the longevity of the product—Ploch said he and his colleagues will specify a certain weight of high-tenacity Dacron. He explained that the warranty Doyle offers on its Bluewater Sails is based on details like the luff slides being sewn on with webbing, the batten patches being reinforced, all the seams being taped as well as stitched, and having large radial patches applied to reinforce the high-load areas like clews and heads. All of this, said Ploch, is standard construction protocol at Doyle lofts.

Stepping up from there, the cruising product line moves into the QuickSilver Genoas and 2+2 Mainsails. The claim that Doyle makes regarding its QuickSilver II headsails is that they offer "the low stretch of laminates with the durability of woven Dacron" at a lesser price. The 2+2 Mainsails, which can be built either of woven panels or laminated fabrics, are intended to satisfy customers who both cruise and race. The idea here, explained Ploch, is to achieve product durability with two full-length battens in the top of the sail and adjustable sail shape with two longer-than-normal battens in the lower portions.

Doyle also offers a proprietary product for roller-furling mainsails that it calls the "Doyle Swing Batten," which is a rigid batten that can be articulated by way of a control line to align vertically for furling or horizontally for sailing.

What sailcloth does Doyle specify for its sails? "We actually use a lot of the latest racing fabrics in many of the cruising sails we sell," said Ploch. "We find that cruising sailors are oftentimes the more challenging customers because they really demand more of the product than a racing sailor. So even though Dacron is probably the material we use most in bulk terms, we use a lot of composite construction materials in our cruising sails. We also build a lot of megayacht sails, in which we often use our new Ocean Weave, and in some cruising sails we're beginning to see an application for our new D4 product."

D4 is a laminated cloth with the base fabric assembled in the Doyle Fraser facility in Australia. It has yarns laminated in between layers of film or fabric, said Ploch. "We specify different components depending upon the order, so in this way the sailcloth is constructed around the needs of the boat." Also among its high-end products, the company offers sails built of a fabric it calls Doyle Vectran, which incorporates Vectran in a laminate between two layers of taffeta that is then cut into a traditional tri-radial sail.

Ploch is keen to stress the importance of tailoring the product to the customer's needs. "It works best that way. With a little information, we can put that person into the most appropriate sail. We can design the inventory to his needs. And honestly, that's the kind of customer that we deal with a lot. Our market is very service-oriented and our buyers are sophisticated."

THE QUOTE Ploch suggested two options for mainsails and headsails. He said the Dacron/Mylar combination mainsail would be great for the more modest budget. The D4 option is "Doyle's best product, and gives you the best balance of performance and durability." Regarding headsails, Ploch offered both the QuickSilver II genoa and a roller-furling sail. He also proffered this important caution: "We feel that something in the neighborhood of a 135-percent headsail is a better sail for the cruiser than a 150-percent. Most of the time they're not sailing with a crew stacked on the rail, and they're usually less concerned about boat speed when there's under 6 knots of true wind than they are about heel in 15-plus knots."

Ploch's quote included a foam luff on the headsail, but he said that he tries to talk most of his southern customers out of this option for two reasons. "The foam luff does indeed help flatten the sail as it rolls in, but you will always have a sail that is compromised. When the sail is rolled up it is sitting behind that fat roll, and when it is totally unrolled, the foam luff makes a thick leading edge, which is hard to read. And, in the warmer southern climates, mildew is an issue within the foam."

For a 329-square-foot mainsail, Option 1 would use 7.62-ounce Dacron with four standard battens, two reefs, a shape stripe, slides, headboard, and a sailbag for $3,122; Option 2 would use D4 Vectran 10 with standard film/taffeta, including four standard battens, two reefs, numbers, a headboard, sail slides, a cunnigham, and a sailbag for $4,210.

For the 497-square-foot headsail (150 percent), the QuickSilver II version would be made from 6-ounce Mylar, including a UV cover and a sailbag for $3,693. The roller-furling version (also 497 square feet) would use D4 Vectran with standard film/taffeta, including spreader patch, UV cover, and a sailbag for $4,779.

▷ **The Bottom Line** Admittedly, there's a lot to absorb here, from technical information to marketing lingo. It's also important to note that none of these major sailmakers take customer service lightly. Anywhere above the basement level, customers can expect personal attention and methodical systems in place for determining the right materials and construction techniques.

We find a clear consensus here that woven-only sails will last longer, but will lose their top efficiency relatively early, while laminated sails will hold their designed foil shape longer but not last as long overall. Standing apart on that matter, with a venerable company track record to back him up, is Tim Woodhouse of Hood Sailmakers.

The major remaining concerns, in order of importance to us, thinking in cruising terms, would be, first, long-term customer service; second, overall durability, meaning resistance to UV, flogging, mildew, poor folding and flaking, and stress at the corners; and third, general shape-holding ability. Oh . . . and cost. Regarding that, it's clear that purchasing new sails involves huge expense. The specific prices we got from these sailmakers ranged from $2,105 to $4,210 for a mainsail, and from $2,360 to $4,799 for a genoa, and due to varying technologies, it's not always an apples-to-apples kind of comparison. However, unless you want to opt for used sails (see "Discount Sail Options," next in this chapter), there's really no way around shelling out this kind of dough.

As all these sailmakers acknowledge, one undeniable key to satisfaction is customer service. But there exists a disconnect here, we think, as far as cruising sailors are concerned. While big-boat racers have long been accustomed to having their sailmaker come along for a ride with a new sail (sometimes several rides, until it's made right), cruising sailors, maybe because they're ordering sails from afar, or buying "stock," or simply don't know when a sail is cut right or not, just don't expect that kind of treatment. But they should. We met a cruiser recently who was worried about where to put leads for his new working jib, but didn't want to "bother" his sailmaker. This is silly—sailmakers expect you to bother them. It's their lot in life. In our view, it's more important for a sailmaker to be willing to work with you and make sure your sails are a good fit, and recut them if necessary, than to deliver those sails for a low price.

Customer service varies from loft to loft, not only among small outfits, but among the big sailmaker groups, and from boat style to boat style. The owner of a Cal 2-29 said in a recent *PS* reader survey, "I have found small, independent sailmakers to be a little less high-tech, but very capable and customer focused." We don't disagree, but we also know that local representatives of the big chains are sometimes more expert and efficient at making certain sails for certain boats. So, there are two questions to ask of any prospective sailmaker: (1) "Have you made sails for my kind of boat before?" and (2) "Will you go out sailing with me?"

Simple crosscut sails are the stock and trade for many discount sailmakers, but that doesn't mean you won't find some reasonable bargains in laminated sails through these sources as well.

Discount Sail Options

Practical Sailor is well aware that not every sailboat owner is equipped with Vanderbiltian wherewithal, a circumstance with which we can readily relate. So, with that in mind, we spent a little time online and Web-surfed our way to some nice bargains on discounted working sails. In the course of our research, we assessed what's available through online discount sail brokers—for both new and used sails—and compared services, prices, and warranties for a suit of working sails.

In an attempt to standardize the information, we chose an established design—the Catalina 320—as our hypothetical boat. The 32-foot Catalina has a 252-square-foot mainsail (give or take a little depending upon the roach you'd like), and a foretriangle that measures 269 square feet. Over 1,000 Catalina 320s have been built since the boat's introduction in 1993, so we felt this boat would offer a relatively stable basis for comparing quotes.

The caveat here is that there are a number of details to be aware of when ordering a sail online. Cloth types and weights should correspond to the kind of sailing you do as well as your expectations for the sail's longevity. Also important are the number of reefs you want, the types of mast attachment hardware, batten configurations, and reinforcement areas. And that's just the mainsail. Regarding genoas,

you will need to specify the appropriate-sized luff tape or hanks, and whether you want UV protection, foam luffs, leech lines and cleats, telltales, and insignias or numbers, as well as sail covers and sailbags. We specified a single-reefed, fully battened mainsail built from 7-ounce cloth, and a 140-percent genoa with a UV suncover and foam luff. We didn't seek quotes for gennakers or spinnakers.

Of course, the customer service that these companies can provide is also important. Even though these folks are selling discounted products, they should nonetheless answer e-mails and return phone calls, and offer advice when requested regarding the details involved in getting a sail right for the clients who are forking over hard-earned cash. Here are the players and their offerings:

National Sail Supply, based in Fort Myers, Florida, deals in new and used sails. It was the first discount online sail supplier we contacted, and frankly, we were impressed with their response time and attention to detail. They got back to us within six hours. The firm's website offers a generic form to complete for quotes, as well as a direct e-mail address and phone and fax numbers that are easy to find.

Dirk Sharland quoted on a new, 7.3-ounce Dacron, full-battened mainsail with one reef and internal mast slides on the luff and a boltrope on the foot for $1,280, including the battens. Despite our attempts

KIWI SAIL SLIDES

No matter how beautiful or well-made working sails are, their efficiency is greatly affected by the manner in which they are attached to a mast or forestay. There are lots of lousy sails in use—partly because they weren't very good to begin with or have been unmercifully stretched, soaked, and wrinkled—but even a lousy sail will function better than a good one if its attachment system is superior. As an engineer would say, sails are your primary source of propulsion, but they have to be set in place properly to work.

We've come a long way from hickory or iron mast hoops and rope grommets with parrels. (The bead-like parrels sometimes were made of lignum vitae, a wood so heavy and hard that it doesn't float in water.) Hoops and grommets were not only picturesque, they were a quantum leap forward from lacing a sail on a spar. Striking sail was not easy for the Vikings.

Nowadays, most mainsails are attached to the mast with metal or plastic slides slipped on a metal track or with a boltrope or slugs that fit in a groove on the mast. And most headsails attach to a wire forestay with metal or plastic piston hanks or snaps or, in the case of furling headsails, the roped or taped luff fits in small grooves in a foil slipped over the forestay.

The problem with the groove approach to either the main or headsail is that the tolerances must be tight. And creatures like spiders love to dwell in these grooves. Dirt, debris, and salt can also accumulate there. When any of those things happen, the sail does not want to go up or down very easily. This is a problem and, in an emergency, it can

mean trouble. In addition, when a jib is equipped with a boltrope or tape, the sail in use must be removed completely when the skipper opts for a substitute sail.

Now, there's a new way, developed by a New Zealand company called Anzam, which is represented in the U.S. by Brian Cleverly, who also sells Reef Rite furlers. Called Kiwi Slides, this new system uses slugs to permit a jib to be preloaded, stored temporarily, all ready for hoisting, whether it's the only sail on a single-groove furler or the second one in a twin-foil arrangement.

"What's best," Cleverly said about this product, "is that they make headsail handling easier . . . and safer." The Kiwi Slides, which can also replace the slugs on a mainsail, are webbed to a sail by sewing the webbing directly to the luff of the sail or by looping the webbing through the existing eyelets or grommets. The slides—made of fiberglass-reinforced nylon—have phenomenal breaking strengths, come in six sizes, and range in price from $2.70 to $4.84 each. They are, of course, standard on Reef Rite furlers.

Cleverly claims the new slides cut friction by 50 percent. Unlike luff tapes, where replacement is difficult if they fail, Kiwi Slides can be individually replaced and extras added if needed.

The six available sizes have breaking strengths from 506 pounds to 1,430 pounds, generally far beyond what a sail would exert. The biggest strain on sail slides, slugs, or shackles occurs not in hard winds, but while slatting—a dynamic load as opposed to a static one—and this happens when a sail pops sharply back and forth in sloppy conditions.

to submit precise and detailed measurements and option preferences, Sharland picked up on an omission we made—sail slide size. He wanted to know whether we needed ¾-inch or ⅞-inch slides.

A new 140-percent genoa made from 6-ounce Dacron and fashioned to fit a Schaefer roller-furling system, including a foam luff and Sunbrella UV protection on the leech and foot, came in at $1,325. Again Sharland's e-mail response asked us for more details. He told us that both sails would come with a two-year warranty covering material quality and workmanship, and that the price included clam cleats, telltales, and flow stripes. The construction included triple-stitched seams as well as large corner and reef reinforcements with a hand-sewn leather finish. We were glad to find pictures on the website that illustrated many of these details.

Sharland told us that the standard delivery time is three to four weeks from confirmation of the order, and the company will ship anywhere in the world. The website also specified how much the extras or upgrades would be, at a glance. An extra reefpoint, for instance, was $75, and a mainsail cover was another $171.

The total price for our test inventory was $2,605. We should note that National Sail Supply places a particular focus on serving Catalina owners, which made this quote easy for that company, but the timely service and insight were well above average.

Cruising Direct, a subsidiary of North Sails based in Portsmouth, Rhode Island, deals only in new sails. The company's website is full of good information, particularly for the DIY owner.

Dan Calore, a sales rep, offered a relatively prompt response, answering one day after our initial e-mail inquiry. He told us his quote would be for a mainsail with only two full battens (the remaining two would be partials), adding, "that's the most we can do for full battens."

This website offered the most extensive technical details in a downloadable, PDF format, which included an outline of the recommended sailcloth—North's NorDac 4800. Standard features for mainsails include crosscut panel construction, two rows of three-step stitching on horizontal seams, stainless

steel rings, solid fiberglass battens with Velcro closure pockets, triangular patch reinforcements, adjustable leech and foot lines, and a sailbag. Extras that are available include reefs, a cunningham adjustment, sail numbers and/or insignias, one or two full-length top battens, and a performance-enhancing roach.

There's no formal warranty, "but we stand behind our products," wrote Calore. The online order form breaks down prices for extras like reefpoints and cloth weight. A 7-ounce Dacron main was priced at $1,297, one reef was $104, and two full-length battens were $150, bringing our total to $1,551.

The standard genoa package includes crosscut panel construction, telltales, hydraulically pressed stainless steel rings, adjustable pre-stretched leech lines, a drawstring sailbag, and self-adhesive spreader patches. For the genoa, we chose a 140-percent sail built from 8-ounce Dacron, priced at $1,429. The UV foot and leech cover (out of Sunbrella) added $264 to the cost, and the reefing pad with reefing patches added another $357, bringing our total to $2,050. The price for the set came in at $3,601, not including sales tax and a $40 shipping cost per sail. Calore told us that delivery times vary seasonally, but the company recommends allowing more time for orders placed from January through June.

Far East Sails sells new cruising sails manufactured by a leading Hong Kong sailmaker, A. Lam Sails Hong Kong, the original sail purveyor for Cheoy Lee Yachts. The form we filled out and submitted via the website was answered five days later by Brad Gunther.

A full-battened mainsail cut from 7.4-ounce Contender Sailcloth, which the manufacturer rates as "offshore quality," with one reef, was $1,176, while a 140-percent headsail built from the same cloth and fitted with a foam luff and Sunbrella UV cover was $1,551. The prices, said Gunther, included air delivery, shipping insurance, and U.S. Customs tax.

Seams on sails over 200 square feet are triple-stitched and come with a leech line and clam cleats, except for the company's high-clew headsails and storm sails. Main and mizzen tacks and headsail clews come with leather chafing protection and anodized aluminum headboards. Slides and hanks are coated with a soft film to protect against chafing while the sails have pressed alloy stainless steel cringles and nickel-plated slide and hank eyelets. Sails have a webbed O-ring at the tack and clew patches with double tape along the leech and foot, with oversize patches at the tack and clew. Full-battened mainsails do not come with battens or batten tensioners, an item that's left to the purchaser to install.

Due to these details, we felt that photos on the website would be a welcome addition.

The lead time for delivery is approximately five weeks from receiving the order, and shipping requires two to four days via UPS. All sails come with a one-year limited warranty. One nice touch is that before production begins, the company sends each customer a computer-generated drawing of the sail as a final opportunity to check all the dimensions prior to approving the order. The total price for our inventory was $2,727.

The Sail Warehouse of Monterey, California, encourages sailors in the market for new and used sails to explore the website carefully to see if their questions have already been answered before making a call. Information on the site specifically states that the company doesn't offer sail quotes by e-mail and cautions against calling if searching for a used sail.

Our first call for a quote met with few results. While we had the measurements, it must have been a busy time at the loft as we were instructed to search the website by square foot for an approximate quote. We called weeks later and our luck changed, that call yielded a quote that was put together in about five minutes while we waited on the phone. And, we were told that the Sail Warehouse was going to begin stocking sails for the Catalina 320 in its inventory.

The mainsail this company builds comes in three versions: a standard OEM, the Coastal Cruise, and an Offshore version, ranging from $1,235 to $1,475. When we mentioned that we were looking for a full-battened main, this tipped the scale to the $1,475 price. (We were also warned that the price would likely soon being going up by 7 percent due to price increases by their cloth supplier.) The Coastal Cruise version has reinforced corners and is intended for coastal and medium-duty cruising and club rac-

ing. The sails are made from performance-grade Dacron with two to three rows of zigzag stitching used throughout. Pressed corner rings are reinforced with webbing, and draft stripes are standard. We were told that a 140-percent headsail would run between $1,400 and $1,700, but a final price couldn't be nailed down as we didn't have the precise measurement of the furler hoist, and thus we were referred back to the website, which has hundreds if not thousands of sails listed. In hindsight, we felt such a small increment—typically inches—wouldn't significantly alter a price estimate for the headsail, and we expected a more accurate quote. The Sail Warehouse offers a two-year warranty and delivery of a sail typically takes three to four weeks. We were told that the total price for our order would run between $2,875 and $3,175.

Atlantic Sail Traders in Sarasota, Florida, is one of the biggest names in discount sailmaking, and deals with new and used sails. Our first inquiry didn't produce a response. Our second e-mail also wasn't answered. So we picked up the phone and twice left messages during business hours. We later found out that the company was in the middle of an unusual transition. We initially abandoned our efforts, but the subsequent testimony of at least a dozen *PS* subscribers who are loyal or longtime Atlantic Sail Traders customers convinced us that the company deserved a second look.

The firm's website does do a good job of instructing how to measure your boat for a sail. The company's cruising sails come with radial corner reinforcements, triple stitching, leather chafe guards, leech line, draft stripe, telltales, and a sailbag. Mainsails come with four partial-length battens, and the batten pockets are reinforced for their entire length. There are slides at the luff and foot, and a heavily reinforced aluminum headboard. Hank-on headsails come with bronze piston hanks, and furling headsails are offered with a foam luff and UV Sunbrella cloth.

The company also had hundreds of used sails listed by leech, luff, and foot size, with their conditions ranging from "usable" to "new." They were also listed by boat type. Atlantic Sail Traders maintains a 30-day return policy, and its loft can also alter a

PROS AND CONS OF ROD RIGGING

Aboard most sailboats these days, the mast or masts are held in place by a combination of fittings and stainless steel wire. Almost all standing rigging (shrouds, headstays, and most backstays) is made from 1x19 wire rope. Stainless steel wire is made from many different grades of stainless, but for standing rigging, *PS* recommends that only 316 stainless be used. Rigging fashioned out of such wire has been around for decades.

About 20 years ago, along came a stainless steel wire with the outer strands flatted so that there is little air space between each strand. This is marketed as Dyform wire. Dyform wire is slightly stronger than conventional wire rope of the same diameter, but also slightly heavier.

A further innovation is solid rod rigging. Principally in use aboard performance sailboats, rod rigging offers a number of advantages. Rod is smooth, so there are no surface crevices for water to be trapped in and later on lead to corrosion. And pound for pound, rod is also stronger than wire rope. There are disadvantages to rod rigging as well. Principal among these is that rod rigging is prone to failure due to fatigue. If rod is made to bend, say, for instance, where a rod cap shroud travels past a spreader tip, that configuration can diminish its lifespan. Rod is also more expensive than comparably sized stainless wire, and it's not easy to stow on board.

A reader once inquired as to how often rod rigging should be replaced. He was concerned because of the well-publicized notion that when rod rigging fails, it doesn't offer any warning, which is usually the case with stainless wire. *PS* responded: "The life span of standing rigging—wire or rod—is not an exact science. There is no formula. We recall that one of the original engineers at Navtec kept the same rigging for around 25 years, sailing north to Labrador with it and experiencing no problems.

"We're not sure it's true that rod gives less warning prior to failure than wire, which tends to fail inside the terminals. If you elect to keep your present rod rigging, at least pull the stick and go over all the critical areas, such as the cold-formed heads, with Magnaflux, which will show up any hairline cracks. If one is found, replace it, and probably the rest, too. Also inspect the rod where it passes over spreader tips. If you have continuous rod, the bends at the spreader tips are critical. Fully articulated discontinuous rod (terminates and starts again at spreader tips) is less likely to have a fatigue problem, except that you have more connections, which are in themselves potential problem areas. That's about all one can do. We'd try to replace any rigging more than 12 years old, particularly if you're planning long ocean passages. Your rig, rudder, and keel are three things you definitely don't want to lose at sea."

sail to fit. Clicking on "view" provided further details like cloth weight, sailmaker, luff type, as well as other details unique to a particular sail.

Proprietor Betty Fahrer provided us with quotes on both used and new sails. A used Sobstad mainsail in "good" condition (70 to 80 percent of its life remaining) was $485. A "good"-condition UK Tape Drive headsail would be $770. She said the company could also design and build us a new mainsail (some sails are built in Hong Kong) out of 7.4-ounce Dacron for $1,368, and a new headsail for $1,403, with delivery time set at about four weeks.

A REPLACEMENT FOR COTTER PINS

A cotter pin is a marvelous little piece of half-round soft metal bent into a round-headed, two-legged sliver whose ends can be flared to keep it in place after inserting it in a clevis pin to close the throat of a toggle or a fork. Of course, these little beggars are wont to jump overboard at very bad times, but unless worn out by repeated bending, they do their job. Even if one loses a leg, the pin still soldiers on.

Their most devilish characteristic is that when one goes overboard, it somehow makes sure that you have no more. And another of a cotter pin's dirty little secrets is that they attack ankles, hands, and sails, and snag lines.

Except for the fanciest ones, shackles require cotter pins. Cotter pins often are "booted," along with whatever device they're mated with, like turnbuckles, tangs, various shackles, etc. It's more common to tape them. After weathering, taping

There are numerous ways to ensure that the barrel of a turnbuckle doesn't turn inadvertently. The customary approach is to use cotter pins or rings. Johnson Marine's new Wrap Pins appear to be an even better solution because they protect sails and people from the potentially harmful effects of cotter pins.

becomes difficult to remove . . . no matter what kind of tape you use. If you trailer a boat, taping is not a good option.

But there is a different approach, thanks to Johnson Hardware. Not long ago, this company trademarked the name "Wrap Pins." Using high-strength glue, cotter pins are perpendicularly attached to a strip of heavy-duty Velcro. To use, insert the cotters (there's no need to flare the legs) and wrap the Velcro round and round. The Wrap Pins are handiest for turnbuckles secured with pins in each of the threaded segments. But they can be used in other ways on shackles; if it's something critical, the cotter still should be flared first.

So far, Wrap Pins come in two sizes, one for $5/16$- to $3/8$-inch clevis pins, the other for $7/16$- to $1/2$-inch clevis pins. Both sizes are sold in kits of eight and are available through chandleries or the Johnson Marine Hardware catalog.

Minney's Yacht Surplus in Newport Harbor, California, also deals in used sails. The company's website offers a veritable online swap meet, and with a little looking, you might find a good buy. The site's layout is a bit dizzying due to the abundance of offerings, but our e-mail quickly drew a response from Ernie Minney, instructing us to look at bin No.

45. That search yielded a 9-ounce mainsail built originally for a J/30. The sail was listed as "in excellent condition" for $695.

Minney, a circumnavigator and experienced ocean racer, has been selling used sails for the past 30 years. He told us that each sail is remeasured before it leaves and can be returned by the buyer for a full refund for any reason. Considering the many details involved in getting used sails to fit your boat, like mainsail slide size and headsail foil size, the odds of finding exactly what you are looking for in a used sail are certainly stacked against you. But if you're looking to find something that, given a little time and effort, might work, it's worth perusing this website.

Sail Exchange Getting in touch with the folks at Sail Exchange in Newport Beach, California, initially proved difficult. Two e-mails we sent went into the void, but we did get a return call from Scott Sheller, the proprietor, after we left a phone message. He's been in this business for 35 years and proved to be quite helpful as well as very patient once we connected with him.

Sheller said his company services every type of sailor from family cruisers to offshore racers. At the time of our conversation, he had over 1,800 sails in stock. His website segments these into mainsails, headsails, and spinnakers, and further lists them by luff length, so finding the right product is pretty simple. He said once a purchase is confirmed, the sails are shipped within two working days and the correct size is guaranteed. The customer pays the shipping charges, and has up to 10 days to try them out and then return them for a full refund or exchange them if for some reason he or she is dissatisfied.

When buying used sails, said Sheller, the actual luff, leech, and foot measurements prove more important than I, J, P, and E measurements that might be listed on a design drawing, because the latter are boat-specific rather than sail-specific. It's also worth noting that what you see listed on Sheller's website doesn't represent the Sail Exchange's entire inventory as sails are bought and sold on a daily basis, so making a phone call is worth the effort.

While the company stocks new sails for Catalina 22s and 27s, it was sold out in the luff and foot size needed for our hypothetical genoa. Sheller did have a used mainsail in stock that closely fit the dimensions of the Catalina 320. As he does with all his sails, he had given this mainsail a rating, in this case a 6 for "good." He said that it still had two-thirds of its life left, or eight to nine years of use by his estimate.

The sail was built by Danish sailmaker Elvström Sails of triple-stitched, 8-ounce Dacron and came with two reefpoints, with a boltrope for the foot, a cunningham, a leech cord adjustment, and internal luff slides. The price was impressive—$495—and tempting, particularly since Sheller told us later that he also entertains "reasonable offers."

Bacon & Associates of Annapolis, Maryland, has one of the easiest-to-peruse and most comprehensive online inventories of used sails that we examined. The company claims to have 10,000 sails in stock, and we don't doubt it. The inventory is updated daily, and there are literally thousands of headsails, mainsails, storm sails, gennakers, and spinnakers listed, not only by the luff, leech, and foot measurement, but also by boat type, including some relatively obscure ones that we've owned and sailed. Headsails were listed in percentages of the foretriangle, along with a helpful blend of I, J, P, and E measurements for boat type.

For the Catalina 320, we found 11 possible mainsail matches (all were for J/30s) ranging from a 7.5-ounce Dacron Doyle main in "excellent condition" to a "soiled, stained, and patched" 6.5-ounce main for $250. A search for genoas yielded some 55 results sorted by luff and foot length.

One possibility looked quite promising—a 136-percent Neil Pryde roller-furling headsail made from 7.5-ounce Dacron, which was listed in "new condition." It came with 3/16-inch luff tape, leech and foot lines, a Sunbrella cover on the port side of the sail, telltale windows, sewn-on draft stripes, and was only lightly stained, all of that in a turquoise bag. It listed for $1,135. The company maintains a policy of offering customers a 10-day examination period that includes hoisting, but not sailing. A full refund is made if the sail, when re-examined, is in the same condition as when purchased, with all shipping costs paid by the customer. And if you have old sails you no longer use, the company buys sails, but charges a 35-percent brokerage fee.

AirForce Sails, based in Mount Pleasant, South Carolina, was established in 2001 as the sailmaking arm of SailNet.com. When the parent company filed for Chapter 11 protection in 2005, AirForce was briefly out of business. It resurfaced after a few weeks, and is now up and running in a new facility. We got an instant quote online, and learned that delivery time was approximately five weeks.

AirForce Sails offers two lines of working sails— Coastal and Blue Water sails—but also builds custom downwind sails, racing sails, and cruising spinnakers. Both the Coastal and Blue Water lines offer two construction and design options: Crosscut and Tri-Radial. Coastal sails carry a three-year warranty and come standard with anodized aluminum headboard, webbed O-ring at the tack, and pressed rings at the reef and leech. Blue Water sails carry a five-year warranty and come standard with anodized aluminum headboard, three rows of stitching on seams, webbed O-ring at the tack, webbed and pressed rings at the clew, leather at the head and clew patches, and double tapes on the luff, leech, and foot.

AirForce would charge $1,226 for the Coastal version of its Crosscut mainsail (282 square feet), and $1,254 for a Coastal Crosscut 130-percent (349-square-foot) genoa. For its Blue Water Tri-Radial mainsail, the company's website quoted $2,164, and $2,423 for a Blue Water Tri-Radial headsail (135 percent, 363 square feet).

FXSails of Charleston, South Carolina, is a relative newcomer to the industry, but the principals here boast 25 years of sailmaking experience. This company, which evolved from AirForce Sails, has the majority of its sails built by a subcontractor in China, but PS had occasion to see some samples and the quality is first-rate, particularly the handwork. Because more than 90 percent of FXSail's business is transacted online, we weren't surprised to get a quote for a Catalina 320 mainsail in about 30 seconds after logging on to the site.

There are four standard option levels for both mainsails and headsails (Inshore Cross-cut, Inshore Triradial, Offshore Cross-cut, and Offshore Triradial), and the company builds spinnakers and gennakers, etc., as well. Inshore sails carry a three-year warranty, and Offshore sails carry a five-year warranty. Standard features include double stitching

RIGGING REPLACEMENT

A *PS* reader wrote to asked about when his standing rigging should be replaced. He said the rigging on his O'Day 39 was 10 years old, and a recent survey had indicated the need for replacement due to the age. He wanted our advice because he was looking at a $4,000 expenditure.

We responded: "Wire rigging can certainly last longer than 10 years, depending upon the use and care it has received, as well as the geographic location where it's spent the bulk of its life. However, older wire in particular should be carefully inspected for meathooks, kinks at the toggles, tangs, spreader ends, etc., and corrosion at the terminals. At any sign of those things, the wire needs to be replaced.

"Of course, if you want to be truly certain, you should confer with a professional rigger and have that person examine your rigging, because some wear and tear (like metal fatigue in rod rigging) is harder to detect. Metal rod is stronger for its size than wire, but unlike wire, it gives no warning before it fails."

throughout the sail, aluminum headboard, draft stripes, leech line with clam cleat, leech telltales, fiberglass battens, sail ties, and a sailbag. Offshore sails also come with web-reinforced pressed rings at the corners and reef attachments, and double tapes on the luff, leech, and foot.

The online quote we received for an Inshore Cross-cut mainsail made of 7.3-ounce Challenge HMD cloth was $1,162. If we wanted a sail with more durability and shape retention, we could opt for the Offshore Triradial mainsail at $1,953. An Inshore Cross-cut headsail (130 percent at 350 square feet) would run $1,176. Again, for a little more durability and better shape retention, the Offshore Triradial headsail (same size) would be $2,046. The company claimed a delivery time of five weeks.

▷ **The Bottom Line** With just a modest amount of talent using a tape measure, you might be able to procure new or used sails for your boat at a substantial discount, but there are drawbacks to all of this. Essentially, you'll lack the advantage of having a sailmaker's trained eye assess your boat (as well as the rest of your inventory). And consider that almost every source we spoke with told us that getting the measurements right is critical, even for well-established boat designs like our Catalina 320. If you end up spending $80 to $100 for shipping the sail from the broker and back because it doesn't fit, there goes a big chunk of the money you saved in the first place.

Our research produced seven firms that could deliver exactly what we were looking for in a new set of working sails: National Sail Supply for $2,605, Far East Sails at $2,727, The Sail Warehouse for somewhere between $2,875 and $3,175, Atlantic Sail Traders for $2,771, AirForce Sails for $2,480, Cruising Direct for $3,681, and FXSails for $2,339. FXSails offered the best price by a slight margin, and the company enjoys a good reputation for customer service, so they get the nod among our options for new sails.

For a budget that favors used-sail options, both Atlantic Sail Traders and The Sail Exchange came in with the most economical options for mainsails. Both offered what we felt would be good, serviceable sails for around $500. For a used headsail, we liked the comprehensive listings at Bacon & Associates ($1,135 for a 140-percent genoa was pricey, but not too far out of line), but the UK Tape Drive headsail that Betty Fahrer of Atlantic Sail Traders quoted for $770 was the best bargain.

If you're willing to spend more, and you require the assurance of aftermarket warranty work, we'd recommend Cruising Direct. This firm's parent company—North Sails—has the most extensive network of lofts, which means that an affiliated service facility won't be too far away.

Turnbuckles

As a rule of thumb, few sailors pay much attention to the lowly but vital turnbuckle, unless, of course, they race their boats regularly. In that case, tuning the rig takes on a whole new level of importance and turnbuckles are apt to be used frequently. The good news for those sailors who don't obsess about turnbuckles is that these devices haven't changed much in recent decades. Though the favored material for their fabrication has swung from bronze to stainless during that time, the design and function of turnbuckles has remained much the same.

Turnbuckles are essentially a hollow sleeve with threads tapped into either ends to accept a threaded stud. In most cases, the threads at one end are normal (right-handed) and the ones at the other end are lefthanded, so that the studs are pulled together or forced apart when the turnbuckle is rotated. Some marine professionals are wary of stainless steel turnbuckles because the threads tend to gall and thus must be inspected closely.

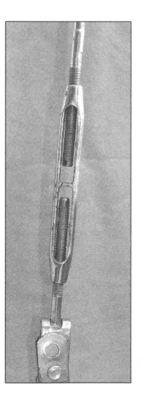

This standard barrell turnbuckle is roughly 10 years old, and it exhibits a design that has been in use for decades. Note that the holes in the threaded studs have not been pinned so this turnbuckle can easily loosen itself through vibration.

WIRE TERMINALS

Not long ago, a subscriber wrote to us to get some advice regarding his new rig. "We've just upgraded to roller furling," he wrote. "This included a new ⅝-inch Dyform headstay. We used our old Sta-Lok terminal ends, with new wedges, the versions specified for Dyform. One of your articles on rigging terminals quoted Phil Garland of Hall Spars & Rigging as saying, 'Using a mechanical fastener with Dyform is not a good idea.' Have we done wrong? We're also getting ready to replace our standing rigging and are wondering about your statement that '304 wire is a false economy.' Can you explain?"

We wrote back: "You've nothing to worry about. Dyform, which is a registered trademark of British Ropes Limited, was developed by BRL and Norseman Gibb, the makers of the Norseman terminal system that competes with both Sta-Lok and Castlok.

"Conventional 1x19 wire rope has a single core wire (called the 'king wire'), surrounded by six more strands, surrounded by the remaining 12 strands (called 'lay lengths'). All strands are the same diameter. Dyform has a single center strand surrounded by nine smaller strands enclosed in nine strands of the same size as the center core. Dyform is then cold-rolled, which compresses the bundle and flattens the circumference. The low-stretch Dyform is stronger, but we've always thought that was because it contains more metal that fits together better and thus creates smaller voids.

"The makers of Sta-Lok say their fittings work well on Dyform wire, too. But a different wedge is used with Dyform wire.

"As might be expected, because they're made by the same folks, Norseman fittings are compatible with Dyform wire, according to Navtec Norseman Gibb, the U.S. importers of both."

Thereafter, we checked back with Phil Garland at Hall Spars. An expert engineer with an enviable reputation, Garland said that there had been, in that earlier discussion, a misunderstanding about what a "mechanical" terminal is. He said all types of terminals work with Dyform wire.

Regarding 304 versus 316 stainless wire, Type 304 is stronger for a given size, but is not nearly as corrosion resistant as 316, which costs about 20 percent more. Wire suppliers and riggers recommend 316, especially for boats kept in warm climes where the saltwater is particularly corrosive.

PS recently surveyed the products of the major players in the turnbuckle game to offer a better understanding of what each company can provide. Included in this brief lineup are turnbuckles from Johnson Marine, Hayn Marine, Sea-Dog Marine, Navtec, Alexander Roberts, Ronstan, and Stay-Loc.

Sea-Dog Marine, out of Everett, WA carries a line of machined, stainless-steel turnbuckles (made with 316 stainless steel with an electropolished bright finish), in both tubular or open body styles. These come in both SAE and metric sizes. SAE models begin at ³⁄₁₆" pin diameter with a breaking strength of 2,860 lbs., and extend up to ¾" pin sizes (28,600 lbs.). The metric sizes begin at 5 mm (1,980 lbs. breaking strength) up 19 mm (35,000 lbs.).

Hayn Marine, based in Rocky Hill, Connecticut, manufactures turnbuckles out of forged bronze and machined stainless steel (all 316 stainless). Both the open-body (bronze) and the tubular style turnbuckles (stainless) can be purchased in various configurations, including jaw-to-jaw, swage-to-jaw, swage-to-swage, eye-to-eye, jaw-to-eye, and eye-to-swage. The tubular bodies have locking nuts, and the open bodies are available in chromed or polished bronze. Hayn also manufactures stainless rigging adjusters for smaller boats (¼ and ³/₁₆ pin sizes), and these can be used without tools.

Navtec Rigging Supplies, headquartered in Guilford, Connecticut, designs, manufactures, and distributes a variety of turnbuckles made of either machined 316 stainless or forged bronze (the latter is thereafter chrome-plated). The company's offerings include both closed-body models with locking nuts and open-body turnbuckles, each in a variety of configurations, including stemball terminals for discontinuous rigging applications. Navtec's turnbuckles are distinct in that they work by way of a center pin with threads (usually made of nickel-plated bronze) rather than a center barrel as in most other makes of turnbuckle. The sizes of these products range from ³/₁₆ to ⅝. The company also manufacturers a range of turnbuckles in various configurations for use with rod rigging.

Ronstan Marine, with its U.S. headquarters located in Portsmouth, Rhode Island, manufactures three models of tubular stainless turnbuckles (all machined from 316 stainless) that can accommodate wire diameters from ⅛" up to 1 inch. Two models come in toggle-to-toggle or toggle-to-stud configurations. The first one relies on a unique coupling nut for adjustment. The second one uses a closed barrel for adjustments. The third model also has a closed barrel, but comes with metric thread sizes and features a fork-to-stud configuration. Ronstan also manufactures a special line of Sealoc calibrated turnbuckles for use primarily aboard one-design racing sailboats. These are available with an integral locking handle so that no tools are required for adjustments.

Johnson Marine, established in 1958, is based in East Haddam, Connecticut. The company manufactures and distributes a broad variety of marine hardware, including numerous styles of turnbuckles. The company's offerings in this realm stem from forged silicon-bronze, open-body turnbuckles for wire sizes from ⁵/₃₂ to ³/₈, to stainless steel (316) tubular turnbuckles that can accommodate wire sizes from ¹/₁₆

to ³/₈. One style of stainless turnbuckle is designed with positive locking rings that cannot be lost overboard. The company also makes thumbscrew adjustable turnbuckles for ⅛ and ³/₁₆ inch wire sizes and a special quick-release turnbuckle for use with inner forestays. That product has a breaking strength of 10,500 pounds.

Alexander Roberts, based in Irvine, California, makes turnbuckles out of chromed forged bronze and machined stainless steel for wire sizes from ¼ to ⁷/₁₆. The company supplies its products to a variety of distributors, including Rigging Only in Fairhaven, Massachussetts.

Sta-Lok Terminals, Ltd., of Essex, England, also manufacturers and distributes a broad variety of turnbuckles, both those made of forged bronze (chrome-plated) and stainless steel (316). In the U.S., these products are carried by Sailing Services in Miami, Florida. The turnbuckles are made in a variety of configurations to fit wire sizes from ³/₁₆ to 1 inch.

Any turnbuckle should serve you well so long as it's properly sized for the application and installed so that the load it sustains runs correctly along its lengthwise axis. When in use, turnbuckles should be able to spin freely, except when under the heaviest loads. The use of cotter pins, ring pins, or locking nuts to secure a turnbuckle in place is vital. Like every other piece of gear on board, turnbuckles require periodic inspections. And unlike many other components, failing to do this could lead to serious consequences.

Shroud Terminals, Swaged or Mechanical?

A reader once wrote to ask: "Has *Practical Sailor* conducted a study of swaged terminals versus screw-on terminals?" She wanted to know if screw-on terminals like the Norseman and Stay-Lok products are preferable because they can't kink the wire (as a swage can if it's not done just right) and can be replaced by the boat owner. She also asked whether or not we'd done any comparisons of the two types regarding cost, safety, and longevity.

Practical Sailor rigorously tested both mechanical and swaged rigging terminals in the early 1990s, and with characteristic candor we titled that article "Wire Terminal Destruction Test." Information derived from those tests can help answer these questions, because the essential data regarding strength remains true today. The four mechanical fittings that we tested included Castlok, Quick Rig, Norseman, and Sta-Lok, which was our top choice.

The wire in the swage fitting we tested began to fail at 7,700 pounds of pull. The first strand of the wire affixed to the Sta-Lok fitting broke at just over 8,000 pounds, and the wire in the Norseman began to break at 7,300 pounds. Wire in the Castlok fitting lasted until the tension reached 8,000, and the wire in the Quick Rig failed at 6,400 pounds.

We told readers that "swaged fittings, applied by an expert rigger, are strong, neat, and fairly inexpensive. . . . The principal liability of swaged fittings is that because dirt and water can enter the terminal, they are more prone to corrosion than sealed mechanical terminals." All of these fittings are reasonably straightforward when it comes to assembling them, though Sta-Lok fittings are slightly more difficult in that regard.

Ultimately, we recommended that the best arrangement would be to put professionally swaged terminals (lighter, less windage) at the upper ends of your shrouds and stays, and Sta-Loks on the bottom ends. That's a recommendation we'd make again. Additionally, if you're inclined to carry a spare shroud or stay on board for emergencies, have an eye or fork swaged onto one end and carry a spare mechanical fitting that can be used on the other end after you've cut it to the necessary length.

The magazine also published a *PS* Advisor on this topic some time later. In that missive, we paraphrased some important information from Phil Garland of Hall Spars & Rigging: a good swage will take 100 percent of the wire strength, whereas a Sta-Lok or Norseman will yield only 90 percent of the wire strength.

As for the advantages of a mechanical terminal over a swage, the greatest edge is that these products (as the reader pointed out) give you the ability to replace the fitting yourself—almost anywhere. As for an improperly applied swage, that's the rub, and the chief reason why it pays to have that kind of work done by an experienced rigger with a good reputation.

Regarding costs, swaged fittings are still slightly less expensive than mechanical terminals. Prices among the latter vary depending upon product, wire size, terminal style (stud, fork, or eye, etc.), and supplier.

CHAPTER 3

Onboard Plumbing

The plumbing systems on board almost any boat can easily be overlooked and forgotten, but they never should be. These important components perform multiple services, and in the case of bilge pumps and seacocks, they're a vital line of defense between you and the sea. We've scoured recent issues of the magazine to provide this offering, a compendium of articles that pertain to some of the most important elements of onboard plumbing systems.

Bilge Pumps

MANUAL BILGE PUMPS

In the marine trade, manual bilge pumps are big business. That's because virtually every boat in the world has at least one, and two or even more aren't unusual. Though the owners of contemporary craft are accustomed to removing bilgewater with electric pumps, should that electric pump fail, or the boat lack electrical power, the importance of a good, working manual bilge pump can't be overstated.

To test such pumps, PS assembled 19 pumps from three major manufacturers, Edson and Bosworth (Guzzlers) of the U.S., and Whale of England, as well as Jabsco, Rule, Beckson, Plastimo, and a Dutch company called Raske & van der Meyde BV. We evaluated functionality and efficiency with each of these.

Most pumps are rated by their makers regarding gallons per minute (GPM) pumped. These ratings are based on horizontal movement, which is almost never the case on board a boat. Our test sought to determine which pump comes closest to meeting its manufacturer's GPM rating, and that gave us an efficiency factor.

In the process of our testing, we also confirmed that bends in the hose and non-smooth hose interiors can impede the flow and diminish a pump's efficiency. It's enough to strongly suggest that when installing a pump, use smooth-walled hose and keep the runs as straight as possible. Also, an air leak, however tiny, in the suction side will drastically reduce a pump's efficiency; on the discharge side, it will be a leak.

PS's testers also disassembled several of the pumps to examine the diaphragm, diaphragm pressure plate, valves, rocker arm, hinge and pressure plates, and to assess how easily each might be serviced. Even a good-quality pump, if it's expected to last a long time, should be dismantled, inspected, and cleaned up every couple of years.

▷**The Bottom Line** These 19 pumps were used vigorously, even roughly. They were clamped tightly to the workbench, usually with but two of their customary four mounting "feet." During the pumping, several of the small plastic pumps bent alarmingly. But nothing broke; there were no cracks, and no handles bent. The conclusion has to be that the pumps are well made and can stand up to fast, strong treatment.

Edson's big 30-GPM classic, whose design hasn't changed in years, ranks first among the large pumps. If you have room for it, this juggernaut (preferably the bronze model) moves water like no other—if you have the arm for it. With the long handle supplied, however, it's not particularly hard work, certainly less than equivalent pumps with shorter handles. Ranking next are the Guzzler 2600, the Whale Gusher 30, and the venerable Henderson Mk V D/A (double action).

If space on board were limited, but you wanted a metal pump that would, with proper servicing, last virtually forever, the best big-pump buy, in our view, would be the bronze Guzzler 2600. Besides pumping 130 percent of its rated capacity, it won praise as the easiest of all to operate. Also a good buy is the very decent-performing Whale Titan.

For a smaller pump, the plastic Whale Urchin moved a lot of water. It is among the easiest to pump and has a modest price—both for the standard version and the through-deck model. It had the highest efficiency rating of all, albeit just a percentage point above the big Edson. Any of these pumps can be mounted on horizontal or vertical surfaces. Through-deck plates are available for many.

ELECTRIC BILGE PUMPS

Bilge pumps are usually out of sight, but they should never be out of mind. They serve two purposes. First, they clear the bilge of incidental water that can cause a variety of problems. Water sloshing around down there is not a good thing. Second, a bilge pump will

Edson's outstanding 30 (not shown here) can be used as a high-capacity emergency pump or to empty a holding tank. In either case, quick-connect hose fittings for the 2-foot hose make stowage easier. Though they lack the Edson's capacity, the other manual pumps shown here will certainly assist you in an emergency.

buy you critical time in an emergency situation—if, for example, you plow into a submerged object (rock, tree, ship container) and hole your boat, or a hose breaks and the engine pumps the boat full of water, or a seacock or other through-hull fitting gives way. In cases like these, pump failure can lead to trouble, even catastrophe.

PS tested 27 pumps that cover a wide range of flow rates and take four different discharge hose sizes. Seven companies participated: Attwood, Rule, Shurflo, Mayfair, West Marine, Whale, and Lovett. We divided the pumps into five groups based on size and characteristics. Three pumps fall into the under-400-gallons-per-hour (GPH) category, and seven range from 500 to 625 GPH capacity. The largest group is rated from 700 to 1,250 GPH, and seven pumps are ranked at over 1,400 GPH. We also included two pumps with internal float switches.

We measured the flow rates and power usage on all these pumps at two voltages while pumping salt water into a tank set 5 feet above the pump. We also ran them without water. ABYC (American Boat and Yacht Council) standards dictate that a bilge pump should be able to dry run at designed voltage, that's 13.6 volts for a 12-volt pump, for at least seven hours without failure. (All the pumps passed the dry-run test.) In the final analysis, we picked the top-rated pump in each group based on performance, warranty, wiring, and price. (The prices quoted here are from 2004, so adjust accordingly.)

Under 400 GPH Rule, Whale, and Shurflo each have a single pump in this category, with prices ranging from $13 for the Rule 24 to $35 for the Whale SS3612. The Shurflo 380 is priced at the low-end: $16. All three pumps have ¾-inch outlets. All did well in performance testing, with the Whale shining brightest. The wire lead lengths on these pumps run from 25 inches on the Whale, to 29 inches on the Rule, to a whopping 69 inches on the Shurflo. The Rule 24 is available with 6-foot leads as the model 24-6, which adds about $2 to the price.

Our top pick in this group is the Shurflo Piranha 380. It edges the Whale with its longer warranty and lower price, and edged the Rule on performance. If you need a low-profile unit due to bilge space constraints, try the Whale. It's the top performer, though pricey.

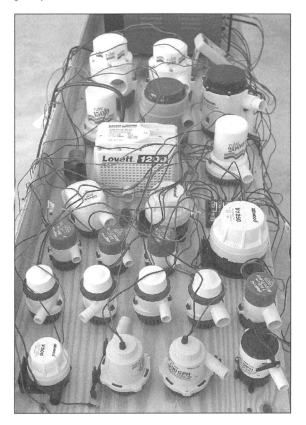

500 to 625 GPH Six of the seven pumps in this group range from $15 to $20. The Whale is much more expensive than the others: $44. Performance varied widely in the group, but ironically, the worst performer was the pump with the highest advertised GPH rating—Attwood's V625. It managed only 188 GPH at 12.2 volts and 251 GPH at 13.6 volts. Even the smaller Attwood V500 outperformed its big brother. So we contacted Attwood to find out why the V625 seemed to perform so poorly. The company told us that the V625 was designed to provide greater output at lower head heights and is expressly suited to vessels with low freeboard. Obviously this pump shouldn't be used in a high-head application.

The best-performing pumps in this bunch were the Whale and the Rule; both pumped at 75 percent of their marketed GPH or more on all tests. The Whale actually bested all others by hitting 99 percent of its rated GPH at 13.6 volts. In this size range, we think the Rule edges the competition based on good performance combined with a good price. This pump is also available with 6-foot leads as the 25D-6, and we'd gladly pay the extra $2 for that.

700 to 1,250 GPH Attwood, Rule, and Shurflo each have multiple pumps in this size range. Mayfair is also represented. Again, prices hold in a tight range, from $27 to $33. There is one exception: the Attwood V750 is the least expensive at $23. The performance in this group was fairly close among pumps with the same outlet diameter, but generally the pumps with the larger discharge pipe pushed more water. The standout was the Shurflo 1000, which was able to pump 85 percent of its rating at 12.2 volts and 93

PS testers put 27 electric bilge pumps through their paces. That's a lotta flow, Florence. Among the under-400-GPH models, we like the the Shurflo Piranha 380. In the 500-to-625-GPH range, the Rule 25D was our top choice. In the 700-to-1,250-GPH range, the Shurflo Piranha 1000 was top dog. And in the over-1,400-GPH pumps, we selected the West Marine 491720. In the last category, pumps with an internal switch, we selected the Lovett 1200 as our top pick. Remember, whichever pump you purchase, make sure it comes with a long electrical lead, at least five feet long. You want that first electrical connection to stay well out of the bilge if at all possible.

During our tests, we secured the pumps inside the circular container. The rectangular receiver tank was set five feet above the pumps.

percent at 13.6. Due to the combination of its performance, warranty, wiring, and price, the Shurflo Piranah 1000 wins this division.

Over 1,400 GPH Among these largest pumps, Rule outnumbers all others here with four pumps, Attwood has a pair, and the Johnson-built West Marine brings the total to seven. The least expensive pump in the group is the Attwood HD1700 at $53. Next is the Rule Model 2 at $60, then the Attwood HD2000 at $66, the West Marine 491720 at $70, and the Rule 10 at $80. At nearly double these prices are the Rule 14A and Rule 56D, both at $155. All pumps except the two giant Rule pumps have 1⅛-inch outlets. The Rule 3700 has a 1½-inch outlet, and the Rule 4000 a 2-inch. Acceptable performance was obtained from all units tested, though these large pumps have a more difficult time than their smaller brethren maintaining their GPH rating at high lift and low voltage.

Our top choice in the large-pump division is the West Marine 491720. It's less expensive than pumps with comparable performance, has a three-year warranty, and comes standard with long leads.

Float-Switch Pumps Lovett and Attwood each have a single pump containing an internal float switch. Though different in most respects, they have at least two similarities. They both have 1-⅛-inch outlets, and they performed the same. The differences begin with pricing; at $130 the Lovett 1200 is $40 more than the Attwood Sahara 1100, which sells for $90. Size and construction are also quite different. The Lovett is by far the largest pump of its capacity we tested, and it features tough, high-quality construction, a rebuildable design, sheath-covered wiring, Monel shaft, and an airlock design with no seals to wear out. However, at 26 inches, the wire lead on the Lovett is too short. Both pumps carry a three-year warranty, but if you've got to have a built-in float switch, we think the Lovett is a good pump.

BILGE PUMP SWITCHES

The automatic bilge pump switch is the lowly guardian of your bilge. Its sole purpose is to switch the bilge pump on when a predetermined level of water is detected in the bilge, and then turn the pump off when the bilge is dry. The job may sound easy, but sloshing, corrosive seawater, oil, fiberglass shards, and other debris typically found in a bilge can foil even the simplest task. And shopping for the ideal pump switch presents its own sticky challenge. At least 30 different bilge pump switches flood the marine market today.

For this evaluation, we kept our focus on stand-alone switches, units that would be suitable companions to the West Marine High Performance 2,200-GPH (part #491720), the Shurflo Piranha 1000, the Rule 25D, and the Shurflo Piranha 380, the pumps that did well in our bilge pump comparison. These types of switches are usually grouped into four basic categories: the pivoting float, the air pressure, the vertical float, and the electronic pump switch. We narrowed the field to 17 switches and did not include the more sophisticated air-pressure types.

We built a simulated bilge, complete with seawater, debris, and motor oil. We mounted a small Rule 350 bilge pump on one side of the bulkhead wall and pumped the seawater over to the opposite side of the compartment. Ten gallons of salt water, one pint of very used motor oil, two handfuls of sawdust, two handfuls of fiberglass holesaw shavings, and a half bag of Doritos were added to the test bilge. To make our test more interesting, we slid a 6-inch-diameter piece of Schedule 40 PVC pipe under the middle of the bilge box, creating our very own "sea-saw" slosh box. This allowed us to really stir the bilge stew and simulate a moderate sea state.

Among the pivoting float switches, we tested five: the Rule 40 Plus (a mercury contact switch), the Sure Bail by Marine Products International (a urethane-foam-filled pivoting-arm switch that contains a large glass vial of mercury that acts as the contact switch), West Marine's Automatic Float Switch (uses a steel ball that rolls up and down a channeled pocket inside of the float's hollow arm), the Attwood Marine Bilge

Pump Switch (a mercury-free design), and the Rule Super Switch Model 37WG. Among these switches, we liked the self-test arrangement and secure wiring on the Rule 40, and the West Marine switch is a solid mercury-free performer, but our top pick in this group—the Sure Bail—is built the toughest and will definitely survive being accidentally stepped on a few times a season.

In the vertical float switch group, we tested eight: the Johnson Electronic Switch and its near twin the West Marine Magnum (both are float switches that use a small sealed plastic pod that floats up inside of the switch's internal chamber when the appropriate level of water is present); Ultra Safety Systems (which makes three versions of its Ultra Pump switch—Senior, Junior, and Mini); Aqualarm's SS-209-12 and PS-309-12 vertical float switches (which mirror the USS's Ultra line but are less expensive); and the Piranha pump switch by Shurflo (which has

The winner's circle included all three types of switches that *PS* tests. Among the float switches, the mercury-free West Marine switch is a bargain (middle row, right); the Rule 40 Plus (back row, right) gets the job done, but our favorite was the more rugged Sure Bail (back row, left). The Johnson vertical switch (front row, center), also marketed by West Marine under its own label, would be a good choice for an upgrade from a float switch. The Ultra Mini (front row, left) is a pricey, bulletproof vertical switch suited for serious cruisers. Offering outstanding performance at a fair price, the Water Witch 230 (front row, right) was *PS*'s overall top pick.

Type and Model	Average Street Price	Price Source	Contains Mercury	Pump Amperage Rating	Pump Delay "On"	Pump Delay "Off"
PIVOT ARM FLOAT						
MPI Sure Bail DEL-30 ✔	$24.99	Boater's World	Yes	15 Amps	No	No
Rule Model 40 ✔	$27.99	Boater's World	Yes	20 Amps	No	No
West Marine 543561 $	$19.99	Manufacturer	No	15 Amps	No	No
Rule Super SW Model 37	$34.99	Boater's World	No	20 Amps	No	No
Attwood 4201-7	$20.99	Defender	No	12 Amps	No	No
VERTICAL FLOAT						
Johnson Pumps 36152 $	$21.94	Boatfix.com	No	15 Amps	No	No
West Marine 3685443	$25.99	Manufacturer	No	15 Amps	No	No
Ultra Safety Mini ✔	$99.00	Manufacturer	No	20 Amps	No	No
Ultra Safety Jr. ✔	$99.00	Manufacturer	No	15 Amps	No	No
Ultra Safety Sr. ✔	$129.00	Manufacturer	No	15 Amps	No	No
Aqualarm SS-209-12	$74.99	Fisheries Supply	No	30 Amps	No	15 Sec
Aqualarm PS-309-12	$49.00	Manufacturer	No	30 Amps	No	15 Sec
Shurflo Piranha	$30.99	West Marine	No	10 Amps	2 Sec	10 Sec
ELECTRONIC						
Water Witch 230 ★	$36.99	Defender	No	20 Amps	6 Sec	14 Sec
Johnson Pumps Ultima SW	$29.99	Defender	No	20 Amps	3 Sec	5 Sec
Touch Sensor Sensa-SW	$34.99	West Marine	No	20 Amps	3 Sec	5 Sec
SeeWater 79701	$40.99	West Marine	No	15 Amps	2 Sec	8 Sec

$ Budget Buy   ✔ Recommended   ★ Best Choice

a small round float ring that rides up the center of a ¼-inch plastic shaft to trip a magnetic reed switch). In our view, the high-quality switches from Ultra Safety Systems have no equal in this field, but for the average sailor, we don't believe this justifies paying $99 for the device. The Johnson and West Marine switches are priced about the same as a pivoting-arm float switch, but perform better when subjected to surging bilgewater. We'd recommend either the West Marine or the Johnson.

Regarding the electronic pump switches, one of the key motivations behind developing these sensors was to prevent the pumping of oil or fuel into the environment. The manufacturers of each electronic switch that we tested claim that their switch can detect if a bilge is full of gas, diesel, or oil and will prevent the bilge pump from automatically activating until the hydrocarbons are removed. Generally, the concentration of hydrocarbons needed to shut down the pump is nearly 100 percent, and the oily mix in our test bilge never triggered this function.

The four specimens included TouchSensor Technologies' Sensa-Switch Marine 20, Johnson Pump's UltimaSwitch, SeeWater's Water Smart Pump switch, and the Water Witch 230. The Johnson UltimaSwitch is sealed in a sonically welded housing, while the SensaSwitch is potted. They should, in theory, outlast the vessel. SeeWater's Water Smart

Current Draw / Standby Mode	Warranty	Test Tank	Quality and Construction
None	5 Yrs.	Pass	Excellent
None	2 Yrs.	Pass	Excellent
None	1 Yr.	Pass	Good
None	2 Yrs.	Pass	Good
None	3 Yrs.	Pass	Good
None	3 Yrs.	Pass	Good
None	1 Yr.	Pass	Good
None	5 Yrs.	Pass	Excellent
None	5 Yrs.	Pass	Excellent
None	5 Yrs.	Pass	Excellent
None	1 Yr.	Pass	Fair
None	1 Yr.	Pass	Fair
None	3 Yrs.	Pass	Good
.006 A	7 Yrs.	Pass	Excellent
.000016 A	3 Yrs.	Pass	Good
.000016 A	3 Yrs.	Pass	Good
.004 A	1 Yr.	Pass	Good

able suds, like Joy dishwashing liquid, so we would hesitate to recommend these units for shower sump pumps, unless the sump is easily accessible.

▷ **The Bottom Line** For less than half the cost of an Ultra Safety Systems switch, the Water Witch 230 electronic switch easily matches the performance levels we observed in USS Jr.'s mechanical switch, with the added advantage of no moving parts. The Witch's seven-year warranty, a 20-amp rating, and a 14-second "pump off delay" are all very compelling reasons to forgo a conventional mechanical float switch and upgrade to an electronic unit. This is also why the Water Witch 230 is our top pick overall for a bilge pump switch.

Marine Toilets

A marine head that works—every time, without fail—doesn't necessarily make a boat a happy place. But if it doesn't work, perdition and pinched faces abound. Those boat owners most likely to avoid the trauma of a "busted head" probably own either a Wilcox-Crittenden Skipper model or a British-made Baby Blake. However, there comes a time when even those two lofty thrones require service.

Practical Sailor evaluated nine manually operated marine heads to determine how well each meets the basic goals of sound, robust construction providing horrendous reliability that requires as little service as possible. We segmented them into three categories: Low-Cost Heads, Medium-Priced Heads, and Premium Heads.

Low-Cost Heads In the "economy" class are three models: the Wilcox-Crittenden Head-Mate, the Jabsco Compact, and the Groco HF. All three have side-mounted piston pumps that are, in our experience, troublesome.

The Wilcox-Crittenden Head-Mate probably is found, more than any other head, aboard boats built in the U.S. due to its low cost, compact size, and easy installation. It has thin, complicated flap valves and a pump that won't stand hard usage, clogs easily, and is difficult to clear. So, it must be used and treated delicately. Jabsco's Compact doesn't enjoy a good reputation either, but at least the Groco HF now

Pump switch uses a 4-inch-long exposed probe that is 1/8 inch in diameter to sense the presence of bilge-water, and that seems precarious given bilge hazards. And the Water Witch 230 was the only electronic pump switch in our test group that performed like a vertical float switch; however, you can mount the Water Witch on any plane and at any angle. When water touches the switch's lower sensing element for six to eight seconds, the switch will activate. The Water Witch's 230 was completely immune to pump stutter and performed flawlessly under the worst of conditions, and the product is backed by an unequaled seven-year warranty. But the Water Witch will activate when covered by nonbiodegrad-

PS testers were very impressed by the Baby Blake (left), shown here with Wilcox-Crittenden's reliable Skipper.

comes with a bronze instead of a plastic base, and it also has good robust valves and seals. *PS* recommends a higher-quality head than these.

Medium-Priced Heads The medium-priced heads are the Lavac, Raritan's Model PH II, and Raritan's relatively new Cricket. The Lavac is exceedingly simple. It is nothing but a toilet bowl with large lip seals on both the seat and the lid. By pumping 15 or 20 strokes, the user builds up a vacuum that draws out the waste matter and pulls in flush water. Raritan's Model PH II is plastic and has a side-mounted pump with an unusually large-diameter piston (2½ inches). The valves are spring-loaded balls, and there is but one rugged flap valve, in the base of the bowl. It looks old-fashioned, but it's very easy to work on. Raritan also makes the Cricket, which has, built in the base, a double-action, lever-operated diaphragm pump. The waste from the bowl is drawn by the pump through a big, thick flap valve and expelled on the next stroke. The flow path is very simple, involving only one 90-degree turn. But to get at the pump's innards you have to remove 10 machine screws, some of which are difficult to reach.

For the money, these medium-priced heads all have good pumps and strong valves. They are far better designed and built than the "cheapies" and much easier to service.

Premium Heads At the top of the heap are the Blake, the Skipper, and the Groco Model K, which range in price from $1,600 to $500, respectively. Both the Groco Model K and the Skipper have bronze pumps below the bowl, which gives them a huge edge over those with small side-mounted pumps. With these pumps, the undesirable matter drops straight down and is expelled through one 90-degree turn.

The Wilcox-Crittenden Skipper has an enviable reputation. It's big, heavy, and reliable. It has a big 4-inch bronze pump operated with a 26-inch lever. The pump piston has a thick leather seal, and the valves are big and tough. With the Skipper, most any clog can be cleared just by laying into the lever. That's good, because if it does clog, it's difficult to work on.

The British-built Baby Blake is a bronze classic that has changed little in 70 years. It has a side-mounted pump built to last. In fact, it has two of them—a lever-operated version for discharge and a piston-type for wash-down. The Blake has a built-in water shutoff valve, which is very handy, and this head comes in right- and left-hand versions.

▷ **The Bottom Line** Don't choose an economy-model head, unless you have no choice. If that's the case, the Groco HF definitely is preferable, and well worth the extra $30. Of the medium-priced heads, the Lavac is simple yet a mite funky. Raritan's new Cricket has a great deal to recommend it, including its looks and the fact that it is the only relatively low-cost head with a diaphragm pump built into the base.

But for day-in-day-out reliability, choose Raritan's Model PH II.

If you want the head that won't fail, pony up for the Baby Blake. It's a tremendously refined and archaically elegant contraption. And the Wilcox-Crittenden Skipper also deserves its lofty reputation. But, if you want something lighter and smaller and for about $300 less, the Groco Model K is the most logical choice.

SIMPLE, PORTABLE HEADS

Aboard boats, head is indeed a four-letter word. Nothing good about 'em. They stink, leak, clog, and break down. But, of course, you have to have a head . . . or do you? Let's examine four popular portable toilets, whose low cost and utter simplicity might make you think twice about a "real" marine head, with pumps, hoses, springs, valves, through-hulls, and myriad other failure-prone parts.

The beauty of the porta-potty is the almost total elimination of moving parts. The only ones of consequence are the pump that draws fresh water from the upper tank and rinses the bowl, and the handle-rod-valve assembly that opens the trap for waste to fall from the top tank/bowl into the bottom tank.

In the U.S., a distinct appeal of the porta-potty is the U.S. Coast Guard's recognition of it as a "legal" head. That's because of its built-in, albeit small, holding tank. Also, appealing is the relatively low cost of these units. *PS* tested four units, and three sell for less than $100. But there is a downside. To begin with, their capacity is limited, and ultimately, you have to find a place to discard the contents of the holding tank, which means looking at, smelling, and coexisting with the stuff.

Looking first at the Thetford toilets—the 735 and the 155—we fail to see justification for the higher price of the 735 "marine" toilet over the standard 155, which has a larger waste tank. The lowest price we could find for the 735 was $119.99, and most online stores wanted upwards of $150. The 155 at $89.99 is a comparative bargain, even without the hold-down brackets and tank level indicator. Priced slightly above the 155 is the big Visa Potty at $99.99, and slightly below is the Sanipottie at $69.99, which

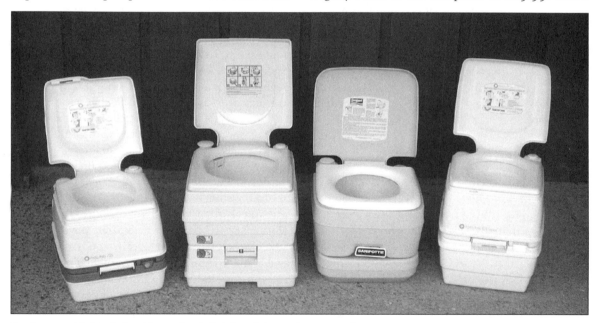

The four portable heads that *PS* tested included (from left to right), the Thetford Porta Potti 735, the Visa Potty 248, the SeaLand Sanipottie 964, and the Thetford 155. The Sanipottie may not represent the best quality product, but it is the best value, in *PS*'s opinion.

Model	SeaLand Sanipottie 964	Thetford 735	Thetford 155	Visa 248
Capacity	3.25 gals. (top) 2.8 gals. (bot.)	2.6 gals. (top) 2.6 gals. (bot.)	2.6 gals. (top) 4.3 gals. (bot.)	3.7 gals. (top) 4.8 gals. (bot.)
Dimensions	16½″ L x 14½″ W x 12″ H	15″L x 13⁹/₁₆″W x 12¹/₁₆″H	14⁷/₈″L x 13³/₈″W x 14½″H	14½″L x 14⁵/₁₆″W x 16½″H
Seat Hole	8¼″ x 9″	7½″ x 9¼″	7½″ x 9¼″	9″ x 10½″
Weight	10 lbs.	7¾ lbs.	8 lbs.	9 lbs.
Strokes to fill	92	160	145	141
Oz. per stroke	3.9	2.1	2.3	3.4
Wt. (full tank)	22¾ lbs.	23½ lbs.	38 lbs.	40¼ lbs.
Warranty	1 year	3 years	3 years	1 year
Price	$69.99	$119.99	$89.99	$99.99

is made from blow-molded polyethylene instead of injection-molded polypropylene. While the Thetfords have a nicer finish, and some clever extra features like the rotating pour-out spout and chemical holder, their seats are small compared to the other two. The Visa flushes better than the Sanipottie and does have tank level indicators (though again we think they're pretty useless). But if saving $30 is important, the Sanipottie continues to represent, if not the highest quality, at least the best value among portable toilets. If you want the biggest porta-potty available (6.1-gallon waste tank), check out Thetford's Aqua-Mate series.

COMPOSTING TOILETS

The U.S. Coast Guard recognizes three classes of installed marine toilets. Type III Marine Sanitation Devices (or MSDs) are holding tanks, pure and simple. Type I and II MSDs are the other types that are encountered on pleasure boats. (Type IIs are for boats greater than 65 feet in length; we'll just refer to Type I here.)

Type I MSDs are flow-through systems: sewage is macerated and disinfected, and then pumped overboard. For these, the USCG requires that "The effluent produced must not have a fecal coliform count of greater than 1,000 per 100 milliliters, and have no visible floating solids." If local regulations

permit dumping of effluent that meets that standard, a Type I unit is a good bet, providing you have the electrical power to run one. More and more localities, though, are instituting "No Discharge" regulations, and the use of Type I MSDs is becoming more and more proscribed.

So, it follows that composting heads offer several big advantages for sailors: They require no through-hull fittings, no plumbing, and no separate holding tank. They have few moving parts. The solids are reduced fairly quickly, and take up less space than the mixed sewage, urine, and flush-water of a holding tank. On the negative side, the toilets themselves take up more space in the head compartment, they require a through-deck fitting and vent, and they need a constant supply of electricity (in very small to moderate amounts) to perform at their best.

Composting heads are essentially Type III MSDs, but with an important difference. Rather than simply storing sewage, composters separate the solid waste from the liquid portion, and convert the solid portion —the one that presents environmental problems— into an easy-to-handle, safe, non-odorous humus. The liquid waste is either stored or evaporated.

When the composting action is complete, what's left is a black, odor-free powder that's free of dangerous bacterial contamination. It's safe and not unpleasant to handle, and can be stored in the MSD itself, or in plastic bags or any other container. The humus, however, cannot legally be dumped overboard within U.S. territorial waters—it must be brought ashore and disposed of on land.

Urine, which presents much less of an environmental and health hazard than does solid waste, is a major problem with composting toilets. It can't be composted, and the boater using a composting MSD has only two choices: store it, or evaporate it. Stored urine, while not particularly hazardous, does develop a strong ammoniacal stink. Urine, though it's virtually sterile, still is considered raw sewage, and can't be legally dumped within 3 miles of shore. Apparently you can't be fined for peeing overboard (unless they get you for indecent exposure) or for peeing while swimming, but you can't pee into a container and then pour it overboard.

PS tested two composting toilets—the Air Head Environmental Toilet and the Ecolet. Both are approved by the U.S. Coast Guard for marine use. The Air Head, made by EOS Design, consists of an upper unit with standard toilet marine seat assembly and a lever-operated trap door; a lower unit below the trap door to catch and compost solids; a liquids jug, with a plastic "shroud" to hide the jug; and a vent hose with a small fan in the end to extract moisture from the solids tank. All up, the empty unit weighs

18.5 pounds. The Ecolet is a somewhat more elaborate device. It's solidly constructed of fiberglass and stainless, and weighs in (empty) at 40 pounds. It has three chambers: a composting drum located under the standard-sized toilet seat; a compost-finishing drawer underneath the drum; and a lower evaporating chamber for liquids. The compost-finishing drawer accepts partially composted material from the composting drum, and allows it to complete the composting operation without any introduction of raw sewage. There's a crank handle for rotating the composting drum and a drum lock arrangement for transferring material from the drum to the finishing drawer. The finishing drawer slides out to simplify emptying. There's a 3-inch-diameter vent with a built-in 12-volt, 4-watt fan.

▷ **The Bottom Line** Anything that can simplify matters of the head compartment—holes in the boat, plumbing, storage space for waste, pumpout hassles, expense—is certainly worth pursuing, and both the Ecolet and the Air Head are worth consideration. The Ecolet will only fit on a boat with a good-sized head compartment. While its footprint is actually only marginally bigger than that of a standard toilet and plumbing fittings, it takes up a lot of cubic feet

The Air Head (left) and the Ecolet (center), stand beside a standard shoreside commode. After four months of use, both these composting toilets issued no unpleasant odors.

and airspace. And it needs plenty of electrical power to work at its best. The Air Head is more suitable for boats with smaller head compartments and less electrical capacity. It will also require a smaller hole to be drilled through the deck for the vent.

The Ecolet is in some ways more "civilized" than the Air Head, in that its size, capacity, and mechanisms are designed to manage waste without much help or attention from you. The Air Head is smaller, a bit simpler, and demands very little electricity. The only trade-off we can find, however, will be a show-stopper for some people: To a certain extent you have to commune with your own waste, and that of everyone else who uses the head. Yes, you can get it to a point where it hardly smells, but you will be inspecting it, pouring it, stirring it, and generally living close to it. In our opinion, it's no worse than having it sloshing around in a holding tank, awaiting a trip to the pumpout station, but many would argue that waste out of sight is waste out of mind. The Ecolet is sold via dealers, with prices ranging from $800 to $1,000; the Air Head costs $770.

CHAPTER 4

Electrical Systems

The foundation of any vessel's electrical system is its battery, or bank of batteries. *PS* has kept a close eye on battery developments over the years by continually testing various models. However, like the proverbial chain, every component in an electrical system serves a vital service, and the weakest link—be it improper wire size or a loose connection—can be its undoing. This chapter examines the more common component areas within an electrical system. We've also included some advice on ancillary products we've tested over the years, like portable generators and power boosters. One caveat need be offered here: Almost anyone can install a new battery or change out a battery selector switch, but no one should work with any portion of an electrical system without first understanding some of the science—and all of the dangers—involved.

Batteries

12-VOLT WET-CELLS

First, let's focus on flooded-cell, deep-cycle marine batteries. Six of the ones we evaluate here are in the popular Group 27 case size and two are in Group 31 size. (The two Group 31s, from Deka and West Marine, are actually the same battery—Deka/East Penn Manufacturing makes West Marine's batteries, which are private-labeled under the Sea Volt name.) Keep in mind that the Group 31 is physically a bit larger, so be sure that such batteries will fit your compartment. Also be aware that major battery-makers not only manufacture for private labels, but may sell the same battery under different brand names of their own.

Flooded-cell (also called wet-cell) technology has been around since the 19th century, yet the electrochemical reactions that drive the generation of flooded-cell battery DC electricity are generally unchanged. The case material, component quality, and material proportions have been optimized for a given battery function, e.g., a starting battery has a different internal structure than a deep-cycle house battery. Battery storage capacity depends upon the area of the plates, while ability to handle deep discharge depends on plate thickness. Starting batteries have more thin plates; deep-cycle batteries have fewer, thicker ones. Output voltage for either is the same.

In the lead-acid battery reaction, each cell within the battery has plates made of sponge lead (called the

Properly maintained wet-cell batteries can last for years—and they're cheaper than AGMs and gel-cell models. *PS* tested eight wet-cell batteries. Top row (left to right): the Deka DC31DT, the Rolls 27 112 XJ, the Deka DC27, and the West Marine Sea Volt. Bottom row: the Trojan 27THM, the Douglas 27 DCM, the U.S. Battery 27TMX, and the Interstate SRM 27B.

active material). These are also the negative plates of the battery, which produce the electrons. The positive plates are made of lead dioxide. All plates are immersed in a strong electrolyte, which provides a mechanism for a charge to flow between positive and negative plates. There are separators (insulators) between the positive and negative plates to prevent inadvertent contact. The most common electrolyte for this type of battery is sulfuric acid or H_2SO_4.

In the discharging reaction, the electrolyte combines with the active material (lead) to produce lead sulfate and water, which dilutes the acid. The voltage developed by this reaction is around 2 volts per cell. By combining (connecting) six cells, you get a 12-volt battery.

Battery ratings can help you determine what you're buying. The only problem is that the rating system is not completely standardized. Many manufacturers stick to similar test conditions and ratings, but some do not. Here are several means by which manufacturers rate batteries:

AMP-HOUR RATINGS apply primarily to deep-cycle batteries. They are considered in a context of the number of amp hours that can be drawn from a battery at 80°F at a relatively slow rate until it reaches 10.5 volts. Moreover, the rate of discharge is non-linear, so a faster discharge will not be a simple division problem, because the battery becomes unable to efficiently discharge at higher rates. Example: A 200-amp-hour battery would not be able to sustain a 20-amp load for 10 hours—it would be more like 6 hours, because of greatly reduced discharge efficiency.

(There is a complicated formula to accurately estimate time remaining, which expensive, chip-driven electronic discharge meters use.) Our testing evaluated the discharge time at various loads to gain a realistic picture of capabilities—something impossible to find consistently among manufacturers.

MARINE CRANKING AMPS (MCA) is a common rating used on marine deep-cycle batteries. This is the number of amps of load that a battery can deliver for 30 seconds at 32°F before it drops to 7.2 volts (1.2 volts per cell). A starter motor is designed to operate at lower voltage because of the huge current demands. This gives you an idea of how much power the battery can supply to start your boat's engine.

COLD-CRANKING AMPS (CCA) is a term more typically used with a car-type battery, and is usually measured for a 30-second duration at 0°F—a tougher standard than MCA. Some makers use Cranking Amps (CA), which is the same as MCA.

RESERVE CAPACITY is the time in minutes that a new and fully charged battery can supply 25 amps of draw at 80°F. This is another test that we ran. By definition, this test is considered over when battery voltage drops to 10.5 volts. This rating allows estimation of the time that your battery can operate essential equipment when your engine or charging system fails.

These ratings should be checked carefully to understand what loads were placed on the battery to determine the rating. Amp-hour ratings can be designated for different rates. We also noted that some manufacturers rate reserve capacity at 23 amps instead of 25 amps. Again, it pays to remember the definitions and read labels carefully.

Diligent maintenance is the true key to a long battery life. If you allow your battery to be stored for a long period of time without charging, sulfating can occur, resulting in a buildup on the battery's plates. This insulates them from the electrolyte, reducing performance. The best way to tell if your battery is charged is by using a hydrometer. (A voltmeter is second best.) As the reaction in the battery takes place, water is generated, diluting the electrolyte. This changes the specific gravity, which is what the hydrometer measures. Care must always be used in testing not to get a spark near the open cells (due to the extreme hazard of explosion).

A well-charged battery would return readings on a voltmeter in the range of 12.4 to 13.4 volts. Around 12.7 or 12.8 volts is a good average.

A battery should rest a minimum of 30 minutes after charging before measuring to get a more accurate reading and allow the surface charge to dissipate. Use of a "smart" chip-controlled charger will optimize both battery performance and battery life, and will pay for itself over the long haul. Also, recharging should occur within 24 hours of discharge to reduce sulfation. And, keep in mind that a discharged battery can freeze because of the higher concentration of water in its cells.

Overcharging is not good for deep-cycle batteries, and fast, shop-style boost chargers are not recommended.

When charging a battery, always make sure that battery plates are covered with electrolyte, and be sure to fill the battery with distilled water—never more battery acid. We found that that after a heavy, deep-cycle use (below 10.5 volts), a higher-amperage charger was required to burn off the buildup on the plates. A 25-amp "smart" computer chip-controlled charger setup with timer or automatic switch is optimal. A 10-amp "smart" charger will also work for this capacity battery because it's capable of higher, but controlled, voltages and current than the simple, cheap chargers.

▷ **The Bottom Line** *PS*'s comprehensive performance tests taught us a number of important lessons.

First, "off-the-shelf" doesn't necessarily mean you're getting a fresh battery. Second, several of the batteries we tested didn't measure up to their manufacturer's claims. Most were close, but a few—including US Battery's 27 TMX and Douglas' Aquatrol 27 DCM—were well off the mark. And third, taking good care of your battery provides as much value as shopping hard for one. All things being equal, finding a good price is the next most important factor. After calling around to a variety of sources nationwide, we found a wide range of pricing for the same batteries. The list prices found online were substantially higher than those offered by "point of sale" representatives.

We suspect that each battery comes with its own history and character. Some may be better than others, even for the same brand and model. Their character may be shaped by the history of the unit—when it was manufactured and how it was stored prior to shipment. Our guess is that the supplier that has the best control of these factors also delivers the best performance at the consumer level. In this case it was Deka and Interstate. The Deka D C27 and the Interstate SRM 27B outperformed the others.

DEEP-CYCLE AGM BATTERIES

There are three basic types of storage batteries used in the marine industry that are constructed of lead and acid: flooded or wet-cell batteries, AGM (absorbed glass mat) batteries, and gel (gelled electrolyte) batteries. Lead-acid batteries are further sub-grouped into three application-based categories: starting, deep-cycle, and dual-purpose. Our focus here is deep-cycle AGM and gel batteries.

Though lead-acid batteries remain the most common source of electrical power on most sailboats today, boat technology and boating habits are changing. Bow thrusters once reserved for only the largest megayachts are now routinely found on vessels under 40 feet, and DC power inverters are almost as common as windlasses. What all of these accessories have in common is an incredible appetite for DC power. As boat manufacturers build larger house battery banks to keep up with the load demands, they are faced with two choices: Build a battery bank out of traditional flooded cells, or embrace new technology

Type	Model	Case Size	Street Price/ Source	Warranty	CCA @ 0(F)	MCA @ 32 (F)	Weight
AGM	Deka Seamate/ 8A27m $	Group 27	$139/ AMS Batteries	3 yrs. Prorated 1st 12M Free Replacement	580 A	810 A	62.5 lbs.
AGM	Energy 1/ NSB-G-2700	Group 27	$225/ Manufacturer	24 Months Prorated	900 A	1150 A	63 lbs.
AGM	Lifeline/ GPL-27TGPL-27T	Group 27	$209.99/ Defenders	5 Yrs. Prorated 1st 12M Free Replacement	575 A	715 A	66 lbs.
AGM	Mastervolt/ AGM 12/90 ✔	Group 31	$213/ Ocean Options	24 Months Free Replacement	1012 A	NA	62 lbs.
AGM	Optima Yellow top/ D31A	Group 31	$199/ Battery Outlet	3 Yrs Prorated 1st 18M Free Replacement	900 A	1125 A	60.5 lbs.
AGM	Trojan/27-AGM*	Group 27	$169/ Manufacturer	12 Months Free Replacement	560 A	760 A	66 lbs.
AGM	West Marine SeaVolt/ 1231406	Group 27	$199.99/ West Marine	5 Yrs. Prorated 1st 18M Free Replacement	580 A	810 A	63 lbs.
GEL	Deka Dominator/ 8G27M $	Group 27	$145/ AMS Batteries	5 Yrs. Prorated 1st 12M Free Replacement	505 A	700 A	62.5 lbs.
GEL	Mastervolt/ MVG 12/85 ✔	Group 31	$344/ Ocean Options	5 Yrs. Prorated 1st 24M Free Replacement	NA*	NA*	68 lbs.
GEL	Westmarine SeaGel/ 437475	Group 27	$210.99/ West Marine	5 Yrs. Prorated 1st 18M Free Replacement	505 A	700 A	63.2 lbs.

$ Budget Buy   ✔ Recommended   ★ Best Choice

*Note: Mastervolt rates its gel coil to Cold Starter Current/DIN standards, which are common in the U.K., but different from the U.S. standard.

and opt for a battery bank that is as progressive as the new components it will serve.

Valve-regulated lead-acid (VRLA) batteries, because of their sealed, spill-proof design, can be mounted in any position, except inverted. If you plan to mount a gel battery on its side, expect to lose 10 percent of its amp-hour (Ah) capacity. When faced with a flooded bilge situation, VRLA batteries will continue to operate submerged up to a 30-foot depth. After the first fathom of water, the point is probably moot. And VRLA batteries' low self-discharge rate is far superior to that of flooded lead-acid batteries, making layup time maintenance free.

PS evaluators used a carbon pile tester from Snap-On Tools (far left) to assess reserve capacity. A row of incandescent light bulbs (foreground) served as the discharge source. The Trojan 27 AGM, which is being tested in this photo, performed slightly below the Mastervolt AGM, but it also sells for about $40 less, so it's *PS*'s top choice in this group.

Rated Amp Hour Capacity	Rated Reserve Capacity at 25 Amp Load (min.)	Observed Reserve Capacity at 25 Amp Load (min.)	Observed Reserve Capacity at 20 Hr. Rate (h & m)	L" x W" x H"	Performance	Quality
92 Ah	175 min.	151 min.	19h 59m	12.7x6.7x10	Good	Good
72.6 Ah	140 min.	113 min.	15h 17m	13x6.5x8.4	Fair	Fair
100 Ah	186 min.	171 min.	18h 25m	12x6.6x9.2	Good	Excellent
90 Ah	160 min.	213 min.	24h 11m	13x6.8x9.3	Excellent	Excellent
75 Ah	155 min.	110 min.	15h 31m	12.8x6.5x9.4	Fair	Good
100 Ah	175 min.	212 min.	23h 40m	12x6.5x9.2	Excellent	Excellent
92 Ah	175 min.	151 min.	19h 55m	12.7x6.7x10	Good	Good
86 Ah	170 min.	145 min.	18h 50m	12.7x6.7x10	Good	Good
85 Ah	Not Specified	196 min.	20h 43m	13x6.7x9.3	Excellent	Good
86 Ah	160 min.	144 min.	18h 45m	12.7x6.7x10	Good	Good

Unlike most automotive-grade flooded lead-acid batteries, AGM batteries will not drop a plate or disintegrate when subjected to pounding in rough seas or excessive hull vibration. This is because the internal plates on an AGM battery receive additional physical support from the compressed fiber mats sandwiched between each lead plate.

Deep-cycle VRLA batteries can cost about double what an average-grade deep-cycle flooded cell battery costs, or about 20 percent greater than a premium-grade flooded cell. If you decide to upgrade, remember to factor in the additional costs required to modify your vessel's battery charging system to satisfy the VRLA's demanding charging regime, unless you are going to install spiral-cell AGM batteries, which are compatible with most alternators.

It is not recommended to discharge your deep-cycle battery below a 50-percent depth of discharge, which is half of your battery's reserve capacity rating. Each time a deep-cycle battery is discharged 100 percent, the battery will lose at least one cycle of the battery's total life-cycle rating.

▷ **The Bottom Line** *PS* selected 10 of the most popular VRLA deep-cycle batteries in the groups 27–31 (about 100Ah) case size. The test field consisted of three gelled electrolyte batteries, six traditional flat-plate AGM batteries, and one spiral-cell AGM battery (see the Value Guide for specific batteries tested). Following the "Standard Test Procedures for Storage Batteries" that is endorsed by the Boating Council International, we arranged a test to evaluate each battery's deep-cycle reserve capacity.

When we evaluated the numbers from our performance test, it became clear that both Mastervolt batteries and the Trojan battery easily exceeded their factory reserve capacity ratings. Although battery reserve capacity is the primary component for determining the merits of a good deep-cycle battery, we also ran an amps-per-pound ratio for each tested battery and then factored in the battery's cost and warranty period.

In the end, we felt Trojan's 100Ah Group 27 AGM earned the Best Choice honors, though in testing it performed slightly below the Mastervolt AGM, which was our best Group 31 battery. Our Budget Buys, the Deka batteries, will satisfy cost-conscious sailors who want to upgrade, but don't need the very best.

The Optima would be a good choice as a house battery for a small sailboat with an outboard or only a basic charging system. And Optimas are a nice alternative to a flooded battery for some applications (a big RIB, for instance) because they're spill-proof and can better take a pounding at high speed. A battery, unlike an engine, cannot be opened up and overhauled or repaired.

Battery Chargers

Fifteen years ago battery technology for vessels whose house battery banks had large load requirements started to slowly shift from automotive-based, lead-acid designs to absorbed-glass-mat (AGM) and gel-based batteries. It was only a matter of time before the battery charger designers caught up with the advances in battery technology and replaced their low-tech ferroresonant, transformer-based battery chargers with something smarter. Now, these chargers can handle not only lead-acid batteries—still the most popular and inexpensive type of battery aboard recreational boats—but also gel and AGM batteries.

Batteries are recharged by the electrochemical reaction that occurs inside them during the charging process. The maximum rate at which a battery can accept a charge is governed by the composition of the battery receiving the charge, and the amount of DC battery charge current applied to the battery. This maximum rate is often referred to as the battery's charge acceptance limit. If a battery charger's output current (including alternators, inverters, and solar panel sources) exceeds the battery's acceptance limit (overcharging), the battery will overheat and its storage capacity will be greatly reduced. Inversely, if

the battery charger does not output enough charging current in relationship to the battery's charge acceptance limit (undercharging), then the electrochemical reaction inside of the battery will never reach its full potential.

All batteries are likely to generate less power over time if they are recharged incorrectly. Most AGM batteries cannot tolerate bulk-charge voltages above 14.2 volts, but can easily accept twice the charging current of a lead-acid battery, which cuts an AGM battery's bulk charge time by 50 percent (AGM batteries have a very high charge conversion efficiency—they charge faster because they convert more of the input voltage into stored energy).

Because AGM and gel batteries have different charging requirements than lead-acid, flooded-cell batteries, the battery charger manufacturers had to engineer microprocessor-controlled charging algorithms. They precisely control charger voltage and current output in three distinct recharge sequences for all three different types of battery styles (flooded, gel, and AGM). Since the cases on both gel and AGM batteries are sealed, most charger manufacturers offer an optional (but highly recommended) battery case temperature probe that allows the battery charger to adjust charge rates according to the case temperature. Charging an AGM battery without a temperature-compensated battery charger contravenes the recommendations of all the leading manufacturers of multi-stage marine battery chargers.

As a result of the manufacturers' need to implement microprocessor-controlled charging sequences, the new-generation smart chargers are fitted with high-frequency AC–DC switching converters that generate the DC charge voltage, instead of old-technology humming transformers (found in ferroresonant chargers). In eliminating the AC transformers from the battery charger design, the engineers were able to reduce charger case weight by over 50 percent and significantly reduce the amount of AC ripple being output by the charger. AC ripple on a battery charger's DC output line is very detrimental to a battery's longevity.

Another benefit: high-frequency converters allow precise DC noise-suppression filtering. Some of the new chargers that we tested are so free of line hum that their manufacturers actually rate them to be used as

	Newmar PT-25	Charles 2000SP	Mastervolt IVO 12/25-3	Charles 5000SP	Xantrex TC20+	Guest 2632A	ProMariner ProTech 1220
Dimensions	12.5" x 8" x 5.3"	8" x 9.5" x 3.7"	6" x 9" x 2.5"	8" x 9.5" x 3.7"	15" x 6.75" x 3"	13" x 10" x 3"	10.5" x 6" x 2.2"
Weight	8.5 lbs.	5 lbs.	3.8 lbs.	5 lbs	6.9 lbs.	15.6 lbs	3.2 lbs.
Current Output x # of Bat. Banks	3 x 25A	3 x 20A	2 x 25A + 1 x 3A	3 x 20A	1 x 20A or 2 x 10A	2 x 5A + 1 x 20A	1 x 20A or 2 x 10A
No. of Charging Stages	3	3	3	3	4	3	4
Current Meter	Yes	Yes	No	Yes	No	No	No
Adjustable Absorption Rate	No	No	Yes	No	No	No	Yes
AC Hum/RFI	None	None	Low	None	Low	Moderate	Low
GP27 Recharge Time	4H 5M	4H 10M	3H 40M	4H 10M	5H 05M	6H 10M*	4H 55M
Battery Types Supported	LA/Gel/AGM	LA/Gel/AGM	LA/Gel/AGM	LA/Gel/AGM	LA/Gel/AGM	LA/Gel/AGM	LA/Gel/AGM
Remote Panel	Opt.	No	Opt.	No	Opt.	No	Opt.
Battery Temperature Sensor	Opt.	No	Opt.	No	Opt.	No	No
Power Supply	Yes	Yes	No	Yes	Yes	No	Yes
Equalization	Opt.	No	No	No	Yes	No	Yes
Price	$319	$289	$449	$354	$299	$329	$339
Warranty	2 years	2 years	2 years	5 years	1 year	2 years	1 year

*We only connected 1 battery to this unit, as the 2nd and 3rd banks were limited to 5A of output current.

stand-alone power supplies for radio communication equipment, without a battery installed in-line.

It is generally accepted that for a battery charger to be categorized as a smart charger, it will have a three-stage charging curve, consisting of a bulk phase, an absorption phase, and a float mode. Taking a flooded battery as an example, the charger applies its maximum rated DC current in the bulk phase until the battery's voltage approaches about 14.4V DC. At this point in the charge cycle, about 75 to 80 percent of the battery's capacity has been replaced.

The charger will then switch over to the absorption phase where the charging voltage is held constant and the charging current is gradually reduced. The absorption phase will take anywhere from one to four hours (depending on battery size and the type of discharge) to "saturate" the battery's internal plates, and restore battery capacity to 95 percent.

Once the battery charger detects that the output current requirements have dropped below 4 amps for three minutes (though each manufacturer has a unique algorithm, 4 amps at three minutes seems to be about the average), the charger will switch over to the float mode. In the float mode, the battery charger applies a precise finishing voltage of 13.3–13.5 volts DC (for lead-acid batteries), which is below the level at which lead-acid batteries will "boil" or "gas." The float mode is considered the maintenance mode in which theoretically the charger can be connected to the battery indefinitely without the risk of over-charging.

A key specification to compare when shopping for a smart charger is the charger's maximum output rating available at each of its outputs. Some manufacturers prefer three independent charging circuits, each with individual positive and negative terminals;

Practical Sailor put seven readily available battery chargers to the test. The specimens included (clockwise from top left): Xantrex TC20+, Newmar PT-25, Guest 2632A, ProMariner 1220, Mastervolt 12/25-3, and the Charles Industries 2000SP (identical in appearance to the 5000SP, which *PS* also tested).

some prefer three "dependent" charging circuits with a full 20 amps or more of available charging power, some less per circuit. How each manufacturer deals with these critical features is an important part of deciding which charger to buy. *PS*'s preference is for each charging circuit to have a full 20 amps available, one for the house battery and one each for up to two starting batteries.

A relatively new mode of charging is "equalization." The equalization mode, as explained by Xantrex, is a manually activated mode that deliberately overcharges the battery. The purpose is to equalize the chemistry in each battery cell by reducing sulfation and acid stratification. Equalization should be performed only on non-sealed, flooded, lead-acid batteries (never on gel-cel or AGM batteries), and

only as often as specified by the battery manufacturer. Our feeling on equalization: If we wanted to boil our batteries, we would just leave our old ferroresonant charger on board.

▷ **The Bottom Line** *PS*'s most recent evaluation included seven chargers, two from Charles Industries, the 2000SP and the 5000SP, and one each from Guest/Marinco (2632A), Mastervolt (IVO 12/25-3), Newmar (PT-25), ProMariner (Pro Tech 1220), and Xantrex (Truecharge TC20+). Our test clearly demonstrated that battery chargers are about as diverse as the different batteries they're built to charge. Truly, there is no one size or model that fits all; something that may change with the introduction of the next generation of digital chargers.

Not to let technology get in the way of simplicity, the Charles Industries 2000SP is a good choice for recharging modest banks of lead-acid batteries. This charger is powerful, compact, and looks like it was designed to be installed on a bulkhead and forgotten about—for many years. Even though the 2000SP has a battery selector switch for gel and AGM batteries, we wouldn't feel comfortable in recharging anything but lead-acid batteries without a battery temperature probe (which isn't available on the 2000SP).

Newmar's PT-25 charger is the best all-around battery charger in this group. It's a versatile unit

PS used a matching pair of Group 27 (100 amp hour) lead-acid batteries as a house battery bank. Each charger, in turn, was connected to a 110-volt AC source and monitored via a Snap-On Tools battery load tester (black box in the back row) as well as a Fluke clamp-on amp meter (in the tester's left hand). The Icom M502 VHF radio (to the right of the load tester) was used to detect if the charger produced any hum or distortion on our DC line.

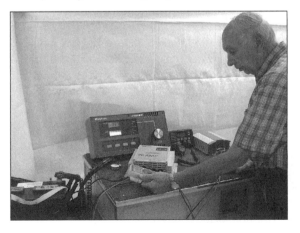

that's well arranged and impeccably built. When you add the optional battery temperature probe and the remote panel, you have a unit that can easily handle complex battery banks. Because of its price—just $30 higher than Charles's 2000SP—and its extended capabilities, this charger is our Best Buy. And we'd recommend the Mastervolt IVO 12/25-3 if you have a few banks of expensive gel-cel or AGM batteries that you want to last as long as possible. The charging profiles of Mastervolt's IVO are very precise and though this specialty charger costs $125 more than the Newmar PT-25, we feel that its subcompact size and programmability justify the price differential.

PS also examined a new charger from Xantrex Technologies, Inc., the XC 5012, which features multiplex charging capability. That essentially means that this one charger can handle different battery types. This one in particular is a 50-amp, three-bank charger.

Here's how it works: Once you program the XC 5012 and tell it what type of battery chemistry that you have connected to each of its three independent banks, the charger will check each battery bank and then start a recharging profile on the battery bank with the lowest state of charge. And once this particular battery bank responds to the XC's charge profile, the charger will put that battery's charge profile on hold and switch its recharge energy over to the next battery bank in numeric sequence and apply a new charge profile. This rolling sequence continues so that the charger can briefly focus all of its energy into one particular battery bank.

Our experience with Xantrex's XC5012 convinced us that this is the best battery charger in its class that we have tested to date. The XC5012 regularly delivered 53 amps in the initial bulk charge phase (more than its rated output) in stone silence. And silence is something that any sailor can appreciate.

It was apparent that this new charger was powerful and capable, but was it durable? The XC series is rated for true reverse-polarity protection, so we reverse-connected one set of the battery output leads (on purpose), stepped back a few feet, and plugged the charger in. The result was uneventful, to say the least. No sparks, no smoke, no Gabriel's horn. All that happened was that a fault message was displayed on the unit's LCD display.

Costing about $335, the XC 30-amp charger (approximately $100 more for the 50-amp XC5012) is one serious battery charger that will finally allow a vessel with perfectly functioning lead-acid start batteries to upgrade the house battery bank to AGM or gel technology without having to add a second battery charger to the system.

Battery Selector Switches

Your vessel's battery selector switch is probably one of the first things that you reach for each time you step aboard your boat. And after you've left, it's the switch that plagues your mind: Did I turn that @$*^ thing off?

A battery selector switch's primary purpose is to help manage the flow of electrical power onboard your vessel. This is accomplished by providing a selectable circuit path between your vessel's batteries and the primary branch circuit, such as the main DC distribution panel or engines. The difference between a battery switch and a battery selector switch is the number of positions on the switch. A battery switch is normally a two-position (On/Off) switch. A battery selector switch is normally a four-position switch (Off, Bat 1, Bat 2, Both).

The selector switch provides the means for isolating the vessel's battery banks to prevent battery drain when the vessel is not in use. In addition, it acts as a master switch capable of shutting down the entire electrical system during an emergency. The battery selector switch also gives you a method of distributing charging currents from generation sources back to the vessel's batteries while providing electrical separation of battery banks.

The battery selector switch is not a particularly glamorous device. It's usually mounted in some dark recess of the cabin or in some surplus space in the engineroom. On older vessels, these switches were consistently sited at ankle height and you almost always needed a flashlight to positively identify the switch's position. But things change. No longer are we finding battery switches limited to the standard colors of bright red, safety orange, or industrial gray. There are switches on the market that now come with white cases that color-coordinate with the engineroom, ones with red and green faceplates, and even ones with luminous dials. The latest trend is toward mini battery switches that can be cluster-mounted directly into the vessel's DC electrical distribution panel.

PS recently tested and dissected a group of battery selector switches from seven manufacturers (BEP Marine, Inc., Blue Sea Systems, Cole-Hersee Co., Charles Marine, Guest, Perko, and West Marine) and came away with some very useful data. Following the manufacturers' lead, we divided these products into regular selector switches and heavy duty ones.

▷ **The Bottom Line** As all of the switches that we tested were either UL1107-approved or rated, it was no surprise that all of the entries met their minimum rated capacities. In looking at the terminal stud temperatures, it is pretty evident that the switches with the copper studs ran the coolest. Thus it would be fair to say, based on terminal stud temperatures and our visual inspection of the interior of each switch, that the BEP and the Blue Sea Systems switches are overbuilt and dissipate a far greater amount of heat than other standard-duty switches of similar rate capacity. In the heavy-duty category, the Perko 8603 switch is almost indestructible.

The interiors of BEP's 721 switch and the Blue Sea Systems switch look similar, but there are noteworthy differences. The plate copper contacts inside the BEP switch are one-third thicker than the ones found in the Blue Sea switch. Also, BEP connects the selector knob to the contact plate with a ¼-inch solid brass shaft, while Blue Sea uses plastic. The copper plates found inside Cole Hersee's M750 are surprisingly thin; thus, the lower continuous amperage rating for such a physically large switch. Minimal components were found on the Charles switch, as well as Guest's 2111A and 2101.

We thought we'd find a much closer comparison in the heavy-duty category between Perko's 8603 and Guest's 2300A. Guest advertises that its switch's sweep design provides 60 percent more contact.

Our test field included 11 models. Beginning with the top row (left to right): Cole Hersee M750, Guest 2300A, Charles 93BS002; middle row: Perko 8501, Guest 2111A, Perko 8603, Guest 2101; bottom row: West Marine 382215, Blue Sea 9001e, BEP Marine 721, and BEP Marine 701S.

However, after poking around inside both of these switches, we can say that Guest doesn't provide 60 percent more contact area than Perko's 8603. The selector plate on the 8603 slides through dual contact plates (one above and one below, much like an old knife switch) at each position stop. So there is twice as much copper plating inside Perko's 8603 switch as compared to Guest's 2300A. The sliding of Perko's selector plate through the contact accounts for the smooth feel as the selector knob is rotated. Conversely, the selector knob on the Guest 2300A takes a good amount of force to turn, to the point that the switch often feels stuck.

The Blue Sea switch is our choice for best value in a standard-duty battery selector switch. It's made in the U.S. with high-grade materials, comes with a lifetime warranty, and is the least expensive switch in our test. When we factored in the Blue Sea's luminous dial, high amperage rating, and the consensus that the switch is overbuilt, allowing cooler terminal stud temperatures, we had no qualms about putting this switch at the top of our list.

Perko's 8603 easily takes top honors in the heavy-duty battery selector switch category. One look at the

	Newmar PT-25	Charles 2000SP	Mastervolt IVO 12/25-3	Charles 5000SP	Xantrex TC20+	Guest 2632A	ProMariner ProTech 1220
Dimensions	12.5" x 8" x 5.3"	8" x 9.5" x 3.7"	6" x 9" x 2.5"	8" x 9.5" x 3.7"	15" x 6.75" x 3"	13" x 10" x 3"	10.5" x 6" x 2.2"
Weight	8.5 lbs	5 lbs.	3.8 lbs.	5 lbs.	6.9 lbs.	15.6 lbs.	3.2 lbs.
Current Output × No. of Bat. Banks	3 x 25A	3 x 20A	2 x 25A + 1 x 3A	3 x 20A	1 x 20A or 2 x 10A	2 x 5A + 1 x 20A	1 x 20A or 2 x 10A
No. of Charging Stages	3	3	3	3	4	3	4
Current Meter	Yes	Yes	No	Yes	No	No	No
Adjustable Absorption Rate	No	No	Yes	No	No	No	Yes
AC Hum/RFI	None	None	Low	None	Low	Moderate	Low
GP27 Recharge Time	4H 5M	4H 10M	3H 40M	4H 10M	5H 05M	6H 10M*	4H 55M
Battery Types Supported	LA/Gel/AGM	LA/Gel/AGM	LA/Gel/AGM	LA/Gel/AGM	LA/Gel/AGM	LA/Gel/AGM	LA/Gel/AGM
Remote Panel	Opt.	No	Opt.	No	Opt.	No	Opt.
Battery Temperature Sensor	Opt.	No	Opt.	No	Opt.	No	No
Power Supply	Yes	Yes	No	Yes	Yes	No	Yes
Equalization	Opt.	No	No	No	Yes	No	Yes
Price	$319	$289	$449	$354	$299	$329	$339
Warranty	2 years	2 years	2 years	5 years	1 year	2 years	1 year

*We only connected 1 battery to this unit, as the 2nd and 3rd banks were limited to 5A of output current.

comparison photo and one turn of its selector knob tell it all. This is the switch to use where failure is not an option.

Guest
Model 2300A

PERKO
Model 8603

Battery Boxes and Trays

Battery boxes are often overlooked, yet these simple devices are an essential and integral part of a vessel's electrical system. A wet-cell battery not held firmly in place cannot perform its intended function, does not comply with U.S. Coast Guard regulations, and in rough seas can be dangerous. *PS* surveyed the market for these devices and purchased two plastic battery boxes (for larger boat needs), two smaller battery boxes (for smaller boats), and three tray-style hold-downs. Then we evaluated each.

The two heavy-duty switches that *PS* tested are shown here without their face plates. This shot clearly reveals Perko's twin thick contact plates and smoother-turning dial.

From Blue Sea Systems we obtained the 4012, which holds two golf cart batteries. (The company also makes boxes to hold a single 4D and a single 8D battery.) Our second big box came from Todd Enterprises, which produces five separate models. We selected the Double Battery Box, designed to hold a pair of group 24 batteries. The three tray-type hold-downs we tested were from Gil Marine, T & H Marine, and West Marine. The small battery boxes came from Tempo and West Marine.

When properly mounted, the big boxes from Todd and Blue Sea should have no trouble meeting CG regulations for security. This means they're capable of a sustained pull on the battery in five different directions with a force of 90 pounds. Both also have vented and secured lids, which is important. Ultimately, our testers preferred the Blue Seas box because it has a double wall molded into the top 2½ inches of the box, helping to secure the batteries firmly in place and increase strength. The bottom is molded to hold the batteries above the actual bottom of the box, which leaves space to hold spilled electrolyte in the event of a leak. Hold-downs are molded into each outside corner and sized for ¼-inch fasteners. The plastic cover is attached with a pair of bolts, one on each end, with large plastic knobs for easy hand tightening. Threaded bronze fittings pressed into the top of the box receive the bolts. They remain with the cover even when it is off the box, held in place by nylon washers. Eight outlets molded into the box rim allow for battery cables to exit, each sized for a single cable. The cover has four matching outlets at one end; it can be flipped in either direction to accommodate a maximum of four cables from the box. We like the sound construction and protective features of the Blue Sea 4021.

Todd Enterprises' Double Battery Box has single-wall construction and is designed to have the batteries sit flat on the bottom. No hold-downs are provided; holes need to be drilled through the bottom of the box so that it can be fastened to the boat's structure with fender washers inside the box and bolts or lags into the deck. A shoebox joint on the cover keeps it from sliding, and two nylon bolts and wing nuts are provided to secure it in place. The nylon bolts were difficult to get through the holes and fit

Battery boxes from West Marine and Tempo (back row) do the job, but the two trays from West and Gil (center) hold batteries more securely and don't block access to the terminals. The T & H Marine tray (foreground) secures its battery with a single strap. Not pictured are the high-end, fully covered boxes from Blue Sea and Todd. *PS* testers felt that the Blue Sea product was best among those.

Manufacturer	Model	Price	Type	Material	Sizes Available	Comment
Blue Sea Systems	4021	$59	Box	Plastic	2xGC, 4D, 8D	A large well-built box, our top pick in large boxes
Gil Marine	913125	$20	Tray	Plastic/SS	24, 27, 31	Tray includes all needed hardware, a top pick
T & H Marine	BH-24P	$10	Tray	Plastic	24, 27	Uses strap to hold battery in place
Tempo	BAT27	$9.99	Box	Plastic	24, 27, 31	Uses small screws and strap to hold everything
Todd	84-1480	$39.95	Box	Plastic	2xGC, 4D, 8D, 2x4D, 2x8D	Not on same level as Blue Sea, but cheaper
West Marine	2235562	$11.49	Tray	Plastic/SS	24, 27	Good tray and a little cheaper than the Gil
West Marine	2235604	$9.99	Box	Plastic	24, 27	Uses small screws and strap to hold everything

poorly. Two 1³⁄₄-inch holes cut into the lid provide for cable exit.

The Todd box is not as well designed or constructed as the Blue Sea 4021, in our view, but it will get the job done for a little less money.

The two smaller boxes we looked are nearly identical in shape and construction—single-wall molded plastic with shoebox lids. Each is packaged with the same plastic strap, a pair of plastic strap hold-downs, and four small screws. The strap clamps are meant to be screwed to the deck at the front and back of the box, and the strap then encircles the box and is tightened. While we've used this type of box and strap on boats for many years, it's not, in our opinion, very secure, especially with the small screws provided. The final drawback on these boxes is that they have high sides, so they require lifting very heavy batteries, in awkward positions, higher than if a battery tray were installed. They're not recommended where space overhead is tight, but at least they're inexpensive. (Both boxes sell for $10.)

Two of the battery trays we examined are nearly identical—the West and the Gil. Both are composite plastic trays designed in two parts. A tray on the bottom holds the battery and is secured to the boat with four large screws. Each end of the bottom tray accepts a stainless steel rod that supports and secures the upper frame, which fits around the top perimeter of the battery. This effectively clamps the battery in place with no movement possible. It's a good arrangement.

Another advantage of the tray is that you'll only need to lift the battery about an inch off the deck to place it properly on the bottom tray, or to take it out for charging or replacement. That's a true muscle-saving feature. However, because the tray-type hold-downs don't have full lids, they require the addition of insulating terminal caps. These can be found at marine supply stores for just a few dollars. These terminal caps can be held securely in place with tie-wraps.

Our third tray-style battery box is from T & H Marine. It's a one-piece molded plastic tray supplied with a strap, selling for $10. The tray is fastened down with four screws placed through tabs molded into the sides of the tray. The strap should be fitted under the tray prior to fastening to the deck. Then it goes over the battery and gets latched. This is not, in our view, as secure a hold-down method as on the Gil and West trays.

We prefer the battery trays available from West and Gil over the strap-equipped T & H tray or either of the boxes. Though they cost a couple of dollars more, and require terminal insulators, they should hold a battery more securely. They also don't require lifting the battery high during installation or a change, and they take up less room inside the boat.

Electrical Distribution Panels

You just finished adding some important electronics to your boat—let's say a new VHF and a combination knotmeter-depthsounder. Now, how do you get electricity to these items? Install a small accessory electrical panel, of course.

	Accessory Circuit Breaker Panels				Water-Resistant Panels		
Manufacturer	BEP	Newmar	Blue Sea	Blue Sea	Blue Sea	Blue Sea	BEP
Product Number	901 V DC	ACCY 1X	8023	8677	8273	4306	CSP6-F
Circuit Protection	Magnetic CB	Magnetic CB	Magnetic	Magnetic CB	Thermal	ATC Fuse	ATC Fuse
Switch	Toggle	Toggle	Toggle	Rocker	Contura	Toggle	Toggle
Circuits	8	8	8	6	6	6	6
Installed Circuits	8	5	5	6	6	6	6
Water-Resistant	No	No	No	No	Yes	Yes	Yes
Panel	Aluminum	Aluminum	Aluminum	Aluminum	Aluminum	Plastic	Plastic
Backlit	Yes	No	Yes	Yes	No	Yes	Yes
Labels, individual	Yes	Yes	Yes	Yes	Yes	Yes	Yes
Night Readability	Excellent	Poor	Excellent	Good	Poor	Good	Good
Quality of Construction	Excellent	Good	Excellent	Excellent	Excellent	Excellent	Good
List Price	$213	$160	$179	$256	$147	$90	$80

Panel boards are commonly referred to as circuit breaker, distribution, fuse, or electrical panels. Depending on the size of the vessel and the complexity of its DC system, power distribution may be centralized on a full-sized circuit breaker panel or branched out to sub-panels. These smaller sub-panels could consist of simple fuse-protected switch panels, accessory circuit breaker panels, water-resistant panels, or any combination thereof. And the latest trend in DC distribution panels is the introduction of water-resistant auxiliary panels for the cockpit. These new panels allow localized control of accessory equipment, eliminating that all-too-familiar trip back into the cabin to turn a circuit on or off at the main distribution panel.

Anyone in the market for one of these panels will first have to determine his or her needs regarding the number of connections and switches. That aside, you'll want to look at the quality of the panel's components, the type of circuit protection provided, the readability of the panel at night, its serviceability, price, and of course, warranty. In a recent evaluation, PS did just that. We looked at 11 panels. These are all three- to eight-position panels with and with-

If your boat's electrical panel has reached its capacity, like this one, one option for accommodating additional electronics is an accessory panel. PS tested 11.

out metering. The smaller DC panels are the choice when 12-volt accessories/electronics are added to a vessel. Our evaluation included two switch-fused panels from West Marine; four circuit breaker panels from BEP, Newmar, and Blue Sea Systems; two circuit breaker panels with metering from Blue

Metered Breaker Panels		Economy Panels	
Blue Sea	Blue Sea	West Marine	West Marine
8081	8401	55344 WM	55342WM
Magnetic CB	Magnetic	Fuse	Fuse
Toggle	Toggle	Rocker	Rocker
5	5	3	6
5	5	3	6
No	No	No	No
Aluminum	Aluminum	Aluminum	Aluminum
Yes	Yes	No	No
Yes	Yes	No	No
Good	Excellent	Poor	Poor
Excellent	Excellent	Fair	Fair
$298	$398	$44	$40

gies circuit breakers. But that is where the similarities end. Blue Sea and Newmar use thicker aluminum stock than BEP on their panels. The thicker stock allows Blue Sea and Newmar to countersink their mounting screw holes, making for a neater installation. The BEP panels must be mounted with panhead screws, which could chip the finish on the panel if small flat washers under the screw heads are not used.

When we took a closer look at the Carling Technologies circuit breakers used on all of the accessory and full-sized panels from our review group, we noticed that Blue Sea is using a different model Carling circuit breaker than both BEP and Newmar. Blue Sea dubs the model of Carling that they are using as their "World Circuit Breaker." The most striking difference of this circuit breaker is that its rated amperage is stenciled right on its face, below the toggle handle and in clear view from the front side of the panel. This location is very helpful in quickly accessing preliminary electrical problems without the need to remove the panel.

In the night readability test, BEP and Blue Sea were the hands-down winners, because Newmar doesn't offer a lamp plate to illuminate their circuit labels. The entire Newmar panel remains dark at night, with the exception of the tiny LED "circuit energized" lamp. Blue Sea does not offer any meter lighting on their No. 8081 twin analog meter panel, just circuit identification and status illumination.

However, Blue Sea Systems is the only manufacturer that offers, in writing, a lifetime guarantee. Simply put, "If you are not satisfied with a Blue Sea product you can return it for a full refund or a replacement, at any time." This is definitely a warranty and a manufacturer that is worth noting. So, because they are backed by an impressive warranty, have excellent

Sea; and three water-resistant panels from Blue Sea and BEP.

▷ **The Bottom Line** When installing or replacing anything electrical onboard your vessel, planning, understanding the system, and knowing your own capabilities are paramount. Every panel manufacturer that we reviewed has a technical support department that welcomes calls and e-mail from both novice and professional alike. And every panel that we reviewed came with installation instructions.

All of the accessory panels that we reviewed (with the exception of the economy panels) are constructed of aluminum and are fitted with Carling Technolo-

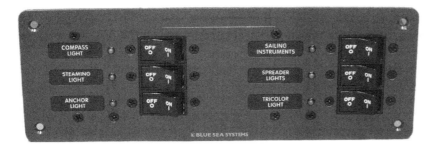

Blue Sea Systems 8677 is one of six panels *PS* tested from this company. This model, which sells for $256, has excellent construction and backlighting, but it's not water resistant. For that quality, you'll have to opt for either the Blue Sea 8273 or 4306, or BEP's CSP6-F.

night lighting, and better labeling than the other panels, Blue Sea Systems' model No. 8023 is our top pick for an accessory circuit breaker panel, and model No. 4306 is our choice for a water-resistant panel. Either of the West Marine switches (both are under $50) are a good choice if you're operating on a tight budget and need to replace a panel of switches on an older vessel.

12-Volt Power Boosters

Not long ago, on board a charter boat, we found that the cardinal battery sin had been committed: The selector switch had been left on "Both," and the electric bilge pump had drawn both batteries down so low that they couldn't start the diesel. Someone ran down the dock, brought back a portable booster box, and moments later the engine was running and recharging the batteries.

These boosters, or power packs, have been available for years, but suddenly they seem to be everywhere. Some are simple and small enough to be slipped under a car seat; many have cigarette-lighter sockets for running 12-volt appliances, and some have several other features. They generally come with a cord fitted at both ends with a cigarette-lighter plug, so they can be recharged from a car's (or boat's) battery banks when the engine is spinning the alternator. And their uses aboard boats are legion—not only to jump-start an engine, but to charge cell phones and handheld electronics, and to be a portable, self-contained power source that can run a pump, a radio, or any number of other things.

With so many brands and models out there, we decided simply to compare a Xantrex booster we had on hand (Xantrex Xpower PowerPack 300 PLUS) with a couple of other models, West Marine's Jumpstart 400 Mk2 and Wal-Mart's EverStart Maxx Heavy Duty Jump Starter. We chose boosters with different cranking-amp and amp-hour ratings, and with different bell-and-whistle capabilities.

The ability of a booster pack to start an engine relies on its available cold-cranking amps (CCA). This is the number of amps a battery can deliver for a period of 30 seconds at a temperature of 0°F, before the battery voltage drops to 7.2 volts (1.2 volts per cell).

The amps required to start a marine engine vary with the type of engine (diesel inboard, gas inboard, gas outboard), as well as the size of the engine, the condition of the engine, the condition of the battery, and the ambient temperature. The bigger the engine and the lower the temperature, the more CCA will be required. Diesels generally require more than gas engines. Engines in good working order, in a warm climate, with nothing holding them back but a dead battery, might need only a couple of hundred amps for two seconds to get going, while an engine with other firing problems, or a big, cold diesel, would need much more. Smaller marine diesels of one to three cylinders require around 300–400 CCA, while bigger diesels might require from 600 CCA on up. That's what these booster packs are meant for— quick jump-starts, not protracted cranking.

Booster packs like those we evaluated use sealed, AGM (absorbed glass mat) lead-acid batteries. All have automatic polarity detection, and all require a minimum voltage in the dead battery in order to activate themselves. This is an excellent safety feature— they won't flow current until a good connection has been made and proper polarity has been sensed. This eliminates sparking. However, the Wal-Mart EverStart comes with a manual override button that allows the user to put power to the cables without any voltage feedback from a dead battery.

Here's how we evaluated them: All three booster packs were given a full charge, then left alone for a week, then used to start a car (142-horsepower gasoline engine) in which a dead battery had been substituted for the starting battery and connections made with jumper cables. The weather was chilly—about 40°F. All three managed the job, and in about the order you'd expect from the boosters' ratings: The one with the most CCA started the engine most easily.

Two weeks later, our friend the shellfisherman couldn't fire up the 80-horsepower John Deere diesel that powers his dredge pump. It was about 12°F, with ice forming in the harbor. We dropped in with the boosters, which had been freezing in the back of the car all night—and accomplished exactly nothing. Neither of the bigger boosters could turn the recalcitrant engine fast enough to fire it off. Later in the day, when the temperature had risen to

	Xantrex Xpower Powerpack 300 Plus	West Marine SeaVolt JumpStart 400 Mk2	Wal-Mart EverStart Maxx Heavy Duty Jump Starter
Starting Power (CCA)	200	450	600
Hieght, Width, Depth	11.8", 12.5", 7.2"	12.75", 11", 5.5"	11.5", 12", 7.5"
Weight	18 lbs.	16 lbs.	20 lbs.
Work light	Two 4-watt fluorescent bulbs	3 LEDs	None
12-volt Cigarette Lighter Sockets	1 (12-amp breaker, auto reset)	1 (20-amp breaker, auto-reset)	2 (10-amp breakers, auto reset)
Reverse Polarity Detection and Alarm	Audible alarm and red light	Audible alarm and red light	Flashing red light
Manual Override to Cables	No	No	Yes
Warranty	6 months	West "No Hassle Guarantee"	1 year limited
Price	$89.99	$79.99	$69.74
Source	ww.amazon.com	West Marine	Wal-Mart
Car start (142-hp gas engine) at 40°F. w. dead, cold battery, and cold boosters	Yes, with a bit of difficulty	Yes, more easily	Yes, easily
80-hp diesel start @ 12°F. w. cold engine and cold boosters	Did not attempt	No way, could not turn engine fast enough	Nope, still not fast enough
80-hp diesel start @ 30°F. w. cold engine and cool boosters.	Did not attempt	Did not attempt	Yes, after 4-second grind
Claimed Amp-hour Reserve	20	19	22
1-amp Bulb Run Time	24.5 hrs.	23.5 hrs.	26 hrs.

a balmy 30°, we tried the Wal-Mart booster and got the engine running after a few seconds of cranking. (Admittedly, the auxiliary engines on most sailboats would likely have less than 80 horsepower, and these boosters would seem adequate to start those.)

All the boosters were then completely recharged and used, in turn, to run a 1-amp incandescent cabin light until the glow went out. The results of this drain test are shown in the accompanying table. All three models surpassed their claims.

▷ **The Bottom Line** Of these three units, the one from Xantrex is the most feature laden. For a few extra dollars you get an inverter to make AC power, two small fluorescent work lights, and an air compressor that will pump 250 psi. It's also the only unit with detachable cables. The unit from West Marine has an LED light that's quite bright, but we'd pick the Wal-Mart booster over the other two, particularly if our primary concern was having significant power

available, for engine-starting or anything else. It's got the most juice, and besides, boats set up to cruise will already have what they need of flashlights, inverters, and compressors on board.

Power Inverters

Quiet and emission-free, DC power inverters can provide a high-quality supply of AC power so you can enjoy most modern-day conveniences while away from the dock. The acceptance of DC power inverters by most leading boat manufacturers is finally starting to make its mark on the marine aftermarket industry. With more and more inverters being offered as a factory-installed option on new vessels, the prices for pure sine-wave inverters are starting to come down. That means that competition between DC power inverter manufacturers is heating up and many new inverter features are hitting the market.

Today's power inverters are pushing the envelope of 90-percent power efficiency. Many inverters contain multi-stage battery chargers, and a few top-of-the-line models are now showcasing active LCD remote monitors that have the capability of sharing intelligence with other onboard power devices via the new NMEA 2000 data network. What this means is that the engineers are designing for the future when onboard power management will be viewed as a complete system, instead of the generator, engine alternator, and house batteries being treated as isolated components.

By definition, marine DC inverters are electronic devices that change low-voltage DC energy (usually from a battery bank) into AC line voltage. Inverters are basically divided into two different classes: True Sine Wave (TSW) inverters, and Quasi or Modified Sine Wave (MSW) inverters. Each of these classes of inverters uses a different circuit design to produce AC voltage. Correspondingly, each inverter design has pros and cons regarding the compatibility of electric appliances to the type of waveform produced.

True sine-wave inverters produce an AC output with a smooth, sinusoidal waveform that is identical to shore power, but command an average 20-percent price premium over modified sine-wave inverters. TSW inverters will power any electric appliance within its load range without restrictions.

In the other camp, modified sine-wave inverters produce an AC output that has a stepped waveform. MSV inverters are considerably more affordable than TSW inverters, but should only be used to power basic electric appliances, those not containing sensitive electronics, due to possible appliance incompatibility with the distorted waveform.

A modified sine-wave inverter uses a system of electronic switches and a transformer to invert stored battery energy into AC power. On paper, this circuit design

will yield a higher conversion efficiency than that of the more complex true sine-wave inverter. The drawback to this design of inverting is that the AC waveform that is output will contain harmonics (frequencies) above 60Hz (cycles). These harmonics or modifications to a true sinusoidal wave can significantly affect the operation of certain AC appliances.

Compromises to consider when choosing a MSW inverter over a TSW inverter might include the following: LCD TVs operating on a MSW inverter will exhibit visible noise lines across the screen. Microwave ovens operated by a MSW inverter will most often not produce full output power, which will effect cook times. In another example, the all-too-popular "wall cube" chargers that recharge everything from your portable VHF to your digital camcorder, will most likely have overheating problems when used with a MSW inverter. Drop-in battery chargers for cordless tools that are powered by a MSW inverter usually do not shut off when the battery has been fully charged, resulting in overcharging and overheating the tool's battery.

A true sine-wave inverter uses a transformer and a case full of specialized electronic circuitry to produce an AC waveform that's clean and symmetrical. The TSW inverter's output is completely comparable with that of the power provided by an electric utility company (and most times superior to it). While TSW inverters are significantly more expensive than

All of the power inverters that *PS* tested are solid products. Here, one of our testers studies the waveform generated by the Charles Industries IQ 2600 (seen at rear).

Product/ Model	Wave Form	Voltage In/Out	Continuous Output	Surge Output	Maximum Efficiency	Weight	Battery Charger	Remote Panel	Warranty	Price
Charles/ IQ2600	MSW	12V DC 120V AC	2,600 W	5,500 W 3 secs.	96%	60 lbs.	Yes 3 stage	Optional	2 years	$2,199
Freedom Marine/20	MSW	12V DC 120V AC	2,000 W	4,500 W 5 secs.	93%	45lbs.	Yes 3 stage	Optional	30 months	$1,199
Newmar/ 12-1801C	TSW	12V DC 115V AC	1,800 W	4,000 W 3 secs.	91%	57 lbs.	Yes 3 stage	Optional	2 years	$2,099
Prosine/ 2.0	TSW	12V DC 117V AC	2,000 W	4,500 W 5 secs.	88%	23 lbs.	Yes 3 stage	Standard	2 years	$1,999
Trace/ SW2512MC	TSW	12V DC 120V AC	2,500 W	4,000 W 5 secs.	90%	90 lbs.	Yes 3 stage	Standard	2 years	$2,795
Xantrex/ MS2000	TSW	12V DC 120V AC	2,000 W	5,000 W 5 secs.	90%	67 lbs.	Yes 3 stage	Optional	2 years	$1,599

MSW units, they are the best choice when powering today's advanced entertainment and communication electronics.

The first step in choosing the right inverter for your vessel will be to define your AC appliance needs. Start by deciding which AC loads you plan to operate at the same time, and then add together the wattage rating of each of these appliances, plus a 20-percent safety margin. The sum of the wattages plus the safety factor will equal the size of the inverter that you will need, expressed as an inverter's continuous power output rating. If you plan on running appliances that draw a large surge when they first start up (plasma TVs and refrigeration units are good examples), then you will also have to check the inverter's surge capacity to make sure that the inverter is capable of handling the starting surge loads that may start at the same time. As a rule, MSW inverters usually have a higher surge capacity than TSW inverters.

The second step in selecting an inverter will be choosing which type inverter, TSE or MSW, will best power the appliances that you intend to use. The last step in inverter selection usually involves price and case size versus weight and performance. Of course, there are certain options to consider, namely integral battery chargers, battery temperature sensors, automatic power management, and remote panel displays. In our view, all of these options are desirable as they can help you extend the life of your house battery, and that's money well spent.

PS put six different inverters to the test get a handle on these devices. Included in our evaluation were Charles Industries' IQ2600, Freedom Marine's 20, Newmar's 12-1801-C, Xantrex Technologies' ProSine 2.0, Trace Engineering's SW2512MC, and Xantrex's MS2000. We devised a test to measure inverter efficiency, and we also evaluated the products' features and warranties (see Value Guide). The prices for these units run from $1,200 to $2,795.

There really were no surprises with five out of the six units submitted for our test. These five were UL-listed, and we can say with certainty that each unit we tested met or slightly exceeded their rated specifications. Of particular interest in the waveform oscilloscope test was the Charles Industries IQ2600 modified sine-wave inverter. Charles Industries claims that they have engineered an advanced circuit into their unit, whereby they are able to break down the stepped waveform of a modified sine-wave inverter into 19,000 individual micro-steps per second. The company claims that this waveform enhancement will be compatible with 95 percent of all AC appliances. We were able to confirm the presence of the micro-steps with the oscilloscope, and when we plugged our 15-inch RCA LCD television into the inverter, there were no bars or lines of interference present.

▷ **The Bottom Line** Every unit included in our test should be considered a recommended choice, which should make your decision easier once you've determined the size of the inverter that you require. If a modified sine-wave inverter fits your intended application, then we would give the nod to the Freedom Marine 20. The Freedom has a long established track record and is attractively priced.

The Prosine 2.0 is an excellent choice for a powerful true sine-wave inverter packaged in a weight-saving 23-pound case. But our overall choice for best quality and value in a true sine-wave inverter would be the Xantrex MS2000, hands down. This unit is priced right, has plenty of power, and is just downright pleasing to the eye, both externally and internally. The Xantrex MS2000 with its Xanabus digital communications network is the very first DC inverter capable of exchanging power management information and commands over a NMEA 2000 network. The MS2000's software pack is upgradable via flash memory, and this unit is so advanced that it can even automatically start your generator when it detects that the voltage in the house batteries has dipped too low. The MS2000 is definitely an intelligent unit, and we give it top honors for its forward-thinking design. The downside is that the fan on this unit is particularly noisy, which is something the manufacturer promised to address in future models.

Solar Panels

Charging batteries is a never-ending problem aboard most boats. Long-term cruisers usually have several ways to replace consumed battery capacity—engine-driven alternators, solar panels, wind generators, and occasionally water generators. Even daysailors and weekend cruisers may profit from a backup means of battery charging.

PS has had solar panels on all of its boats for roughly 15 years and we view them favorably, more so now that wire leads are better sealed and 10-year warranties are common. At the least, a solar panel can charge your battery while you're away. And at best, it can reduce engine running time to a more tolerable level.

We've also run tests on a number of panels, through which we discovered several that we liked, including the Solarex MSX-18 with its glass cover, robust aluminum frame, and large junction box; the Siemens SM-50 and SM-46; and the Kyocera KC 200GT. However, our most recent assessment of these products involved a reader survey, and we think the results were quite informative. Before we look at the details of that survey, let's delve into a little background on solar panels.

Essentially, the greater the amount of light that falls on a panel, the more power available from the panel. The output of a panel is comprised of two measurable quantities, voltage and current. While solar panel voltages are fairly insensitive to light levels, the output current will double for each doubling of the light intensity. Since power is the product of voltage times current ($P = V \times I$), and since the voltage is pretty constant, the power output is directly proportional to the current. Monitoring the

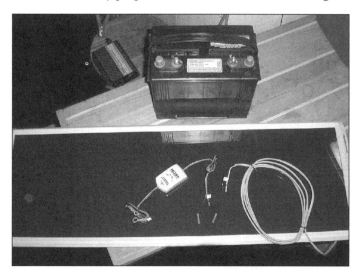

This is as simple as it gets for power generation: a solar panel (in this case an ICP 15-watt, all-weather panel, rated at about 1 amp at peak output, which weighs 9.3 pounds, comes with a five year warranty and 10-foot positive and negative wires), a 7-amp charge controller with two LED indicator lights (the ring terminals go on the battery) and two butt connectors to hook the panel wires to the controller wires. Behind the battery is an inverter, which can be hooked up to provide some AC power.

This solar panel system—two Siemens 55-watt panels—is mounted on a folding bracket made by Hotwire Enterprises of Madeira Beach, Florida. The panels are deployed via a single control line led through a cam cleat. The bracket can be angled toward the sun through 120 degrees and weighs 18 pounds, or 42 pounds with the two panels.

current will be a close analog of the panel's output power.

The angle of the solar panel to the sun will have a fairly large impact on the panel's power output. For the best results, the light should hit the panel perpendicularly to its surface. As the sun's angle moves away from perpendicular, the light intensity falls off as the cosine of the angle. Additionally, below a certain angle, the sunlight will just reflect off the panel's surface without producing electricity.

The silicon material used in the production of the solar panels is also sensitive to variations in temperature. As the panel temperature increases, the power output goes down. As a rule of thumb, the power output goes down 0.5 percent/°C (or about 1 percent/°F). The panels, since they are absorbing solar energy, will be warmer than the surrounding air. Therefore, air temperature will not be a good indicator of panel temperature. Also, some panel ratings are given at 20°C (68°F). Hence, on a warm summer day of 90°F, and ignoring the increase in the panel's temperature due to solar absorption, the output power will be about 20 percent less than the rated power. This is why many solar panel installations allow air to circulate beneath the panels.

Regulators can be very simple and inexpensive, like the 7-amp ICP Charge Controller—it simply lies between the panel and the battery, starts the charging when the battery voltage drops to 13 volts, and stops it at an upper end of 14.2 volts. Or they can be more sophisticated and energy-efficient themselves. Several survey respondents spoke highly of their Flexcharge controllers.

Solar energy systems for marine use are now a fully matured, reliable, and not-too-expensive technology. This is a most welcome evolution—especially at a time when banging, smoking, fossil-fuel-burning engines are regarded with even more distaste than usual. As we said at the top of the section, it's difficult to think of any battery-carrying sailboat that wouldn't benefit from collecting some energy from the sun's rays for use on a rainy day.

There are now dozens of excellent online information sources for sailors interested in adding solar panels to their power arsenal. Start with the manufacturers' websites to get an idea of product range and specs. For person-to-person advice on how to specify a system that will meet your boat size and type, your sailing area, and your amp-hour demands, get in touch with the folks at Jack Rabbit Marine in Stamford, Connecticut, or with Hotwire Enterprises in Madeira Beach, Florida, or with any reputable local alternative energy purveyor who can walk you through the details and help you get set up and energized.

Portable Gas Generators

While mid-sized and even small rack-carried generators don't seem to have a place aboard sailboats—they're too heavy to lug around, too big to stow, too noisy, and too noxious—portable generators make sense in this context. And from our perspective, they're more practical for most boats than the big, high-capacity, permanently mounted gensets (usually diesel fueled) with dedicated wiring and through-hull exhausts, which are used to make electricity when the main engines are idle in the yachts of the idle rich. (Resentful? Us?)

Portable generators, which produce up to, say, 2,000 continuous watts, aren't big enough to do a huge amount of work, but they're so light, clever, and compact that they just seem like something we ought to have. Even the idle rich pause when they see these things in a catalog or hardware store.

A standard portable generator produces AC power directly. It contains a small engine (gasoline-powered, four-stroke in the case of the models evaluated here), which turns at 3,600 RPM to produce, via an alternator, 120 volts of AC power at 60 hertz, thus mimicking a household current—although voltage and hertz frequency do vary somewhat with load. The engine RPM is kept steady by a governor, which feeds the carburetor more fuel as the electrical load comes on (as when you switch on a sander), and decreases fuel when the load decreases. A voltage regulator helps smooth the output and prevents wild spikes. You simply plug your appliance into the socket on the generator, and away you go. There are plenty of other details, of course, but those are the basics.

In recent years, some companies have been trickling-down engineering from their bigger gensets to their smaller models, in the form of variable-speed technology, or VST. With VST, a generator rectifies the AC output from its alternator into a powerful DC current, then feeds that DC current into a sophisticated inverter, which changes it back to AC, and you plug your appliance into the inverter. It sounds like a bass-ackwards way of doing things, but there are two advantages to the technology: It allows engine speed to vary, so that it can run at optimum revs to answer the load. This makes the engine more efficient at producing power, which means that a smaller, lighter engine can do the job. Thus, the second advantage.

A third potential advantage is that the strong DC current can be used to boost starting and house batteries very quickly. The downside is that with all those amps flowing, if you don't monitor things carefully, you'll fry your battery in short order—maybe in a matter of minutes. The safer way is simply to plug a dedicated battery charger into the AC socket, then hook it to the dead 12-volt battery. It's slower, but the charger's regulator will save you an expensive mishap.

Portables are a good option if you can justify them for both surf and turf. They're handy on a boat, yes, but also in the boatyard, as well as for the distance cruiser liable to visit remote locales where AC power

PS's test of portable gasoline generators was limited to models under 75 pounds. All of them had to have a protective plastic case and carrying handle. Clockwise from top right: The Yamaha EF1000iS, the Coleman Powermate 1850, the Briggs and Stratton 900 Watt Elite Series, the Honda Super Quiet EU2000i, and the Honda Super Quiet EU1000i.

is hard to come by. They're useful for charging batteries—not only the boat's 12-volt batteries but, rechargeables used for tools, flashlights, and so on, because you can plug AC chargers into them. They're useful for powering tools directly via AC power, generally one at a time—a drill, a grinder, a sander, etc. They can also be useful for lighting, pumping, and other spot projects as they occur. And their portability means they can be slung into a dinghy and carried ashore, or to a friend's boat.

However, these generators are not always well suited for directly powering sensitive electronic equipment like computers or TVs, because their AC output waveform tends to be quite rough. Household AC appliances are designed to run best on a normal, power-grid-supplied AC current. Small generators have historically been crude in supplying power, and their output waveforms translate into electrical noise like hum in audio equipment and fuzz on screens. Today, the more advanced VST generators are engineered at least to approximate a perfect sine wave in forms that are sometimes called "modified" sine waves.

	Coleman Powermate New Pulse 1850	Honda Super Quiet EU2000i	Honda Super Quiet EU1000i	Briggs & Stratton 900 Watt Elite Series Portable	Yamaha EF1000iS
Price	$459	$1,080	$790	$499	$749
Price Source	samsclub.com	portable-electric-power-generators.com	portable-electric-power-generators.com	briggsandstratton.com	amazon.com
Weight	73 lbs.	46.3 lbs.	28 lbs.	61 lbs.	29 lbs.
Cylinders	one	one, 98.5 cc	one, 50 cc	one, 80 cc	one, 50 cc
Horsepower	3.5	3.5	1.8	2.4	1.67
Wattage (max.)	1850	2000	1000	1000	1000
Wattage (continuous)	1500	1600	900	900	900
Hertz	60	60	60	60	60
Charging Amperage	13 amps	8 amps	8 amps	8.3 amps	8 amps
Dimensions (L,W,H)	20.5" x 14" x 18.5"	20.1" x 11.4" x 16.7"	17.7" x 9.4" x 15"	18" x 13.5" x 15"	17.7" x 9.4" x 15"
Warranty	1 year	2 years	2 years	2 years	2 years
Fuel Capacity	1 gal.	1.1 gals.	.61 gal.	1.2 gals.	.66 gal.
Voltage Stability	Fair	Good	Good	Fair	Excellent
Portability Rating	Fair	Good	Excellent	Fair	Excellent
Noise Level (audio)	78 decibels	62 decibels	61 decibels	74 decibels	67.5 decibels
Tested Run Time	2.75 hrs.	5.25 hrs.	4.25 hrs.	6.75 hrs.	4.5 hrs.
Minutes Per Gallon	165	286	418	337	409
Claimed Run Time	Not stated	4 hrs.	3.8 hrs.	6.4 hrs.	4.3 hrs.
No Load Voltage	137 volts	126.4 volts	124.8 volts	135 volts	122.6 volts
Light (vltg. drop/ stabilized vltg.)	130 volts/ 135 volts	123 volts/ 125 volts	112 volts/ 122.2 volts	124 volts/ 129 volts	61 volts/ 122.6 volts
Light, Fan	126 volts/ 128.5 volts	124.7 volts/ 124.7 volts	117 volts/ 121.7 volts	120 volts/ 126 volts	102 volts/ 122.6 volts
Light, Fan, Drill	108 volts/ 126 volts	111 volts/ 124.5 volts	95 volts/ 120.6 volts	105 volts/ 126 volts	84 volts/ 122.5 volts
Light, Fan, Drill, Sander	80 volts/ 99 volts	86 volts/ 124 volts	Overload tripped	60 volts/ 60 volts	Overload tripped

One important caveat: If you operate one of these things in an enclosed space, or even a space with poor ventilation, you're liable to kill yourself. Common sense would suggest that taking a generator down into the cabin to work on something would be no problem. Don't do it. Carbon monoxide is a killer with a long, proven track record on boats.

PS tested five portable generators—two standard and two VST types. These vary in size and output as well as features (see the Value Guide). The two non-VST units were the 3.5-horsepower Coleman Powermate New Pulse 1850, and the 2.4-horsepower Briggs & Stratton model 1923. Among the VST units, we tested Honda's Super Quiet EU1000i

PS's test methodology included the use of an oscilloscope (far right) to analyze the AC sine waves, a decibel meter (bottom right) to record the noise levels, two Fluke multimeters (adjacent the oscilloscope) to track DC and AC voltage, and numerous appliances and tools to apply varying loads to the chargers. In this photo, the Yamaha EF1000iS (far left) is being load tested, while the Honda SuperQuiet EU 1000i (rear) stands ready.

All generators—except for the Yamaha—started with one pull of the cord. The Yamaha required two or three pulls about 50 percent of the time. Which ran the longest? The Briggs & Stratton, but it also has the largest fuel tank—1.2 gallons. The most economical was the small Honda, followed by the Yamaha. The least economical was the Coleman Powermate (see the chart for minutes per gallon). And the quietest? The Hondas, by far. The Honda EU1000i was 6.5 decibels quieter than the Yamaha and a whopping 17 decibels quieter than the Coleman Powermate.

The VST types have overload protection mechanisms to shut down the generator when too much current is being drawn. This is a good safety feature that will prevent you from damaging the engine. The non-VST types have circuit breakers, but not electronic overload protection.

All of these generators get the job done. The VST types do it differently—and each type has its pluses and minuses. The VSTs are quieter and lighter, but much more expensive. The non-VSTs are cheaper but loud, bulky, and heavier. Despite its slightly noisier operation, we like the Yamaha EF1000iS best among the VST models because of its spotless sine wave, excellent voltage stability, low weight, and economical operation. The Briggs & Stratton is our top non-VST generator. It's lighter, quieter, and more economical to run than the Coleman Powermate. In addition, the Briggs & Stratton carries a two-year warranty, compared to the Powermate's one year.

and Super Quiet EU2000i, and Yamaha's EF1000iS. They range in size from 28 to 73 pounds.

▷ **The Bottom Line** Among the VST units, the Yamaha had the cleanest sine wave, followed by the two Hondas. The Coleman showed the roughest sine wave, as was expected. The Yamaha also had the best voltage stability, meaning its voltage level with loads remained at its normal operating voltage level of 122.6 volts. The runner-up was the Honda Super Quiet EU2000i, which put out 1 to 2 fewer volts with various loads. And even though voltage varied for the two non-VST types, they were still generating plenty of voltage.

CHAPTER 5

Navigation and Electronics

As wonderful as they are, today's electronics can be complex, and they're increasingly inter-dependent. Inexpensive radar, chartplotters, and GPS receivers have led to an alarming decrease in piloting skills. At the same time, they have taken much of the anxiety out of navigation. Though we editors at *PS* aren't Luddites bent on demeaning labor-saving devices, we'd be remiss if we didn't point out that prudent navigators never rely on a single method to determine position. Navigation is the art and science of safely conducting a boat from one point to another. You may be convinced that your most important navigation tools are electronic, but there's always a place for paper charts, a straightedge, and a pencil on board. Thus, in this collection, we've attempted to cover more than the latest handheld GPS unit.

Compasses

HAND-BEARING COMPASSES

Aboard ships and boats, compasses with which to take bearings by hand have always been central to the navigator's tool kit. You can get by without them in a pinch, but it's better not to. Unfortunately for the Phoenicians and other ancient mariners, compasses didn't come along until the 12th century.

Aboard pleasure boats, the bearing compass once was a beautiful, expensive, flat-card, prism-sighting instrument kept safe in a mahogany box. With "D" cells stored in the long handle, it resembled Julius Caesar's scepter. Like sextants, there must be thousands of these instruments stowed away in lockers and closets. Although cumbersome, such instruments were often used when rounding points, to make sure the course being steered didn't take the vessel into dangerous water, or to adjust courses (by steering no more or less than a carefully developed bearing) to avoid shoals and hazards.

When you mention a hand-bearing compass, many sailors envision a "hockey puck," the first of which was called a Morin Opti, and it burst out of France in 1975. A simple, accurate compass, it is still sold as the Vion MiNi 2000. These initially sold like popcorn, until competitors like Plastimo, Plath, Silva, Suunto, and others fragmented the field.

Next to explode on the scene in 1987 was the Auto-helm Personal Compass, a thin, flat fluxgate instrument that was a sensation (30,000 sold the first year) because it was so very different. The Autohelm stored nine bearings and had glow-paint sights and lithium batteries to illuminate the digital display.

Maker	Model	Price	Type	Marks	Reciprocal Bearing	Night Lighting
Davis	#215	$38	Domed	5°	No	LED/Battery
KVH	Datascope	$350	Fluxgate	1°	No	Fiber Optic
Brunton	Sightmaster	$69	Compact, Prism	1°	Yes	Photoluminous
Brunton	15TDCL	$50	Flat Folding	2°	Yes	Luminous Marks
Nexus	70UNE	$93	Dual Purpose	5°	No	Diode/Battery
Nexus	#80	$75	Compact, Prism	1°	Yes	Diode/Battery
Plastimo	Iris 100	$89	Dual Purpose	5°	No	Optional Kit
Plastimo	Iris 50	$60	Compact, Prism	1°	No	Photoluminous
Ritchie	Sportabout	$25	Domed	5°	No	Lightstick
Speedtech/Brunton	Outback	$56	Fluxgate	1°	No	LED/Battery
Suunto	KB-20 Vista	$65	Compact, Prism	1°	Yes	No
Suunto	KB-14/360R	$160	Compact, Prism	.5°	Yes	Optional Kit
Suunto	DP-65	$70	Matchbox	2°	Yes	Luminous Marks
Suunto	M-9	$29	Wrist	5°	No	Luminous Marks
Vion	MiNi 2000	$100	Compact, Prism	1°	No	Luminous Tablet
Weems & Plath	#2004	$100	Compact, Prism	1°	Yes	Photoluminous

Next came the Datascope, originated in the late 1980s by a little company called KVH, on the same island in Rhode Island as *Practical Sailor*'s early offices. In the mid-'90s, another fluxgate compass, the Outback (first called the Wayfinder), elbowed its way into the market. It was made in the Far East and wasn't much to begin with, because it ate batteries like a sumo wrestler eats rice. Now trained to be more conservative, the Outback has been widely marketed by several sales organizations.

To get a handle on the current market, we gathered up all the hand-bearing compasses we could find, including a few that really are for use on land, and ran them through some simple tests. The lot includes an unusual number of compasses made by Suunto and Silva, two Scandinavian companies that, if you count marine and landsman's compasses, make an outsized percentage of the world's compasses.

As was the case among Orwell's animals, all these compasses are equal, but some are more equal than others. In other words, they were acceptably accurate across the board, with the single exception of the

For all-around accuracy and utility, *PS* prefers the hockey-puck style hand-bearing compass, like the Plastimo Iris 50 being used here.

Night Operation	N/S Measured Bearing 000°. Compass Read:	E/W Measured Bearing 306°. Compass Read:	Bringing To Bear	Ease of Reading	Comments
Good	000°	307°	Excellent	Good	Proven, simple, cheap, foolproof, Best Buy.
Excellent	000°	307°	Fair	Excellent	Still king of the hill, but for many, overkill.
Fair	358°	305°	Poor	Poor	On a rolling deck, would be difficult to use.
Poor	000°	299°	Fair	Poor	Venerable, but better for land use.
Excellent	358°	304°	Excellent	Good	A good dual-purpose globe card instrument.
Good	002°	305°	Excellent	Excellent	Top puck. Good scores, all categories.
NA	000°	304°	Excellent	Excellent	This is our choice in a universal-mount.
Good	001°	304°	Excellent	Excellent	Good puck. Could use better lighting.
Good	005°	318°	Fair	Good	Small, tough, but not accurate in our test.
Excellent	001°	307°	Excellent	Excellent	Simpler to calibrate and cheaper than KVH.
NA	002°	304°	Excellent	Fair	It floats, but too hard to read the numbers.
NA	002°	306°	Excellent	Fair	Pricey, but many options in KB series.
Fair	000°	302°	Good	Good	Many-featured, but for hikers, hunters, etc.
Poor	000°	305°	Good	Fair	Surprisingly good, inexpensive, and handy.
Good	359°	305°	Excellent	Excellent	A trusted instrument; excellent track record.
Fair	001°	306°	Excellent	Excellent	Another excellent hockey puck.

Ritchie Sportabout, whose errors seemed excessive. The accuracy of most of these instruments made it even more important to consider how easy each compass was to bring to bear and, then, how easy the bearing was to read—with judgments made in good daytime visibility. We didn't deem significant the fineness of the graduations on the card. Graduations of 5 degrees certainly are not preferable to 1- or 2-degree graduations; that's because the 5-degree marks call for a level of visual and mental extrapolation that may make errors more likely than with 1-degree marks. As a practical matter, utilizing 1-degree fineness is almost impossible (even though it's nice), and that goes for our test procedure, too.

▷ **The Bottom Line** The hockey-puck type remains our favorite. A puck embodies the best combination of accuracy, stowability, ruggedness, and readability in lumpy conditions. All the pucks in this evaluation are good. We'd rank them thus: (1) Nexus Model 80, (2) Vion MiNi 2000, (3) Plastimo Iris 50, (4) Weems & Plath 2004, (5) Suunto KB-20, (6) Suunto KB-14, and (7) Brunton Sightmaster. If you're a dollar-conscious consumer, the Plastimo Iris 50 comes first, with the Suunto KB-20 second and the Nexus Model 80 third. And if you're really concerned with cost and want something absolutely foolproof, your choice should be the Davis, which is both simple and accurate. It's not a thing of beauty, but what a bargain.

If you have a smaller boat and want a combination steering and bearing compass (or wish to mount the bearing compass over

The Vion MiNi 2000, shown here, sells for around $100 and has an excellent track record of service.

the chart table so you can keep an eye on the helmsman), the choice is between the Nexus Model 70UNE and the French-made Plastimo Iris 100. Both are excellent, but because the Plastimo has better damping, it gets the nod.

One oddball is the Suunto M-9, a wrist compass that was surprisingly pleasant to use, very accurate, and under $50. It's basically a top-reading flat card, but has a crafty rim-reading feature and a rotating bezel that makes it grid-steering. It might make a good compass for one-design racing.

And finally, there are the fluxgate instruments—the KVH Datascope. If you truly like and are adept with somewhat complicated electronics, the KVH is a trophy piece. It's amazingly waterproof and very accurate. It can keep nine bearings, which it will average for you. It has a five-power scope, a chronometer, and a range finder. The only downside, we later learned, is that it's difficult to service, which can be disappointing for such an expensive item.

STEERING COMPASSES

In the age of GPS, DGPS, WAAS GPS, and handheld GPS systems, how important is the magnetic steering compass? Just ask anyone who has been disoriented at night, turned around in the fog, or been on the receiving end of an electrical storm. Magnetic compasses are installed at almost every helm for a reason—to provide a reliable heading by which to navigate, independent of all the other onboard systems. When referenced against today's technologies, the heading from a magnetic steering compass is a silent backup that carries a significant amount of clout.

Ship's steering compasses can be broken down into two basic groups, electronic and magnetic. In the electronic group (compasses that require electrical current to operate), you have the fluxgate compass, the standard gyro compass, the digital gyro compass, and the ring laser gyro compass. In the magnetic group, there is the basic flat-top magnetic compass and the spherical or domed magnetic compass. *PS* gathered up a bevy of spherical magnetic compasses to compare them, principally because they're the most common kind found on recreational vessels from 16 to 60 feet. We looked at compasses

for mid-sized vessels from Brunton, Ritchie, C-Plath, Danforth, and Plastimo.

After contacting manufacturers, we learned that there is no industry-standard performance test that is applicable to recreational magnetic steering compasses. Every manufacturer builds to its own self-imposed level of performance. However, it seems reasonable to expect that since magnetism is a phenomenon of nature, each similarly sized compass will respond similarly to the Earth's magnetic field. Our test results point to quite a different conclusion.

We evaluated several important elements about each of these compasses. The first—friction error—we assessed by placing each compass on a smooth, level, non-magnetic countertop and allowed the compass's card to come to a complete rest. Keeping our eyes sharply on the exact heading that the compass's lubber line was oriented to, we slowly and gently rotated the compass clockwise a fraction of a turn and then counterclockwise a fraction of a turn. We were looking to verify that the compass's card remained absolutely stationary during this slewing, indicating that the compass's jewel movement is free of defects. Any movement of the card during this test would yield a failing grade.

Then we assessed sensitivity by lining up each compass's lubber line precisely with a card gradation mark. We introduced a mildly magnetic jeweler's screwdriver into the compass's field from the starboard side of the lubber line, just enough to deflect the compass card clockwise by 1 degree. We then removed the screwdriver from the compass's field and observed if the card returned back to its exact original position relative to the lubber line. We repeated the procedure, but this time deflected the card 1 degree counterclockwise. If the compass card didn't freely come back to rest at the exact lubber line reference point, or if the card appeared to "stick" as the screwdriver entered the compass's field, then the sensitivity of the card's jewel movement was unacceptable and a failing grade was recorded. Stickiness could be caused by either an imperfect fit between the pivot and the jewel bearing, or dirt/impurities in the jewel cup. Either way, it is nearly impossible to accurately adjust a sticky compass, so those should be avoided.

The field of 16 compasses that made up *PS*'s test include: (top row, left to right) Danforth C561, Brunton 150, Ritchie FB500, Plastimo Olympic 135; (second row from top) Danforth C402, C. Plath Merkur SE, Plastimo Offshore 135, Ritchie FN201; (third row from top) Danforth C399-3, Ritchie SS-1002, Ritchie FN203, Ritchie SS2000W; and (bottom row) Ritchie HF742W, Plastimo Offshore 105, Plastimo Offshore 90, and Plastimo Olympic 100.

standards require that "...the line thickness and the heights of figures and letters shall allow a person with normal vision to read the card, in both daylight and artificial light, at a distance of 1 meter." Our test adhered to the 1-meter distance, and we scored the daytime legibility of each compass card (using our tester's late-40-something, 20/20 vision) and the nighttime legibility with each unit's DC illumination turned on.

▷ **The Bottom Line**

In the large-compass field (4¾-inch to 6-inch cards), the Brunton and Plath stacked up well against the Plastimo 135

Next we examined each product's dampening characteristics. Following the U.S. Navy Bureau of Standards 1945 document, we deflected and held the test compass's card at +30 degrees from rest (using a medium-strength flinder bar that we salvaged out of an old flat-top compass). We then removed the flinder bar, which released the compass's card and recorded the number of degrees of overswing past the zero mark. The procedure was repeated again with a card deflection of -30 degrees from rest.

Then we investigated each compass's period in accordance with the Navy Standard as follows: "After release of the card from the ±30 degrees, the time required for 25 degrees (from 25 to 0 degrees) swing shall be not less than 5.5 seconds and not more than 6.8 seconds." We disregarded the Navy's numbers, and created an average of our own given that our compasses differed in size with the ones the Navy standards were meant to test.

And finally, we assessed each compass's readability, both during the day and at night. Navy

Offshore and the Ritchie Globemaster. Danforth's heavy damping and long period on its 5-inch Constellation cost the product a spot among the top four.

The card movement on the Brunton 150 was the smoothest of the 16 compasses tested. When we approached the Brunton with our bar magnet, its card repelled against the magnet in a predictable manner, without jumping or dipping. Brunton also boxes the north indicator on its card with a large red arrow, making it possible to identify north at distances greater than 10 feet. But, because the price ($795) seems such a hefty investment and because local support and customer service remain unresolved issues with Brunton's products, we're inclined to look elsewhere.

Plath and the Globemaster are solid compasses, readily supported worldwide. The Globemaster would be our top choice in this category, but it didn't pass our sensitivity test—it was off by ±2 degrees. We like that the Plath has a glass dome, but it's also quite pricey with a shorter warranty period.

	Apparent Card Size	Card Type	Friction Error	Sensitivity	Dampening (degrees)*	Period (seconds)†	Nighttime Readability	Daytime Readability	Warranty	Retail Price
Brunton 150	5.91"	Flat	Pass	Pass	12	6	Excellent	Excellent	10 Years	$795.00
C. Plath Merkur SE	4.75"	Flat	Pass	Pass	12	9	Excellent	Excellent	3 Years ‡	$671.99
Danforth C561 Constellation	5.00"	Flat	Pass	Pass	5	13	Excellent	Excellent	3 Years	$600.00
Plastimo Offshore 135	5.20"	Front	Pass	Pass	9	9	Fair	Excellent	5 Years	$197.95
Plastimo Olympic 135	5.20"	Flat	Pass	Pass	15	6	Good	Excellent	5 Years	$230.95
Ritchie FB500 Globemaster	5"	Flat	Pass	Fail	9	10	Excellent	Excellent	5 Years	$489.99
Danforth C399-3 Corsair IV	3.75"	Flat	Pass	Fail	10	8	Fair	Good	3 Years	$180.00
Danforth C402 Constellation	4.50"	Flat	Pass	Pass	7	8	Good	Good	3 Years	$345.00
Plastimo Offshore 90	3.25"	Flat	Pass	Pass	15	6	Fair	Good	5 Years	$98.95
Plastimo Offshore 105	3.64"	Front	Pass	Pass	14	7	Fair	Good	5 Years	$130.95
Plastimo Olympic 100	3.50"	Flat	Pass	Pass	15	5	Excellent	Good	5 Years	$184.95
Ritchie FN201 Navigator	4.50"	Flat	Pass	Pass	10	9	Excellent	Excellent	5 Years	$249.99
Ritchie FN203 Navigator	4.50"	Front	Pass	Pass	10	10	Excellent	Poor	5 Years	$259.99
Ritchie HF742W Helmsman	3.75"	Flat	Pass	Pass	13	12	Excellent	Good	5 Years	$139.99
Ritchie SS2000W Supersport	4.50"	Flat	Pass	Pass	10	9	Excellent	Excellent	5 Years	$294.99
Ritchie SS1002 Supersport	3.75"	Flat	Pass	Pass	11	11	Excellent	Good	5 Years	$159.99

*Navy standards stipulate that readings shouldn't exceed 11 degrees   †Navy standards stipulate between 5.8 and 6.6 seconds   ‡Unlimited on dome

So, that leaves us with the Plastimo Offshore 135, which at under $200, is not only the least expensive one, but it racked up commendable scores in all areas except for nighttime viewability. We think it would be prudent to inspect the compass at the store before making a purchase, a caution we'd apply to any compass you intend to buy.

In the 4½-inches-and-under card category, Danforth's Corsair IV could have been a contender, but the compass that we evaluated had a sticky movement. We set the Corsair's lubber line on north, deflected the card 30 degrees, and then released the card. The card then settled at anywhere from 356 degrees to 005 degrees. When the movement didn't stick, the compass turned in the best performance numbers of its peer group, but it took five or six tries (on each test) to get the card to float. We sent that compass back to Danforth for further evaluation.

Our suspicion is that we simply received a unit with individual defects. And, we questioned the Corsair IV's nighttime visibility. You have to adjust the sunshield—it has the bulb on its underside—to illuminate the back half of the card and the lubber line. In our tests, the back remained dark when the shield was fully open.

Based on these tests, the better choices in the smaller compass category are Danforth's Constellation, Ritchie's flat-view Navigator, and Ritchie's flatview Supersport. Each of these compasses turned in very similar test scores (save for the Constellation's viewability ratings). Both the compasses from Ritchie had excellent viewability ratings, and both have a longer warranty than the Danforth. Though we prefer the Supersport's blue card, the price favors Ritchie's Navigator, which is our choice in this category.

Barometers

It takes very little skill or technology to know that you're in the midst of a storm. It takes considerably more to know that a storm is coming. That information, however, can be a lifesaver if you're on the water.

Prior to the early 17th century, a mariner's only tools for predicting weather were his senses and a collection of rules on the order of, "Red sky at morning, sailors take warning." The reliability of these methods left a great deal to be desired.

Torricelli's invention of the mercury barometer changed all this. Now it was possible to predict an impending storm with some accuracy many hours before it struck. And the barometer, to this day, remains a fundamental tool for weather prediction.

The barometer, in most of its forms, is a simple gadget. Early ones were all made of glass tubes with one end sealed and evacuated and the other immersed in a pool of liquid—usually mercury, because it's dense enough to permit the tube to be short. Liquid from the pool, which is open to the atmosphere, is forced up into the tube by the ambient atmospheric pressure until the downward pressure exerted by the liquid exactly equals the atmospheric pressure forcing it up into the tube. A scale—just an ordinary ruler attached to the side of the tube—made it easy to read how far the liquid level had dropped (or risen).

This type of liquid barometer is still the most accurate one available. If the level in the glass rose, atmospheric, or barometric, pressure was increasing; if it fell, pressure was decreasing. Sailors around the world learned very quickly that when the "glass fell," foul weather was on its way.

Over the next 350 years, only a few changes were made to this very basic instrument. To help overcome the fragility of the glass-tube barometer, variations on the theme were developed that used thin curved sealed tubes or bellows. When the pressure dropped, the bellows expanded or the tube straightened. The movement of these aneroid (the word means no liquid) devices was generally transmitted to an indicating needle through a geared mechanical linkage that converted the sealed container's small movement to a larger, easier-to-read needle. This type of barometer is still the most popular one today.

A further refinement was the barograph. But in the past few decades, electronic barometers have appeared on the scene. The pressure-sensing element of these devices works on the same principle as the aneroid barometer's bellows, but consists of a thin membrane formed onto a silicon chip over an etched, sealed recess in the chip. Strain gauges on the membrane sense any movement of the membrane, and display it as electrical signals. Microprocessors take the electrical signals and convert them to a readable form, usually on an LCD display. Because microprocessors have memories and computational capabilities, these electronic barometers also can "remember" former readings and keep track of pressure changes, as well as use other on-the-chip sensors to monitor such items as date, time, temperature, and relative humidity, in addition to air pressure.

We were particularly curious to see how the newer electronic barometers stacked up against the classic aneroid barometers and barographs, so we concentrated our product search on electronic models. We found four: two older versions—the Perception II and the Weather Monitor II—from Davis, which has been making weather instrumentation for quite some time now, and a couple of newcomers—the Altitude Electric Barometer and the Speedtech WeatherMate Electronic Barometer. We compared them to two representative instruments from Weems & Plath, a well-known manufacturer and distributor of quality marine instruments, an Atlantis aneroid barometer model #200700, and a Dampened DeLuxe Quartz aneroid barograph.

Essentially, we tested all the devices by lining them up side-by-side and using them. We adjusted each to a sea level zero setting, and noted their readings, comparing them to NOAA radio reports from a local station.

We ran them for a period of several weeks, noting any differences in readings and/or other aspects of performance. We checked to see how useful each unit was for predicting weather and noted how easy each was to use.

Finally, since we knew that temperature sensitivity is a possible problem with electronic devices, we tested all the units in a large fish tank, using ice, then a heater, to create temperature extremes.

We found that all the units are inherently accurate to within 0.02 inch of mercury—or precise enough. All could be adjusted for changes in altitude, although there were differences in the convenience of making the adjustment. This isn't an adjustment that you'll make frequently, unless you trailer your boat between the seashore and mountain lakes. Further, it's not critical in predicting weather—actual pressure readings are important but not as important as accurately tracking the pressure changes.

All the units tested can give some indication of trends in barometric pressure changes; there are major differences in how conveniently they do this, and how much operator attention is required.

All operated consistently over a wide temperature range.

A barometer, particularly one such as the Speedtech or Altitude that allows you to monitor pressure trends at a glance, makes an excellent backup to a dedicated weather radio.

If you're a weather hobbyist, Davis's Weather Monitor II is much more versatile than the Perception II for not much more money. If you don't opt for a Weatherlink and computer, you'll find that the Weather Monitor isn't as handy for tracking barometer changes as the less expensive Speedtech and Altitude instruments.

If you want to do it the traditional way, a nicely polished brass aneroid barometer will certainly do

the job. And while we are certainly in favor of tradition, we'd probably supplement one with either the plain-Jane Altitude or Speedtech for planning our next day's cruise.

Handheld GPS Units

Today, inexpensive handheld GPS receivers are marketed to a wide range of users, not just sailors and power boaters. Most carry generic software of little specific value to mariners. Even marine designations are more marketing than content, it seems. Still, they all do one thing very well and that is track GPS satellites.

For the mariner, they can serve as a viable backup to a permanently installed onboard navigation system, with a sextant safely on board, but tucked away. Accurate position, speed, and course information supplied by a handheld GPS used in conjunction with paper charts should be all any sailor needs to complete a long, planned voyage. When so equipped, these devices also do well at supplying accurate lunar, solar, and tidal data in an easy-to-access, user-friendly format—information that's critical for making landfall in unfamiliar ports.

What they don't do well is display easy-to-read map data. Past testing has shown the charts on handheld units to be lacking in accurate marine details. Two factors contribute to this problem. First, the screen size on a handheld unit is simply not large enough to display the huge volume of data needed to make a chart display useful and accurate. Second, memory and processor capability is limited in a small handheld device, and unfortunately a good map display requires lots of both. We don't see either of these problems going away anytime soon in low to moderately priced handheld GPS units.

For this evaluation, we cast our net around a broad group of handheld GPS units, each specifically chosen because it does not use cartography on a card. Our goal was to keep the price point at the lower end of the market, though some units have additional features that push their prices higher. Two units come in under $100 (these prices are from 2004)—the Garmin eTrex and the GPS 100 from Cobra. Our mid-range units, between $100 and $200, include the Garmin Fortrex 201, Garmin

HANDHELD HOLDERS

Ever try banging upwind in a steep chop while reading a GPS position on a handheld unit? If you have, you know that sensitive electronics like this can hit the deck with alarming regularity. These situations obviate the need of some place to put handheld units where they'll be both safe and immediately accessible, but few sailboats offer that. Enter the handheld holder.

PS visited chandleries and scanned the Web to find 14 different such holders from 10 manufacturers. That's just a sampling of what's available, but it's a good enough collection to give us some clear ideas about what works and what doesn't.

These things come in varying designs, materials, sizes, and holding mechanisms. Some are very well made. Some are cheap and should never be taken aboard a boat. We limited our test to holders that could be mounted with

The Ram dual-ball mount holds two electronic devices at once. On the left is a Ram GPS cradle designed specifically for a Garmin 48. The unit's other arm is holding a small FRS radio. Notice the radio's raised position, necessary so the holder's side paddles don't activate the radio's buttons. Despite the compromised grip, the Ram holder still easily passed *PS*'s shake tests.

screws because we wouldn't trust a suction cup or adhesive to hold an expensive piece of electronics.

After screwing them into our test board and shaking, pounding, vibrating, and generally mistreating all 14, we determined that the Ram Mounting Systems are top-notch, particularly the Ram B-138. We later learned that every Ram product carries a lifetime warranty.

If you only need a holder for your cell phone, we'd recommend the Clipmount Cell Phone Holder from Good-to-Go. The phone does require a belt clip or swivel clip on its back—which explains the name. But it's simple and strong, and it works. For anything else, we recommend a holder from Ram. National Products, Inc., which makes these devices, offers several models. Yes, these units are the most expensive products we tested, but they're worth it.

Geko 301, Garmin GPS 76, Garmin GPS 60, and the Magellan eXplorist 200. In the upper echelon, at $250 is the Magellan SporTrak Pro Marine, and the highest-priced unit in the test is the Brunton Multi-Navigator at $299. Position-locating accuracy is a given with current GPS technology. Therefore, we didn't specifically test this, but instead compared all the systems against each other to determine that each

was precise in this regard. All the units consistently self-located within a 10-foot circle of the group.

We did, however evaluate the quality of each unit's display, how pertinent the information is that each unit offers, and how easy each is to operate. All of these products claimed to be waterproof, so to verify this we fully submersed each unit in a tank of fresh water for five minutes. Every handheld

The specimens that were included in *PS* test of handheld GPS units include, top row (l. to r.): Magellan eXplorist 200, Garmin's GPS 76, the Brunton Multi-Navigator, and the Cobra GPS 100; bottom row (l. to r.): Garmin's eTrex, Garmin's Geko 301, Garmin's Fortrex 201, Magellan's SporTrak Pro Marine, and a prototype of Garmin's new GPS 60. Garmin's GPS 76, which has been in production for several years, came out on top.

worked properly after the water immersion; we even inspected the battery compartments and discovered no water in any unit. (One, however, failed to operate the day after the immersion test.) We also examined prices and warranties.

▷ **The Bottom Line** The map pages found in these handheld units are not very useful to the mariner, and we shy away from them when navigating with a handheld. The information supplied on even the easy-to-read displays like the Garmin GPS 76 is still too small and too difficult to use while under way. We recommend sticking with navigation pages that supply the necessary data in crisp large text.

Another area of concern is the continual reduction in the size of these units. At some point, especially for mariners, who have no real need for the smallest screens available or push-buttons sized for children's digits, it all becomes rather ridiculous. The rule of diminishing returns definitely applies here. Our preference is for units that fit and feel solid in hand, have push-buttons big enough for adult fingers, and screens we can read without a magnifying glass.

With those thoughts in mind and after a critical review of each unit's features, we have settled on the Garmin GPS 76 as our top pick. It has five main

pages which arrange information in a sensible, easy-to-use fashion. This unit also boasts the highest-resolution screen in our test and one of the biggest at 2.9 inches (diagonal). It has finely defined letters and numbers with clean edges even when displaying small type or curved lines, and we found the viewability very good under all conditions. Because all named push-buttons are supplied with backlighting, they're easy to read in the dark. (Garmin also makes a GPS 60. It, too, has great screen resolution and user-friendly operation, but the push-buttons are too small for our taste.) A second choice, if you can overlook the small push-buttons, would be the Magellan SporTrak Pro. Among the less expensive units here, we'd opt for the Cobra GPS 100, because its extra navigation page bests the other units priced under $100.

Big-Screen Chartplotters

We've been saying now for several years that bigger is better in chartplotter display screens. The ocean (as well as other bodies of water) is rarely stable, and waves can be jarring, thus making reading small screen graphics, letters, and numbers difficult or impossible. Ultimately, the difference in viewability

Model	Furuno GP1900C	Garmin GPSMAP 3010C	Raymarine C120	Simrad CP44
Price (Configured as Chartplotter)	$2,579	$2,857	$2,575	$3,885
Unit Dimensions (inches) W x H x D	14.2 x 9.3 x 7.1	13.1 x 8.8 x 3.0	14.0 x 10.4 x 4.5	14.6 x 8.7 x 3.0
Screen Dimensions (inches) Dia.	10.4	10.4	12.1	10.4
Screen Resolution (H x V)	640 x 480	640 x 480	800 x 600	640 x 480
Screen Orientation	Landscape	Landscape	Landscape	Landscape
Max No. of Split Screens	3	4	4	4
No. of Pushbutton Controls	27	26	16	30
No. of Soft Keys	5	5	5	0
Rotary Enter Knob	Yes	No	Yes	No
Alphanumeric Key Pad	Yes	Yes	No	Yes
Cursor Input Device	Trackball	Cursor Pad	Cursor Pad	Cursor Pad
No. of Screen Brightness Levels	8	26	64	15
Electronic Interface	Network/NMEA	Network/NMEA	Network/NMEA	NMEA
Radar Optional	Yes	Yes	Yes	Yes
Sounder Optional	Yes	Yes	Yes	Yes
Weather Data Optional	Yes	Yes	No	No
Video Optional	Yes	Yes	Yes	Yes
Waterproof	Yes	Yes	Yes	Yes
Warranty Period Years - Parts/Labor	2/1	1/1	2/2	2/1
Day View	Excellent	Excellent	Excellent	Excellent
Night View	Excellent	Good	Good	Excellent
Cartography	Furuno, C-Map, Navionics	Garmin Blue Chart	Navionics	C-Map
Waypoint Storage Capacity	999	4000	1000	10000
Route Storage Capacity	200	50	100	1000
No. of Waypoint Symbols	16	68	36	18
Characters in Waypoint Name	6	10	16	25
Characters in Waypoint Comment	13	20	32	0
Plotter User Interface	Good	Good	Good	Good

between 5-inch and 10- or 12-inch displays is stark. That's why we rounded up three chartplotters with 10-inch screens (Garmin's 3010C, Furuno's GP-1900C, and Simrad's CP44, which has since been replaced with the CX44; they have identical screens and similar software), and one with a 12-inch screen (Raymarine's C120) for an evaluation. These units range in price from around $2,600 to $3,900.

With these units, viewability—both during the day and at night—is a chief concern, as is the functionality of their user interface. We evaluated each chartplotter for user interface by performing various operations with each display unit and gave our highest ratings to the units with intuitive software, alphanumeric keypads, and numerous dedicated function keys.

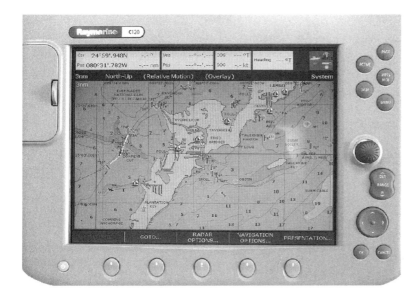

The Raymarine C120 seems to have it all: a large display area (12.1-inch diameter screen), good viewability day and night, and easy-to-use functions. Its only drawback is the lack of an alphanumeric keypad, but that's an option.

▷ **The Bottom Line** All four units had excellent for daytime viewability, but there's still a pecking order. We'd rank the Furuno No. 1 in this regard; it's definitely brighter than all the others. The Simrad would rank No. 2; it's not quite as bright as the Furuno, but like the Furuno, it suffers no ill effects from viewing with polarized sunglasses. The Garmin and Raymarine units, which we'd rank a bit behind the Simrad in screen brightness, are very close in overall daylight brightness levels. Both darken a bit when viewed through polarized sunglasses.

Bigger differences appear in night view ratings. Here we'd rank the Simrad No. 1, followed by the Furuno. The Garmin and Raymarine units are somewhat less sophisticated in night lighting control.

All four units garnered good ratings in user interface, but again there are differences. The Raymarine is No. 1, even without an alphanumeric keypad as standard equipment. In our estimation, the Raymarine software in the C120 is the most intuitive of any unit in this test group. It makes good use of its five soft keys and numerous dedicated push-buttons. We cranked up this machine and started using it right away without any reference to the operating manual. Cartographic data from the Navionics card is well presented. We especially like the increased letter and number size used for the display of water depths on the map display. Of the others, the Garmin would rank No. 2, the Furuno No. 3, and the Simrad last. Though the Simrad has a superb screen and decent software, we'd eliminate it first. It costs over $1,000 more than any of the other three and has software that's harder to use.

The Furuno, Garmin, and Raymarine products are priced competitively, and in our opinion, you can't go wrong with any of the three. However, we must whittle, so every minor difference and operational nuance must be considered. Though the Garmin viewability ratings are equal to the Raymarine, we'd eliminate it next. It's priced a bit higher than the other two, has a shorter warranty period, and garnered a viewability rating below the Furuno's.

The Raymarine C120 has a larger screen area for the same price and software that is a step ahead of the Furuno. So the C120 is our top pick. But the runner-up, Furuno, has a lot going for it, including a proven track record of reliability with several years out in the field compared to the C120's mere months (at the time of our test). Even though the C120 screen is larger, the Furuno 10-inch NavNet display remains the brightest during daylight and a slightly better performer at night. Still, the extra screen area and the intuitive nature of the Raymarine software ultimately won us over.

Marine Radar Units

The best way to avoid running into an object or avoid being hit by another vessel is to have a radar reflector and a marine radar system on board. Like GPS units, marine radar systems for sailboats have improved in quality, power consumption, and price in recent years.

Radar is an acronym for "RAdio Detection And Ranging." A radar system operates in the microwave part of the radio-frequency spectrum used to detect the position and/or movement of objects. It works in a similar fashion to your voice echoing in a large open room. Essentially your voice is the transmitter. When the energy from your vocal cords hits an object, some of it is reflected back. That reflected energy is perceived by your ears. The longer the sound takes to return, the farther away the object is from you. Also, the louder the return echo, the bigger the object is that the energy hit.

When you are choosing a radar system for your boat, there are a couple of specifics you should keep in mind. While transmitting range and power are important, they are not the only factors that should influence your decision. The range of a radar system depends on several variables, and the height of the scanner above the waterline is chief among them. Radar range is directly related to height—the higher up the radar is, the farther it will see. Mounting your scanner well up in the rig can be a great asset. Keep in mind, however, that by doing so you're creating a greater circle around the vessel that the cone-shaped energy beam issued from the scanner will not see. Thus any targets in this circle will not return echoes. Of course these are close-in targets, and they're the ones that are most important for you to be aware of. Who cares if you can see a passenger ferry 48 miles away? You want to see that powerboat screaming toward you in the fog on your 2-miles-or-less scale.

Another critical consideration regards the installation of the scanner. It should be put it in a location where the beam that it issues will not pass through GPS sensors, Loran or weather fax couplers, and most importantly, people. Keep the antenna at a minimum of 2 feet above and least 5 feet from where you, your crew, and your passengers spend the majority of your time on board.

When you are looking at the power output of radar systems, in most cases a 2-kilowatt radar system can give excellent target imaging for inshore applications on 20- to 50-foot vessels. Higher power ratings like 4- and 6-kilowatt systems may have a longer "range" than a 2-kilowatt system; however, the real performance gain is seen when the weather conditions are bad.

Rain and snow have a tendency to reflect and absorb radar energy. When the energy is reflected, we are able to see the size and the pattern of the storm. Because rain and snow absorb radar energy, they can block your view of targets and landmasses. This is where additional power becomes an advantage. The increased energy punches through the weather and allows you to see the targets. Fishing

In *PS*'s most recent evaluation of radar units, our testers looked at the systems arrayed here—all 4-kilowatt systems that sell between $3,878 and $5,407. They are, clockwise from bottom left: Raymarine's E120, Northstar's 6000i, JRC's JMA-5104, Simrad's RA41C, Garmin's 3010C, and Furuno's 1834C NavNet VX2. Among these displays (and their radome counterparts), the testers deemed Furuno and Raymarine's products the best options.

Model	$ ★ Furuno 1834 Navnet VX2	Garmin 3010C W/GMR-40	JRC JMA-5104	Northstar 6000I RAD4K	↗ Raymarine E120 M92652-S	Simrad RA41C
Display Size/Type	10.4" Color TFT	10.4" Color TFT	10.4" Color TFT	10.4" Color TFT	12" Color TFT	10" Color TFT
Range	⅛–36 nm	⅛–36 nm	⅛–48 nm	⅛–36 nm	⅛–48 nm	⅛–36 nm
Radome Weight	17.6 lbs.	27.5 lbs.	23 lbs.	25.5 lbs.	19 lbs.	25.5 lbs.
Beam Width Horizontal/ Vertical (Degrees)	3.9/20	3.6/25	4.0/25	3.9/25	3.9/25	3.9/25
System Power Consumption Standby/TX	2.9A/5.1A	2.0A/3.2A	3.9A/5.1A	3.9A/4.9A	2.7A/4.8A	2.0A/3.1A
Antenna Cable Length (Meters)	15 m	15 m	20 m	10 m	15 m	10 m
Close Range Target Resolution	Excellent	Excellent	Excellent	Fair	Excellent	Excellent
Long Range Target Detection	Excellent	Good	Good	Good	Excellent	Good
Display Brightness/ Sunlight	Excellent	Excellent	Fair	Excellent	Excellent	Excellent
Display Brightness/ Night	Excellent	Good	Excellent	Excellent	Excellent	Excellent
Human Interface/ Menu Operation	Excellent	Good	Excellent	Fair	Excellent	Good
Product Quality	Excellent	Good	Good	Good	Excellent	Excellent
Street Price	$3,878	$4,298	$5,407	$5,348	$5,048	$4,729
Source	boatfix.com	Boater's World	boatfix.com	consumersmarine. com	defendermarine. com	consumersmarine. com
Warranty (Parts/Labor)	2/2 years	1/1 year	2/2 years	2/2 years	2/2 years	2/2 years

$ Budget Buy   ↗ Recommended   ★ Best Choice

vessels, for example, like to use higher-power radars to see indicators like birds working an area of bait.

The size of the radar antenna is another important variable to look at when choosing your radar system. The antenna transmits the energy at a "wide" vertical angle to cover the entire target range area with radio waves. The antenna also transmits at a "narrow" horizontal angle. This allows the system to see targets that are close together, so that the targets are perceived as individual items as opposed to one large mass. This discrimination of targets is called resolution. A vertical beam angle of about 25 degrees is common to most systems. The length of the antenna determines the horizontal beam width. The longer the antenna,

the more narrow the beam's horizontal width, creating greater target discrimination or resolution. Short-length antennas (18 and 24 inches) typically housed in domes provide approximately 6 to 3 degrees of horizontal angle. Open-array antennas, typically 2 to 12 feet, produce a horizontal beam from 3 to 1.9 degrees.

PS has evaluated radar units on a number of occasions. Our two most recent tests involved entry-level radar units—2-kilowatt systems that list for under $3,000—and 4-kilowatt systems that sell between $3,878 and $5,407. First, we'll look at the less expensive models.

We chose to evaluate radar units that a majority of sailors could afford and install in about a weekend.

The test specimens included both monochrome and color displays. Among the monochrome systems we selected are the Furuno 1623, the Furuno 1712, the JRC RADAR1000 MKII, the JRC RADAR 1500 MKII, and the Raymarine SL72 Plus. We tested two color systems: the JRC RADAR 1800CP, and the Simrad RA30.

We tested these systems under real-world conditions, and evaluated them for product construction, installation and setup adjustments, menu navigation, functional control, and target resolution. All of the systems evaluated have NMEA 0183 inputs. This is a valuable feature to have in your radar because you can interface the unit with your position finder and view your own vessel's position on the radar screen. And this interface will give you range and bearing to a waypoint, if you have one selected. If you have NMEA-capable instruments on board, you can also display that information on your radar display.

We'll note right here that the color displays offer distinct advantages. These offer much greater detail and target discrimination than is possible with 8, 12, or 16 shades of gray. We also found the viewing angles of the color LCD displays much improved.

Because it had the best combination of menu navigation and system control, and superior target resolution—even though it has a monochrome display—our overall top choice is the Furuno 1712. Subsequent to our testing, Furuno discontinued its 1712 and replaced it with a model that has identical specifications. Except for a larger radome, the differences between the new Furuno 1715 and the 1712 are cosmetic. These changes, say company representatives, were made so the new system better fits the design of other products that the company makes for the helm station.

We should note that after purchasing and installing a new radar system, it's vital that you spend some time learning how to use it properly. The operation manual that accompanies the unit is a valuable resource, as are the many aftermarket instructional videos available. After that, practice using the radar unit in good conditions, especially when transiting in and out of harbors. This will help you learn to recognize landmasses and key targets that can be important landmarks later on when you find yourself out there in the soup.

The 4-kilowatt models we tested included Furuno's 1834C NavNet VX2, Garmin's 3010C with GMR-

40 Radome, JRC's JMA-5104, Brunswick's 10.4-inch Northstar 6000i, Raymarine's E120, and Simrad's RA41C. Among these, the best performer also turned out to be our Best Buy: Furuno's 1834C NavNet VX2. Not only is it priced right at $3,878, it's a well-built, professional-grade radar system. When we opened up the 1834's radome, we were greeted with the cleanest and most organized design of our test group. In the performance arena, Furuno's 1834C scored highest in both close-in and distant-target detection when operated in the manual mode. The initial setup of the 1834C is slightly more involved compared to its market rivals. The Furuno required that we access an installation menu and select the radar scanner type, radar antenna height, and perform a radar optimization test. This sounds involved, but the NavNet VX2 is fitted with an on-screen installation wizard menu that guides you through each step.

Regarding the other units, the Raymarine E120 also performed excellently. If you don't mind paying $1,000 extra for Navionics platform and other bonus features, it's a good choice. We also like the rotary controls on JRC's JMA-5104, and found this unit's performance and intuitive operation to be quite good. For helm mounting, look for an alternative sunlight-viewable LCD monitor. Other than that, Simrad's RA41C is a good performer that allows the operator to adjust the picture with relative ease. The multi-view feature, in our opinion, still needs refinement. The good news is that Simrad seems on the verge of launching a radome that should improve this feature.

Marine Radios

FIXED-MOUNT VHF RADIOS

VHF marine radios remain the most common and useful communication devices found aboard recreational boats. They have no monthly user fees, and can be used for routine voice traffic as well as emergency calls. Plus, with the advent of Digital Selective Calling (DSC) several years ago, limited digital information can now be sent via VHF. Other methods of communicating by voice, via cellular phone, for example, have become popular and do have a place on a boat—just not as the primary communication tool. A cellular phone offers one-on-one communication

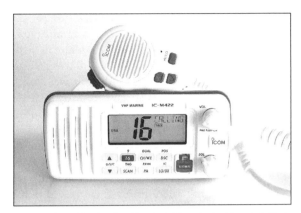

Among the mid-priced radios that *PS* evaluated (models that sell from $160 to $299), we crowned the Icom M422 king for its stellar transmitter, receiver, and audio performance. Over the years, Icom has proven to be the Steady Eddie in marine radios. What these products may lack in pizzazz, they more than make up for in utility.

through a connection that's often poor, particularly offshore, while a "Mayday" on Channel 16 goes out to everyone within line of sight. Smart sailors always have a working VHF aboard their vessel.

The electronic circuits in today's marine VHF radio transmitters and receivers have remained virtually the same for years. But the implementation of DSC—a required function in any VHF radio designed since 1999—has altered the landscape recently in the VHF marketplace. Today, even the least expensive VHF radios can have an extensive list of DSC capabilities.

PS has kept a close eye on VHF radios over the years, both the fixed-mount and the handheld ones.

This is another area where rapid evolution requires that kind of vigilance. In less than a year's time between 2005 and '06, we published four feature articles that collectively reviewed and evaluated 25 radios. We segmented those products into the following categories: radios that sell for less than $160, those that sell for $160 to $299, and those that sell for more. As one might expect, basic communication is available at all product levels, but the more expensive units offer ever more features, like remote-mic capability, hailer function, and DSC (digital selective calling), all in a compact design.

PS tests VHF radios in a comprehensive fashion. We characteristically use a Ramsey COM3010 communications monitor to measure transmitter power output, frequency accuracy and stability, and receiver sensitivity. We conduct our tests on Channel 16 at room temperature (75°F), but we also measure performance at temperature extremes near the max ranges of each radio. To reach the cold extreme, each radio is placed in a freezer (at 15°F) for hours prior to testing. We used a food smoker as an environmental chamber to get the radios to high-temperature extremes—two hours at 122°F. And we evaluate each unit's user interface as well as its display features.

▷ **The Bottom Line** Among the more economically priced VHF radios (those under $160), we evaluated six: Icom's M302, Raymarine's Ray48, Standard Horizon's Quest GX1255S, Uniden's Solara and Oceanus, and West Marine's 500 VHF, which is also built by Uniden. Within this group, the Icom M302 distinguishes itself with excellent transmitter, receiver, and audio performance. Those facts, coupled with the unit's full DSC capabilities, and a significant list of features, make it our top pick in this range. Our second choice is the Standard Horizon Quest.

In the mid-priced category, we examined 11 models: Icom's M402, M402S, and M422, Navman's

Among the high-end radios, Standard Horizon's Quantum GX2360S and Uniden's 625c (not shown) are both priced close to the minimum ($299), and both offer excellent overall performance and a full list of features, including a hailer with automatic fog signals and a horn function.

VHF7100 and VHF7200, Raymarine's Ray 54, Standard Horizon's Quest+ GX1256S, Phantom PS1000, and Matrix GS1280S, Uniden's UM525, and West Marine's VHF600, which is made by Uniden. We have always favored radios with exceptional overall performance, and thus our testers favored the Icom M422 for its stellar transmitter, receiver, and audio performance. Over the years, Icom has proven to be the Steady Eddie in marine radios. What these products lack in pizzazz, they more than make up for in utility.

We'll acknowledge that things in this segment of the market are shifting. The features provided in some of the mid-priced radios tested here are amazing. For instance, the Navman 7200 offers a barometer and a thermometer. But it's Uniden that seems to be leading the pack in innovation. This company has managed to couple a decent basic radio with an outstanding number of added features in the UM525. For around $200, you can get a VHF radio with a screen displaying large, easy-to-read letters and numbers, a hailer with automatic fog signals, a well-conceived and user-friendly menu, and a rotary channel selector. The UM525 is easily our Best Buy.

Only two radios disappointed our testers, and each in their audio quality. The Ray 54 and the West Marine VHF600 both achieved the lowest scores in audio output, though otherwise each offers good features at a reasonable price.

Moving on to the highest-priced radios, we examined eight models: one from Furuno (FM3000, which is built by Icom), one from Uniden (UM625c), and two each from Icom (M502 and M602), Raymarine (215 and 240), and Standard Horizon (Quantum GX2360S and Quantum GX3500S). These are all feature-rich products, most of which boast sophisticated DSC features, built-in hailers with automatic foghorn capabilities, alphanumeric keypads to quickly select functions or enter data, and superior transceiver performance.

Two important elements of marine radio performance that are often overlooked are the audio amplifier and speaker. Sailboats can produce a lot of noise, and if you can't hear the output, it doesn't really matter how well the receiver works. To rate the audio system of each radio, we measured the sound pressure at maximum volume while generating a

(above, left) Priced at $250, the compact HX600S from Standard Horizon isn't the most economical option, but it offers excellent performance coupled with features like multi-band technology and DSC capability. (above, right) Listing at $200, the Icom IC-M72 is more economical and *PS* testers deemed it a more ergonomic radio than the HX600S. It combines light weight (9.9 ounces) and a powerful battery (2000 MAH), and boasts one of the most powerful outputs among handheld VHF radios at 6 watts.

1-KHz tone with our COM3010 and inputting that into the radio. Measurements were taken at a distance of 1 meter using a Radio Shack decibel meter. Our testers also rated each audio system with a voice input by monitoring a weather channel and rating the quality of sound reproduction.

It's hard to overlook Icom's M602, even though it's one of the most expensive units in this group ($513). It's packed with features, including a hailer capable of producing automatic fog signals when needed and an alphanumeric keypad to quickly select your desired function or type in MMSI numbers and names. But most importantly, it has the best transceiver performance of this elite group. When coupled to a quality antenna and hailer horn, this unit will do everything but wash your boat. It also carries a three-year warranty, as do most of these high-end products.

Two units in this group offer particularly good value for the price: Standard Horizon's Quantum GX2360S and Uniden's 625c. Both are priced close to our minimum price ($299), and both offer excellent overall performance and a full list of features, including a hailer with automatic fog signals and a horn function. But Uniden's product is less expensive and comes with a color display, which earns this radio Best Buy honors.

HANDHELD VHF RADIOS

Handheld VHF radios are another of those areas in the marine electronics market that exhibit continuous change and improvement. Most of the models that appear in this section are still marketed, but some new ones have been introduced since our most recent test took place.

Most models are now waterproof or at least represented as such. The size of these radios continues to decrease, and battery capacity has increased markedly. Compared to radios tested several years ago, the current models perform much more like high-end commercial products and not low-priced consumer items. However, *PS* discovered two manufacturers who represented radios as "waterproof" or "submersible" when, according to our tests, they weren't.

We made the rounds through the various boating catalogs and marine websites and identified 13 models from six manufacturers: Standard Horizon, Uniden, Simrad, Raymarine, Icom, and Shakespeare. We bench-tested each radio against its published specifications using an IFR COM-120B communications service monitor and translated our findings into numerical ratings. We also listed the features that we consider important for this product category. In the case of VHF handhelds, these include:

12-VOLT DC CHARGER—Some manufacturers include a DC charger with their radios; others require you to purchase one. Given that DC power is the standard on board, we consider the inclusion or availability of a 12-volt charger important.

AA BATTERY PACK—AA battery packs provide the availability of instant power. Alkaline batteries can be stored for long periods and provide the maximum operational capacity.

The eight VHFs that *PS* tested are, from left to right: Standard Horizon's HX471S, Icom's IC-M88 and IC-M72, West Marine's VHF 250, Standard Horizon's HX500S, and HX 370S, and Raymarine's Ray 101F.

RAPID CHARGER—All types of rechargeable batteries normally take longer to charge than to discharge. A rapid charger will recharge a handheld in 1 to 3 hours versus up to 16 hours for a regular charger.

BATTERY TYPE—Until recently, NiCad (nickel-cadmium) batteries were the standard in rechargeables. Now NiMH (nickel–metal hydride) batteries, and most recently LiIon (lithium ion) batteries offer increased capacity, decreased size, freedom from memory effects, and an increased number of charge/discharge cycles.

BATTERY CAPACITY—The higher this number, the more hours you can run your radio between charges. Note that some models offer more than double the capacity of others.

ANTENNA CONNECTOR—In an emergency, the ability to connect your handheld to your fixed antenna could save your life—especially in a sailboat with a mast-mounted antenna, which would greatly extend the handheld's range. While most of us have never heard of an SMA connector, knowing that it's standard and that an adapter is available is very important.

Finally, we believe a waterproof device should be usable in the rain—without a plastic cover. It should also survive immersion in shallow water—such as a puddle or bilge—without damage. Each radio was briefly immersed in a bucket of clean water. It was tested immediately and then retested the next day.

▷ **The Bottom Line** Many of the models tested in this round performed very well. Icom and Standard Horizon remain at the top of the pack. Their radios are all well made and very competitive in both performance and price. Raymarine has also continued to produce a good radio. Of the aforementioned, our testers were particularly impressed by the Icom IC-M1V ($250). It's compact, full of features, submersible, and it performed exceptionally well. Icom supplies a drop-in charger and 1,600-mAH LiIon battery with the M1V. This battery should easily last through a long summer day, especially when transmitting on low power. Despite the fact that its one of the most expensive radios on the market, we think

its higher cost is justified. It has since been joined in the market by Icom's M88, which is also very compact, waterproof, and carries a long-lasting LiIon battery (this unit sells for $300).

Our testers also liked Standard Horizon's HX350S. They felt it had excellent performance. It's waterproof, and comes complete with most common accessories, and earned our Best Buy status. Since our test, that unit has been replaced by the HX270S, which offers all the same capabilities, and sells for $120. Standard Horizon has also added two other products to its line, the rugged HX500S ($200; comes with a three-year warranty) and the HX600S ($250; also with a three-year warranty). And the Raymarine Ray102 is also a good all-around radio. It has since been replaced by the Ray 101, which we recommend without reservation.

Stand–Alone Depthsounders

If you're installing a depthsounder (and through-hull transducer) for the first time, and have space for such an instrument, it makes sense to at least consider a sounder that will paint you a picture of the bottom as well as give you depth numbers and (usually) water temperature—especially because monochrome fishfinders are priced about the same as single-purpose sounders, or even less. (If you're a fisherman as well as a sailor, so much the better.)

However, there are also plenty of reasons to choose a numbers-only sounder. They take up little space; they can be, and usually are, members of instrument systems from the same manufacturer; and they admirably fill the holes in bulkheads left by sounders that eventually give up the ghost after years of service.

PS investigated nine digital-display depthsounders from six different manufacturers in two categories: those with large displays and those with small displays, and two different ranges, which could simply be called "more expensive" and "less expensive." For this evaluation, we focused on samplings from those ranges. Not every sailor needs a depthsounder, but the information they provide can lessen your anxiety, especially if you're in unfamiliar waters. For that alone, one of the less expensive models might be attractive, provided it works well. On the other hand, there are features and capabilities in some of the more sophisticated sounders that may be worth the added expense. Obviously, if your instrument system consists of several displays from one manufacturer, it will make sense to consider adding or replacing an instrument that fits technically and visually with what's already there.

The sounders we looked at include four "small" models, which have round bezels and will fit a standard 2⅛-inch instrument hole: the Lowrance 3500, the Teleflex TFX IDD, the Norcross Hawkeye, and the Uniden QT206. Ranging in price from $90 to roughly $150, these four units are far less expensive than the other five large units that range from $179 to $399. From Raymarine we got the ST40 and ST60 displays, and from Standard Horizon the DS35, DS45, and DS150. Each unit was tested with its transom-mounted transducer, which was mounted to a board that was submerged alongside our test boat. (All these instruments are also available with through-hull transducers.) We looked at how each unit functions, as well as how easy their displays are to install.

▷ **The Bottom Line** All these sounders have at least one type of depth alarm; we operated them on every unit. The alarms did work as advertised, and this can be an important feature, but in our opinion, none of them were loud enough to get your attention were it noisy on deck or were you a sound sleeper using this as an anchor alarm.

We found the overall performance of the two Raymarine units superior to the others tested. We selected the ST40 as the top pick because we don't think the bigger ST60 has $150 worth of extra features, which is the price differential.

Sailors looking for a less expensive unit simply to display depth should consider the Norcross Hawkeye or the Uniden QT206. They both do the job accurately.

Nautical Charts

ELECTRONIC CHARTS

In addition to providing finely detailed charts for display on screen, today's cards supply a plethora of additional information that mariners find extremely useful. A few years ago, we might have told buyers to look first at what plotter they liked and then live with the cards that it came with. After all, they were all pretty much the same. Not today. The latest releases from C-Map and Navionics have so much additional information that it takes a chartplotter with a very powerful processor and a high-resolution screen to fully exploit all of the cards' capabilities. Today, picking your chart card is just as important as picking the plotter that will display it.

To achieve the most useful evaluation of electronic charts, we contacted vector chart card makers C-Map, Navionics, and Garmin and asked each to supply their latest and greatest chart card along with a large-screen plotter capable of showing all the features and capabilities the card has to offer. C-Map elected to send an NT+ Max card installed in a Standard Horizon CP-1000C. Garmin choose to send a BlueChart 7.5 card and a Garmin 3010C chartplotter to display it. Navionics' most

PS relied on a powerboat to cover more ground quickly when testing four different electronic cartography cards: the Garmin BlueChart, loaded in the Garmin 3010C (top left); the Navionics Platinum, in a Raymarine E120 (top center); the C-Map NT+ Max, in a Standard Horizon CP-1000C (top right), and Navionics Gold, in the Northstar 6000i (flush-mounted in the console, lower right).

MARINA GUIDES

From time to time, we try—with middling success—to keep track of and report on chart books and cruising guides. Regarding cruising guides, it used to be that most of the cruising guides were onetime efforts by experienced sailors to bolster their cruising kitties. These often excellent (and frequently charming) books were about waters with which they had intimate knowledge. Because of limited sales, some books never, or rarely, got properly updated. More common now are professionally done books that, because of computers and electronic databases, can be updated easily, as need be.

PS once made a determined effort to round up and evaluate a lot of these books. However, researching those articles convinced us that this topic is so vast and so mutable, that it shouldn't really be tackled in the print format.

What remains important are the basic differences in these books. For instance, one set of guides may attempt to do everything—from noting the locations of marina fuel docks, to listing the best waterfront restaurants and nearby tourist attractions. Others seem to concentrate on quiet anchorages, the resident avian population, and snippets of historical lore. (And a few attempt, not very successfully

in our view, to combine chart books with cruising guides.)

To get the guides that suit your style of cruising, it's best to visit a nautical bookstore, grab some guides, find a quiet corner, and spend a half hour deciding which kind most closely match your needs.

However, there's one series of books that truly distinguishes itself from the hoi polloi—the Atlantic Cruising Club's set of marina guides. Most recently, the company issued one for Florida's East Coast. Delayed for a year by the hurricanes Charley, Frances, and Jeanne (which rearranged a lot of docks), the new book required the ACC staff to revisit 95 percent of the 226 marinas excellently detailed in the book. (The ACC guides, four on the East Coast, one for the Pacific Northwest, include facilities that have transient docks for boats of 30 feet or longer.)

The ACC guides accept no advertising and come with CDs that include color photos. The guides currently available from ACC are for New England, Long Island Sound, the Pacific Northwest, The Chesapeake Bay, and the new one for Florida's East Coast. Published by Jerawyn Publishing of Rye, New York, the new guide is available online ($29 for both book and CD-ROM).

recent release is its much-heralded Platinum chart card. As of early 2006, the only machine capable of fully utilizing this card was Raymarine's E-series plotter. We reviewed the card on an E120 display. Because the market for the Navionics Platinum card is currently limited to only one plotter, we elected to evaluate the Navionics Gold, as well. This card was assessed on the 10-inch Northstar 6000i. All charts covered a similar area of the southeastern U.S. and Bahamas.

As with most *PS* tests, we attempted to be comprehensive, investigating not only the functionality and accuracy of these cards, but also how easy they are for the average user to manage. We mounted the plotters and their respective GPS antennas on our test boat and took them to sea off Islamorada in the Florida Keys. To be as practical as possible, we minimized any variability in position data by mounting all the GPS antenna modules within 2 feet of each other. Then we rated the cards based on the readability,

Manufacturer	C-Map	Garmin	Navionics	Navionics
Type	Max	BlueChart	Gold $	Platinum ★
Model Number	NA-M008.2	MUS603X	1G906XL3	CF/906P
Card Price	$300	$643	$200	$500
Plotter Used	Standard Horizon CP1000C	Garmin 3010C	Northstar 6000i	Raymarine E120
Coverage Area	Hatteras to Tampa including the Bahamas	Jacksonville, FL, to Bahamas, through Turks & Caicos, west through Mobile Bay	Cape Fear to Turks & Caicos to Cedar Keys, including Florida Keys Dry Tortugas, Cay Sal Bank	US Southeast and the Bahamas
Data Depth	Good	Very Good	Excellent	Excellent
Navigation Aids	Good	Very Good	Excellent	Excellent
Tide Data	Excellent	Excellent	Excellent	Very Good
Shoreline Accuracy	Good	Good	Good	Excellent
Harbor Information	Very Good	Fair	Fair	Excellent
Aerial Photos	Good	N/A	N/A	Excellent
Current Data	Excellent	N/A	N/A	Very Good
Wreck Information	Poor	Poor	Poor	Fair

$ Budget Buy   ✔ Recommended   ★ Best Choice

usefulness, and accuracy of the data displayed. For instance, we picked a lighthouse or beacon in our local area and checked how each chart card displayed the name, color, shape, light sequence, and light sectors. We also confirmed that each unit was giving us the correct position data for each nav aid we checked. We combined all the ratings and data collected by checking numerous lights, buoys, and day beacons into an overall "navigation aids" rating.

For the cruising crowd, we came up with a harbor-information rating by looking at marina information, diagrams, photos, and zoomed-in cartography.

▷ **The Bottom Line** Finding highly detailed, glitch-free cartography should be your No. 1 priority when choosing a card for your plotter. Both the Garmin BlueChart 7.5 and Navionics Gold cards make the grade here. We'd gladly use either to traverse our local waters and take an occasional out-of-area trip. We found that depth contouring and spot soundings on the Navionics card were accurate in all the areas. Depth contour detail was good in deepwater areas

and clearly superior to the C-Map cartography in several nearby areas we checked. These areas have usable small-boat channels running through flats. Both the Navionics and Garmin cartography showed the channels, and the C-Map did not. And though the Garmin has a slightly larger coverage, it is three times the price of the Gold card. Given that, we'd go with the Gold card from Navionics.

If you're shopping for a card and plotter at the same time, you're in a position to look beyond the basics and go for the latest and greatest. The Navionics Platinum takes the prize here. We think the extensive photo library alone is worth the extra bucks for a cruiser. Just the peace of mind one will get from seeing an aerial shot of an unfamiliar harbor or a particularly treacherous section of coastline is worth the price of admission—to say nothing of the variable photo overlay, 3-D view, and current predictions. The Navionics Platinum card only works in Raymarine E-Series plotters at the time this book was published, but soon we'd expect to see several other machines with Platinum capability.

CHAPTER 6

Steering and Propulsion

An auxiliary engine is the heart of any vessel's non-sailing propulsion system. But there are numerous other elements that support and aid the operation of these engines. Over the years, *PS* has examined the engines themselves and the various supporting components. In this chapter, we've grouped propulsion items with steering system components due to their close association aboard most vessels. First, let's consider the ubiquitous diesel engine.

Diesel Mechanics' Forum

Ghosting along in a bit of breeze—everything silent except for that hiss and burble of bubbles polishing the counter—is one of the powerful allures of sailing. But when the wind retires and the water turns into a huge sheet of dark steel, you must sing out, "Engine room, Bridge here." And with a turn of a key, that noisy, smelly Beast-in-the-Bowels rattles its bones, chuffs out a puff of smoke, and goes dutifully to work.

That's when you appreciate the perseverance of Rudolf Christian Karl Diesel, who in 1893 built the first engine that came to bear his name. He first used coal dust as fuel, but blew out a brick wall in his shop and almost killed himself. He recovered, got backing from Friedrick Krupp, and made a fortune.

Reliable, powerful, and long-lasting, diesel engines did not replace the renowned Atomic Four gasoline engines aboard sailboats until the 1970s and even the '80s. That's when diesels became small and light enough to be practical in sailboats.

Much of the credit for making small diesels goes to a onetime farm boy, Clessie Cummins, who fell rich in about 1920 when the introduction of his "lightweight" engines coincided with the nation's first energy crisis.

Diesels in boats work hard. And everyone expects them to be devoted to duty—unfailing, infallible, and up to any challenge. They'll do that, too, as long as the master is meticulous about clean fuel, proper lubrication, and adequate cooling.

So, which makes of diesel engines best do the job? It's a daunting question. And to answer it, we turned to those who should know—the mechanics who maintain and fix these engines when they fail. We surveyed a group of professionals that includes mechanics, lead mechanics, and mechanic supervisors.

Though there are a couple of dozen diesel engine manufacturers, including familiar names like Alaska, Bukh, Caterpillar, Cummins, Deere, Faryman, Izuzu, Lehman, Lister-Petter, Mann, Nanni, and Vetus, five companies rise to the top as

A conclave of diesel mechanics—like this group at the Jamestown Boatyard in Jamestown, Rhode Island—usually has a lot to say about which engines are the best. *PS's* less-than-scientific but nonetheless useful survey indicated that Perkins engines are the best among smaller diesels.

those whose products are most often used in sailboats: Perkins, Volvo, Westerbeke, Universal, and Yanmar. We asked our survey respondents to limit their considerations to small engines—from around 15 to 50 horsepower.

Gordon Murphy, for years the resident diesel wizard on Goat Island in Newport, Rhode Island, is known in New England and beyond as a consummate diesel doctor. He's now in his early 70s, and worked with Ken Simas (another respondent) for over 35 years. These two, and the other professionals we surveyed, told us that, in their collective view, Perkins is the best small diesel. It ranked first in five categories, including the important categories of reliability and durability.

Perkins's signature marine engine, the 4-108, is no longer made, and the company is now owned by Caterpillar Diesel in the U.S. Their marine engine division is Perkins-Sabre, which is represented in the U.S. by Penske, the automotive conglomerate out of Detroit. Several mechanics were quite forthright in their dismay over this arrangement. One said that when Penske took over in the U.S., "everything went to hell for Perkins."

Another lead mechanic said Penske "hasn't got Perkins back up to the position it had when it was making the 4-108." Others told us that the company's

parts distribution is sorely lacking. Perhaps ominously, Perkins suffered a poor rating only in the "parts availability" category.

Westerbeke was ranked second by our cadre of mechanics, and most referred to this company's products as good, solid engines. In the survey, Westerbeke engines outranked Perkins in a few categories. And most significant was the mechanics' view that Westerbekes are very smooth-running engines. Westerbeke also enjoyed a reputation for its careful work to make parts available (the company ranked first in that category) and relatively inexpensive.

Another old reliable—Universal—was ranked third. Universal was once the maker of the ubiquitous Atomic Four marine gas engine. They made 155,000 of them up in Oshkosh, Wisconsin, and thousands of them are still plugging away. The last Atomic Four went out the door in 1985. Universal makes a couple of diesels, including the M-25XPB, as drop-in replacements for the Atomic Four, and this has done much to keep the name alive.

Universal, which is now owned by Westerbeke, enjoyed not a single first-place rating in the 10 categories. But it hung right around the middle all the way.

Volvo took fourth-place honors. This could be considered a special case, because without its miserable showing in two categories—low-cost parts and

REPOWERING, BUT
HOW MUCH HORSEPOWER?

A subscriber once wrote to *PS* in need of advice about repowering. He owned a 1970 Ericson 35 MK-II, and the original engine was an Atomic Four. He had settled on a 14-hp Universal diesel as a replacement, he said, and wondered if that might be a little skimpy in the power department. His boat displaced 11,500 pounds. Given that, he asked, what should the overall horsepower be?

We wrote back that 14 horsepower seemed a little lean, but we added that yacht designer and boatbuilder Tom Colvin recommended 1 horsepower per long ton (2,240 pounds). The idea behind Colvin's formula is to use the engine only for powering into difficult anchorages and to recharge batteries. However, in actuality, few sailors really do that.

We also said that designer Ron Holland recommends horsepower of four to six times a vessel's displacement tonnage. So, between the two, you get recommendations of 5.1 and 30.6 horsepower. Certainly the recent trend has been to overpower boats, mostly because so many sailors motor so much of the time—when the wind is too light and when it is too strong. A large engine also may be required to run accessories such as refrigeration compressors and high-output alternators. If your sailing style is otherwise, 14 to 18 horsepower may suffice.

---

easiest to work on—Volvo would have ranked very close to the second-place Westerbeke.

"It's hard to find anyone who handles what you need," said Murphy of Volvo's parts distribution. "The parts have two or three part numbers, and when you do find what you need, the stuff is ridiculously priced," he said. Murphy told us that Volvo has some other quirks: "They stick you $470 for an oil cooler that otherwise might cost maybe fifty or sixty bucks. And Volvo gets five or six hundred dollars for a simple water pump."

Volvo has for years been widely known (or reviled) for the truly outlandish price tags on both its marine and automobile engines. If you lack good fortune and need a major repair, Volvo parts will make you weep.

And last in the view of the mechanics surveyed was Yanmar. A considerable success story in its entry into the marine markets more than two decades ago, and now a formidable occupant of a position envied by other diesel makers, Yanmar has greatly improved its engines. No longer are they known as "Yammering Yanmars" that vibrated so violently that they broke standard engine mounts.

PS editors have generally had very positive experiences with Yanmar diesels (despite the noise), and we wonder how much of the mechanics' relatively negative response to these engines stems from the track record of early models shipped out of Japan. There's no question that a brand name can suffer for years because of a poor start in the market, and this may be what happened in this survey. Mechanics, in our experience, have long memories, and can hold a grudge.

Clearly, boatbuilders feel differently—Yanmar engines are probably those most often installed in new production boats, and have been for some years. This begs the question: Could Yanmar engines be in less favor with these mechanics simply because more of them come under mechanics' care than other engines? We don't know. All that can be reported here is that Yanmar was rated easiest to work on, and had the silver-medal cooling system. Otherwise it ranked poorly.

Each of the mechanics we spoke with was careful to impart some essential knowledge regarding engine care. They told us that unlike an automobile engine, which has a relatively easy job apart from getting tons of steel into motion, marine engines never get to loaf. Any engine installed in a boat, especially a displacement sailboat, must be a brute with big muscles and a strong desire to sweat ceaselessly. It is, in effect, accelerating all the time. That's because for each waterline length the displacement boat moves, the engine must move a volume of water equal to the boat's weight. That's a lot of water—on a full day of motoring in a calm, a diesel aboard a typical cruising boat might move 25,000 tons of the stuff.

Though diesels are a lot lighter than they used to be, they're still heavier than gasoline engines. They also take up more space and are more expensive to buy and to repair. However, because diesels are long-lasting, powerful, reliable (they need no elaborate electric ignition system), and (perhaps paramount in many boat owners' eyes) use sparingly and efficiently a fuel that doesn't explode, they are and undoubtedly will continue to be the engine of choice for sailboat owners.

Use your diesel hard. It's built to work that way. Give it nothing but clean fuel. Change the oil as specified. Keep a close eye on the temperature. And remember—it's an auxiliary. That means it's there to help the sail plan, not replace it.

Picking a Prop

Readers often write to *PS* to determine what sort of prop they might use to replace one that they own. Or they contact us to find out if a two-bladed prop is better than one with three blades for their boat. Or, they want to know the difference between two makes of propeller.

Here's an example: The owner of a Newport 41 wrote to find out what kind of prop would maximize his boat's speed under power and not impair the boat's sailing characteristics. He said that cursory research was pushing him toward a three-bladed feathering prop as the best solution and wanted to know if we agreed.

In our response, we referred him to two lengthy articles on propeller technology that *PS* had published (October 1, 1993 and January 1, 1995). Both articles detail the research and findings of a propeller study this magazine conducted in conjunction with researchers at the Massachusetts Institute of Technology. In those articles, we revealed that a feathering prop has less drag than a fixed prop, but a bit more than a folding prop.

Our findings showed that a feathering prop such as the Max-Prop, however, has better performance in

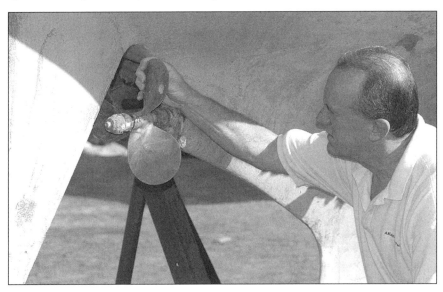

Fixed props like this one are the least expensive option in most cases, but if performance under sail is important to you, consider the advantages of a folding or feathering propeller.

In *PS*'s tests, feathering props, like the Max-Prop shown here, exhibited better performance in reverse, which may be important for those owners who keep their boats in a marina.

reverse, which may be important for those owners who keep their boats in a marina. We wrote: "The Max-Prop's efficiency in forward isn't quite as good as a fixed or folding prop because its blades are flat; the solution is to apply more throttle . . . if the horses are available. Nonetheless, the Max-Prop is an excellent, all-around choice, albeit an expensive one."

In our experience, folding props are fine for moving the boat forward in open water, but when you have to get to a dock it's a different situation, particularly getting the boat to slow down. The makers of the Martec folding prop, however, insist that a boat with a folding prop can stop quickly enough, and that the secret is in applying lots of revs to the engine.

Fixed props are the least expensive and are probably the most efficient for motoring. But the drag, which varies by boat but probably costs 0.3 to 0.8 knot on the average, is a serious drawback for one who likes to sail as fast as possible.

Yet another choice is the self-pitching Autoprop, an unusual design that automatically changes pitch to match loads. It, too, feathers under sail. Cost is about the same as a Max-Prop.

In the aforementioned studies, *PS* tested both the Autoprop and Max-Prop at MIT's hydrodynamic tunnel. Because of its flat blades, the Max-Prop is not as efficient in forward as fixed props or the Auto-

prop. In reverse, however, the flat blades are better than shaped blades that would otherwise (on fixed props) be angled in the wrong direction. That's why a lot of people like the Max-Prop—for maneuvering in tight marina quarters. They also feather nicely and reduce drag under sail, though the large hub creates more drag than a folding prop. The low efficiency in forward means you have to apply more RPM than you would with a fixed prop with shaped blades. Because most boats are overpowered, this is generally not an issue. It would only cause a problem if you had a small engine for your boat and didn't have the reserve power necessary.

The Autoprop is ingenious in that it automatically adjusts pitch to the speed desired, so it does require a bit less RPM than a Max-Prop. This was confirmed by a *PS* reader who had his boat and a friend's (identical 41-footers) equipped with an Autoprop and a Max-Prop, respectively. In powering side-by-side in identical conditions, the boat with the Autoprop turned at a few hundred less RPM.

The reputed downside to the Autoprop is that it requires a bit more RPM before it gets a "bite" on the water but, as soon as it does, digs in voraciously. Under sail, drag with the Autoprop is a bit more than the Max-Prop. Performance in reverse also is supposed to be good.

So, what about a three-bladed prop versus a two-bladed prop? A three-bladed prop will produce stronger, smoother thrust than a two-bladed prop, which means it will be better at pushing the boat into strong headwinds and chop. Feathering props are a bit less efficient than fixed-blade props at driving the boat forward, mainly because they have less twist built in so that they present less drag when feathered. Even so, a feathering three-blade should be more efficient than a fixed two-blade, and a lot better in reverse.

Boat speed is another question with more components. If, for example, your boat's maximum hull speed is 7 knots and you can reach that speed in flat water with your two-bladed prop, you'll probably be able to reach it more easily with the three-bladed prop at the same RPM, and cruise at 6 knots at a lower RPM (depending on how your engine is geared). The three-bladed prop won't have much of an effect on top speed in flat water, although it might muscle the boat ahead a bit faster at the cost of fuel and engine

When *PS* Editor-at-Large Nick Nicholson installed a Max-Prop VP feathering prop on his 40-foot, heavy displacement cruising sailboat, he did so with two purposes in mind: to reduce drag under sail and to increase maneuverability in tight quarters, particularly in reverse gear. Later, when he had the boat surveyed, prior to turning it over to new owners, Nicholson was reminded of yet a third advantage of this versatile propeller, the ability to change propeller pitch without hauling the boat.

Neither the Max-Prop nor the Max-Prop VP is cheap, mind you. A 17-inch, three-blade standard Max-Prop retails for about $2,700. The same size VP version of the prop—the size and model on Nicholson's vessel—retails for a whopping $3,200.

And like most sailors, he had never paid much attention to the details of prop pitch and diameter.

Diameter, of course, is a no-brainer. Any boat that does a significant amount of motoring should have as big a prop as you can install, subject to the normal requirement that the minimum vertical clearance between the prop tip and the hull or aperture be at least 15 percent of the prop diameter. For example, there should be at least 2.7 inches of tip clearance for an 18-inch prop. But determining correct propeller pitch, as any designer will tell you, is somewhat of a moving target. Yes, there are well-established formulas—both simple and complex—for determining proper pitch, but these generally give you only a starting point. We sailors generally take what the boat comes with, and don't give it a second thought. If the boat moves ahead at about the speed we expect, that's good enough for us. It really shouldn't be.

wear. Again, it will be a good deal better at getting you home in a headwind.

Sail-Drive Pros and Cons

Are sail-drives viable alternatives to the conventional engine and shaft arrangement? The editors at *PS* think so, but we're not entirely sold on them. Yes, we're aware of their primary advantages (reduction in vibration thus quieter running, fixed alignment, and less underwater drag), but we also know that there are significant corrosion and maintenance issues associated with these units, and those must be addressed.

When a reader recently queried us on how viable sail-drive units are, we did the sensible thing and quickly deferred to our resident engine expert Capt. Mike Muessel of Oldport Marine in Newport, Rhode Island.

Muessel told us: "Sail-drives are neither fish nor fowl in the sailboat propulsion field, and are a close relative of the popular powerboat out-drive units. For the sailboat manufacturer they represent a quicker, more versatile, and non-technical engine installation route as compared to a conventional inboard installation. Gone is the propeller shaft, along with its attendant coupling, stuffing box, cutless bearing, stern tube, and strut. Also missing are the alignment procedures between the engine and shaft that must be done on the production line.

"The sail-drive can easily be mounted facing forward or aft, and because it isn't constrained by shaft angle or aperture location, it offers the builder more versatility in engine placement.

"There's also a certain propulsion efficiency in the sail-drive, because the thrust is parallel to the boat's waterline, whereas the downward angle on a standard shaft means that some of the propeller's thrust is wasted.

"On the other hand, sail-drives are usually made of aluminum, one of the least noble metals, and they are constantly immersed a hostile marine environment.

What that pre-sale survey indicated was that Nicholson had grossly over-propped the boat, to the point that he was unable to pull much horsepower out of the Perkins 4-108 without overloading it. He simply couldn't get the engine far enough along on its power curve to use it effectively if it became necessary to power into strong winds or a head sea. He had known that all along, but had never gone through the exercise of putting it right.

The engine RPMs he normally used for motoring in calms weren't sufficient to punch the boat through building seas, but running the engine up higher on the power curve led to rising temperatures—the classic signs of an overloaded, over-propped engine.

The survey revealed that Nicholson's boat could barely turn more than 2,200 RPM at full throttle. So, he knew the prop pitch had to be adjusted. This is when the advantage of a variable-pitch prop like the Max-Prop VP really comes into play. With a fixed prop, changing pitch means hauling the boat, taking the prop to the shop for a repitch (or simply buying a new prop, which might be easier), and reinstalling. With the Max-Prop VP, all that was required was a thorough external cleaning of the external pitch adjusting ring, as any fouling on the prop hub would make it diffi-cult to adjust the pitch. "I then removed all the lubrication plugs from the prop hub, screwed in my grease gun, and gave the hub a fresh shot of grease," wrote Nicholson in his Offshore Log column. "Because the pitch ring hadn't been moved in a year and a half, it required some gentle prying to free it up, but all of this was done underwater, with no prop disassembly. It was also done by free-diving, rather than using scuba tanks, which had already been removed from the boat. If the prop had already been lubricated and cleaned, the whole job would have taken about a minute. And the cost was zero. The price differential of about $500 between the standard Max-Prop and the VP was almost paid for by avoiding a single haulout."

After repitching, Nicholson reported that the he had increased engine speed under load by almost 800 RPM, and the engine was running significantly cooler when pushed hard. "The new owners now cruise under power at about 2,200 to 2,300 RPM, something we could never achieve. This is very close to the optimum cruising RPM for this engine, according to several 4-108 experts we consulted, although it is still below the 70 percent of rated RPM that most engine manufacturers quote as an ideal speed for diesel engine efficiency and long life."

Because aluminum is anodic, it will corrode when it remains in contact with nearly every other metal while it's immersed in an electrolyte, seawater in this case. And, if placed too far forward of the rudder, a sail-drive will offer little prop-wash on the rudder for low-speed steering; if placed well aft of the keel, it can increase drag. And don't forget the large hole that must be cut in the hull to accommodate the sail-drive. We installed a Yanmar saildrive unit on J. P. Mouligne's class-winning 50-footer *CCP Cray Valley* in the Around Alone Race six years ago, and I must tell you, I didn't want to be the one to cut a huge hole in his beautiful Finot-designed carbon fiber hull to slide the leg through. Still, sail-drives were still the required emergency power packages of choice in that race, so we had to do it. We strapped a huge 200-amp alternator and a large water ballast pump to that little 18-horsepower engine, and it never failed him during that race.

"Some competitors thought the units needed more fairing and proceeded to sand through the factory-applied barrier coating in an attempt to reduce drag. I was quick to point out that messing with the barrier coat is a recipe for electrolysis, and it must not be disturbed even though small scratches can be repaired with out-drive barrier coat.

"Because of the short shaft length in the sail-drive legs, one should be careful to pick a prop that is rubber-bushed to reduce shifting shock on the drive system. Some folding props also feature shock-absorbers on the blades to further reduce clunking.

"A good boot seal to keep the ocean out of your boat is essential with these units, and I recommend you look for a double seal with a water detecting alarm between them, like Yanmar uses.

"Follow the maintenance instructions carefully, and be sure to use the recommended oil. Different units use different oils, so be careful."

So the answer is yes, we definitely consider sail-drives to be a viable alternative to the standard shaft/strut/prop system, though we prefer the latter in most cases for cruising applications. As always, it's necessary to balance the trade-offs. The proper use of zincs should protect your sail-drive unit from galvanic corrosion, but if your boat is kept in a marina that's apt to have stray currents, those can damage metals kept underwater in very little time. Keep in mind that neither zincs nor a galvanic isolator will fully protect your boat and its parts from a bad case of stray currents, so wise sailors will monitor their sail-drive units closely.

Shaft Seals

For ages, keeping the water out of boats where the propeller shaft pierced the hull was the job of a stuffing box. In most of these, flax packing is wrapped and then compressed around the shaft to create a seal. The nut is tightened until the flood of incoming water is reduced to a drip—about two or three per minute—indicating that the seal material is being properly lubricated.

The problems with stuffing boxes are twofold: The least of the two is the need to pump out the water that leaks in. That's annoying enough. But along with the lubricating water comes silt and sand, which never quite makes it into the bilge because they are trapped by the flax seal. And, because we don't see these materials, we're not bothered by them until, perhaps, years later when we discover our shaft has been heavily scored. All along, we've been retightening the nut to keep the drip at the correct rate when we were also increasing the pressure on the trapped abrasives that enhance the scoring.

This process can go on for many years with no real problems. All we have to do is periodically pick out the old flax, which also removes the collected abrasives, and replace it with new flax. When we tighten the nut, the flexible flax properly seals the shaft . . . even with the scoring. Fortunately, there is a better solution.

Some seals employ a positive lubrication system in which cooling water is piped from the raw-water pump into the seal housing and made to flow out the stern tube rather than in the conventional method used on stuffing boxes. Some units use the prop shaft for the sealing surface while others take the seal completely off the shaft and place it elsewhere. And one unit doesn't use water as a lubricant at

The best shaft seal systems move the seal off the shaft and provide substantial shaft-bearing surfaces for automatic alignment, like the Lasdrop original and Gen II systems shown here. However, a sealing surface off the shaft is great, but if it is not properly aligned, it is destined for excessive wear and premature failure.

all. Rather, it imitates the seals found in the lower housings of outboard motors and outdrives. On a sailboat, a well-designed shaft seal can mean the owner will not have to worry about shaft leaks other than to take a periodic peek to see if anything is wet. But keep in mind that all of the shaft seals evaluated here employ a hose or other mechanism intended to connect to the stern tube. Before you charge ahead to retrofit an existing stuffing box, be sure to examine your particular setup so that proper connection to the stern tube can be established. Not all stuffing box configurations are alike, and your through-hull hardware may have to be changed.

We evaluated shaft seals from six manufacturers, all of which take the sealing responsibility away from the stuffing box and place it within the shaft seal unit. None use flax packing or require periodic adjustment, and all should make for a dry bilge over a long service period. They included the Norscot from

REPLACING PACKING GLANDS

O.K., so you want to stick with your conventional stuffing box. No problem, a lot of sailboat owners opt for this route, but you will have to learn the proper procedure for replacing shaft packing.

Conventional bronze stuffing boxes (or packing glands) are attached to a stern tube in the hull ('glassed in, on fiberglass boats) by means of a rubber hose and secured with hose clamps. This allows the gland to center itself on the shaft.

To replace the packing, first buy the right thickness lubricated flax; it has to fit between the shaft and the inside of the gland—say, ¼ inch. You don't want to cram it in because tightening the gland will force it to expand somewhat. At the same time, you don't want it loose.

Back off the lock nut and the compression nut, and remove the old packing. Then insert at least three rings of flax around the shaft. To ensure a good watertight joint where the two ends of the flax meet, cut each end at 45 degrees so you get a

scarf. You can do this on the shaft outside the gland. Once you're satisfied the flax is the right length, push it into the gland with a blunt object that will fit between the shaft and gland. Work your way around the shaft, shoving a little flax in at a time.

When you've filled up the gland, screw down the compression nut and lock nut onto the gland body. That's it. Check it soon thereafter; conventional packing should leak a drop or two of water every minute, but never overtighten as you may score the shaft by doing so.

New materials, such as Drip-Free packing, that contain hydrocarbons and Teflon, are designed not to allow any dripping. The Drip-Free works well, but it's expensive at about $50. Still, it's guaranteed for the life of your boat. We've used it for years with good results. Enough other water manages to find its way into the boat without intentionally introducing it through the packing gland!

Ibsen Co., a Strong shaft seal from Tide Marine, one from TrellCom Marine, one from Duramax, PYI's Packless Sealing System, and Nautical Specialties' Lasdrop. We wondered, what might happen when these seals fail, and what would make them fail? Also, are they easily repaired? Can they be repaired in the water like a stuffing box or does the vessel have to be hauled? And how easy is it to install and maintain them? We also checked to see if they come with clear instructions, what they cost, and what warranties, if any, they carry.

Our investigations confirmed that all of these products work and should keep one's bilges dry. However, a water-lubricated seal that uses a simple O-ring around the shaft—like the Lasdrop Dry Seal—isn't

the best approach, in our opinion. Whether your shaft seal has forced water lubrication or not, there is always positive pressure on the wet side of the seal. The positive pressure on the non-forced system still exists because the seal is below the waterline. And the water still contains the same silt and sand that aggravates stuffing boxes. But because there is no drip flow under the O-ring, the abrasives will not collect at the same rate. However, the seal will eventually begin to leak because of wear, the abrasives will collect, and shaft scoring will occur. The longer you let it go, obviously, the worse it will get.

Now, to repair it, you have a dilemma. A new O-ring simply will not properly seal a scored shaft. This means that the O-ring will have to be moved

CHANGING IMPELLERS

Nearly every sailor we know has a horror story involving a failed raw-water pump, usually one that centers on a broken impeller. Though the magazine has never tested the full range of replacement products available for impellers, these products are commonly available nearly everywhere. However, for quick, safe, reliable impeller changes, we do have two favorite products—the SpeedSeal and the Jabsco Puller.

Naturally, most raw-water pumps are mounted in a place where three of the six screws that hold the plate over the pump bore are impossible to get at. You have to contort your body, invent techniques, and jury-rig tools to finally get all the screws backed out. This just won't do in an emergency situation, when you need the engine fully operable to claw your way off a lee shore in little breeze. Most sailors know that it's situations like this when your engine is most likely to fail. Call it Murphy's Law with an agenda. So, what can you do?

Do as we did, and order a SpeedSeal, properly sized for your boat's water pump. These simple devices, fashioned from marine brass, come with two holes and two slots, so they really require only four fasteners to be dogged into place. The advantage they offer is that you can significantly accelerate changing an impeller, and you can almost do it blindfolded, they're so well engineered.

Despite the fact that the SpeedSeal comes with a plastic lever-type tool for removing the impeller, we prefer to use a Jabsco puller, which is made in two sizes for impellers up to 2.5 inches. Like we said, this is no time to mess around.

The SpeedSeal makes changing an impeller a straightforward and speedy process. Here, at left, the SpeedSeal cover plate is ready, with its nitrile O-ring lubricated and set in its channel. In the center, the cover's slots are slid behind two of the knurled screws, placed in the least accessible holes. At right, the Speedseal is now in place. Only four screws are needed for a six-screw cover replacement.

to a cleaner place on the shaft or the shaft will have to be replaced (expensive). In most installations, we think repairs can be accomplished by shortening (or lengthening) the connecting hose plus replacing the O-ring, but the number of times this can be done is obviously limited.

We think a better system is one that moves the seal off the shaft and places it elsewhere to completely avoid shaft scoring, like the PYI Packless Sealing System. And we think the best systems move the seal off the shaft plus provide substantial shaft-bearing surfaces for automatic alignment, like the Lasdrop original and Gen II systems. A sealing surface off the shaft is great, but if it is not properly aligned, it is destined for excessive wear and premature failure.

The Lasdrop (¾ inch to 4 inches) and PYI (¾ inch to 3¾ inch) products are the best performers. Both are off-the-shaft sealing units. The PYI units employ a polished bearing surface on a carbon graphite flange that is connected to the stern tube with a flexible hose employed as a spring bellows. The flange is pressed against a stainless steel rotor bearing surface that itself is O-ring-sealed and secured to rotate with the shaft with set-screws.

These simple yet elegantly designed units should yield a long service life with little or no maintenance. If any seepage were to occur, it is easy to compress the bellows and wipe away contaminants that may have collected on the sealing surface, and then let the seal reseat itself with usage.

We reviewed three Lasdrop units, all forced-water lubrication models in two types; one uses the shaft for sealing with a hefty O-ring, spare seal provided (Dry Seal model); two employ an off-the-shaft sealing mechanism with a graphite compound against a stainless steel bearing surface. All use a cutless bearing–like section built into the connecting hose for shaft alignment.

The difference between the two off-the-shaft seal types is how the sealing surface is loaded. The Original model employs a sturdy flexible hose as a spring bellows that presses the graphite seal against the stainless bearing that in turn is clamped to the shaft with a hard rubber split ring and sealed with an O-ring. The Gen II model uses a specially made shaft fixture with a built-in stainless steel spring that makes the stainless surface press against the graphite bearing surface, which is affixed with a rigid hose to the stern tube.

▷ **The Bottom Line** Clearly, any shaft seal that provides a dry bilge is better than one that does not. A dry bilge also eliminates the headache of figuring out what to do with oily water that by law cannot be discharged over the side.

On a sailboat hull, any of the units tested should perform satisfactorily with a long service life, but we still recommend those units with off-the-shaft sealing mechanisms as opposed to those that seal against the shaft—especially if the vessel is to be used in silty and sandy waters. None of the manufacturers we talked to have run extensive tests-to-failure in silty and sandy waters, although most have bench-tested them for many thousands of hours. All tell us that the flushing mechanism in a forced-water lubrication system is all that is needed to keep the seals free of abrasives. Maybe so, but when a seal does eventually fail, we'd prefer it not damage our shaft, no matter how slight. Because these products are integral to your boat's security, engineering and reliability are what counts here, not price.

Soundproofing Materials

Engines make noise. Crew—especially when they're trying to hold a conversation, sleep, or just relax—don't like noise. The solution? Isolate the crew from the engine noise and vibration. So we investigated 10 different sound-attenuating products.

Noise and vibration are inseparable. Noise exists because vibration causes variations in the air pressure that reaches the ear. This is perceived as sound. An effective control deals with both the vibration and the airborne noise.

Noise levels are measured in decibel units, usually referred to as dBA (the A denoting that the measurement is adjusted for the frequency response of the human ear, rather than the total sound level energy). Everyday sounds fall into a range from roughly 25 dBA (a suburban bedroom at night) to 100 dBA (a chainsaw at a distance of 3 feet). On a boat, an unshielded diesel genset will produce sound levels of 100 dBA at 3 feet; an inboard typically raises the noise in the engine room to about 110 dBA. The object is to drop those levels to approximately 75 dBA for more-or-less normal conversation, and another 20 dBA for comfortable sleeping with the engine running.

There are three basic approaches to making your boat quieter. The first step is to use flexible mounts to isolate the vibrating machinery from the hull. These help prevent the transmission of vibration through the solid structure of the boat, and the consequent reverberation of hull sections that can act like amplifiers. Correcting any engine-shaft misalignment will certainly help.

The next step is to surround the noise-producing machinery in a tight, insulated enclosure to reduce air-transmitted noise.

The final step is to line enclosed living quarters, such as cabins, with sound-absorbent materials.

There are only three things that can be done with the air vibrations that we regard as noise. They can be reflected, transmitted, or absorbed. The first two don't do you much good on board a boat. Sound, after all, is a form of energy, and you can't just make it vanish. You can, however, convert sound energy into another form of energy—heat. The energy dissipates when the absorbent material becomes displaced or compressed. Materials like lightweight foams and fiberglass wool have good damping but not enough mass to be effective by themselves. More specialized sound-absorbers are more effective. These are composite materials with a high-mass layer, one or more damping layers, and (usually) a thin plastic film at each face to protect the damping layer(s) from mechanical damage and moisture.

The products we tested ranged from 1/4-inch-thick fiberglass sheets to plywood with a built-in sound-deadening layer, to 2-inch-thick foam/lead/foam composites. For comparison purposes, we also included exterior-grade plywood, which is typically used for engine enclosures. Based on their effectiveness, these products fell into three groups,

Silent Running is a paintable sound-deadening material that sells for about $150 a gallon. That's certainly not cheap, but this product does the same work as its foam competitors, but takes up much less space.

and those generally carry prices that corresponded with their performance. The most effective products tended to be the most expensive, although there were some notable exceptions. The most effective products gave a 12–15 dBA noise reduction, the least effective about 3–5 dBA.

None of the products showed any signs of degradation after several days of exposure to any of the liquids we applied to them. All were easy to work with and apply; the foam products were physically stronger than the fiberglass ones and could be glued, which gave them an advantage. On the other hand, the fiberglass products can withstand much higher temperatures than the foams and are all flame-resistant (although the facing material on some may support combustion). All the foams burned when exposed to a flame.

▷ **The Bottom Line** The most effective sound barriers were three 2-inch-thick composites—Soundown 2-inch Lead/Foam, Soundown 2-inch Lead/Fiberglass, and Hough Marine Sonovinyl Supreme. Any one of these products should do a good job of suppressing noise at its source.

If all you're looking for is the maximum in noise control, Soundown 1-inch Lead/Foam is your choice, though not by much. Hough Marine's Sonovinyl Supreme performed as well for a gas engine, almost as well for diesel, and costs less. If you're concerned about fire protection, Soundown 2-inch Lead/Fiberglass will provide comparable performance combined with fire retardance at a comparable price, but you won't be able to glue it.

If all you need is a sound barrier for quieting a cabin or the like, Hough Marine Acoustical Fiberglass is effective and inexpensive. And if you're starting from scratch, Greenwood's dB-Ply is a good choice.

In a separate test, *PS* editors evaluated a relative newcomer to the soundproofing market—Silent

WIZ OIL FILTER CUTTER

All too often, boat owners keep tabs on the condition of their engines by simply running them: If they start and run smoothly enough, all must be well. But there are several more specific maintenance procedures worth considering that can help head off trouble before it gets serious. One is oil analysis, in which a used-oil sample is mailed off for spectroscopic examination; this is best done as an ongoing program that provides you with baseline information and warns of any sudden changes in the makeup of your oil.

A second, complementary procedure, which you can perform yourself, is inspection of the contents of the oil filter itself. While the oil analysis looks for micro-contamination, it's possible for macro-contamination to exist either along with or without micro-contamination. Excessive carbon from blow-by can show here as carbon granules, which means potentially big trouble is not far off. Poor assembly practices show up as silicone gasket pieces which can block oil holes. Metals show up in several distinguishable forms that are easily visible to the naked eye.

But one reason that you don't hear about sailors conducting oil filter inspections often is because it's a nasty, messy job. Hacksaws and chisels are both messy and also tend to contaminate the filter element.

Until the last few years there was only one specialty tool (designed for aviation use) available for this job, which made the process quick and easy. Unfortunately, it was also very expensive. Many airplane owners are as thrifty as boat owners, so fortunately several lower-cost tools have come on the market. These tools are designed to open the outer shell of spin-on filters, making the inner pleated element easily removable for inspection. One such cutter tool is the Filter Wiz.

Basically, the Wiz is a simple purpose-built pipe cutter, with a bushing to hold the filter in place (the filter should be placed in a vise) and the cutting wheel positioned to slice through the outer layer of the filter at just the right point—above the thick steel base but where the skin won't buckle either. The tool is made of $\frac{1}{8}$-inch steel plate.

Filter Wiz is available only from the maker for around $50 postpaid, satisfaction guaranteed. The package includes written inspection information, as well as a 20-minute instructional video. This is primarily an aviation-oriented product, but will cut open any spin-on oil filter with a ¾-inch-by-16 thread, $^{13}\!/_{16}$-by-16 thread, or 18 thread count, male or female. There are several other filter cutters available, primarily through aviation shops, such as Aircraft Tool & Supply, and costing between $50 and $100 or more, but this is the least expensive we've found.

The Wiz Oil Filter Cutter makes a messy job a lot easier.

All of the engines that *PS* tested in this four-stroke round-up vibrated at mid-throttle settings, a symptom of their single cylinders. From left to right, the Suzuki, the Mercury, and the Yamaha. In this gathering, we deemed the Suzuki the best option due to its easy starting, solid performance, smooth shifting, and long tiller. It also carries a slightly lower manufacturer's suggested retail price.

Running. This product is a paint-on soundproofing, which means it may be more versatile for some applications. The product is advertised as nontoxic, VOC-free, fireproof, and able to withstand temperatures from minus 30°F to 375°F. It's reportedly resistant to gas, oil, and most chemicals. At $150 per gallon, it's not cheap, but it does take up less space than other sound-deadening systems (only a layer $\frac{1}{16}$ inch thick is needed to reduce noise say its makers). We found it to be very easy to apply, and quite functional. It may not outperform its thicker rivals, but it does offer an appealing alternative for aftermarket installations.

Four-Stroke Outboards

In the product evaluation business, it's easy to get ambitious because there are so many items on the market. *Practical Sailor* once attempted to review small four-stroke engines from 4 to 9.9 horsepower by surveying 30 separate products. We looked these over in the showrooms, examined their respective data, and then reported on them. Because we know that actual hands-on testing produces more useful information, we whittled that group down to three of the more popular models and ran those through a series of field tests.

We actually covered six 4-horsepower engines by testing only three: one from Suzuki, one from Yamaha, and one from Mercury. These are all single-cylinder engines with 15-inch shafts. Suzuki's DF 4 is the same motor as the Johnson 4. The Mercury 4 is actually built by Tohatsu, which also markets it as a Nissan product, and Yamaha 4 builds its own 4-horsepower. (Honda does not make a 4-horse-power model.) Since some of the manufacturers use the same power head for their 5- and 6-horsepower versions, most of the comments concerning the 4-horsepower models would apply to their higher-horsepower brethren—not performance, of course, but certainly ease of carrying, storage, and access to maintenance components like oil fill and spark plugs.

To conduct the testing, our editors spent a full day with these engines. They were lifted, mounted, and

It's more difficult to stow the Yamaha engine (at left) in a stable position, relative to the Suzuki (at right).

MR. FUNNEL

Clean air, clean oil, and clean fuel are the three main support legs of a healthy engine, especially a diesel, and of those three it's the fuel that will let you down the fastest if it's contaminated with water, dirt, bacteria, or sludge. It's important to be scrupulous about putting in clean fuel in the first place, and keeping the tanks topped up to prevent condensation. (It's water in the tank that breeds the beasties that cause the sludge....)

We have reported many times on that first line of defense—the deck-fill fuel filter—and in recent years we have favored Mr. Funnel, a.k.a. the Fuel Filter Funnel, made by Smart Tech LLC in Alaska and sold under different names by West Marine and other outlets. It's a plastic funnel with a filter element made of Teflon-coated stainless steel, set in a cylindrical arrangement over a sump. The sump catches any amount of water that might be in the fuel, and the filter catches particulate matter and water droplets that might be held momentarily in suspension (although water settles almost immediately to the bottom of any fuel vessel).

The funnels are sold in several sizes and flow rates range from 2.5 to 15 gallons per minute. (The flow rate should be calibrated to the patience levels of the skipper, the fuel-dock attendant, and the attitudes of the people waiting in line behind you for fuel. The faster the flow, the better, but you'll pay for it.) The smallest version is about $18 and the largest about $65.

Since we began reporting on Mr. Funnel, several readers have written to ask what's supposed to be done with the fluid that collects in the filter sump. In a pinch, it can be absorbed with a few paper towels or a piece of fuel-absorber pad like those made by 3M. Those absorbers must be disposed of properly. A better plan is to keep a clean glass jar with a lid on board, and pour the sump fluid into that. It will give you a chance to inspect the fluid for debris.

---

removed, carried, started, run, checked for features, and examined under the hoods. Basically, we got to know them well. We put each engine on a 10-foot Apex inflatable and ran it at various throttle settings with one or two people aboard.

▷ **The Bottom Line** We found that all these engines vibrated noticeably at mid-throttle settings, a result of their single cylinders; all had throttle friction lock and steering friction lock; and all lock in the down position when shifted into reverse. We made sure of this by slamming each engine into reverse and cranking the throttle. None of them kicked up.

Admittedly, all of the engines have their drawbacks and strengths. We rated the operational aspects of each slightly ahead of portability. The fact is, none of the engines is fun to carry around or put on the transom of a boat, though the Yamaha is easiest.

For our money, however, the Suzuki is the top pick due to its easy starting, solid performance, smooth shifting, and long tiller. Its drawback—no front carrying handle—can be dealt with. Just keep a glove around to protect the hand that endures the tiller elbow. This engine rests nicely on two side-mounted storage pads and its propeller. The hood fits snugly on this engine and is held in place by two latches, one in front and one at the rear. The oil fill/dipstick is easy to access, and there are even instructions printed nearby on how to read the dipstick. As with the Merc, a funnel with a long neck or hose attached makes spillage less likely. The single spark plug is on the back of the engine and easily accessible.

We found that one-pull starting was the norm once the Suzuki warmed up. The tiller arm is the best of the group—it's angled outboard and extends 17 inches from the transom.

As for its performance, under full throttle, the Suzuki and the Mercury were even. The Suzuki planed the dink easily with the heaviest tester on his own, and nearly so with both testers aboard. Shifting is clean and crisp. Tilting the engine up and down is easy. We noted no sticking or jamming. Noise levels on the Suzuki were 70 decibels at idle, 79 at mid-throttle, and 88 at wide-open throttle. It also has the largest internal fuel tank (nearly half a gallon) but has no external tank connection. The Mercury comes in a close second, held back by its somewhat rough shifter and no backside-carrying handle.

The Yamaha finishes third. It may be easy to carry, but it doesn't stow in a stable position, was harder to start than the others, and exhibited less kick than the Mercury and Suzuki during our day of testing. And the other downside of the Yamaha is its price. We were able to find both a Suzuki 4 and a Tohatsu 4, identical to the Mercury, for around $900 on the Internet. The cheapest Yamaha we found was $999. However, if portability is your main concern, the extra money might may well be worth it.

Trolling Motors

PS once experimented with using a small electric trolling motor as the source of power for one of our workboats. This little motor made a worthy replacement for a recalcitrant 15-horsepower gasoline engine, so we wrote about the experiment. That piece prompted a deluge of letters and e-mail from readers. A significant number of boat owners, it turned out, appreciate that these quiet, efficient devices are almost ideal for propelling small to mid-sized dinghies. What was really surprising was the number of people who wrote to tell us that they use an electrical trolling motor as the main source of auxiliary propulsion aboard sailboats, including one 30-foot loa.

That interest on their part prompted an evaluation of these products. To determine if these products perform as advertised, we gathered up four representative models to determine the facts on each. We obtained models from two manufacturers dominant in the marine electric trolling motor marketplace— Minn Kota and MotorGuide. MotorGuide sent us two motors from its Great White Saltwater Series: a 24-volt SW82 HT and a 12-volt SW46 HT. To compete against this pair, we also obtained two Minn Kota Riptide Saltwater trolling motors, a 24-volt RT80/S-3X and a 12-volt RT50/SC/S. These four motors fit nicely into two groups for testing. The pair of 24-volt, 80-pound-thrust motors in the $550 to $600 price range formed one group, while the two 12-volt, near-50-pound-thrust motors, both priced at $300, formed the other.

We opted to test all four motors on a 16-foot skiff. We examined speed at maximum thrust for each

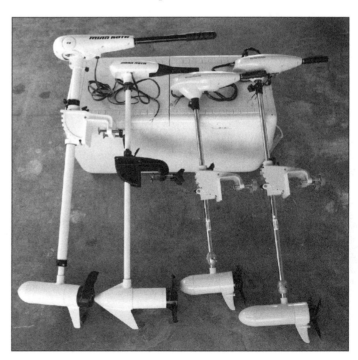

The test specimens that *PS* examined include, from left: the Minn Kota RT80/S-3X, the Minn Kota RT50/SC/S, the MotorGuide SW 46 HT, and the MotorGuide SW82 HT.

product as well as amp draw. Then we evaluated the static thrust of each. Then we examined the operation and handling of each unit.

▷ **The Bottom Line** Ultimately, our testers favored the Minn Kota RT80/S-3X, which weighs in at 34.5 pounds, carries a three-year warranty, and is available in the both a 42- or 52-inch shaft length. One major operational enhancement on the RT80/S-3X —not found on any of the other trolling motors we tested—is the 3X steering. By its very nature this feature makes this motor unique compared to the others tested. Essentially what happens with the 3X steering is that when the operator moves the tiller handle to redirect the thrust of the motor, the handle need only be moved one-third of the desired amount. For example, if you wish to change the direction of the thrust from straight astern to directly to port, a 90-degree direction change, the tiller handle need only be moved 30 degrees. In actual operation this makes the job of steering very easy, as only small movements are needed even for large course changes.

The RT80 did well in our performance testing, too, even though it lacks the brute horsepower of MotorGuide's 80-pound-thrust motor. At maximum thrust, the RT80 managed to push our test boat along at a respectable 3.6 MPH while drawing about 45.5 amps. In our static thrust test, it produced 59 pounds of thrust. Overall we found the RT80 had more than enough power to move our test boat around easily.

In the 50-pound-thrust class, we picked the Motor-Guide SW46 HT over the Minn Kota RT50/SC/S. Priced the same, these smaller units fared almost identically in our tests, but the transom mount on the SW46 was stout and secure while the RT50's was plastic and pliable.

When selecting a trolling motor for your boat, no matter the style of mount you choose, it's important to get the correct shaft length. Follow the manufacturer's recommendations and make sure that when properly installed on your boat, the trolling motor propeller can be set well below the water's surface. Minn Kota recommends that the top of the motor housing be at least 12 inches underwater to alleviate any problems with propeller ventilation.

Even though the Minn Kota RT80/S-3X was slightly outperformed by the MotorGuide SW82

HT and is about $40 more expensive, we think it handily beats the competition with a long list of exclusive features. We liked the long, adjustable tiller handle, tilting control head, built-in battery monitor, back-troll feature, and its 3X steering. These features make the product easier to use and more versatile, which is important given the wide variety of dinghies and sailboats aboard which it might be used.

Tiller Autopilots

Tiller pilots and cockpit-wheel pilots are the low-cost alternatives to belowdeck pilots that attach directly to the rudderstock and often employ hydraulic rams to provide turning power. Abovedeck pilots, on the other hand, use small, energy-efficient, high-speed, low-torque electrical motors. They are comparatively inexpensive but not as robust. Between the two, the tiller pilot has several distinct advantages over the wheel pilot: there's no belt to slip and much faster hard-over times. For these reasons, a good tiller pilot will probably do a better job steering your boat in sketchy conditions than a wheel pilot.

But what if your boat has wheel steering? Well, you might be able to rig the emergency tiller (and when was the last time you tried that?!) for attachment of a tiller pilot. When self-steering isn't needed, simply remove the tiller and the pilot and stow.

If buying a new boat, you might reconsider the tiller versus wheel question in light of the tiller pilot's superiority. Remember, however, that a boat that's easy for you to steer will also be easier for the autopilot. The converse, of course, also is true.

PS has tested autopilots throughout the years as these products have evolved and new models have come to the market. Most recently, the magazine tested four of the six tiller pilots available from Simrad and Raymarine (each company offers three). In our tests, which focused on pulling power and current draw, we examined Simrad's TP10 and TP30, and Raytheon's ST2000 Plus and ST4000 Plus. We left out the Raytheon 1000 Plus and the Simrad TP20. The apple among oranges was the ST4000, which is operated by a separately mounted display and has a fluxgate compass that must be located away from the drive unit. The ST4000 is designed

The tiller pilots that *PS* tested included these four models, from left to right: Simrad's TP10 and TP30, and Raytheon's ST2000 Plus and ST4000 Plus. Our testers felt that, if what you need is a simple helping hand and don't care about connecting to other instruments—or about a particularly rapid response on the helm—then Simrad's TP10 would make a good, sturdy choice.

to accept and process more sources of data than the other units; it's targeted more toward ocean passage-makers than the normal cruiser-racer. Even so, we were testing drive units, not peripheral functions, so we included it.

To derive our findings, we bench-tested these units. We hinged a tiller to an upright and put a bench underneath it. At one end of the bench we clamped a stack of wood with a hole drilled for the bearing cups that accept the pins at the outboard ends

of the pilots; at the other end we rigged a gantry with a hanging block through which we could swing 20-pound and 44-pound weights to oppose the pilots, while measuring hard-over times.

All the manuals were clear about how these units should be mounted in real boats. The watchwords are "straight" and "level." Understanding the variety of cockpit and tiller arrangements possible, as well as owner preferences, engineers for both companies provide plenty of mounting options and accessories to cover the gamut. In our tests the distances to the fuse panel, and thence to the battery, were short. We used 14-gauge wire throughout. We made repeated tests in series in order to account for the inaccuracies inherent in eyeballing the multimeter readings and in working a stopwatch with one hand while holding down the directional buttons on the tiller pilots with the other. We recorded the results of each series of tests separately, without reference to the performance of the other units tested.

▷ **The Bottom Line** If what you need is a simple helping hand and don't care about connecting to other instruments—or about a particularly rapid response on the helm—then Simrad's TP10 would make a good, sturdy choice. The price is right. It is controlled by five buttons on the keypad—one for calibration, one for toggling between Standby and Auto (a push of this one locks the boat onto the current course); two for course changes to port or starboard (one push gives a 1-degree change, a hold-down gives changes in 10-degree increments); and one for auto-tacking. For another $200 you could add interface capabilities and a bit more power by purchasing the TP20, but at that point we think it would be wise to spring

To test each tiller pilot, *PS* testers used a tiller mounted on a bench, linked to a gantry with a hanging block that supported 20-pound and 44-pound weights.

Tillerpilot Model	Simrad TP10	Autohelm ST2000 Plus	Simrad TP30	Autohelm ST4000 Plus
Mfg. Suggested Price	$620	$929	$1,075	$1,399
Average Discount Price	$395	$630	$670	$900
Drive System	Drivescrew	Recirculating ball	Recirculating ball	Recirculating ball
Max. Suggested Disp.	11,000 lbs.	10,000 lbs.	14,000 lbs.	14,300 lbs.*
Max. Suggested Boat Length	34'	36'	42'	45'
Max. Thrust Claimed	143 lbs.	170 lbs.	187 lbs.	185 lbs.
TEST DATA				
Operating Stroke	9.75"	9.38"	10"	10"
Electrical Consumption in Standby Mode; no load	0.06A	0.06A	0.08A	0.05A
Moving, no side force on tiller	1.57A	1.30A	1.07A	1.33A
Pulling, 20 lbs. side force	2.65A	2.20A	1.85A	3.43A
Pulling, 44 lbs. side force	3.80A	3.16A	2.74A	3.48A
MECHANICAL POWER AND SPEED				
Hard-over Time, no load	8.6 secs.	3.8 secs.	4.2 secs.	4.0 secs.
Hard-over Time, 20 lbs. side force	9.9 secs.	4.5 secs.	4.5 secs.	4.9 secs.
Hard-over Time, 4 lbs. side force	12.1 secs.	5.2 secs.	5.2 secs.	5.9 secs.

*20,000 lbs. with optional GP drive unit
Notes: 1. Amperage was recorded during the "pull" stroke. Current peaked as the pull started and varied by as much as half an amp through the pull, decreasing after the tiller had moved through the 'midships position. Data shown here is averaged from the draw near the 'midships position. 2. We used a new West Marine SeaVolt dual-purpose 65-amp-hour battery and charged it to 12.9 volts for the series of tests on each unit. All connections were made with 14-gauge wire. 3. For the weighted pulls we used a 20-lb. York dumbbell and a 44-lb. jerry jug of water (jug included), swung free through a ball-bearing block and tied straight to the tiller about 2" forward of the pin location. We took care to ensure that the pull from piston to block was straight. No account was made for the friction of the hoisting line through the block.

for a recirculating ball drive—either the Raytheon ST2000 or the Simrad TP30.

Between those two, the choice is difficult. The street price of the TP30 is currently a bit higher than that of the ST2000. The five-button control area on the TP30 is arguably simpler, although these are always matters of personal preference. Meanwhile the ST2000 offers a valuable information display. Both units are well engineered, both come with full interface capability, both are typically offered with handheld remote controls.

In our weighted pulling-power tests the two units were identical, with the TP30 having a slight edge in current consumption and operating piston length. According to the strict test parameters, then, the

Simrad TP30 gets the blue ribbon by a nose: It pulled a twitch farther in the same time, with less effort. It could, as noted earlier, benefit from a display.

Tiller Extensions

Despite the proliferation of wheel-steering systems aboard small sailboats, the traditional tiller is making a comeback. Tillers have some advantages. They are quick, virtually foolproof, and visually obvious as to whether the rudder is amidships, hard-over, or in-between. And, for the purist, a tiller also provides that heralded "feel" which tells you if the boat is making way gracefully or is struggling—constantly falling off or griping.

Often, to give a helmsman more choices about where to plant his weight—as ballast, for good visibility, or just for plain old comfort—a tiller usually needs an extension. Whether you call it a tiller extension or a hiking stick, these devices should have a universal joint and a good handle. We gathered up 16 of them for a close examination.

Competition in this realm is international, with one U.S. manufacturer (Forespar), three British (Spinlock, Holt Allen, and RWO), one Australian (Ronstan), and one French (Wichard). A fourth British maker, Barton, has a U.S. distributor that does not stock the company's tiller extensions. There also are a few long hiking sticks—GRP Arribas and aluminum Silver Sticks—in the catalog published by Murrays, a California firm that caters to fast catamaran owners.

With almost any brand of tiller extension you prefer, the manner in which the joint is attached to the tiller is a choice. These joints must swivel 360 degrees in a hemisphere above the tiller. The simplest and cheapest is an elastic joint (rubber, urethane or elastomeric polymer) that tends to make the tiller, when not in hand, stand straight up or wave around in a generally vertical position. The elastomer versions claim to be good for millions of bends before failing. RWO even offers two densities of the elastomer to provide more or less flexibility.

There are also stainless steel universal joints, a U-shaped hinge on a base with a post. There's a hang-up point, but it's rarely a bother. These two-hinge-post joints will outlast the wood into which are driven the customary two mounting screws (bolts are better).

Finally, there are, mostly on the more robust tiller extensions, the double-U joints; one with adjustable tension to make it stay where you last left it; the post-and-socket types; and several ball joints, all of which usually have one or more through-bolts.

A further refinement is the means used, usually an elastic pad or collar, to prevent the stick from dropping much below a horizontal position, where it can jam up against a coaming or a corner of a seat. The ideal is full, unfettered articulation through a hemisphere.

Consumers will have to determine whether to have a simple fixed-length hiking stick or one whose "reach" can be varied—quickly and easily while under way. The fixed-length sticks are generally the cheapest way to go. Forespar's very serviceable Swivel Stick, a black anodized aluminum tube with a foam-ball grip and an elastomer joint, is an example. Others are Ronstan's X-10 fixed, RWO's Fastac, and several new blue and white models from Wichard.

If you don't trust the trendy, thin, black-anodized aluminum tubes, there are fatter tubular models some made from composite materials. Various sizes and even do-it-yourself cut-to-length-and-glue models are included in the more exotic straight sticks, whose prices get up above $100 or more. Included in these premium versions are Ronstan's "Battlestik," a carbon fiber/Kevlar extension that can set you back more than $150; RWO's carbon fiber/GRP "Carbo Stik," another hot-dog stick that lists for $85; Forespar's "Ultimate Graphite" for $65; and Forespar's husky carbon fiber/Kevlar "Cobra Stick," whose price ranges from $78 to $168.

There are also several twist-lock models available if you prefer simple adjustability. Both Ronstan and Forespar make these. Forespar has a white-powder-coated aluminum stick in several sizes, with either a quick-release swivel that is first class or the patented StaFAST™ joint. Ronstan sells three sizes of its black anodized aluminum X-10 extendibles with several grip options and either elastomeric or stainless steel joints.

Twist-locks should never be lubricated. If we were to use one on a boat, we'd make sure it was demountable and stowed in a protected place when not in use—to prevent the accumulation of dirt, salt, and other crud that is bad for any twist-lock joint. Considering the options, twist-lock does not seem the best way to go with something that gets the continual stress involved with steering a boat.

High-end tiller extensions primarily consist of the powerful "ladder" and "saddle grip" type. The eight in our collection run in price from $86 up close to $300. The manufacturers make them brutally strong and seem to concentrate on comfortable grips on which the helmsman can use two hands, when needed. Also important, the tiller extensions for larger boats are, with one exception, extendable.

Ronstan's X-10 ladder extension comes in two fixed lengths and has a three-step ladder for gripping at different lengths. The black-anodized aluminum shaft is fluted for extra strength. The fairly hard Hyperlon on the three handle positions feels like it would last a long time. For the money, this simple Australian product is a lot of tiller extension.

The Wichard comes in two sizes, is moderately priced, has a comfortable molded saddle handle, plus a nice intermediate foam grip. The one-finger trigger, cleverly recessed in a crescent in the handle, works stainless steel stop pins. Both parts of the arm are powder-coated, and it seems likely that the paint on the smaller one will get worn and a bit unsightly. It comes with but one simple swivel.

The old reliable (but with a newly designed handle and a great new joint option) is Forespar's OceanRacer. Available to three extending ranges, this U.S.-made tiller extension has stainless steel adjustment pins; the adjustment mechanism is rugged, but a little balky. The OceanRacer is available with Forespar's StaFAST joint, which can easily be adjusted to have just enough tension to stay put when temporarily released. It's also available with a carbon fiber outer tube.

Somewhat similar (in that they use very modern, light materials) are the two British tiller extensions—RWO's Mighty Stik and the Spinlock, a new design that uses a common shaft, many joint options, and interchangeable handles to produce a range of extensions. RWO's Mighty Stik, with a trigger-finger extension mechanism with Torlon balls, is slick, the smoothest operating of the lot. It has a carbon-reinforced ball joint (they call it an Omniball) that rotates in any direction, has a rubber collar to preclude drooping, and even has a push-button Quickpin for easy demounting. The Mighty Stik comes in four extendible ranges and two fixed-length models. The Spinlock tiller extension, available in four lengths, is a shaft system with three easily changed handles (one straight, one saddle, and one asymmetrical saddle) and several stainless-steel-in-plastic-sleeve joints, all with two through-bolts (a good idea) and rubber cushions to prevent the handles from drooping. The extension mechanism is smooth, with push-button controls and Torlon balls.

▷ **The Bottom Line** Fixed-length tiller extensions made of aluminum tubing may well be adequate to the job. If price is important, any of the fixed-length models would do, as long as it's equipped with whatever grip and swivel you prefer and rated for your size vessel.

However, if you've ever seen aluminum tubing collapse when kinked even slightly, you might be, as are we, inclined to favor a straight stick made of sterner stuff—like carbon fiber, fiberglass (GRP), or Kevlar. Among such sticks, we favor Forespar's fat "Cobra," for its modest weight and price, but even more because it looks indestructible. We'd prefer it equipped with the StaFAST swivel.

However, unless we were still sailing a small one-design, the choice would be one of the extendible ladder/saddle models. The rugged, proven Forespar OceanRacer would get our vote if we were going to sea and absolute reliability ranked first. If it was coastal cruising, it would be tough to pass over RWO's very slick Mighty Stik with Omniball joint, but our choice is the new Spinlock, because of its excellent asymmetrical handle and the rubber-cushioned, stainless steel quick-release swivel.

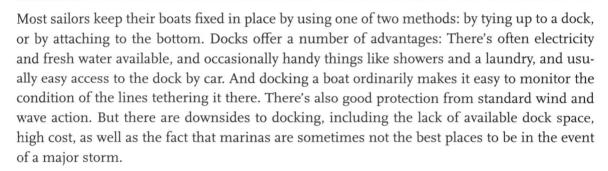

CHAPTER 7

Anchoring and Docking

Most sailors keep their boats fixed in place by using one of two methods: by tying up to a dock, or by attaching to the bottom. Docks offer a number of advantages: There's often electricity and fresh water available, and occasionally handy things like showers and a laundry, and usually easy access to the dock by car. And docking a boat ordinarily makes it easy to monitor the condition of the lines tethering it there. There's also good protection from standard wind and wave action. But there are downsides to docking, including the lack of available dock space, high cost, as well as the fact that marinas are sometimes not the best places to be in the event of a major storm.

Permanent moorings or well-tended anchors have two main advantages: They're relatively inexpensive in equipment terms, and they allow the boat to swing bow-on to the prevailing forces—usually wind, but often tide. This greatly reduces a number of stresses on the boat, as well as the dangers of dings and gouges from pilings and poor boat handling on the part of one's dockmates. But there are disadvantages, and chief among those is the corrosive nature of the elements that surround that single, slender tendril affixing your boat to the bottom. There are several components in a vessel's ground tackle system, all of which can fail. We'll start with one that's often overlooked, but shouldn't be. We're talking here about anchor and mooring chain. (We could make a crack here about weakest links, etc., right? But we won't. Too obvious.)

Anchor Chain

Our attention was forcefully drawn to the subject of chain when the one anchoring our paint test raft parted in a storm and we lost the raft. The chain was less than four years old, but our local dockmaster told us that our loss wasn't uncommon. Despite a compulsory inspection of mooring rigs every three years, one or more boats in that harbor lose their moorings each year. High time for investigation, we thought.

First, some background. A little cursory catalog research led us to five basic types of anchor chain: proof coil, BBB, high-test, vinyl-coated proof coil, and stainless steel proof coil; all except the stainless are zinc-coated using a hot-dip galvanizing process. The vinyl coating on the vinyl-coated chain is applied

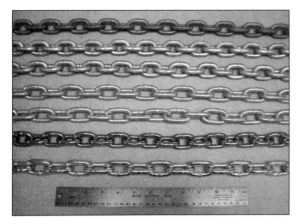

The mooring/anchor chains that *PS* tested most recently include, from top to bottom: Acco proof coil, Acco BBB, Acco Hi-Test, Campbell proof coil galvanized, imported Chinese proof coil galvanized, Suncor stainless steel, and Campbell proof coil zinc-plated.

after the chain is galvanized. While chains with other protective coatings, such as electro-galvanizing and cadmium plating, are available, they're generally unsuited for marine application, so we didn't test any of these.

Almost all chain used for permanent moorings is made of welded steel alloy, galvanized to forestall corrosion—not, in the long run, to prevent it. The common hot-dip process involves first "pickling" the raw welded chain in acid baths to clean it, then immersing it in molten zinc, which bonds metallurgically to the steel surface and forms a protective barrier. The zinc also acts as a sacrificial element against galvanic corrosion, an all-too-familiar process, especially in salt water.

This is a common refrain among the pros: American-made chain is good, or at least predictable, while imported chain can be a hit-or-miss proposition. There's a lot of imported chain on the market, but most is used for dry-land purposes like truck tie-downs and industrial applications.

Chain types are defined primarily by the length of the individual links. All our samples are open link. (Stud link is excellent but hard to find in the right sizes for yachts.) Proof coil chain is probably the most commonly used type for moorings, though its relatively long, open links may make it incompatible with some anchor windlasses. The link design is shared with vinyl-covered proof coil chain and stainless steel proof coil chain. BBB chain has thicker, shorter links. BBB chain is roughly 20 percent heavier than proof coil chain on a per-foot basis, but doesn't exhibit any improvement in tensile strength.

Proof coil chain, as well as its vinyl-covered sibling and BBB chain, is made of low-carbon steel—a tough, moderate-strength steel that tends to bend rather than break under severe load. High-test chain is made of a higher-carbon steel that gives it a higher strength/weight ratio than low-carbon steel. High-test chain has slightly longer links than BBB chain. High-test chain is about midway between proof coil and BBB in terms of strength for a given weight; it's about 50 percent stronger than either of the others on a per-foot basis. But if you're concerned about getting one or the other of these to match your windlass, don't worry. Most windlass manufacturers can match the wildcat to your chain. Still, it's wise to check before buying.

So, what's the main advantage of vinyl-coated chain? Its soft plastic coating won't mar a deck or gelcoat. Stainless steel proof coil chain has the obvious advantage of not rusting. It's midway between proof coil and high-test on a strength-per-foot basis; on a strength-per-pound basis (which is of relatively little importance in a mooring rode that doesn't get handled often) it's even stronger than high-test.

Now, a word about strength ratings. The strength of chain, like rope, is usually listed in two ways: breaking (or ultimate) strength, and working strength. The former is the load that will break a sample of new chain, in good condition, under laboratory conditions. Because chain, generally speaking, isn't new, isn't necessarily in good condition, and is seldom used under laboratory conditions, a "working load limit" is also supplied. This figure, about 25–30 percent of the chain's breaking strength, is the basis for selecting chain. It's not as conservative a derating factor as it appears: A chain's ultimate strength is only a valid number if there's no rust or corrosion of the chain.

In our test, we wanted to determine which types of chain are best; not in a brand-by-brand comparison, because chain is among the items not generally purchased by brand name. We ordered all our chain samples from the same catalog. All the chains were manufactured by the same manufacturer, Acco, the preeminent supplier of mooring chain to the recreational marine industry. Acco's galvanizing process is careful and costly, but effective at covering all cracks and crevices. This initial resistance to corrosion is what makes the difference in terms of longevity in the marine environment. (There are other domestic chain manufacturers, including Campbell [Cooper Hand Tools], Columbus McKinnon Corp., and Chicago Hardware & Fixture. Because marine chains conform to ISO standards, we'd expect other manufacturers' products to behave similarly to the ones we tested.)

We took a 15-foot length of ⁵/₁₆-inch chain of each of the five types, attached one end to a 75-pound mushroom anchor by means of a stainless steel swivel, attached the other end to a stout raft, and waited. The raft was moored in a shallow section of eastern Long Island Sound off the Connecticut shore in Captains Harbor. Mean low water depth here is about 3 feet, and tides average about 7 feet, so there's always enough slack in our mooring chain and a fairly extensive degree of abrasion between the chain and the bottom, as well as between sections of the chain. Every couple of months during the boating season (May to November) we went out and inspected the chain. During the off-season, when the raft was out of the water, we fastened the chains to 6-foot 2-by-4-inch winter sticks. At the end of a full year, we pulled the mushrooms and inspected the entire length of each chain.

While none of the chains failed, there were some dramatic indications of things to come—bad things. The vinyl-coated proof coil lost a significant amount of its coating along the entire section that was totally submerged. Worse, the underlying chain showed some very noticeable pitting. It appeared as though

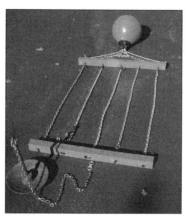

The *PS* test rig has the five galvanized in the middle, the zinc-plated chain at the buoy, and the stainless steel chain at the anchor. After six month's immersion, the Acco proof coil chain looked the best, and all the chains exhibited some corrosion or wear.

the vinyl coating, instead of providing additional protection, trapped water under the peeling plastic and made the situation worse. The most severe attack occurred in the 2 feet or so nearest to the surface. This contradicted prior experience in which the chain most often failed in the length that collapses on the bottom and continually lifts and falls with the tide; the reason is presumably due to the physical damage the chain caused itself.

The proof coil and BBB chain fared better. We found that each had sections with a rust-colored slime, but this wiped off easily, leaving a smooth, black finish with no perceptible pitting or roughness. The high-test chain stood up even better—in appearance, at least—retaining a smooth, black finish along its entire length.

The stainless steel proof coil showed no signs of corrosion whatsoever. It went in shiny; it came out shiny. It did, however, prove to be an excellent breeding ground for barnacles and, near the surface, seaweed. Apparently, the zinc on the surface of the galvanized chains dissolves sufficiently to provide an antifouling action; the stainless steel didn't. Growth on the chain didn't weaken it, but we expect that hard-shell mollusk growth buildup might eventually prevent the chain from flexing. And, of course, to handle such chain, you have to wear gloves.

▷ **The Bottom Line** As expected, vinyl-covered chain is not what you want for a mooring. It may have some application in a working anchor rode if used sparingly. Stainless steel proof coil appears to hold up best, if you can live with the wildlife that it collects. The other three chains are in the so-far-so-good class.

Possibly the most applicable criteria we garnered is cost versus strength. While there's really never a problem in selecting a strong chain, as long as weight and bulk aren't a consideration, heavier chains can cost considerably more per foot than lighter ones. In the chain size we tested, high-test chain is the clear winner, providing over a ton of breaking strength per dollar-foot of chain, as compared to 1,827 pounds for galvanized proof coil, 1,670 pounds for BBB, 618 pounds for stainless, and 616 pounds for vinyl-coated. Or, in other terms, if you're seeking a breaking strength of at least 10,000 pounds, you'd need to go to with ³⁄₈-inch chain in proof coil, BBB, or stainless (at per-foot prices of $5.49, $5.99, and $20.99 respectively), while you could achieve the same result (or better) with ⁵⁄₁₆-inch high-test at $5.99 per foot.

Anchors

Without really meaning to, over the past six plus years, *Practical Sailor* has acquired a considerable reputation for testing anchors. On more than a dozen occasions anchor makers have sent anchors to be included in these *PS* tests. When we first looked at this situation back in 1997, there had been dozens of tests run by manufacturers, other magazines, independent authors of books on the subject, and even government-allied groups. Among these were the French APAVE, the U.S. Navy tests, the RNLI (Royal National Lifeboat Institution) in England, the BOAT/U.S.-Cruising World magazine strength tests, the Dutch tests (done in a huge sandbox), the ongoing tests by naval architect and author, the late Robert A. Smith, and the extensive "Seattle Tests" co-sponsored by the Safety at Sea Committee of the Sailing Foundation and West Marine.

Close examination of the results of these tests, plus careful readings of books like Earl Hinz's *Complete Book of Anchoring & Mooring*, Don Bamford's *Anchoring*, and the revered *Chapman's Piloting*, suggested to us that the tests were too omnibus (in most cases, the bottom was not even known or varied). Generally, these tests tried to do too much.

In our due diligence, we also checked several other books for their respective guidance on anchor performance and use, including International Marine's *Small-Boat Seamanship Manual*, Brian Fagan's *Staying Put*, and John Rousmaniere's *The Annapolis Book of Seamanship*. All of these sources offer differing information regarding what type and size of anchor to use for a given vessel. We also consulted another

authority, Steve Dashew, who in his huge (1,232 pages) *Offshore Cruising Encyclopedia* tap-dances for a half dozen pages around the subject of anchor loads, but summarizes with: "You should carry the largest possible anchor and use it for everyday anchorages." He also "suggests" as a main anchor "the largest Bruce you can carry, twice the size of what everyone else suggests…," and a big Fortress as a second anchor. He also likes a chain rode. We think it's good, conservative advice.

Because of all the conflicting and imprecise data, we concluded that anchor testing should be broken into many sections that can be used by a boat owner to suit his or her needs. So, anchor testing should examine these principal areas:

1. Setting (if an anchor doesn't set, it isn't an anchor).
2. Holding (with dragging as a derivative).
3. Resetting (or holding) when veered.

And four other factors need to be considered: (1) difficulty of breaking the anchor out; (2) the anchor's weight; (3) the quality of the anchor as it pertains to long-term utility; and (4) the anchor's ease of handling and stowage.

We didn't get too far along in our assessment before we realized that the next question to grapple with is, of course, how do these anchors perform in different bottom conditions? Will the same anchor that holds well in fine and coarse sand get an equally good bite in solid mud, gravel, or that soupy ooze encountered in the tributaries of the Outer Banks of the Carolinas? That question led to the decision to conduct separate tests in clearly identified bottom conditions. Of course, you also have to factor in the kind of boat for which you're considering a particular anchor as well as that vessel's hull configuration and displacement, along with the wind and water conditions where you'll be anchoring. Those are, indeed, a lot of factors, but that's the nature of the beast. This is a topic fraught with variables.

For our first foray into the realm of anchor evaluation, we tested the initial setting ability of nine anchors in wet, packed sand. Setting is the key to any anchor's functionality. If an anchor doesn't set, we reasoned, it isn't an anchor. So, using a land-based winch with a rode led down the beach to our test specimens (and a Dillon dynamometer to gauge our pulling power), we repeatedly tested nine anchors in hard, wet sand on shore. Then, we moved them into the water and repeatedly tested them at scopes of 3:1, 5:1, and 7:1. To each we applied 200 pounds of pull and measured the distance required for that anchor to set.

The clear winner was the Bruce, followed, in the order of how they did, by the Super Max, Claw, Fortress FX-11, West Marine Performance2, Delta, Danforth 20-H, and CQR. We noted that in tests by other groups, the Bruce was not as good at ultimate holding power, but it was indeed (and still is) a ferocious setting anchor.

Our next test examined holding ability. Of the 15 anchors tested in that outing, two new ones—the French-built Spade Model 80 and the Bulwagga—did best, holding to 1,000 pounds and 880 pounds, respectively, as measured on our Dillon dynamometer. Then followed the CQR, Delta, Fortress, West Marine Performance2, Super Max, Danforth Deepset II, Bruce, Vetus, Claw, etc.

After that we conducted a test of 17 anchors in mud. This time the Barnacle and CQR anchors triumphed, followed by the Bulwagga, Spade, Danforth Deepset II, Delta, Vetus, Bruce, etc.

Then our testers examined the abilities of 18 anchors to reset themselves (in muddy sand) when set initially at 200 pounds, then veered 140 degrees and pulled again. The best in this test—those that reset with little or no breakout or movement—were the Bruce, the Fortress, the Super Max (with adjustable shank), and the Spade Model 80.

At that juncture, we added the Kingston QuickSet and Digger anchors to our group of specimens, and we modified our testing methodology by using a powerboat with twin Suzuki 90-horsepower outboards to do the pulling instead of a land-based

winch. In 8 to 9 feet of water over a sandy mud bottom, we found that the QuickSet lived up to its name, then held very well in a straight line, popping out at 600 pounds, then resetting and holding to 780 pounds before we backed off the throttles to keep from pulling cleats off the boat. The worst, we learned, was the Digger; we could not get it to set after many attempts.

Some of our test efforts to that point had been criticized because a number of the anchors involved had differing weights. However, that was essentially by design. Years before, we had deliberately decided to approach these tests from a consumer-advocate point of view. So, we devised a scenario wherein the boat these anchors were intended to be used aboard was a 30-foot displacement boat anchored in sheltered water, with up to 40 knots of wind blowing. We simply asked every anchor maker that submitted a specimen to furnish us with the proper anchor for that job. The first batch or two of anchors we gathered ranged in weight from about 10 pounds up to 35 pounds. But each of them, the makers told us, would do the job for our scenario.

Those disparities in weight revealed over the years that weight can make the difference in some

This group of anchors—one of numerous groupings that *PS* has tested (in this case in loose sand over packed sand)—includes, upper row, (left to right): the heavy stainless steel Wasi anchor with universal swivel, two HydroBubble anchors (only the larger one was tested), and the galvanized Davis Talon XT plow. The two anchors below are the Spade Oceane (left) and intriguing XYZ anchor (right).

Anchor Model	Price (Source)	Weight	Suggested Boat Length	Style	Set Rating 3:1 SCOPE	Holding Power 3:1 SCOPE	Set Rating 7:1 SCOPE	Holding Power 7:1 SCOPE
Bruce ✔	$169 (westmarine.com)	23 lbs.	28–32 ft.	Bruce	Excellent	450 lbs.	Excellent	450 lbs.
Barnacle	$179 (bluewaters.com)	29 lbs.	33–38 ft.	Single Fluke	Good	80 lbs.	Good	100 lbs.
Box	$179 (boatersworld.com)	25 lbs.	31–40 ft.	Hybrid	Good	100 lbs.	Good	100 lbs.
Lewmar Claw ★	$79 (westmarine.com)	22 lbs.	28–32 ft.	Bruce-style	Excellent	400 lbs.	Excellent	470 lbs.
Lewmar Delta Fast Set	$195 (boatersworld.com)	24 lbs.	25–41 ft.	Plow	Excellent	300 lbs.	Excellent	480 lbs.
Danforth Standard ✔	$69 (boatersworld.com)	16 lbs.	30–36 ft.	Danforth	Good	400 lbs.	Good	450 lbs.
Danforth Hi-Tensile ✔	$199 (boatersworld.com)	22 lbs.	30–36 ft.	Danforth	Good	400 lbs.	Good	425 lbs.
Danforth Hooker $	$34 (boatersworld.com)	17 lbs.	31–34 ft.	Danforth	Good	350 lbs.	Good	450 lbs.
Fortress FX-11	$129 (boatersworld.com)	7 lbs.	28–32 ft.	Danforth-style	Good	350 lbs.	Good	425 lbs.
Fortress FX-16	$189 (westmarine.com)	10 lbs.	33–38 ft.	Danforth-style	Good	375 lbs.	Good	350 lbs.
Fortress Guardian G-16	$109 (westmarine.com)	8 lbs.	28–33 ft.	Danforth-style	Good	400 lbs.	Fair	375 lbs.
Fortress Guardian G-23	$169 (westmarine.com)	12 lbs.	34–41 ft.	Danforth-style	Good	350 lbs.	Good	425 lbs.
Hans-C Hans-C	$149 (Hans C-Anchor)	15 lbs.	24–29 ft.	Hybrid twin fluke	Fair	60 lbs.	Good	380 lbs.
Kingston Quick Set	$169 (rivermarine.com)	22 lbs.	25–40 ft.	Plow	Fair	200 lbs.	Poor	0 lbs.
Sascot Plough 30	$199 (westmarine.com)	32 lbs.	20–34 ft.	Plow	Poor	0 lbs.	Good	125 lbs.
Spade Oceane 0-12	$189 (westmarine.com)	27 lbs.	25–28 ft.	Plow	Excellent	380 lbs.	Excellent	250 lbs.
West Marine Performance ✔	$189 (westmarine.com)	25 lbs.	30–44 ft.	Danforth-style	Fair	500 lbs.	Good	500 lbs.
West Marine Traditional ✔	$79 (westmarine.com)	24 lbs.	28–44 ft.	Danforth-style	Good	400 lbs.	Good	450 lbs.

$ Budget Buy   ✔ Recommended   ★ Best Choice

A top performer with a fair price, the Lewmar Claw is our best choice for soft mud. Of our recommended Danforth-style anchors, the West Marine Performance offers superior holding power, while the Hooker is easiest on the wallet.

These four plow-style anchors—from left: Lewmar's 22-pound Delta Fast Set, Kingston's nearly identical 22-pound QuickSet, the Spade Model 80, and the 35-pound CQR—are all well-established models. With the exception of the Kinston product, which didn't fare well in soft mud, these anchors have consistently performed well in *PS* tests.

instances—but so too can shape and design dynamics. We've seen the Spade Model 80, a large but lightweight aluminum anchor, perform consistently well. It's not the weight, but the shape that makes that anchor so functional, at least in the bottoms we've encountered. There are bottoms like packed sand covered with heavy grass in which the Spade might not get set well, but the 35-pound CQR would certainly bully its way down.

So it was that we instituted a further test—one conducted in soft, fine sand 15 inches thick, layered over hard, packed larger-grain sand. This test included anchors up to 58 pounds. We pared our number of specimens down to just 13 anchors by using representative models from each type of anchor (Danforth style with flukes, plow style, etc.) and introduced five new designs in that particular test: the XYZ Anchor from DI Research and Design, the HydroBubble from Anchor Concepts, the Oceane Anchor from the makers of the Spade, the all-stainless Wasi Anchor from SwissTech (our 58-pounder), and the Davis Talon XT.

Again, we used a boat and outboard motor to pull and set these anchors. For a rode, we used 10 feet of $^5/_{16}$-inch proof coil galvanized chain, shackled to $^5/_8$-inch Samson Braid. Each anchor was set at a 4:1 scope in the immediate vicinity of an anchored inflatable boat, which served as a support vessel for our SurfaceDive rig. This rig allowed a diver to remain on the bottom for the better part of the workday, observing the initial sets and subsequent pulls, and reporting on each via frequent trips to the surface.

As it turned out, these conditions were very good for setting, and very poor for holding. All 13 anchors

set quickly in the soft sand at a 4:1 scope. Then we applied our 90-degree veer tests, pulling this time with a land-based winch from the nearby wall of the canal. With minor exceptions, all 13 anchors stayed buried in the soft sand when they were veered. But as the winch applied pressure, only a few of the anchors could maintain a solid grip in the hard-packed sand underneath. Most were simply dragged—shank, flukes, and chain, still buried in the top layer of loose sand—across the hardscrabble underneath. The diver could see it happening, and our tester onshore could feel the chattering through the taut rode.

The XYZ Anchor (17 pounds), which looks more like a sculpture than an anchor, set and buried almost instantly, but it couldn't penetrate far into the harder substrate. The HydroBubble, which has a stainless plow, aluminum shank, and lead weighting in the plow, relies on an air-filled plastic bubble (flotation chamber) to keep it upright as it settles to

These three anchors, which take their basic form from the popular Bruce anchor (far left), have each performed reasonably well in *PS* tests. At the top is the adjustable-shanked Super Max 16, at the bottom is the Bruce look-alike that Lewmar markets as the Claw. *PS* testers recently labeled the Claw a bargain buy at $79.

HOLDING POWER

One obvious conclusion from *PS*'s testing is no secret: soft mud makes for lousy holding ground. Rather than dig in and hold tight, anchors, particularly plow types, do just that, they plow right through.

To get an idea of what level of security these tested anchors actually offer in soft mud, you need only consult the American Boat and Yacht Council's "Design Loads for Sizing Deck Hardware" which calculates the loads that ground tackle would transmit to the hardware to which it is attached in a given breeze. The table assumes the anchorage is sheltered, and takes into account yawing of up to 30-degrees off the wind. According to the ABYC, a "working anchor" should hold in 30 knots, and it calculates that the loads of various-size boats in this wind as the following: 20 feet, 360 pounds; 25 feet, 490 pounds; 30 feet, 700 pounds; 35 feet, 900 pounds; 40 feet, 1200 pounds; 50 feet, 1600 pounds; 60 feet, 2000 pounds.

Our best anchors met the ABYC'c definition of a "lunch hook," one that should hold in a 15 knots of breeze. The ABYC calculates that the corresponding loads under those conditions as: 20 feet, 90 pounds; 25 feet, 125 pounds; 30 feet, 175 pounds; 35 feet, 225 pounds; 40 feet, 300 pounds; 50 feet, 400 pounds; 60 feet, 500 pounds. The complete table appears in section H-40 of its *Standards and Technical Reports for Small Craft*, which you can download (for a fee) at *www.abycinc.org*.

---

the bottom. We tested a 16-pound model, which flew down to the bottom and buried smartly. But in our veer pull, it tipped over and wasn't able to penetrate far into the harder stuff. The Oceane is a heavier, galvanized alternative to the aluminum Spade. It, too, didn't perform as well in this test as its larger, lighter sibling and failed to penetrate the substrate. The 58-pound Wasi Anchor is extremely heavy. Its shank is tipped with a "Wasi Powerball" universal-joint swivel, also in solid stainless, and this anchor did bury and hold hard, using its weight to tip its sharp single point down into the hard sand. And the Davis Talon XT, 35-pound galvanized plow did quite well in the pull to determine holding power. It pulled to a maximum of 550 pounds.

This test taught us why the Danforth-type anchor has proven itself for decades in many conditions. We admit that the lightness of the Fortress version hasn't always been an advantage, but it sure didn't hurt in this test. And the Spade Model 80 performed admirably as well. If we anticipated anchoring a lot

in this kind of bottom, those are the two anchors we'd choose. Alternatively, we'd get the Spade and a heavier, galvanized Danforth type or a Bulwagga (in the 27-pound version) just because it doesn't seem versatile to carry only light aluminum anchors. It makes sense to have at least one anchor with some heft to it.

Lastly, our most recent evaluation looked at the performance of anchors set with a short scope in pudding-like soft mud, the kind you're apt to find in the Chesapeake Bay and other popular estuaries around the U.S. and elsewhere. Using first 3:1 then 7:1 scope, we tested 17 anchors that sell for no more than $200. Our group varied from twin-fluke, Danforth-style models to hunks of steel that resemble bear traps. We used this test to introduce several new models: The hinged-fluke Barnacle, the Box, the Bruce-like Claw, the Hooker, and the Sascot Plough.

"As it turns out," we wrote, "wacky-looking designs don't live up to their billing. Bruce-type anchors and

Danforth-style anchors seem the best for this sort of duty. However, when handicapped by the challenging conditions of our short-scope test, only the 25-pound West Marine High Performance anchor met the minimum holding power we'd need for a 30-foot cruiser, although it took several tries to set. In other words, if you value your boat, be wary of soft-mud-bottom anchorages, don't skimp on scope, and use heavy ground tackle—an all-chain rode would be a start."

As a group, the steel Danforth-style anchors did very well in the muck. Both anchors from West Marine and the pair of Danforth's from Tie Down Engineering performed best out of the twin-fluke group. All were relatively easy to set and provided good holding power. The genuine Bruce and its knock-off the Claw are right in there too. They set even better than the steel Danforths and held exceptionally well. We'd opt for any of these anchors as a mud hook, but given its $79 price tag and slightly better performance, the Claw is our top pick. For an even more inexpensive yet reliable option, the 17-pound Hooker yielded above-average performance results while carrying a price tag less than half of the next expensive anchor. It's a good bet that this anchor might not last as long as the more expensive models, but at $34, it's hands-down our Budget Buy.

Anchor Rode Kellets

What exactly does a kellet do? In deference to Earl Hinz and his authoritative work, THE COMPLETE BOOK OF ANCHORING AND MOORING, we'll offer his response: "Sometimes your available anchorage area may be just too small or the water too deep to let out all the scope you really need for the occasion. This situation will arise more frequently with the combination rope-chain rode than with the all-chain rode. The solution is to place a concentrated weight along the anchor rode that tells it to behave like a heavy chain rode. . . . The function of the kellet is to steepen the initial drop of the rode and to flatten out the rode on the sea bottom to decrease the anchor lead angle. A kellet should weigh about 25 to 30 pounds for a 40-foot boat, and it should be located so that it is about halfway along the rode from bow roller to anchor ring. If better holding is what you want, place the kellet closer to the anchor. If more cushioning of surges is needed, place the kellet slightly higher on the rode."

PS examined two readily available kellets: the 20-pound Rode Rider, sold by Ada Leisure Products, meant for rope only (3/8 to 3/4 inch diameter; $189.50); and the 30-pound Kiwi Anchor Rider, Model CAR 30, meant for both rope and chain rodes and boats up to 60 feet ($219). We were interested in seeing what would happen if we set an anchor and measured the pull it took to break it out, then reset it, rigged a kellet on the rode, and pulled again. Would the kellet make a difference? Would it help set an anchor in the first place?

Our "testing" of these two products got a bit absurd, as anchoring matters sometimes do. Armed with our trusty Dillon dynamometer, a willing crew, and capable powerboat, we made 16 to 20 sets (we lost count) with two anchors, in two locations, and only once

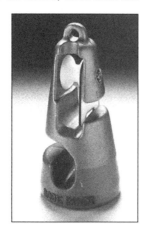

The 20-pound Rode Rider, which is meant to be used only on rope, is cast from bronze and has soft plastic adhered to its bottom so that it won't ding decks. We like all that, but it is on the expensive side at $189.50.

The Kiwi Anchor Rider is made of a heavy aluminum and zinc composite (non-magnetic and corrosion-resistant) and comes in models for chain or rope. It's made in 20-pound ($179) and 30-pound ($199) models and comes with a carrying handle and a 50-foot line for retrieval.

ADVICE ON ANCHOR SHACKLES

Some time ago, we were surprised to discover that the shackle pin on the high-tensile galvanized shackle connecting the anchor chain on one of our test boats to the 60-pound CQR was rusting after only six months of use. Fortunately, we could still get the shackle apart, and a careful examination with a high-powered magnifying glass revealed some disturbing problems.

Although the shackle bow is hot-dipped galvanized steel, the high-tensile shackle pin has a thin electrocoating that is unsuitable for prolonged immersion in salt water. After half a year, this coating had virtually vanished, and although the pin showed no structural wasting, it will have to be monitored, and replaced on a regular basis. Furthermore, it appeared that the threads in the shackle bow were recut after the bow was galvanized, and that area had no anticorrosion protection. By comparison, a different hot-dipped galvanized anchor shackle that we had previously used was still in perfect shape, with virtually no corrosion on the bow or the pin. This standard $^7/_{16}$-inch hot-dipped shackle was galvanized after all threads were cut.

The thread profiles on standard and high-tensile shackle pins are slightly different. Threads on both the pin and bow of the standard shackle are "softer" in profile, with more clearance to accommodate the roughness created in the galvanizing process. This makes it difficult—fortunately—to screw the high-tensile pin into the standard shackle, or the standard pin into the high-tensile shackle bow.

We originally chose these high-tensile galvanized shackles because their strength more closely matched the working load limit of our $^3/_8$-inch high-tensile galvanized chain. But we learned that a caveat must be added: if you use high-tensile shackles, you should lubricate the pin threads with waterproof grease prior to assembly, and disassemble them on a regular basis for inspection and relubrication. And for boats that live on the hook, particularly in tropical waters, this examination should take place at least every three months.

If you intend to use high-tensile galvanized shackles, carry plenty of them. You'll be replacing them much more frequently than standard galvanized anchor shackles. However, another option is to use a forged stainless steel shackle in place of a galvanized shackle. The best forged stainless shackles, hands down, are from Wichard. For $^3/_8$-inch high-tensile chain, you can use either the 10-millimeter bow shackle (part #1245), which has a working load limit of 4,190 pounds and a breaking strength of 9,480 pounds, or the 12-millimeter bow shackle (part #1246), with a working load limit of 5,730 pounds. The pin of the 12-millimeter shackle may be too large to fit through some $^3/_8$-inch chain. Of course, the downside of stainless steel shackles is that they will chafe the galvanizing off your chain and anchor. This will probably not present a structural compromise for the anchor, but could mean that you will need to cut off the last link of anchor chain every year or so—not a bad idea in any case.

Unless you use high-tensile chain, the best choice of all for anchor shackles is a U.S.-made, drop-forged, hot-dipped galvanized bow shackle meeting federal specifications as a Type IV shackle. Use one size larger than the nominal chain size—$^7/_{16}$-inch shackle with $^3/_8$-inch chain.

got what we could deem a quantifiable result—so it should be taken with a big chunk of salt.

Our findings emphasized that kellets can be helpful, not so much in high-load conditions, but in helping anchors set with limited scope and in iffy bottoms. Aside from weight, and the rope-only versus rope-and/or-chain difference, the two kellets are distinguished mostly by different design details. The smaller Rode Rider is made of cast bronze, which is both non-magnetic and virtually impervious to corrosion in salt or fresh water. The bottom is covered in soft plastic to keep it from dinging decks or woodwork. It has a hook cast in the bottom so that it can be hung temporarily on the bow rail while anchoring ops are underway. Height is 10.75 inches, diameter is 4.75 inches, and it comes for now in only the one size.

The Kiwi Anchor Rider is made of a heavy aluminum and zinc composite, also non-magnetic and corrosion-resistant. It has two halves, bolted together, and the top parts form a carrying handle—very convenient. The rode is inserted into the channel and the kellet is given a quarter-turn in order to seat the pulley on the rode. Then the locking lever (made of stainless steel) is put in place. A 50-foot line for lowering and retrieving the kellet is included, made up to the handle. The Kiwi also comes in models for rope rode only, the AR20 at 20 pounds ($179) and the AR30 at 30 pounds ($199).

We like the cast bronze and thoughtful anti-ding measures of the 20-pound Rode Rider, but the equivalent 20-pound Kiwi AR20 comes with the 50 feet of line, the carrying handle, and the stainless gate. It's also a bit less expensive. If you regularly anchor in places where you think you need a kellet, it makes sense to invest in one of these products. If you're apt to use one only occasionally, for about one-fifth the price you can make your own. Just purchase a stout canvas bag, add 15 feet of chain, a shackle, snap-hook, or carabiner, and a length of any old line. The beauty of this is that all these kelleting components can serve other purposes on board.

Anchor Rodes

What a sailor expects from a rope anchor rode is not very complicated. The rode should have great strength, stretch liberally, stoutly resist abrasion, be easy to handle, kink rarely, and never hockle. Although other newer kinds of man-made fibers might satisfy some of the requirements, the stretch requirement dictates the use of one of the oldest kinds of thermoplastic material—nylon.

This highly refined synthetic polyamide—very tough, very strong, very stretchy—comes in sheets, bristles, filaments, and fibers. It's the filament version we find so useful in making nylon line. In any form, nylon resists abrasion, ignores chemicals, is low in moisture absorbency, cares little about how it's stored, and doesn't get upset about mildew. So, it's just the ticket for an anchor rode—and much cheaper than an all-chain rode.

For this test, *PS* gathered up 17 kinds of nylon line from seven manufacturers. We examined laid and braid lines, both standard and premium, as well as one additional line—a single piece of polypropylene. This was partly out of curiosity, but also to discourage the use of this kind of line for anchoring. Then we subjected each to a stint on our abrasion machine. This 3-RPM device draws a sample of line over a sharp, stainless steel scraper under a 5-pound load imposed by shock cord. The loss of fiber is measured as a percentage of the original cross section.

Most anyone can pick up a piece of three-strand, twisted nylon and tell—by feel and by looking closely at its fibers—whether it was made by what is called a three-stage or four-stage process. Three-stage line usually is soft and limp. It's so limp, it's difficult to splice because the strands must be continually twisted while tucking. Four-stage rope, which includes a lot of extra bundling and twisting, is firmer, more compact, and has more twists in a given length.

Of course, any line can be made to appear firmer by setting up the machine to increase the twist and tension. The machine can be adjusted to produce a soft, medium, or hard "lay." Mountain climbers use hard line that is much stiffer than that usually chosen by a sailor. A cowboy's lariat is so hard and stiff (that's why he can lasso those frisky steers) that it can't really be knotted.

Single-braid or plaited line made of nylon is less susceptible to the soft–hard considerations. In fact, some of the loose braids, like Yale's Brait, make ideal anchor rodes with amazing energy-absorbing qualities. However, they still require careful manufacture to assure that each filament and strand has the same tension.

Although they are ideal for the purpose, braids and plaits are not used as anchor rodes nearly as often as laid line—the three-strand, twisted variety. It may be because braids and plaits are more expensive and are more difficult to splice, or that when someone sees a braided line, the assumption is that it's Dacron, which lacks the stretch to make a good anchor line.

Good nylon, however, stretches about 25 percent of its length at 50 percent of its breaking strength, and when very heavily loaded can visibly be seen to have a reduced diameter. Nylon line recovers from such loads better than any other line. Its only "negative" is that when wet, it temporarily loses about 15 percent of its strength. But with the safety margins usually selected by boat owners looking for a good anchor rode, that shouldn't matter much.

There are but a few manufacturers of the raw nylon filament, but each rope manufacturer boasts of combining a coating (to waterproof and lubricate the filament) and careful machine work to produce a balanced assembly that assures that every filament is doing equal duty. The coating, by the way, means that it's not a good idea to wash lines in detergent.

Generally speaking, nylon also has better abrasion resistance than other synthetics. There is a considerable difference of opinion about whether laid line resists chafe better than braid. The laid-line argument is that less of the surface of the line is in contact with whatever is trying to damage it. The braid makers claim that laid line tends to chafe because the high points of the strands concentrate the wear, whereas braid has a smooth even surface that spreads out the wear. However, compared with double-braid, laid line is stretchier, has superior chafe resistance, and is easier to splice. Braid is stronger (for a given size), stows better, and is nice to handle. Single-braid or plait is more difficult to splice, but stows well (because it is so limp) and is a whiz at handling shock loads.

If it's braid you prefer—and why not?—we'd be tempted, if we had a big boat, to use New England's handsome Mega Braid (⅝-inch is the smallest it comes). We'd also like to try a rode of Yale's Brait

(very similar in feel and appearance to Mega Braid), because Yale claims it has outstanding energy absorption (78 percent greater than laid line and 85 percent greater than double-braid). However, for braid, the conservative choice is Samson's 2-IN-1 double-braid, mostly because Samson seems to have the edge in abrasion resistance. It's expensive. For a lot less money, either Wellington's Braid-on-Braid or Samson's Super-Strong seems close enough in abrasion-resistance to earn a Best Buy classification.

If it's laid line you like, we think New England Ropes' Premium nylon is the best in the business. The line seems to have the right combination of coating and density to be nice to handle and easy to splice. Most importantly, for abrasion resistance, braid or laid, it's in a class by itself.

▷ **The Bottom Line** What's the ultimate choice for an anchor rode when it's 4:00 a.m. and your vessel is caught in an exposed anchorage with 4-foot swells and a 30-knot wind shrieking in the rigging? Ignoring any braid/laid preference, our choice would be New England Rope's Premium three-strand nylon, with any chafe point wrapped and taped with our favorite sacrificial chafe guard—torn-up strips of cotton toweling, tightly wrapped and taped securely at the ends. With chafe resistance superior to any other line, New England Premium is the one that will come closest to giving you what is hard to come by at anchor—a good night's sleep.

Chafing Gear

The most vulnerable spot in any anchor or mooring system never touches the water. It's actually where the anchor rode or mooring line climbs aboard the boat via a bow chock, which the French call a *galoche d'avant* and the Germans, whose marine terms surely are the most comical-looking, say, "*Bug-Aufklotzung.*"

Bow chocks come in numerous forms and designs, but there are few that are so foolproof that they won't cause some chafe to your anchor or mooring line. For ultimate peace of mind in these situations, there's only one source—good, reliable chafing gear.

In ye olden days, the drill was "worm, parcel, and serve," meaning that small line was fitted in the

STOWABLE FENDER

Whether you take a minimalist approach to sailing and limit the complexity of the maintenance and systems on your boat, or you're more inclined to swamp yourself in gadgetry, there are some things you simply can't do without. Fenders fall into this category. Even sailors who own small dry-sailed boats have need for a fender now and then, if only for those few moments when the vessel is tied to a dock while they're parking the car and trailer. But, the downside of owning fenders is that they inevitably occupy space, and space is almost always at a premium aboard sailboats.

That's one of the reasons we like the Easystow fender made by Seoladair in LaGrange, Illinois. We also like it because it's a simple, rugged device. It marries an inflatable composite film bladder with a thick extruded PVC exterior (reinforced with polyester fabric), and a screw-type valve. In several months of testing alongside a more conventional vinyl fender, the Easystow left no marks whereas its distant cousin did. The Easystow's no-marking exterior is a one-piece tube with no seams except at the top and the bottom of the fender, and those are capped with thick polyester webbing (with loops for attaching lines) that's sewn closed using industrial strength, UV-resistant thread. When inflated, these fenders take on a rectangular pillow

The Easystow Fender from Seoladair is a unique product given its shape and its ability to be stowed so easily. It's made of a durable extruded PVC exterior (reinforced with polyester fabric) surrounding an inflatable film bladder. The simple screw-type valve (inset) is protected by a flap of the same rugged material as the exterior. These fenders come in five different sizes.

shape. When deflated, they can be folded up into compact stacks.

Ted Corlett, who runs Seoladair, said his customers particularly like these fenders for protecting boats in storm conditions. Because of the fenders' pillow shape, they tend to stay in place and don't roll when set against a piling or dock.) One owner, said Corlett, even used an Easystow fender to jack up his onboard generator, because a conventional jack wouldn't fit in the limited space.

Easystow Fenders come in sizes ranging from 8 by 27 inches to 12 by 60 inches, and come in black, dark red, green, and blue. Corlett and his colleagues make both the standard fender and a heavy-duty line as well, the largest of which, he said, are popular with boat owners who use them in lieu of fender boards. The products range in price from $49 for the smallest standard fender to $179 for the largest heavy-duty one. Seoladair also sells fleece covers for each (from $22 to $50). The fenders are relatively light; the smallest one weighs just 3 pounds, 8 ounces. And Seoladair also offers a double-action pump with three different nozzle sizes for inflating the fenders ($12). Easystow Fenders are sold only through the company's website and at select boat shows.

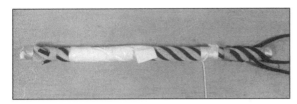

Chafe protection done the old-fashioned way with worming, parceling, and serving. The outer layer—the marling (in this case tape and twine)—was considered sacrificial to spare the actual line itself.

grooves of the anchor or mooring line, the bundle was wrapped with canvas, and the whole thing was tightly bound (or marled) with serving line. Sometimes the layers were tarred to make the whole section waterproof. The outer layer—the marling—was considered sacrificial and was redone as needed.

You can get an approximation of that old-fashioned chafing gear by just worming the standard three-strand nylon line and covering it with several layers of good-quality marine tape. The worming should be big enough to make the bundle as smooth and round as possible, with the worming standing a bit proud. The roundness doesn't reduce wear, but it discourages the wear from concentrating on one strand. Or you can opt to purchase purposely designed chafing gear. We tested 10 types. Eight of these are commercially available products—two hoses, four made of woven fabric, a sewn leather cover, and an expensive marine tape. Also included was a piece of common garden hose and a cover made of strips of an old towel, taped in place. The hose-type guards come either as slip-on tubes that must be positioned before any eyesplices are constructed, or as split extrusions that can be applied anytime. (The tubular hoses can be cut, of course, to permit installation, but, if done so, the line should be taped to preclude any sharp edges from sawing the line.) The woven material guards come as tubes or shapes considered removable because they are fixed in place with hook-and-loop edges. These are particularly useful when anchoring.

We first positioned and secured each piece of chafing gear on properly sized, three-strand nylon line, then we subjected each to *Practical Sailor*'s abrasion machine. We used a rod-like hacksaw blade as our abrader, and set up the machine so that the blade would move back and forth across each chafe guard in a perpendicular orientation. The blade is embedded with bits of tungsten carbide. In one direction, the stiff rod was lightly drawn sideways over the chafe guards, but the pressure on the return stroke was much heavier. Admittedly, this action isn't a substitute for what might happen in a real anchoring situation. If moored or anchored in difficult conditions, it seems likely that this much damage could be done in a few minutes. We subjected each chafe guard (or at least those that could withstand it) to eight hours of scraping, or 2,880 strokes.

▷ **The Bottom Line** So, which products fared best? In a little more than four hours, the blade sawed a narrow slit through the leather. The two layers of tape, applied in a spiral, lasted only an hour. The toweling wore through in six hours—probably because it had some flexibility to slip back and forth. So, what about the hoses and fabric tubes? The fabric guards fuzzed up; strands broke until the material was tattered and worn—sometimes completely through. The best of the fabric guards was the Davis removable, whose woven nylon was backed by a solid layer of "hook" material (part of the hook-and-loop fastening). It finished second.

Aside from the Davis removable, the natural or synthetic hoses generally performed considerably better than the fabric guards. Each behaved somewhat like a pencil eraser. Tiny bits of rubber were shaved off with each pass of the abrasive rod. After a few hours, the bits made a neat pile. These products lost the lowest percentage of wall thickness, with the neoprene Perma Buoy sample suffering less percentage loss than the rubber Seafit or the common garden hose.

For placement as needed to protect an anchor rode, it would be nice to have aboard the removable version of the nylon Davis guard. It's particularly helpful on lines with eyesplices, over which you can't slip a tube. On a rough night aboard, we'd inspect the guard fairly often.

For a mooring line or permanent docking lines, the test strongly suggests that flexible rubber or neoprene hose is by far the best. And, of the several versions, the Perma Buoy seems preferred—not only because of its thicker wall, but because it tested best against abrasion. Just check first to make sure it fits in your chock.

Power Windlasses

Around *Practical Sailor*'s offices, one test often leads to another. Guess what came to mind as we broke our backs all day in a recent anchor test? That's right—power windlasses.

Many, if not most, heavy-displacement cruising sailboats carry windlasses on the foredeck, but the decision whether to mount one on a smaller, lighter boat has to be based on several factors, including the size and type of anchor and rode used (a 35-pound CQR on an all-chain rode is a bit of a hardship to hoist bare-handed); the depth of the water and type of bottom in your anchoring grounds; how much electrical current you can spare; where to mount it; what kind of lead you'll have over the bow—and, of course, expense.

Windlasses are categorized as horizontal or vertical. Generally, a vertical windlass is mounted with its motor and electrical connections below decks. These windlasses ordinarily take up less deck space, and because most of the machinery is sealed out of the elements, they're more resistant to weather-related problems. Verticals also tend to have fewer problems with rope slippage because the rope passes through the gypsy for at least 180 degrees. Most horizontal windlass gypsies only have contact with the rope for 90 degrees of travel. However, vertical windlasses are usually more expensive than comparable horizontal windlasses.

Perhaps the most important difference between these two styles is the fact that a vertical windlass can accept leads from almost any side-to-side angle, while a horizontal windlass must have a lead straight from the bow roller. So, if you're in the market for a windlass, don't make a move until you've sussed out your mounting and lead situation. The lead must be fair, and you need to have sufficient space below decks for the motor on a vertical model.

Practical Sailor has tested power windlasses on numerous occasions. In each instance, we've evaluated these products by looking at several criteria. First, we assess their ease of installation, then we test their pulling ability—both loaded and unloaded—while keeping a close eye on their power consumption. We also take note of warranties and price.

During one of our early assessments, we gathered a field of four verticals and five horizontals, all but one under $1,000. This grouping included two verticals from Lewmar's Sprint series, the 400 and 600, and two of the company's horizontals, the Horizon 600 and 600GD. We also looked at three other horizontals, the Lofrans Dorado, the Muir 600 (slightly more than $1,000), and the Quick Genius 600, plus two other verticals, the Lofrans Marlin and Maxwell Freedom 500.

Our testing methodology, which has essentially been duplicated in all of our power windlass tests, involves mounting each unit (one at a time) on a plywood test deck screwed to the top of a stand that is firmly secured in place. Customarily, all electrical connections are made with the switches, solenoids, and circuit breakers provided with each windlass,

In one *PS* test of windlasses, our testers evaluated nine models—four with vertically oriented drums and five with horizontal ones. These products were, top row, left to right: the Quick Genius, the Muir 600, Lewmar's Horizon 600GD and Horizon 600; middle row, the Lofrans Dorado, Lewmar's Sprint 600, and the Lofrans Marlin; bottom row, the Maxwell Freedom 500, and Lewmar's Sprint 400.

Maker	Lewmar	Lewmar	Lewmar	Lewmar	Lofrans	Lofrans	Maxwell
Model	Sprint 400	Sprint 600	Horizon 600GD	Pro-Series 1000	Marlin	Dorado	Freedom 500
Type	Vertical	Vertical	Horizontal	Horizontal	Vertical	Horizontal	Vertical
Cost	$739	$929	$829	$769	$1,020	$915	$992
Power Rating (watts)	150	250	400	1,000	400	400	600
Circuit Breaker Rating (amps)	25	35	50	70	35	35	80
Warranty Period (years)	3	3	3	5	2	2	3
Adjustable Clutch	No	Yes	Yes	Yes	Yes	Yes	Yes
Claimed No Load Speed (ft./min.)	98	98	98	105	79	79	None Made
Tested No Load Speed (ft./min.)	99	85	99	83	58	62	112
No Load Current Draw (amps)	6.5	7.5	17	16.5	22	25	50
Claimed Working Speed (ft./min.)	70	82	89	88	46	46	45/62
Tested Working Speed (ft./min.)	60	60	69	57	45	48	105
Working Load Current Draw (amps)	22	25	35	35	32	35	75
Start-up Current Draw (amps)	61	73	136	187	85	95	210
Claimed Maximum Pull (lbs.)	400	600	625	1,000	695	695	500
Maximum Pull with Rope (lbs.)	500	640	600	430	550	550	550
Maximum Pull with Chain (lbs.)	800	900	900	1,400	Unit broke	1,000	650

and wires are sized according to the manufacturer's specifications. The power is supplied by marine batteries backed by a 35-amp power supply.

For this test and most of our other windlass tests, each windlass manufacturer sent its preferred rode, and that was led from the windlass through an anchor roller mounted several feet in front to simulate a boat's ground tackle setup. To obtain no-load measurements, about 60 feet of rode was stretched straight in front of the test stand. Then, we timed each windlass for 30 feet of retrieval, calculated the speed, and recorded current draw. For this working load test, we used a trailer as our anchor and timed how long it took each windlass to pull the trailer 30 feet up a slightly inclined pavement. Current draw was also recorded. It took 200 pounds of force to get the trailer moving and 100 pounds to keep it rolling.

Then we tested maximum-pull capacity by securing our dynamometer between the end of the chain rode and the trailer hitch on a pick-up truck. With rope in the gypsy and a small amount of slack in the line, we ran the windlass until either the rope slipped or the circuit breaker popped. Maximum pull was recorded in feet per minute (FPM). The test was repeated a second time with chain in the gypsy.

In that test, the Maxwell Freedom 500 won overall top honors due to its performance, construction, warranty, and price. This vertical windlass was the only one we tested that had a clutch handle which could double as a manual retrieve handle should the unit lose power. The Freedom 5000 achieves its high retrieve rates (112 FPM with no-load and 105 FPM with working load) by using a lot of electricity. The start-up current draw in the working load test was 210 amps, with continuous working amperage of 75 amps. We also like Lewmar's Horizon 600, which proved to be the top horizontal windlass in performance. It also carries a three-year warranty and is reasonably priced.

We followed that test with another that examined windlasses under $1,000. We included the same

Maxwell	Powerwinch	Quick	Quick	Quick
HRC8	40	Genius 600	Genius 1000	Crystal 1000
Horizontal	Horizontal	Horizontal	Horizontal	Vertical
$920	$999	$599	$749	$849
600	300	500	800	800
70	25	40	80	80
3	3	3	3	3
Yes	No	Yes	Yes	Yes
108	75	48	99	93
121	82	36	62	68
35	8.5	14	17	25
108	75	43	67	60
90	56	26	42	58
56	24	25	34	40
175	40	92	185	200
900	900	1496	1,984	1,808
1,100	450	250	620	1,500
1,170	600	1,070	1,520	1,500

adequate maximum-pull capability. However, if your use of a vertical windlass demands more pulling power than fast retrieve speeds, we'd opt for the brute strength of the Quick Crystal 1000. This windlass is a virtual stump puller with nearly three times the pulling power with rope or chain of the speedy Maxwell. It carries a three-year warranty and sells for $924.

If you just can't fit a motor and gearbox belowdecks on your vessel, then a horizontal windlass is the style for you. Among the horizontal windlasses we tested in this group, the Maxwell HRC8 is our top pick. It sped past all competitors in no-load speed testing and was only a bit slower than the Freedom 500 in working-load speeds. Plus, it has a powerful max pull with either rope or chain, and a three-year warranty. And, it's also about $70 less expensive.

Then it was time to turn our attention to windlasses for larger vessels. We gathered a group of seven vertical models, some of which are able to put more than a ton of force on an anchor rode. If you're

eight windlasses and added four more horizontal models and one vertical to the group. The new horizontal models included Lewmar's Pro-Series 1000, Maxwell's HRC8, Quick's Genius 1000, and the Powerwinch 40, and the vertical was Quick's Crystal 1000.

At the end of all our tugging and measuring, we still felt that Maxwell's Freedom 500 was the top choice for this price range and size if your boat has the space belowdecks to accommodate the machinery associated with a vertical windlass. This unit has high retrieve speeds, quality construction, easy installation, and a good warranty, along with

PS testers mounted each windlass in turn atop its custom-made test platform. To test maximum pull, a forklift was used (with chocked wheels) as an anchor. A Dillon dynamometer linked into the run of chain from the windlass to the forklift measured the pulling power in pounds. Here, Lewmar's V3 Gypsy undergoes testing.

CHOOSING A WINDLASS

There are a number of important considerations that go into choosing the proper windlass for your boat. First, you need to decide on the type and style. Is an electric windlass what you want, or are you fit enough—and are your vessel, anchor, and rode appropriately small enough—to handle a manually operated windlass? Will a horizontal windlass fit the space on your boat best, or should you opt for a vertical one? Then, do you want just a gypsy, or a gypsy and capstan combination, or just a capstan?

Those are each important questions, but also critical are the size of your boat and the weight of your anchor and rode, particularly the later. Most windlass manufacturers will specify a range of boat size for which their particular products are suited. Some also consider vessel displacement. But most companies will recommend that you choose a windlass with a maximum load (or pull) capacity that is at least three times that of the normal working load—the weight of your anchor tackle. For instance, if the primary anchor on your boat is a 40-lb. plow coupled to 250 feet of $\frac{5}{16}$" high-test chain, then you need to select a windlass with over 900 lbs. of pulling power (265 lbs. of chain plus a 40 lb. anchor equalls 350 lbs., and multiplied by 3, that's 915 lbs.). Lewmar, incidentally, recommends using a factor of 4 to determine the normal working load.

Remember that windlasses are not intended to pull boats against heavy winds and chop, but are specifically designed to raise the weight of a particular anchor and its attendant rode. They're also not designed to break out anchors that are heavily buried in mud or sand. That's a job for the momentum of the vessel under engine power. And windlasses are usually not designed to take the strain of the boat at anchor. For that there are chain stoppers and cleats.

looking to lift a hefty anchor set deep in a muddy bottom and then carry hundreds of pounds of chain, anchor, and mud to the surface, these are the tools you want.

Collectively, the windlasses we tested at this stage are suitable for a range of boats from 25 to 60 feet loa. They're priced from $1,300 to $3,400, and each has the ability to handle both chain and line. The test specimens included Lewmar's V2 Gypsy and V3 Gypsy, Lofrans' Project 1000 and Project 1500, Maxwell's Freedom 800 and Liberty RC2500, and Muir's Atlantic VRC1000.

Among the winches that sell for under $2,000, we were impressed by the Lofrans Project 1000 and the Maxwell Freedom 800. Both combine fast retrieve speeds and enough pulling power to lift a hefty anchor. They're reasonably priced, too (Lofrans is $1,320; Maxwell is $1,500). The Project 1000 is not perfect, though. We'd like a longer warranty and would prefer to see it ship with a remote switch and the appropriate circuit breaker. The Maxwell Freedom 800 is a tad faster, but trailed in the maximum-pull test. However, it comes standard with the needed installation items and has a three-year warranty, so we gave it our top honors and named the Lofrans, which we feel is an excellent choice for boats from 29 to 45 feet, as our Best Buy.

For windlasses priced over $2,000, our top pick was the Lewmar V3. It is quite fast under minimal load and only a few FPM slower than the fastest with a working load. Plus, it's smooth, quiet, and pulls like a 20-mule team. This windlass, which sells for $2,064, also comes with many accessories and carries a three-year warranty.

In our final effort, we concluded our winch evaluations by considering a trio of horizontal windlasses: Lewmar's H2 and H3 and Muir's Cougar HR1200. These heavyweight pullers are designed to handle relatively high loads aboard boats not well suited for a vertical windlass or where having a horizontal capstan would prove valuable for other winching duties. The windlasses ranged in price from $1,300 to $2,500 and are recommended for boats from 20 to 55 feet in length.

We again employed our "patented" windlass testing system to assess these units. Our initial impression was that we like the standard package of accessories Lewmar ships with the H-series windlasses, and it's hard to overlook the fact that the company backs these products up with an impressive three-year warranty. The performance of both the H2 and H3 was good, and our testers felt that they'd be happy to pay the few hundred extra dollars for the more powerful pull and faster retrieve speeds found on the H3. It was therefore our top pick among these hefty horizontals.

The Muir Cougar HR1200 is a well-built product, but we deemed the gypsy's inability to handle nylon rode under load unacceptable, particularly for owners who use anything but all-chain rodes. We wrote that "Muir needs to resolve this apparent design problem before we can recommend that windlass to anyone who intends to use a combination rope-and-chain rode."

Boat Poles

A strong, functional boathook is handy to have on board. And even nicer is its more versatile cousin, the boat pole; one that telescopes and accepts multiple heads for various specific functions. Hyped as space-saving tools that morph from hooks into mops, squeegees, and paddles, these poles are made by several companies. *PS* tested seven such products that telescope from 3 to 6 feet: Star brite's Extend-a-Brush, West Marine's Heavy Duty Pole, West Marine's Signature Series Pole, Taylor Made's C-Mates (one aluminum, one stainless), The Swobbit Perfect Pole, and the Shurhold Pole.

Telescoping poles differentiate themselves by their lock mechanisms, materials, and diameter. Twist-lock poles have an internal offset cam that locks and releases when the inner and outer tubes are counter-rotated. Pin-lock poles are secured via a pin in the inner tube that pops up through a hole in the outer tube. Poles are made of aluminum or stainless in $7/8$-inch and 1-inch diameters. *PS* tested these poles for strength, bending, deployment time, flotation, and corrosion resistance.

The twist-lock and pin-lock poles each have inherent advantages and disadvantages. The twist-lock designs are faster to deploy, don't come apart if extended too far, and can be extended by feel in darkness. But twist tools are friction-locked and may inadvertently collapse or extend when pushed or pulled during use as a boathook. If locked tightly, they can be difficult to unlock. Under pressure, people may confuse which way to twist and forget to lock them after extension.

Pin-lock tools withstand pushing and pulling forces well and lock securely. But, with the notable exception of one tool (the Perfect Pole), pin-locks

Boat poles need to stand up to heavy stresses yet be easy to manipulate and offer some versatility. That's a tall order, but the Swobbit Perfect Pole, shown here, is up to the task.

FENDER BOARDS

A reader once wrote to us for advice on fender boards for his 55-foot boat. He specifically wanted protection from the dirty pilings he anticipated tying up to on an impending trip to Nova Scotia.

There's no big mystery to fender boards, we told him. They can be as plain or fancy as you like, but plain is better. The idea is for the board to span the gap between two vertically hung fenders, and take the load of the piling along its length. Go with a soft wood like pine (no knots) for more cushioning, or a harder wood for more durability. We'd choose construction-grade pine planks. Length should be 4 to 6 feet (or whatever is convenient to stow on a particular boat). We advised him to radius the corners so they won't have any points to dig in or catch, and we instructed him to drill holes to accept the lines that would hang the board.

We also said he could paint or varnish the boards if he wanted them to last (and to make them easier to clean), but we advised not spending a lot of time on that as the boards would get trashed pretty quickly. You could also attach rubber strips or lengths of old fire hose to the boards, we told him, for extra cushioning and protection outboard.

It's likely that users of fender boards will hang them from the vessel's lifelines and stanchion bases, but if you take the time to set up a system where you can suspend everything from real cleats, or at least from preset shackles or clips on the toerail, life on board will ultimately be easier.

---

require you to look at the holes. In addition, some people have difficulty pushing in the pins far enough. Pin-locks are slower to deploy, come apart if extended too far, and, except for the Perfect Pole, can't be operated in darkness.

All of the tools we tested operated satisfactorily despite salt buildup. We did not have problems unlocking twist-lock tools with wet hands, although we did with soapy hands after wringing out a mop. Not surprisingly, the $7/8$-inch-diameter tools bend noticeably more than the 1-inch tools. And only one tool in our test group floats—the West Marine Signature Series.

Ultimately, there isn't an ideal telescoping pole, but MPS's Swobbit Perfect Pole comes close. When used as a boathook, you can operate it quickly by feel. It's strong and locks securely. It's the only pin-lock tool that can be telescoped in the dark. Although not as easy to extend as the twist-locks when used for cleaning, it's quick enough and ergonomic.

On the downside, it doesn't float, and it skips holes when extended quickly (the company is addressing that issue). Some people find it hard to push pins. Still, it would be our first choice, especially if you plan to use it primarily as a boathook.

Their light weight and ease of extension make the Star brite Extend-a-Brush and the West Marine tools good choices if primarily used as cleaning tools with occasional use as a boathook. If used as a boathook, they're more appropriate for smaller boats, or as a backup on a larger vessel.

Bear in mind that some poles are sold as a package with attachments nearly equal to the cost of the pole itself.

CHAPTER 8

Safety and Survival

There are many elements of safety for sailors to consider, and myriad products that support safe practices at sea. Though having and using the proper equipment is an important factor, safety on the water is equally reliant upon the proper outlook and the right knowledge. Perhaps chief among the many gems of advice any sailor can receive regarding this topic is that invaluable yet hackneyed phrase, "Stay with the boat." If you're attached to the boat, it's hard to be lost overboard, and going overboard is the primary culprit for loss of life among sailors. The U.S. Coast Guard estimates that a third of man-overboard incidents end in fatalities. And let it be clearly understood that the most seasoned offshore sailor can easily find him- or herself in just as much trouble as the least experienced amateur. All it takes is a lapse of judgment regarding safety.

Because safety pertains equally to mundane, non-life-threatening situations, in this chapter we've tried to address a broad spectrum of safety considerations for sailors. Let's start with gear that can help you stay on board, in this case, jacklines.

Jacklines

At sea, the most obvious way to stay attached to the boat is to wear a harness and to make sure you are hooked onto something strong enough to take the strain if you suddenly find yourself at the end of your tether. The offshore racing regulations are a good place to start for guidelines on these matters, and those regulations require jacklines to run the length of the boat, with an unobstructed route from bow to stern. Aboard most boats, jacklines are almost always made of flat webbing. The advantage of webbing is that it lies flat on the deck, and will not roll underfoot when you step on it. However, there are also some significant caveats when using webbing.

Webbing should be polyester, not nylon or polypropylene. It should have a minimum breaking strength of 6,000 pounds, and should have heavily stitched eyes at either end. You obviously must have strong points for attachment on the boat at either end like bow cleats or stout padeyes. Of course, the jacklines themselves must be somewhat shorter than the length between points of attachment to allow for a tensioning device. We recommend using small line like 1/4-inch Spectra cord at one end for this purpose. And keep in mind that when they're wet, webbing jacklines stretch dramatically. It's vitally important to keep jacklines tight to minimize the distance you will fall before fetching up.

While the jacklines offer good security when moving fore and aft, you should really clip to a fixed strong point when you're in a single location for an extended time, such as working on the bow, steering, or sitting near a winch to trim a sail. Make sure that what you clip into is capable of withstanding severe shock loads, like stout bails or firmly secured pad-eyes. You should be able to clip onto one of these strong points, or onto the jacklines, from the security of the companionway. Other than when working on the foredeck, you are most vulnerable to going overboard when coming on deck. And never attach yourself to your boat's lifelines. Despite the name, these lines can't be trusted to stay intact under severe loads.

Harness Tethers

PS regularly evaluates safety products. However, sometimes we defer to or collaborate with other organizations. Several years ago, the Sailing Foundation of Seattle instituted a test of 19 harnesses and tethers, and we shared the organization's findings with our readers. The tethers tested were from Captain Al's (Single and Three-point), Forespar (Passagemaker), Holland Yacht Equipment, Helly-Hansen (Three-point), Jim-Buoy, Lirakis, Raudaschl, SOSpenders (Three-point), Survival Technologies (Single and Shock Arrest), West Marine (four different models), Wichard (two different models), along with the Miller Industrial 216 M. (A three-point tether is actually two tethers conjoined, with three total attachment points, one at each end and one at the harness.)

To conduct dynamic load testing, each tether was attached to a harness on a 220-pound dummy and dropped 6.6 feet. Each harness and tether was soaked in water before the test, per the ORC regulation. It should be noted that this improves the shock-absorbing qualities of nylon webbing. Failure criteria include "flaws, defects, or deterioration after testing that would jeopardize the safety of the wearer." There were some harnesses and tethers that either had bent or slightly deformed hardware

and one instance where the webbing was shredded, but the equipment held. Still, fully 47 percent of these devices failed in such a way as to endanger the wearer. That's an alarming rate of failure.

Only the following tethers passed without failures: Jim-Buoy, Lirakis Newport, SOSpenders, Survival Technologies (6-foot and Shock Arrest), West Marine 6-foot tether with snapshackle, West Marine 6-foot basic tether, West Marine 6-foot tether with snapshackle and Gibb Hook, Wichard Model 7015 tether, and the Miller 216 M.

PS generally considers a tether with a quick-release shackle at the inboard end to be an important feature; however, we tried to test as broad a spectrum of hardware as possible to see if there might be any lessons learned. We did come to this conclusion: Quick-release snapshackles are robust, as are the locking, gated snaphooks (the Wichard and Gibb hooks). Snaphooks without a gate, even the well-respected Wichard forged models, and most of the other non-locking hardware, have too high a failure rate to trust your life to them. Also, snaphooks have been known to pick up a lazy jibsheet while walking along the deck, and can come undone if twisted on a padeye. And some tethers have quick-release hardware; others do not. When wearing a tether without a quick-release, crew should always have a knife within easy reach in case they get trapped and need to release themselves.

Our ideal tether would have a quick-release snapshackle at the inboard end, and both a 3-foot and 6-foot leg. The 6-foot leg might have some shock cord built into it to help keep it from getting in the way while working on deck. One skipper in the 1998 Sydney-to-Hobart Race thought it ridiculous that his crew had to unhook from a windward padeye, and drop knee-deep into water on the leeward side before finding a padeye and then easing a sheet. A dual tether would have solved that problem. The boat end of the tether would have either the new Wichard patented locking snaphook or the Gibb snaphook with locking gate, which is preferable to a snapshackle that may take two hands to attach. The stitching would be at a minimum 2 or 3 inches long, and a contrasting color to the webbing for easy inspection. The snapshackle would have a very substantial cotter ring, and the release line would have an easy-to-grip feature such as a plastic ball. At the time of this test, none of the test specimens had all those features.

Safety Harnesses

The Sailing Foundation of Seattle also conducted comprehensive tests on harnesses, both conventional ones and inflatable PFDs that double as harnesses. This test consisted of three elements: an in-the-water test to determine towing characteristics; a static test to determine comfort and ease of use; and a dynamic load test to ascertain compliance with ORC regulations. The harnesses were also evaluated for desirable features such as reflective tape, stitching, quick-release capability, and general quality. For comparison, several rock-climbing and industrial harnesses were also examined.

Testing consisted of both subjective and objective criteria. The former was mostly an evaluation of comfort and ease of use and adjustment, and how well the harnesses worked while the wearer was being dragged through the water. When used while being towed through the water, most of the harnesses were fairly comfortable. The exception occurred when a Type III PFD was worn underneath each harness. The PFD kept the support straps from riding up under the armpits, which placed the load heavily on the lower back and caused quite a bit of discomfort. The sailing harnesses did a good job of keeping the wearer's head above water, while the rock-climbing and industrial harnesses did not. The objective criteria consisted of weight, magnetic properties, and a dynamic load test where the harness or tether is attached to a 220-pound dummy and dropped 6.6 feet. It was this last area of dynamic testing that yielded the most noteworthy results. Of the 22 harnesses tested, two failed, though one was a prototype. And none of the harnesses met the committee's criteria of an "ideal" harness, although several came close.

Among the regular harnesses were models from Holland Yacht Equipment, Captain Al's (which was identical to the Holland Yacht Equipment model), Gill, Forespar, Jim-Buoy, Lirakis, Musto, Raudaschl, Survival Technologies (two models), and West Marine (three models).

The ideal conventional harness would be easy to adjust and lightweight. It would be easy to don and not be too hot. It should have reflective tape on the shoulders and a place to attach or stow extra gear, such as a whistle, strobe light, and a flare. We prefer two attachment rings for redundancy. Again, the

This sailor is demonstrating the proper way to clip his harness tether into the weather side jackline that's just visible running alongside the coaming. If he were actually under way at sea and fell, the fact that he's clipped into the weather side would keep him from going very far to leeward.

What this sailor is wearing is actually a combination auto-inflatable PFD and harness. He's using a single snap-in tether, but many offshore sailors prefer to use two tethers.

stitching would be a contrasting color from the webbing for easy inspection, and the material would be supple for comfort on bare skin. None of the harnesses we tested fit all these wishes, although the Raudaschl, Survival Technologies Deck Pro and Pelican 2, and the West Marine Ultimate did come close.

The best scenario for most sailors, however, is a harness with built-in inflation. All the inflatable ones that were tested turned out to be good products, although the Stearns 1143 seemed to lack sufficient hook-and-loop material to hold it closed, and the Survival Technologies seemed stiff compared to the others. There are advantages and disadvantages to having automatic inflation. Obviously, automatic inflation gives you a better chance if you get knocked unconscious while going overboard.

Among the best-performing inflatable harnesses were the SOSpenders 38MHAR-P-1, and the West Marine Ultimate Harness. The Jim-Buoy 922 was the one that failed. Its webbing gave way in the dynamic tests, and the weld on its D-ring had begun to crack.

Lifelines

Lifelines, stanchions, and pulpits are an integral part of any boat's crew-overboard prevention system. The weakest link in the lifeline chain is, almost inevitably, the lifeline wire. Unfortunately, vinyl-coated 7x7 stainless steel wire is a poor choice for this task. The reason is simple: the vinyl coating can trap water, which then wicks along the wire. This can lead to accelerated corrosion of the wire, dramatically decreasing its strength. And the corrosion will not necessarily be visible, as it can be hidden under the vinyl coating.

Coated lifeline wire is generally made from type 302/304 stainless. For uncoated standing rigging, type 304 stainless offers adequate corrosion resistance, although it is less corrosion-resistant than type 316 stainless. But type 316 stainless steel wire has its own shortcomings: it is both significantly more expensive and weaker than type 304 stainless wire of the same diameter.

Switching to bare 316 wire of the same diameter would increase the wire cost for a basic 40-foot boat by only about $25. However, bare wire of this size is hard on the hands, and the lower strength of type 316 wire would make lifelines of this size marginal in strength. Instead, for lifeline use you should increase the bare-wire diameter to $1/4$ inch for the upper wire and $3/16$ inch for the lower wire. This would add about $100 to the cost of the wire for a 40-footer. And, you also have to consider that the end fittings for larger-diameter wire are somewhat more expensive.

Going up in diameter improves the feel of the wire and gives you an additional safety margin. Your basic $3/16$-inch coated lifeline wire has a breaking strength of 3,700 pounds. Bare type 316 wire $1/4$ inch in diameter has a breaking strength of 6,900 pounds, a comfortable increase.

If you must have coated lifelines, we would recommend replacing them if they are more than five years old. With new coated lifeline wire, we would protect the interface between the wire and any end

With just a single set of lifelines running around the periphery of this boat, the sailors on board are at greater risk than if the boat had both upper and lower lifelines, which is conventional.

terminal by using adhesive-lined heat-shrink tubing over the joint, installing this before the lifelines are ever exposed to any moisture. Do not use heat-shrink tubing without adhesive, as this may still allow moisture penetration.

It should go without saying that lifeline stanchions, bases, and pulpits must be strong. We would recommend that upper lifelines and pulpit rails be at least 28 inches off the deck on any boat used in exposed waters. However, taller stanchions are more susceptible to bending than shorter stanchions, since the lever arm of the stanchion is substantially longer.

And whether they're cast or welded, stanchion bases should have strong bracing bails. Of course, stanchion bases and pulpits must be strongly through-bolted, with substantial backing plates.

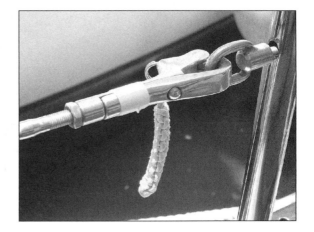

Lifeline attachment points, like this pelican hook, need to be secured when under way. *PS* has long favored taping pelican hooks in this fashion so that there is less chance they'll inadvertently be released.

Personal Flotation Devices

TYPE IV THROWABLE PFDS

Each year in the U.S., there are numerous man-overboard incidents, and not all of them end happily. If someone goes over the side unnoticed from a boat moving at 6 knots, he or she will be a football field away in 30 seconds. Let's hope they're wearing a personal flotation device (PFD). Meanwhile, assuming that someone on board did notice them go overboard, and the person in the water didn't have a PFD, one of the principal considerations is to get flotation to the victim as quickly as possible.

PS has tested a number of throwable, Type IV devices (which the Coast Guard requires be on board every vessel). In one evaluation, we checked out a new cushion developed by two Californians, Don Anderson and Jim Way. It's called the Lifeline PFD. It looks like a standard boat cushion but has a Velcro-closed pouch on one side that stores 42 feet of polypropylene line. The cushion end is spliced into a loop of webbing, heavily sewn on both ends inside

the cushion. The far end also has a spliced loop for the tosser to hold. The Lifeline is U.S. Coast Guard approved. We also tested throwable cushions from Kent and Stearns, along with two life rings (24 and 30 inches) made by Jim-Buoy, and two horseshoe rings, one from Jim-Buoy and one from Forespar.

The hands-down winner of the distance toss was the white Jim-Buoy life ring. It has the best combination of weight and aerodynamic ability, and flew well when tossed with a backhand throw, more or less like a Frisbee. Two of the tosses took it to about 40 feet, directly upwind, with decent accuracy, and two of the crosswind tosses took it to about 60 feet with decent accuracy. The orange Jim-Buoy life ring was also good at flying, but it was just too hefty to make it as far. The best toss for that was about 35 feet, with decent accuracy. Most tosses were in the 25-foot range.

The Jim-Buoy and Forespar horseshoes both tossed surprisingly well, although technique varied. Some throws were backhands, some were discuss-style. The best tosses seemed to be with a grip on the fastened cross-strap, but in an emergency situation that strap would probably be undone after the horseshoe came out of its bracket.

The Jim-Buoy horseshoe is a bit larger than the Forespar, and filled with hard Styrofoam. The Forespar is filled with softer foam. There was some debate about which tossed easier, but they performed about the same. Most tosses were in the 40-foot range upwind, and slightly better crosswind, with decent accuracy.

In the cushion competition, we weren't very surprised to confirm that these suckers just plain don't fly, either upwind

PS testers threw rings, horeshoes, and cushions upwind along a 50-foot range in moderate breeze. The Jim-Buoy 30-inch ring, shown here, had the best buoyancy of any device in our test, but it's too bulky to throw very far, especially from a smaller boat.

Manufacturer/Brand	Price	Dimensions	Weight	Throw Rating	In-water Effectiveness/ Fit	Comments
CUSHIONS						
Lifeline PFD	$26–$30	15" x 15" x 2¾"	1¼ lbs.	Good	Good	Versatile, good all-around device, well-made, one solid piece of foam inside
Kent cushion	$10	15" x 15" x 2¾"	1½ lbs.	Fair	Fair	Standard boat cushion, multiple layers of foam
Stearns cushion	$15†	16" x 15' x 2½"	1½ lbs.	Poor	Fair	Also standard with multiple foam layers, but looser cover makes it too flexible and slippery
HORSESHOES						
Cal-June Jim-Buoy 920	$52†	23½" x 23½" x 4¼"	3¼ lbs.	Good	Excellent	Hard foam inside, excellent buoyancy, throws well
Forespar Horseshoe Buoy	$80	22½" x 22" x 23"	2¼ lbs.	Good	Excellent	Softer foam interior, very well made, throws well, good buoyancy
RINGS						
Cal-June Jim-Buoy 30	$48†	30" diameter	5½ lbs.	Good	Excellent	Top buoyancy in test, too bulky to throw far.
Cal-June Jim-Buoy 24	$58†	24" diameter	2½ lbs.	Excellent	Excellent	Throw-distance record holder, good buoyancy; excellent in water
THROW ROPES						
West Marine‡	$45	50' line	1 lbs.	Excellent	NA	Excellent accuracy, same as SOSpenders but overpriced
SOSpenders	$40†	70' line	1¼ lbs.	Excellent	NA	Excellent accuracy, best price
Forespar	$44*	70' line	1¾ lbs.	Good	NA	Excellent accuracy, bag more water-resistant, lacks tube-covered MOB grip, heavier to throw

*Retail price, all others are in store or catalog prices. †BoatU.S. 2002 catalog price—less expensive than West Marine 2002 catalog price.
‡West has improved the 70' model with reflective tape and a bright day-glow bag.

or crosswind. In fact, in some of the early upwind throws we were lucky not to have them land behind the tossing point. They toss better downwind, of course, but don't have enough mass to stay aloft for long, and it was hard not to throw them wild.

The best among these devices was the Lifeline. It was the most rigid of the three, and flew farthest, even with its line attached. In fact, it had a couple of fairly decent flights, and might have even traveled farther than its 42-foot line permitted it. We were surprised to see the thin polypropylene pay out as well as it did; we never encountered any significant snarls.

We also evaluated these products from the victim's point of view in the water. While all Type IV devices are intended for use in quick recoveries, things don't always work out that way, and often MOBs are in the water for a long time. Logic suggests that the big orange Jim-Buoy ring would walk away with that award—it had the greatest buoyancy of all the devices. However, it was actually too big to offer a close fit, and a close fit in these matters is a good thing. The white Forespar ring, the Jim-Buoy horseshoe, and the Forespar horseshoe were better at offering a sense of security in that regard. Among those, it was tougher to choose.

The tricky part was figuring out the best ways to hang on to the things. You're not supposed to wear them, just hold them—but of course most people will try to wear them somehow anyway. A medium-sized man can fit through the hole in the Forespar ring, but a man bigger than about size 40 will have a tough time. That leaves what—a head and one arm? Or lying across the ring, forearms folded? The horseshoes offer more options—lying backward in the curve, lying forward in the curve, lying on top with arms folded across, etc. One swimmer even found it comfortable to lie backward in the curve with both knees supported against the buckled strap.

The Lifeline PFD, which resembles a standard boat cushion, but has a pouch on the side that stores 42 feet of polypropylene line, was among our top performers. It had no trouble traveling 40 feet despite carrying the line.

Among the cushions, the winner again was the new Lifeline. Being stiffer, it was easier to maneuver in the water, yet it was still flexible enough to conform to the curve of the swimmer's body, offering steadier support. Its self-draining pouch also retained some water after each toss, which had the effect of slowing its speed across the surface in the wind, and making it act like a mini-drogue.

▷ **The Bottom Line** Of the two life rings, we prefer the smaller Jim-Buoy unit. Between the horseshoes, it's a toss-up. The Forespar is very nicely built and slightly easier to work with; the Jim-Buoy has a more utilitarian look and greater buoyancy. They performed about the same in the toss testing and in the water with the swimmers; however, the Jim-Buoy has better buoyancy and costs less.

Among the cushions there's a clear winner, at least if you intend to rely on a cushion as a Type IV device: the Lifeline cushion. As one tester said, "It doesn't do anything really well, but it does everything pretty well. If I had to pick only one of all these things, I'd pick that."

BELT-STYLE INFLATABLE PFDS

Belt-style inflatable life jackets are no doubt the most comfortable personal flotation devices (PFDs) on the market. They weigh only a few pounds, and as their name indicates, you simply strap them around your waist like a fanny pack. The rolled-up package that holds the belt's inflatable chamber(s) is intended to sit just below your belly button, protruding only a few inches. Belt-style inflatables also can be had for under $60, which is roughly a third of the cost of some vests. But—and this is a big but—some of these comfortable and cheap belts have limited buoyancy ratings, which makes a significant difference if you've fallen overboard and are struggling to find your next breath. And there's one important caveat with these devices: Because someone who is injured while falling overboard may not be able to don a belt-style inflatable PFD, we don't feel these devices are preferable to those worn as vests.

All belt-style inflatable PFDs are limited to Type III classification by the U.S. Coast Guard, even if they meet the automatic deployment and buoyancy requirements of the higher rating. Why? Because the user has to put on the inflated device after it's inflated.

In a recent test, *PS* evaluated belt-style inflatable PFDs from four manufacturers: Mustang (MD3025), Seapro (SSB25), SOSpenders (38MBP), and Stearns (340 and 375), all of which are manually deployed. We also examined Stearns' auto/manual belt, the 575 and a manual unit from West Marine (Manual Inflatable Belt Pack, model No. 3742103), which is manufactured by SOSpenders.

The size and shape of the belt packs vary widely. The manual firing mechanisms used on all but one

Brand Name	Crewsaver Crewfit	Crewsaver Crewfit	Mustang AirForce	Mustang AirForce	Stearns Ultra 4000	*SOSpenders World Class	SOSpenders Sailing Series	SOSpenders Sailing Series
Model	275N	150N	MD3003	MD3031	1439	38A LNG	38M HRN	38A HRN
USCG Approved Type	N/A	N/A	5	5	5	5	5	5
Operation	Auto/Man	Auto/Man	Man	Auto/Man	Auto/Man	Auto/Man	Man	Auto/Man
Chest Size (inches)	34–50	34–50	30–52	30–52	30–52	30–52	30–52	30–52
Weight (pounds)	>88	>88	>80	>80	>90	>80	>80	>80
Buoyancy (pounds)	61.8	33.7	33.7	33.7	33.7	35	35	35
Cylinder Size (grams)	60	33	33	33	33	38	38	38
Number of D-Rings	1	0	0	0	0	0	2	2
Reflective Tape (sq. inches)	86	48	46	46	22	12	12	12
Warranty Period (years)	3	3	1	1	None	1	1	1
Price	$274.65	$164.52	$109.95	$159.95	$151.25	$113.88	$119.60	$139.95
Re-Arm Kit Price	$35.05	$27.63	$19.27	$24.36	$24.99	$15.21	$12.03	$15.21
Price Source	High Seas	High Seas	pyacht.com	pyacht.com	westpac marine.com	pyacht.com	pyacht.com	pyacht.com

RATINGS

Donning Ease (On/Off)	Fair	Good	Good	Good	Good	Good	Excellent	Excellent
Comfort/Fit on Land	Good	Good	Good	Fair	Good	Good	Good	Good
Comfort/Fit in Water	Good	Excellent	Good	Good	Fair	Fair	Fair	Fair
Re-Arming/Repacking	Good	Excellent	Excellent	Excellent	Excellent	Good	Good	Good

*West Marine model 5328786 is the same as the SOSpenders 38A LNG. It sells for $179.99 and $22.99 for the re-arming kit. Prices from westmarine.com

of the belts differ in detail, but operate on the same principle. The user pulls a cord connected to the mechanism that allows a pin to penetrate a CO_2 cylinder and inflate a bladder. Manual inflators are held to a strict inflation standard that requires they reach design buoyancy within five seconds of activation.

We rated each PFD for ease of donning—how easily did the buckles and waistband operate? Did they feel secure? Were they easy to adjust to the proper size? Did they slip? And once donned, the not-yet-inflated belts were rated for comfort and fit. To select an overall winner, we considered the ease of donning, comfort/fit on land, comfort/fit in water, ease of re-arming/repacking, and buoyancy. Warranty details were also taken into account. Additional testing included a spray test to determine if automatic deployment would occur in rain or sea spray.

We'd opt for the SOSpenders 38MBP because it delivers the most buoyancy for the dollar ($61). Other belt-style inflatables are slightly easier to don in the water and some are certainly a bit more comfortable to wear, but the SOSpenders performed best in real-world conditions, which were sloppy enough offshore to cause one of our testers to become seasick. The SOSpenders belt is also comfortable to wear on land and easy to adjust.

VEST-STYLE INFLATABLE PFDS

The U.S. Coast Guard estimates that more than half of the people who drown following a fall from a boat would have survived had they been wearing a personal flotation device (PFD). Unfortunately, standard life vests can be very uncomfortable and are thus not

THROW BAGS

Seamanship authority and occasional *PS* contributor John Rousmaniere maintains that one of the most important pieces of safety gear aboard any boat is a throw bag, and his advice regarding these products is, "buy one and practice throwing and repacking it with your crew..." Because contact with a person in the water is vital to successful man-overboard rescues, the importance of this advice cannot be overstated.

PS recently tested eight different throw bag products from seven manufacturers to offer advice on which ones work best and would be appropriate for certain vessels. Our test included one 50-foot bag—the Kwik Tek Life-line— and seven that are at least 55 feet long: the Marsars 2-in-1, the NRS Rescue and NRS Pro-Spectra, the Plastimo Rescue, Seattle Sports Co.'s Slant Six, Stearn's Rescue Mate, and West Marine's Deluxe Throw Rope. Our testers evaluated these products, which range from $11 to $70, for ease of deployment, accuracy, and distance by throwing them multiple times at a fixed target. We also examined the construction of each product.

The Seattle Sports Slant Six, Plastimo, Marsars, and NRS Rescue all performed well overall and have specific features that we like. (Most have reflective tape or patches and mesh drainage areas.) However, the Kwik Tek and the West Marine Deluxe were the best performers by a substantial margin.

PS testers evaluated eight different throw bag products with lines from 50 to 75 feet. Here, West Marine's Deluxe bag (70 feet) is about to get launched. That product was the smoothest operating, in deployment, retrieval, and repacking.

(The Stearns Rescue Mate was less than impressive because the line snagged several times while being deployed in our tests. We deemed that a matter of poor packing, and a strong example of why every owner of these devices should pack them him or herself.)

Those with lines that deployed most smoothly out of the bag—the Kwik Tek, Plastimo, and West Marine—do offer an advantage in accuracy and distance, but mostly on the first toss. On subsequent throws, all of the products suffer a loss of distance, and most a loss of accuracy.

We think some throw bags are better suited to certain boats. If you own a small boat, or you primarily use your boat for day trips, the inexpensive Kwik Tek Life-line would be the best product for your use, in our opinion. It consistently deployed well out of the bag and threw reasonably well when unpacked. It lacks drainage and doesn't have any reflective material, but at $11 it's a good value and our Budget Buy.

If you're an offshore boater, or your boat is longer than 30 feet, we think you'd be better served by a throw bag with mesh drainage and reflective material. Several of the bags we tested worked well enough, but we found West Marine's Deluxe Throw Rope to have the most consistent performance. Yes, at $66, it's the second most expensive, but we think it's worth it.

always worn by the average boater. In an effort to improve this situation, the U.S. Coast Guard began certifying inflatable PFDs as lightweight—though not inexpensive—alternatives to the bulky foam-flotation life jacket. Here's the bottom line: Because they're smaller and more comfortable, sailors are more likely to wear these devices more often.

Of course, inflatable PFDs come in two types: manually activated and automatically activated. Technically, according to Underwriters Laboratories Inc. (UL), which set the standards that PFD manufacturers must meet, the automatic inflatables are actually manually inflatable vests with automatic backup. That's not how they're being marketed in some cases, and not how the public perceives them.

According to U.S. Coast Guard/UL standards, an automatic inflatable must provide a minimum of 33.7 pounds of buoyancy, or 150 Newtons (1 Newton equals a mass of 1 kilogram times an acceleration of 1 meter per second). That sounds like a lot, since the average adult only needs 7 to 12 pounds of buoyancy to stay afloat in calm waters. But waters often aren't calm, and the extra buoyancy mandated for these devices keeps your head farther out of the water and away from waves; it also keeps you face up to prevent drowning even if you're unconscious. PFDs of this type must activate within 5 seconds of immersion

and inflate to the designed buoyancy level within 10 seconds.

Manually deployed inflatable devices with a Type III performance rating must provide 22.5 pounds of buoyancy (100 Newtons), but may offer more (we specify inflatable here because non-inflatable Type IIIs are only required to provide 15 pounds of flotation). Manuals are held to a stricter inflation standard than their auto-deploy brethren. They must reach designed buoyancy within 5 seconds of activation.

All Type V inflatables must also carry an oral-inflation tube for backup. As a protection against premature or inadvertent inflation, Type V PFDs must withstand 120°F temperatures at 80 percent humidity for seven days without self-inflating. (That's a sliding scale; at 90°F, the humidity would rise to 100 percent.)

PS gathered nine vest-style inflatable PFDs in adult sizes, leaning toward units with both automatic deployment capability and manual mode. Seven of the nine fit that description. These products ranged in price from $110 to $275. We obtained our specimens from four manufacturers: Mustang (the manual MD3003, and automatic MD3031), SOSpenders (the 38A LNG and the 38A HRN, both automatic, and the manual 38M HRN), Stearns (automatic Ultra 4000), UK-based Crewsaver (Crewfit 150N, and Crewfit 275N, both automatic), and West Marine (World Class, model no. 5328786), which is an exact copy of the SOSpenders 38A LNG and is made by SOSpenders.

Admittedly, inflatable PFDs aren't for everyone. Users must be at least 16 years old and, depending on the model, weigh a minimum of 80 to 90 pounds, and have a chest size ranging from 30 to 52 inches. And choosing a manual or automatic inflatable PFD itself is a tough call. If you get knocked unconscious or are injured, then you'd want the automatic PFD, which will turn you face up and keep you afloat. But if the boat capsizes and traps you under it, an automatic PFD will make it virtually impossible to swim down and resurface.

The Crewfit 150N is an automatically inflated PFD. *PS* testers were unanimous that it was the most comfortable vest in the water.

Making this decision depends upon a number of factors, including the type of boat you have, how you use it, as well as the sailing conditions you generally experience. For instance, if you sail offshore aboard a lively design—often in rough conditions—an automatic PFD might be the better choice because the risk of getting injured is greater. Manual-style vests may be better for slower boats where the risk of injury is not as great. As we said, it's a tough call.

Our testers donned and deployed each product several times. They rated the vests for comfort and fit (both in and out of the water), and commented on how each was to swim with and whether or not the PFDs could turn them face up if they started out face down. An additional test included spraying the vests with water to determine if automatic deployment could occur in rain or sea spray. We hit each automatic vest with a freshwater hose for a full two minutes with enough water flow to simulate heavy rain or sea spray. None of the vests inflated. To select a winner, we used all ratings and each vest's warranty period, buoyancy, and area of reflective tape.

▷ **The Bottom Line** Given the high price of these devices, it's unlikely that many owners will outfit their boats with a full complement of vest-style inflatable PFDs. More often than not, the owner will buy one for himself and stock up on less-expensive PFDs to satisfy U.S. Coast Guard regulations. So, with the boat already in full compliance, we see no reason not to recommend the Crewsaver 150N in spite of its lack of Coast Guard approval. It scored high in all testing areas. It also has lots of reflective tape and carries a three-year warranty.

The Crewsaver 150N is more expensive than the others, but we think its excellent comfort and fit—especially in the water—and its easy repacking and re-arming, make it worth the price. For those sailors who prefer sticking with Coast Guard–approved vests, or want a less-expensive alternative, we'd recommend purchasing either one of the inflatable PFDs we tested from Mustang.

PFDS FOR KIDS

When it comes to safety precautions, kids usually think less is better. Fortunately for them, parents (and the U.S. Coast Guard) disagree. Since you have to have them on the boat, and parents often want them on their kids, we decided to have a close look at children's PFDs.

Type I PFDs provide maximum buoyancy (minimum 11 pounds) and perform well in rough water. Type I PFDs are the only flotation devices acceptable for offshore use. Type II PFDs are collared jackets with flotation behind the neck and on the chest. They are required to provide a minimum buoyancy of 11 pounds for children weighing 50 to 90 pounds, 7 pounds for children under 50 pounds. These devices are acceptable for calm waters near shore, where rescue is not far off. The design offers head support and good buoyancy distribution; the collars are also designed to enhance freeboard (height of the head out of the water) and provide a grab-hold for parents—but they tend to be awkward and, well, dorky-looking.

Vest-shaped Type III "Flotation Aids" were the top choice of most of our testers. They have the same buoyancy requirements as Type IIs. Recommended for active boaters who can swim, Type IIIs are a good choice for active pastimes like water-skiing or kayaking. Kids like them because they look pretty cool, permit movement, fit well, and usually have no leg straps. Type IIIs rely on fit to prevent riding up.

Type V PFDs are a special class of life jackets that must be worn at all times on the boat in order to meet Coast Guard requirements. Frankly, the one model we tested looked so silly that we can't imagine kids wearing it as a Halloween costume. The company told us it meets the same buoyancy standards as a Type III PFD.

Our testers looked at two Type I PFDs (the Safeguard and Cal-June's Jim-Buoy); six Type II PFDs (Coral's Kiddie Safe, Stearn's Splash Zone Heads Up, Mustang's Lil Legends, the Extrasport, and Kent's Buoyant Vest and Kent's Classic); four Type IIIs (Kent's Casad, Mustang's Lil Legends, Extrasport's Youth Jacket, and Stearns' Illusion); and one Type V (Future Products' Aqua Force). We tested both child (about 30 to 50 pounds) and youth (40 to 90 pounds) PFDs. We found that children in the 40–50-pound range felt safer and were more comfortable in the larger sizes, provided they could get a snug fit.

SOSpenders 12AYH PFD is one of the few models in existence that combines both foam floatation and inflatable chambers. Due to this combination, the SOSpenders vest offers much more buoyancy than any other vest that *PS* tested. Sailors who rely on this vest will have to make sure that they properly maintain its inflation equipment.

This child's PFD from Stearns, the well-known maker of safety gear, has excellent buoyancy, comes in bright colors, and has some reflective material on it for nighttime visibility. *PS* testers deemed it the best choice in a recent test.

SAFETY WHISTLES

When it comes to survival at sea, the more tools you have at your disposal, the better. And that includes, in addition to high-tech items, such low-tech devices as a reflecting mirror or a simple whistle. We tested five different whistles to see which ones can really get some attention.

Using a digital decibel meter at a distance of 10 feet, we sounded each whistle in turn. Then we dunked them in water and saw how well they worked afterwards. We also considered such factors as size, design, ease of use, etc.

The ACR Res-Q whistle is a small, flat device that produces reasonably good volume, but doesn't seem to have the penetrating pitch of several other models. The diminutive Fox 40 gave out a shrill scream that was both loud and penetrating. It's a three-chambered whistle with a sound that can rise above ambient noise, which is

The safety whistles that *PS* tested include, left to right, bottom row: ACR, Seven Seas, the top-rated Fox, and the West Marine model. Top: the second-place Storm.

why it's the official whistle of the NFL. The Seven Seas whistle is a pretty pedestrian affair, and not much of a noisemaker. The makers of the Storm whistle claim that it's the "loudest in the world!" It was loud, with a distinct pitch, but it's larger than the other whistles and oddly shaped, making it somewhat awkward to handle. The model from West Marine is very similar to the Seven Seas, and offers similar performance; however, this one is less expensive and comes with a lanyard.

All of the whistles worked reasonably quickly after being submerged for some time in water, but we noticed that those that rely on an internal pea took a bit more clearing. Also, it seems, the smaller the whistle (i.e., the Fox), the less water that needs to be expelled from the chamber. Our first choice is the Fox, followed by the Storm, and the ACR a distant third.

PFD nomenclature can be confusing. Some labels specify appropriate weights, others use chest sizes (which can vary in range), and yet others refer to their models as "child" or "youth" devices. Read the UL label printed on the inside of the jacket (make sure there is one), which will specify the amount of buoyancy provided.

The Coast Guard says that snug fit is critical to the effectiveness of a PFD and suggests you test for ride-up in the store by pulling the device up by the shoulders; the wearer's chin and ears should not pull through. Children are especially subject to ride-up because their chests are often smaller than their lower bodies. The Coast Guard further suggests that you test the jackets in shallow water to see how well they keep the head above water, and also for ride-up.

▷ **The Bottom Line** After all our testing, we offered our hard-working testers their choice of life jackets for helping us out. One 12-year-old tester told us he would choose the Safegard to save his life, but preferred the Casad for looks and comfort. That particular vest was a favorite with several testers because of its comfortable fit and good range of motion. There are better performing vests in this category, but this one looks the coolest. And if it looks cool, your kids are more likely to want to wear it.

If safety is your primary concern, go for the Type I Safegard—it's a serious lifesaving device. If you know your kids will only be in calm waters near to shore, and if you're always going to be with them, we'd try the Casad or the Extrasport Type IIIs for older, more active kids. For a younger kid who might need to be yanked out of the water, the Type II Mustang Lil Legend is a good, if expensive, choice.

Personal Strobe Lights

Every couple of years, *PS* gathers and tests personal strobe lights just to stay on top of the offerings in this important market niche. Not long ago, two new lights caught our attention when we went hunting for safety gear to take along on an offshore race.

The HydroStar MultiStrobe, from Seattle Sports Co., is a unique animal in the realm of strobe lights because it's designed and built to do triple duty as a strobe, a flashlight (with three power settings), or a set of navigation lights for a small vessel.

Built in China, the MultiStrobe is powered by four AAA batteries, with a claimed life span of 72 hours. The batteries power five combinations of the nine LED lights that sit within the unit's dome. The base of the unit serves as the switch. It can be rotated from "off" to various settings depicted by symbols representing "strobe" (120 times per minute), "nav" (red and green LEDs), or one of three flashlight settings.

To enchance its versatility, the HydroStar Multi-Strobe is equipped with a short bungy lanyard and

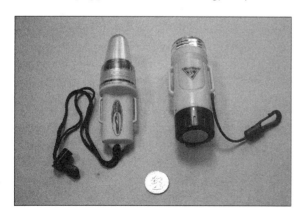

plastic clip, a metal clip for mounting on pockets, and has fixed slots in its body so that it can be lashed using webbing or hook-and-loop straps. It also has a magnet built into the bottom of the base, which mates with another magnet in a socket-like suction cup mount, included expressly for using the device as a nav light. The interior circuitry seems well built, and the case and dome are rugged. The HydroStar MultiStrobe is 4.25 inches long (without the suction cup mount), weighs 8.4 ounces, and retails for $29.95. The only downside of this product is that the LED lights aren't as bright as the xenon tubes used in most other strobes.

The Princeton Tec Aqua Strobe is another rugged product, but its sole function is as an emergency light, flashing up to 70 times per minute. The Aqua Strobe's xenon tube is powered by a single AA battery, which its manufacturers say will run the light continously for 8 hours.

Unique to the AquaStrobe is that it has no dedicated switch, but relies on the user to tighten the dome down sufficiently so that the reflector assembly (which houses the tube) comes into contact with the battery. You simply tighten the dome until the light begins to flash. To turn it off, back off the dome until it stops. In this position, the strobe is off, but the guts of the unit are still protected from water intrusion by the O-ring seal. The Aqua Strobe also floats with its lens up.

The Aqua Strobe weighs 3.4 ounces, and is sold with a battery, a hook-and-loop strap and buckle, a short nylon lanyard, and a spring-loaded cinch stop. The light carries a 90-day warranty and retails for $29.95. (For storage, the manufacturer recommends removing the battery.)

We ran only a cursory test of these two products. The Aqua Strobe's flash is brighter than the MultiStrobe's

The Aqua Strobe (left) from Princeton Tec, is built expressly as a safety strobe. The Hydrostar MultiStrobe (right) from Seattle Sports Company, has a variety of functions, including flashlight (with two intensity levels), running light (for a small boat), and strobe. The U.S. quarter at the bottom of this photo is there to indicate size.

(the latter also lacks a reflector), and both units easily survived a five-hour dunking in fresh water.

Fire Extinguishers

Consider how a fire might start aboard your boat—a spark into an engine fuel leak, a spark into a propane leak, a burning bit of ash into a dry trash bin, a spoonful of flaming stove alcohol into the paper goods, an electrical short—the possibilities are many. Now consider how far and how fast the fire might progress—through curtains, cushions, vinyl headliner, oiled and varnished wood, into more fuel supplies. No need to imagine further: A fire that gets out of control on a boat is a nightmare, and has been so since the days of wooden ships with tarred rigging and gunpowder down below. Today we have plastic boats, which means very flammable hulls that can generate toxic fumes, and there are usually all manner of flammable materials aboard, including propane. So the seriousness of fire aboard stretches right through the ages, as does the difficulty of running across water in order to escape.

Regarding fires on board, it's well known that the faster and more effectively you can attack a fire, the better chance you'll have of beating it, saving your boat, and surviving. Some of the success will depend on crew training and preparedness. The location of the fire extinguishers is also critical. One rule of thumb is never to mount an extinguisher where you might have to reach through fire to get to it. In other words, don't mount one on the far side of the stove. And some success will depend on the performance of the equipment itself.

Over many years we've become convinced that the best fire extinguisher is the one that shoots the most stuff for the longest time. When you put out a fire, you really don't want it to rekindle; you want to make sure it's good and out, and sometimes a few extra seconds of ammo can make that difference. So to us it makes sense to buy the biggest fire extinguishers you can manage.

There are various classes of fire extinguishers. For Class A fires (where solid combustibles like wood and fabric serve as the fuel), it's hard to beat good, old H_2O, which is found in cheap abundance around boats. Aqueous foam extinguishers are also effective on this kind of fire, but may not be Coast Guard–approved. CO_2 fire extinguishers are effective on Class B (combustible liquids like gas and oil) and Class C (electrical) fires, and leave no messy residue, but have some drawbacks. The CO_2 is under high pressure, yet the extinguishers are bigger and heavier than their dry chemical counterparts. While CO_2 is effective in enclosed spaces, it disperses quickly in open air, so it isn't particularly good against fires where there's significant ventilation. The ventilation meanwhile provides oxygen to the fire, further negating the smothering effect of the CO_2. And because there's no fire-retardant residue, a fire only partially smothered by CO_2 can more easily rekindle itself.

By far the most common and least expensive handheld fire extinguishers found aboard small boats are the dry chemical type. The extinguishing agents are usually sodium bicarbonate or potassium bicarbonate for Class B and C fires. Extinguishers that are also rated for Class A fires usually contain mono-ammonium phosphate. This is a highly corrosive chemical, so if you use an ABC unit to put out a live electrical fire in the nav station, you're likely to damage your electronics.

Because of the ban on Halon that went into effect a few years ago, the firefighting industry has come up with a number of Halon-replacement chemicals. One of these replacements is Halotron, made by the American Pacific Corporation; another is FM-200, made by the Great Lakes Chemical Corporation; a third is FE-241, made by DuPont. What distinguishes these firefighting agents is that they're safe for the environment, leave little or no residue after discharge, and, unlike CO_2, don't pose the threat of thermal shock if used on a hot engine. They also make for mighty expensive fire extinguishers.

PS gathered several handheld fire extinguishers that use the new "clean agent" chemicals, and compared them with our previously favored, U.S. Coast Guard–approved Kidde UN 1044 and the Kidde Spray Foam extinguisher (model 466620). Among the new products was Kidde's Pro Plus 5H Halotron-based extinguisher, Fireboy-Xintex's Model 70551 (a 5-pound portable), and Sea-Fire's 5-pound C-50 unit. All of these fire extinguishers are Coast Guard–approved, with the exception of the Kidde Spray Foam unit. Interestingly, the Kidde engineer we talked to said that

Manufacturer	Metalcraft/Sea-Fire Marine	Fireboy-Xintex	Kidde	Kidde	Kidde
Model	Fire-Hawk C50	70551/Buckeye 5F SA	Pro Plus 5HM	Dry Chemical	Spray Foam
Classification	5 B:C	5 B:C	5 B:C	1-A:10-B:C	8A, 70B
Extinguishing Agent	FM-200 (heptafluoropropane)	Halotron I	Halotron I	Dry Chemical	Foam
Gross Weight	9 lbs., 12 oz.	9 lbs. 8 oz.	8 lbs. 10 oz.	3 lbs. to 3 lbs. 5 oz.	7 lbs. 8 oz.
Chemical Weight	5.75 lbs.	5 lbs.	5 lbs.	2-3/4 lbs.	4.4 lbs.
Price	$439	$309.05	$144.99	$20.99	$39.99
Price Source	Manufacturer	Manufacturer	West Marine	West Marine	www.shop.com
Warranty	1 year	3 years	2 years	6 years	5 years
Recharge Cost	$112, plus shipping	Not rechargeable through Fireboy	$209†	Not rechargeable	$50‡
Stated Coverage Area	150 cubic feet	700 cubic feet	700 cubic feet	Not stated	Not stated
Claimed Discharge Time	8 to 10 seconds	9 seconds	None stated	8 to 12 seconds	12 to 15 seconds
Tested Discharge Time	8.4 seconds	11 seconds	12 seconds	11.5 seconds	22.5 seconds
Time to Extinguish*	5.9 seconds	5.75 seconds	3.8 seconds	2.25 seconds	7.3 seconds
Ease of Use	Good	Excellent	Excellent	Excellent	Good
Accuracy	Excellent	Good	Good	Good	Excellent

*Average time of two attempts. Conditions varied, two different testers, two different fires. Both fires were gasoline burning on top of water.
†Pricing provided by Suncoast Fire, Sarasota, FL.   ‡Unit is rechargeable, but recharging costs more than simply buying a new unit.

he keeps Coast Guard–approved dry chemical extinguishers aboard his boat to fulfill the letter of the law, but also carries one of his Spray Foam units as a first line of defense for Class A and B fires.

Two of the five extinguishers tested—the Kidde Spray Foam and the Sea-Fire C50—have short hoses attached to their nozzles. The hoses allow for a more accurate shot, but the setup does require two hands—one to hold the canister and the other to point the hose. Our testers preferred the units without hoses, figuring that on a boat, you may need your other hand for balance—and your balance will affect your accuracy.

All of the extinguishers are easy to operate. They require you simply to pull a pin, squeeze a lever, and shoot (using a sweeping motion). One tester had difficulty removing the Sea-Fire canister from its bracket because its hose is held in place with a separate clip. The lesson here is to practice removing the canisters from their brackets.

The clean-agent extinguishers worked very well. They seemed to surround the fire and smother it. Testers preferred the Halotron extinguishers from Fireboy and Kidde because they dispersed wider sprays than the Sea-Fire. Still, there were no discernible differences in effectiveness among the three. The discharge times for both the Kidde Pro Plus 5HM and Fireboy Halotron were two seconds longer than the Sea-Fire. The Kidde Chemical and Kidde Spray Foam were also effective, but they did not envelop the fire like the clean-agent extinguishers. Testers had to "move in on the fire" to extinguish it.

The clean-agent units will not stop reignition. The drawback of the foam unit is that it cannot envelope the fire like the Halotron units or the Sea-Fire extinguisher. And, the foam and chemical units are messier and can damage sophisticated equipment. The clean-agent extinguishers won't damage computers, engines, or electrical panels, but they can form toxic by-products when applied to a fire. Each clean-agent extinguisher warns the user not to discharge the product in confined spaces. The Sea-Fire should not be used in spaces smaller than 150 cubic feet; the Kidde and Fireboy Halotrons should not be used in spaces under 700 cubic feet.

▷ **The Bottom Line** For many boats, the ideal situation would be to have three fire-extinguishing alternatives on board. We'd love to have a permanently mounted, clean-agent automatic system in the engine area and a portable clean-agent at the helm, close to our electronics and other sophisticated equipment. Among those, we prefer the one-handed operation of the Kidde Pro Plus 5HM and the Fireboy. Both are equally effective, but we'd go with the Kidde simply because it's less expensive.

The Sea-Fire can be used safely in smaller confined spaces, so we'd opt for this model if we had a boat with particularly small enclosed areas.

MAN OVERBOARD!

"Can any two words chill a sailor's heart like 'man overboard'?" John Rousmaniere posed that question as the introduction to his report from the 2005 Crew Overboard Retrieval Symposium held on San Francisco Bay. Given the inherently narrow margin between life and death, attempting to rescue a person who has gone overboard is the most agonizing, demanding challenge that any sailor will ever face. Among the many truths that participants at the symposium discovered was this: most rescues are long, physically taxing (if not plain difficult), and require good equipment, fortitude, and (most important) good boat handling.

The testers and volunteers at that symposium learned or relearned a number of valuable lessons, and ultimately identified several reliable products. The lessons:

- Buy a throw bag, practice throwing and repacking it with your crew, and hang it off the binnacle so you can get to it quickly.
- If you sail at night, purchase small emergency lights to give to your crew to carry in their pockets or clip to a safety harness, or PFD. Strobes may be good for short ranges, but to be visible over

a long distance, buy a focused light like the VIP Safety Light or Laser Flare.
- If you buy a device that depends entirely on inflation (like a MOM—man overboard module) or electronics (like an alarm/crew monitoring device), understand that there's a trade-off between the enhanced visibility or more accurate locating of the crew overboard (COB) that these devices purport to offer, and their inherent complexity.
- Improve your sailing skills. When you're on the water, spend some time practicing tacks, jibes, heaving-to, and stopping the boat. Know how long it takes to bring your boat to a halt within heaving-line distance (10 to 20 feet) of an object in the water.
- Buy good safety harnesses, and develop and enforce rules for their use. For instance: hook on when you have a two-handed job, like coming up and down the companionway or changing sails.
- The well-known Lifesling continues to be the most reliable crew retrieval device on the market; and its smaller, less-expensive sibling, the Inflatable Lifesling, worked well as an initial contact and buoyancy device once testers became accustomed to it.

The Kidde Spray Foam is still a must-have for boaters, in our opinion. It worked well in our tests, and had the longest discharge time of any in the group. It's cheaper than the clean-agent extinguishers, and its ability to stop reignition cannot be overlooked. But, as we said, it's not Coast Guard approved, so you'll have to stock up on the required number of Coast Guard–approved units.

406-MHz EPIRBs

Nick Nicholson, *Practical Sailor*'s well-traveled Editor-at-Large, has often shared his opinion that the most important safety item on any offshore sailboat is the 406-MHz EPIRB (emergency position indicating radio beacon). These devices are essentially small radio transponders that, when turned on, connect to a global satellite network to alert search-and-rescue agencies that a vessel is in dire trouble. EPIRBs are intended to be used only as a last resort, when other means of rescue or communication aren't available or have failed.

EPIRBs in the 406-megahertz (MHz) band transmit digital signals to low-orbiting satellites, which allow the transmission of additional data, including a UIN (unique identification number). When coupled with proper registration, the UIN allows rescue agencies to confirm the need for assistance prior to launching expensive SAR assets. However, EPIRBs are sophisticated pieces of gear, so it shouldn't surprise anyone that they're not 100 percent reliable. Most do work, and work well. Still, even a fully functioning EPIRB won't help you at all if you haven't properly registered the device beforehand. (EPIRB owners in the U.S. can register their products at www.beacon-registration.noaa.gov.)

The latest incarnations of the 406-MHz EPIRB contain an internal GPS receiver to increase position accuracy. In addition to the UIN, a GPS-equipped EPIRB also transmits the unit's latitude/longitude coordinates. The Coast Guard recommends this type of EPIRB. With a non-GPS equipped EPIRB, the satellite system generally requires at least 45 minutes to calculate the position of an activated beacon. Plus, once calculated, the position is not as accurate as the transmitted position of the more sophisticated GPS EPIRB. The USCG estimates that the area needing to be searched with a position-reporting EPIRB is a mere 0.008 square mile. But with a non-position-reporting unit, the search area increases to 12.5 square miles. In rough seas, or restricted visibility, this is a big difference. Though opting for the internal GPS does add expense, doing so makes sense for everyone who gears up with an EPIRB. After all, this is your last-ditch Mayday device, for use when you have a big, bad problem on your hands. If you ever have to use it in earnest, that extra couple hundred dollars will seem like money wisely spent.

There are two classifications of 406 EPIRBs. The first are Category 1 units, which have brackets that automatically deploy the beacon when it is immersed 3 feet deep in water. The second, Category 2 units, need to have the bracket released manually for deployment.

EPIRB test specimens from ACR and Pains-Wessex McMurdo stand ready for baseline evaluation at the Imanna Laboratory. All functioned as expected in this environment, but some flaws were uncovered during real-world, marine tests. Those flaws, which pertained to the self-locating aspect of some devices, and not the alert functions, have since been addressed by the manufacturers.

ABANDON-SHIP BAGS

If the worst happens while you're offshore and you have to consider getting into a life raft, having to frantically hunt for safety and survival gear could waste precious time. That's why you should store the equipment in one easily accessible place. The abandon-ship bag helps get that job done. It also is a necessary supplement to a life raft's survival kit, which may fail to include all pertinent equipment.

PS rounded up four of the most widely marketed bags, one from each of the following manufacturers: Survival Technologies, West Marine, ACR Electronics, and Landfall Navigation. We examined each bag's construction and overall design, looking for features that enhance value and ease of use. We tested each bag's buoyancy by throwing them into a pool—with dumbbells inside—and observing how long they floated. These bags range in price from $90 to $200. Though they're available in a variety of sizes, the ones we evaluated are roughly the size of a standard gym bag.

Among these four, the pricey ($200) Landfall Navigation Dri-Bag, with its waterproof design that keeps everything dry and maintains buoyancy, is our top choice. Because it's tightly sealed, it easily supported 100 pounds of dense materials with the zipper closed. If you want to be sure the bag will float with just about anything you put into it, this bag's for you. Since it is waterproof, you can also be somewhat less concerned where you store it.

Of the conventional abandon-ship bags, we prefer West Marine's practical, well-thought-out model. It's well built; the good tether is icing on the cake. Priced reasonably, it's our Best Buy.

PS has tested EPIRBs on a number of occasions. We've done this on our own, and in conjunction with the Equipped to Survive Foundation, a nonprofit organization that exists to evaluate and report on safety products (www.equippedtosurvive.org). One recent test included three units: ACR Electronics' Global Fix 406, Northern Airborne Technology's Satfind 406 Pro, and McMurdo Pains Wessex's Precision 406 EPIRB. Only the Satfind 406 Pro wasn't equipped with internal GPS, and that company's products are now branded as ACR Electronics.

In that evaluation, we considered each unit's cost, battery replacement cost and downtime, warranty, and GPS capability. All three units were activated and tested using the U.S Coast Guard's testing equipment. Our top pick in this group was the ACR Global Fix, which sells for $1,000 in the automatic configuration and $849 in the manual version. This unit worked as advertised with very good accuracy, and it carries a five-year limited warranty. However, the battery replacement cost is high (about $300) and requires shipping the unit back to the manufacturer.

Subsequent to that test, we participated in a further evaluation conducted by Doug Ritter and his colleagues at Equipped to Survive. That comprehensive evaluation took place both on land and at sea. The results of those tests indicated that "all the beacons provided the minimum acceptable level of distress alerting expected from non-location 406-MHz emergency beacons." However, Ritter wrote: "the McMurdo Fastfind 406 PLB [Personal Locator Beacon] and McMurdo Precision 406 GPS EPIRB generally failed to provide location information except under ideal conditions.... These beacons failed to provide a location unless the sky view was unimpeded, and there was little or no movement of the beacon due to the motion of the water." Officials from McMurdo disputed those findings and subsequently conducted their own tests.

We should be clear here that at issue was the functionality of these units' GPS locating capability. These EPIRBs otherwise functioned properly as distress alerts. The upshot of all this is that EPIRB units should continue to get more reliable, and with time, their prices should continue going down. For now, *PS* stands by its endorsement of the ACR Global Fix.

Personal Locator Beacons

With the price of 406-MHz EPIRBs having dropped a great deal in recent years, these devices make great sense for any offshore vessel. But 406-MHz EPIRBs do carry a big drawback—they're too large and too bulky to strap on a PFD. Moreover, most EPIRBs just aren't very practical for smaller boats. However, more compact 406-MHz beacons are gaining in popularity. These devices are called PLBs (personal locator beacons). After years of opposition from the FAA, the U.S. Air Force, and others, which prevented the sale of PLBs in the U.S., these valuable safety devices are now available to U.S. sailors.

The PLB is a pocket-sized, manually operated emergency beacon providing essentially the same alerting capabilities as a 406-MHz EPIRB for less money. These PLBs are compact enough to carry easily on your person, and most manufacturers provide a pouch that can be attached to your PFD. The larger ones weigh about a pound; the smallest are about half that weight and not much larger than a cigarette pack. As with most electronics, there is an inverse relationship between cost and size; smaller is more expensive.

In the U.S., PLBs must include a 25-milliwatt, 121.5-MHz analog homing signal, not required by COSPAS-SARSAT standards. While less powerful than an EPIRB's 121.5-MHz signal, the 406-MHz primary beacon transmission provides increased accuracy, so this doesn't represent any decrease in safety or effectiveness. Inserted into the homing signal at the insistence of the FAA is a Morse Code P to distinguish a PLB from an ELT (Emergency Locator Transmitter, strictly an aviation beacon) or a standard EPIRB, for that matter.

Generally, PLBs have various attributes, which in turn affect performance and price. The specifications delineate Class 1 and Class 2 PLBs, the former providing a minimum of 24 hours of operation at -40°C; the latter, 24 hours at -20°C. For most boating purposes, a Class 2 PLB will be adequate. By comparison, an EPIRB is required to transmit for 48 hours at -40°C.

Category 1 PLBs are inherently buoyant. That is an obvious advantage for marine use, but a secure tether would also likely suffice (and a tether should be used in any case). The buoyant PLBs are not the smallest available, so depending upon your priorities, you might want to depend solely on a tether in exchange for smaller size. It's important to note that the buoyant PLBs will not float upright in the transmitting position, like an EPIRB, but they also won't sink.

For someone floating in a PFD, the PLB will need to be held or secured on top of the vest with the antenna pointed skyward and out of the water for the most part. Some PLBs have adjustable antennas; others are fixed. With an inflatable PFD, some of the PLBs can be wedged between the inflated chambers. Those thinking ahead may want to secure some Velcro on the PFD and the PLB to make this easier.

PLBs are manually activated—they can't be activated by a water-sensing switch. So you must be conscious to activate one, which limits the PLB's usefulness as a man-overboard device. The manual activation requirement was driven by a desire to cut down on false and inadvertent alerts that plague the system. Perhaps the future will bring a solution, once the authorities become comfortable with the technology.

Self-locating PLBs may accept GPS coordinates from an external GPS, or they may have their own integrated GPS chip and antenna. The former is less expensive; the latter is a more compact solution, though you will pay a premium for the capability.

Self-locating PLBs must be operated optimally for GPS to work to its best advantage, or even at all. As with any GPS receiver, it requires a clear sky and a reasonably stable antenna pointed skyward. Too much motion, as in heavy seas, will defeat the very basic antennas included in either the integrated beacons or most handheld GPS receivers, preventing the GPS from receiving enough satellites to determine an accurate location. All are "fail-safe," in the sense that they will not transmit an unreliable location. In any case, the 5-watt 406-MHz distress signal will still punch through and provide location accuracy of less than a 3-mile radius, and experience suggests it is often far better.

PLBs use lithium-based batteries (meeting DOT requirements) with a minimum five-year replacement interval, though actual service life may be longer. As with 406-MHz EPIRBs, PLBs must be registered, for free, with NOAA. (For online registration of PLBs and EPIRBs, go to www.beaconregistration. noaa.gov.) Registration also allows inputting a float plan that is immediately provided to Search and Rescue in case of an alert.

The prices of these devices do fluctuate. In mid-2006, Landfall Navigation listed the compact ACR AquaFix 406 PLB with GPS for $650, and without for $550. The McMurdo Pains Wessex FastFind Plus PLB with GPS sold there for $550, and without GPS for $470. And all these units were priced similarly elsewhere.

Life Rafts

With lives at stake, we expect manufacturers of safety equipment to value our lives, and those we care about, as much as we do. Unfortunately, past tests have proven that this isn't always the case. *PS* has evaluated life rafts on numerous occasions, and though the rafts tested could save your life if everything goes right, we're inclined to believe that is not likely to be the case all the time. Otherwise, why would you bother with a life raft in the first place?

In an ongoing series of articles several years ago, *PS* reported on a comprehensive evaluation of rafts, including: three inshore, eight coastal, and fourteen offshore life rafts, in four- or six-person capacities, from nine manufacturers: Crewsaver by Eurovinil (Italy), DBC Marine Safety (Canada), Givens Marine Survival (U.S.), Plastimo (France), Survival Products, Inc. (U.S.), Switlik Parachute Co. (U.S.), Viking Lifesaving Equipment (Denmark), West Marine by Zodiac (France), Winslow LifeRaft Co. (U.S.), and Zodiac International (France). At the time of this test, which was conducted in cooperation with the Equipped to Survive Foundation

PS has been involved in testing life rafts on numerous occasions. Here, testers use a fire hose to ascertain how much pressure the entry flaps on a particular life raft can sustain. This kind of thorough testing is vital to ensure the safety of those who trust their lives to these products.

(www.equippedtosurvive.org), Avon declined to participate, citing the unavailability of their completely revised product line with manufacturing just underway in Hungary. RPR Industries, which formerly manufactured the Givens rafts and now is manufacturing a similar raft on its own, declined, citing pending legal issues involving Givens. Eastern Aero Marine also declined, and RFD/Revere and BFA failed to return our calls or e-mails at the time we researched our article. And officials from Givens subsequently requested that any information pertaining to its products not be included in this book.

Performance tests were conducted in a wave pool to ensure consistent conditions. Volunteers attended from throughout the U.S. and Europe. They ranged from unsuspecting "life raft virgins" who had never been in a life raft before, to experienced survival instructors. Following three days of exhausting in-water work, we conducted detailed evaluations of the rafts and their survival equipment. The evaluations were conducted in cooperation with the Equipped to Survive Foundation, and the U.S. Coast Guard had two representatives on hand who participated in the testing.

You can't expect a small valise or canister weighing from 12 to 100+ pounds to afford the luxury of a yacht. The option of last resort, a life raft should be capable of delivering its occupants to safety, even through weather and seas that may have contributed to the loss of the mother vessel. That's a lot to ask of anything, let alone some inflatable contraption made of fabric and little else. These rafts ranged widely in price, features, and capability. But when all was said and done, our overriding concern focused on capability—would it save our lives?

As we spent hours, days, and weeks with these rafts, a related concern came to the fore. The raft must be designed and equipped to take care of the survivor; it should demand little or nothing of the survivor, who may be unable to do much on his or her behalf. Everything should be obvious and intuitive to survivors who most likely have no survival training.

A life raft is an integrated system in which the performance of individual features, or lack thereof, can significantly affect overall performance. The devil is often in the details. And, with little in the way of standards for noncommercial rafts, manufacturers can pretty much make whatever claims they want to.

Our testers evaluated these products for a number of attributes: ease of deployment and operation; seaworthiness and stability; ease of entry, both from the vessel and the water; protection from the sea and elements; functionality; livability; comfort; survival equipment selection and quality; and of course, price.

The space available to each survivor has a huge impact on livability. SOLAS/Coast Guard–approved rafts use, as one measure, a minimum of 4 square feet per person. While popular opinion seems to be that non-approved rafts often don't meet this standard, virtually every raft we reviewed did, though only a few exceeded it by any significant amount. Winslow's Ocean Rescue took top honors with half again more space per person. While configuration can make a difference, any way you slice it there isn't

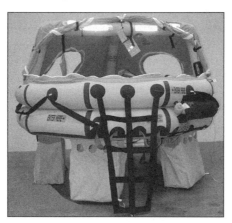

This raft exhibits a number of the attributes that *PS* testers favor in these devices: it has double tubes, a canopy supported by inflated tubes, an abundance of reflective material, a broad entry area, and portlights so that the occupants can see out. However, this raft would appear to be difficult to enter because it lacks a boarding platform.

much room. Think sardines. Lay open a magazine on the floor and multiply it by three. Imagine spending a few days in that space.

If you can afford a few extra dollars, pounds, and a few inches, seriously consider going up one or even two sizes, but only if you purchase a well-ballasted raft. For example, if you need a four-person raft, upgrade to a six-person, which is essentially what Winslow has done with its Ocean Rescue model. In a raft with minimal ballast, it is better to stick with the rated capacity, maximizing the ballast effect of the survivors.

There are numerous other concerns. For enhanced stability, a raft should have a drogue, and these are particularly critical with boat-shaped or elongated rafts. Unfortunately, drogues are often lost in heavy weather. If a round raft loses its drogue, it may carousel, but it generally has no inherently less stable configuration. Lose the drogue on a boat-shaped raft, and it is likely to quickly turn broadside and settle in a wave trough, as would a boat without steering. Unless the ballast compensates, it is then more likely to capsize in conditions that might otherwise not cause a problem. And, while some manufacturers require the survivor to deploy the drogue, we prefer self-deploying drogues—one less thing for the survivor to worry about. Only Winslow, Switlik, and West Marine use swivels on their drogues. These are essential to eliminate twisting of the rode, which is believed to be the primary cause of drogue failure. The drogue rodes one some of the rafts we tested were too short, and none of the drogues on a short rode performed well. We consider 75 feet the minimum, and double that wouldn't be too much. We also prefer the heavier line used with many of the drogues, as opposed to lightweight parachute line found on the Winslow rafts and many of the Switliks.

Multi-sided equilateral rafts, especially those with six or more sides, can have a structural advantage over round or elongated rafts. The short-coupled reinforced mitered joints can provide significant added rigidity, which was evident reviewing videotapes of our tests.

Another obvious distinction between rafts is whether they have a single tube for flotation or if they use two stacked tubes. Many coastal rafts have only a single tube. The difference in freeboard is significant. In rough weather, the more freeboard you have, the better. With double-tube rafts, larger tubes provide greater freeboard and more reserve buoyancy. And twin tubes also offer a much more supportive backrest; the single-tube rafts were deemed much more uncomfortable. Also, higher sides are necessary to brace oneself against the violent motion of the raft in bad weather.

Inflatables, while pretty darn tough, are still subject to puncture by any number of means. Even in closely supervised training, rafts are often punctured. We feel strongly that there must be means to ensure that if there is a puncture, then some buoyancy remains. Whether by having multiple tubes or by dividing up a single tube internally, puncturing one buoyancy chamber should not sink the whole raft. The DBC and Plastimo coastal, and all three inshore rafts, were deficient in this regard.

Other concerns include weight and volume; those aspects of a raft are affected by its capacity, its design, additional features, and the materials from which it is made. Shape plays a part in to overall weight: a canister is generally heavier and more bulky than a valise. The selection of survival equipment also can make a huge difference in overall weight.

And deploying a raft is something any owner should be familiar with. Our tests revealed that neither written nor pictorial instructions alone seem to be entirely adequate. If possible, anyone owning a

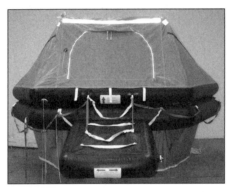

The inflatable boarding platform on this raft will make it much easier for those sailors who are in the water to enter the raft, and that's a vital concern.

life raft should attend a deployment demonstration. The Zodiac and West Marine rafts came with instructional videos, which while not great, were better than anyone else provides.

We also learned that the raft's painter should be at least 50 feet in length, and probably not more than 70. It should lead directly to the main boarding station. Also, though it doesn't happen regularly, rafts do inflate upside down and then need to be righted. Most rafts don't have clear instructions printed on them for this task, but they should. If you're abandoning ship at night and your raft is upside down, you'd be out of luck with most rafts except for those from Winslow, which have excellent righting aids and an exclusive "righting locator light."

Our testers also evaluated how easy it is to jump into the raft from the boat. The Winslows and the Switlik SAR Mk II have large canopy openings, making this method of boarding easy. (However, it's not necessary to jump into the opening, you can simply jump onto the canopy of any life raft and then enter the opening afterward.) Some rafts, the DBC for example, have small openings that would make it more difficult and potentially dangerous to board in this way.

And, for boarding from the water, the effectiveness of the boarding aids is absolutely critical. Some rafts with minimal aids and little more than a few loops of line for assist—Givens, Zodiac, and Viking—were virtually impossible for some volunteers to board without assistance, which may not be available. Without considerable upper-body strength, you're in trouble. Short and bottom-heavy volunteers especially had difficulties, but anyone who is injured or exhausted from fighting a storm could have difficulty. A few rafts made it relatively easy, including Winslow with its ample outside and inside ladders, stirrups, and grab handles; Switlik's "step" on most of their rafts; and the West Marine Offshore and DBC Swiftsure Global with their inflatable "ramps."

MORE LIFE RAFT OPTIONS

Subsequent to the massive life raft test we reported on, another comprehensive test was conducted in which testers examined some entirely new life rafts and updated elements on existing models. The new rafts included products from Avon, (Open Ocean), Viking (RescYou Pro 6), Zodiac (Class Ocean), and Switlik (Rescue Pod 8). Switlik no longer makes the Rescue Pod 8, but its smaller sibling, the Rescue Pod 4 is still available.

The Avon Open Ocean ($2,950) is an uninspired raft at an inexpensive price, a generation behind the other designs, with nothing in particular, except price, to recommend it. The raft's low canopy and single small door made the interior feel constricted and caused claustrophobic feelings among our testers. We think the West Marine Offshore raft (built by Zodiac) that we tested previously represents a far better raft overall, and a better value.

The six-person, boat-shaped Zodiac Class Ocean ($3,800) is very similar to Switlik's SAR 6 Mk II, and the only element keeping it from surpassing that product is the ballast. The Class Ocean's ballast is not even close to being as effective as Switlik's toroidal shape. In other areas, including boarding aids, integral bailer, and nice insulated canopy, the Class Ocean is superior. The foam floor isn't as comfortable as Switlik's optional drop-stitched or air mattress style, and there's that reflective finish, which could be good or bad depending on where you're cruising.

Nobody beats Switlik's fabric for toughness, even Zodiac with its PVC. On the other hand, the Zodiac raft is less expensive than the SAR 6 Mk II

(6,695), without an insulated floor, but with a more capable standard equipment package. That's a big difference, tipping the value scale toward Zodiac. While still not the performance equal of the SAR 6 Mk II or the well-equipped Winslows, this raft is head and shoulders above previous offerings from Zodiac.

Viking's RescYou Pro 6 ($3,150 in valise) has some very nice features, especially its self-righting design. Our testers liked the open, airy canopy and feeling of spaciousness that it provided. It's stoutly constructed, and we don't see the lighter-weight fabric as an issue. It also has a good offshore SEP and a bit of extra room. The improved ballast helps to compensate for the boat shape. The entry aids, better by far than the company's previous raft, remain a concern. They're fine for sailors in reasonable shape or not already exhausted from fighting a storm, but there's significant room for improvement based on what we've seen on other rafts. The revised canister is beautiful, and that alone may prove an important selling point for some. We think it's a product well worth consideration—and our Best Buy in this group.

Among the important updates to existing models were the inflatable boarding platforms that Winslow added as standard equipment on all of its Offshore rafts. Even the shortest and heaviest testers were able to board these rafts easily using the new platforms and the robust interior boarding ladder. This is especially important to note because the Ocean Rescue has 20.33" of freeboard, far more than any of the other rafts.

EMERGENCY RIG CUTTERS

Among a sailor's worst nightmares of what can happen at sea, dismasting is right up there. When a mast comes down at sea there's tremendous potential for further damage. Few things will sink a boat more quickly than the end of a mast holing a vessel. When such a calamity occurs, speed is of the essence, and the number-one priority is getting rid of the danger as quickly, and safely, as possible. Sometimes, the only option is to cut away the rig.

We used common sizes of wire cable and Navtec rod rigging in different diameters to test three emergency cutters as well as a standard hacksaw. A hacksaw will work, particularly on smaller rod, but it does take the most time and effort. We took 20 seconds to cut through $^3/_{16}$-inch 7x19 wire, 40 seconds to cut ¼-inch 1x19 wire, 25 seconds to cut –4 (0.172-inch) rod, 70 seconds to cut –40 (0.5-inch) rod.

The Swiss-made Felco C-16 Cable Cutters are a big step up from a hacksaw, both in ease of use and price ($350). These are not intended for rod, but if you're strong enough, there's enough leverage with the 22-inch-long handles that you will be able to cut smaller cable straight away.

We also tested Huskie Tools' model S-24 hydraulic cutter, which sells for a whopping $1,200. The S-24 is basically a hydraulic jack with the ram providing 7.2 tons of shearing force, enough to cut –40 rod,

the thickest we had to test. Husky provides a five-year limited warranty.

And we evaluated the German-built Toolova Shootit 12, a unique tool that fires a .27-caliber rimfire blank cartridge, which drives a piston against an anvil integrated into the forward end of the tool, cutting whatever wire or rod has been placed in the slot between the piston and the anvil. The Toolova was extremely effective, instantly severing all the cable and rod up to –22 (0.375 inch). But the 13¼-inch-long, 6-pound Shootit 12, which sells for $585, is somewhat awkward to use.

Ergonomics, safety, and other issues aside (because everything is a compromise), the Shootit 12 is the easy choice for best emergency rigging cutter. Despite what we consider a relatively awkward design, it produced the quickest results with the least effort at a cost that, if not inexpensive, is less than half the hydraulic cutters.

If you buy a Shootit 12, take to heart the company's recommendation to practice first before having to use the tool in an emergency. There are too many safety and functional idiosyncrasies to expect anyone to be able to grab it and use it effectively in an emergency.

For wire rigging, the Swiss-made Felco cable cutters are effective and affordable, though they're not easy to use. The larger the wire, the more difficult it will get.

The stability of any raft is critical, and ballast is the primary means of preventing capsize. From a practical standpoint, ballast in a raft is limited to the people and equipment in and on the raft, and some means of retaining water below the raft to counteract the tendency to capsize as it lifts out of the water.

Ballast effectiveness is determined by the capacity of the water retention devices, their configuration, and their placement. All the non-U.S.-manufactured rafts use similar, marginally effective ballast systems V-shaped bags hanging below the raft. Capsizing them was a trivial matter. U.S. manufacturers provide more capable, higher-capacity ballast systems, ranging from box-shaped bags on the Winslows and Switliks to the unique Switlik "toroidal" ballast on its SAR MkII, and Givens' "hemispherical" design. Another consideration, particularly with regards to boarding, is how quickly they fill with water. With the exception of Winslow and Givens, all had weights to assist in rapid filling, though results were mixed.

Our testers felt that having a rigid arch to support the raft's canopy was essential for comfort, and two were vastly better than one. Ideally, some form of interior illumination like a light or several view ports is also beneficial. Of course, a canopy that leaks is not nearly as comfortable or effective as one that really keeps the weather out. Two issues arose here— effectiveness of the closure system on the canopy openings, and ease of use. All the closure systems are a compromise, but overall we prefer ease of use that doesn't require much manual manipulation. Digital dexterity is one of the first things lost as a result of exposure. So openings that seal with large zippers (and helpful zipper pulls), such as Winslow's and Switlik's, are the easiest to use and fastest to close up.

Also important to survival and comfort is an insulated floor, even in temperate waters. Some rafts don't offer insulated floors. Zodiac and West Marine use a thin layer of foam with a reflective surface integral in the floor. The effect of UV on the reflective surface in the tropics gives us pause, and the foam was ripped up in places even from our short test period. The Plastimo Offshore Plus had a tied-in foam sheet that was a real nuisance. (The company has since replaced that with an inflated floor panel.) Winslow, DBC, and others offer integral inflatable floors, some with reeds (fabric attachments that connect the top of the floor with the bottom), others without, a less desirable design. Crewsaver, Viking,

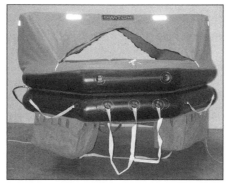

Multi-sided equilateral rafts, especially those with six or more sides, like this model from Switlik, can have a structural advantage over round or elongated rafts. The short-coupled reinforced mitered joints can provide significant added rigidity to protect the raft's occupants.

and Switlik offer drop-in inflatable floors, much like an air mattress. Switlik also offers a drop-stitch drop-in inflatable floor on higher-end models. This floor becomes an almost rigid structure 2.5" thick, easily the most comfortable of the options, though they are quite heavy. In our experience, the Zodiac foam floors aren't as effective or robust as the best inflatable floors, with Winslow's and the drop-stitch from Switlik leading the pack.

The testers found that the quality of the survival equipment in some rafts is questionable. Inshore and coastal rafts especially were short-changed. Many didn't include the most basic device, a signal mirror. And the raft repair supplies on some models were insufficient, particularly those made outside the U.S. All the U.S. and West Marine rafts included mil-spec raft repair clamps that are very effective. Generally speaking, you'd best plan on supplementing the raft's equipment with your own. The less expensive the raft, the more equipment you'll need to provide yourself.

Other considerations include whether the raft should be stored in a hard container, or in a valise, and that decision is guided in part by where the raft will live onboard.

Coastal life rafts provide reduced capability compared to offshore rafts, but are generally lighter, have smaller pack sizes, and are often less expensive. For those who never venture far from shore and for those with limited room or budget, these rafts represent a reasonable compromise. The coastal raft concept is based on assumptions that, close to shore, you will be able to make it to a safe port before a major storm hits, or, if sinking for other reasons, such as collision or leak, that help is minutes away. That's not always the case. Whether 20 miles offshore or 500, you still need to survive until rescued, and the raft and survival equipment must be up to the task.

▷ **The Bottom Line** Among the eight coastal rafts we evaluated, only the one from West Marine had double tubes. Plastimo has since discontinued the Coastline and only offers two life rafts to the U.S. market: the Cruiser ORC+ ($2,497 for six-man version in the valise) and the Offshore+ ($2,900 for the six-man version in the valise). Both come with double tubes, but we haven't tested these rafts yet. Offering double tubes in a coastal raft at an economical price is commendable, but these rafts have some deficiencies. The West Marine raft is notably difficult to enter from the water unaided. (We much prefer the boarding ramp used on the Offshore model the company sells.) And Plastimo's Coastal raft has a minimal canopy that must be deployed by the occupants.

We liked the sleeved design of the Switlik CLR6 USCG Mk II ($5,095), which is well made and sturdily constructed. Even if it isn't 100 percent effective at keeping water out, it is a huge improvement over other single-tube designs. The entry aids are a big advantage. The double-arch canopy makes for a much more comfortable raft, though we prefer the more weather-tight entry used on the SOLAS version. Its biggest drawbacks are weight, pack size, and, to a lesser degree, price. A bulky coastal raft that weighs in at more than some offshore rafts doesn't make a lot of sense to us. And the Switlik MD-1 also is very well made, but has inadequate boarding aids and proved very uncomfortable due to the low canopy. We thought it had too many deficiencies for its price.

The biggest problem with the DBC Life-Pac ($2,076 in a valise) life raft is that it is a single-cell design. In addition, the DBC was not easy to board, the drogue orients the entry toward oncoming waves, and the interior lifelines were uncomfortable. Plastimo's new life rafts are built with double-walled tubes, and do have a canopy. The company also offers vacuum-packing, and these rafts do now come with a drogue and retro-reflective material.

Despite the drawbacks of the single-tube design and single-arch canopy, the upgraded Winslow Canopied Coastals—the Plus ($3,520 for six-man version) and Premium ($4,895 for six-man version)—are our top choices. Our testers, to a man and woman, felt the same way. Winslow's coastal rafts are octagonal, dual-cell, single-arch, dual-color canopy designs. They are constructed of a bright yellow material. With five boxy ballast bags (83 pounds, 415 pounds total), the rafts were moderately difficult to capsize. A "Cape Horn" option ($87) increases ballast to 640 pounds, making the raft very difficult to capsize. A length of line attached to each bag allows them to be tied up when desired. Winslow's compact, lightweight pack; attention to detail; unique features; and overall quality are compelling. And Winslow now offers the option of vacuum-packing on all of its life rafts ($265) to seal them against the marine environment. If you're on a budget, the base Winslow Canopied Coastal would be our choice, but we strongly recommend the optional view ports.

Among the 14 offshore rafts we examined and tested, those from Winslow, the Offshore Plus ($4,635 for six-man version), the Extended Offshore ($5,795 for six-man version), and the Ocean Rescue ($7,595 for the Maxi 4 and $8,195 for the Roomy 6) were also impressive. Quality, performance, light weight, and attention to detail make this company's rafts our top choice; they were also the near-unanimous selection of our volunteers. We were impressed with Winslow's many innovative, industry-leading features, as well as the company's obvious consideration of human factors in design and equipage. One example of this is the auto-inflating floor on the Ocean Rescue (a $250 option on other models). The floor, incidentally, is built with 21 reeds that enhance comfort while requiring that less air be used to fully inflate the floor. (Reeds essentially work like tufted panels in furniture to connect the top and bottom panels of the floor.) And the flexibility to tailor a Winslow to your particular needs is a welcome option, as is their upgradeability. All Winslow's offshore rafts have inflatable boarding platforms as standard equipment.

The Winslow Ocean Rescue is our top choice for an offshore life raft, albeit at a premium price, followed closely by the Extended Offshore, which provides perhaps the best value in their line, in terms of standard features and capability for your dollar. The Offshore Plus, in its standard configuration, represents the best of the single-arch-canopy rafts,

HANDHELD EMERGENCY FLARES

For any sailor in distress, flares are the most effective close-range signaling tools. Both aerial and handheld flares can attract attention at night (and in some conditions during the day), and these devices usually do so better than flags, lights, dye markers, mirrors, or smoke-generating devices. Aerial flares help rescuers locate mariners in distress, and handheld flares guide the already-alerted rescuer to the rescuee. The U.S. Coast Guard makes no distinction between the two types of devices, only that they burn a red flame with an intensity of 500 candela for at least 60 seconds. (The international SOLAS standard requires a minimum of 15,000 candela for a burn of at least 60 seconds, and requires only that a vessel have on board three of either type.) What's important is that these devices burn brightly enough and long enough to permit a raft or disabled vessel to be found, even under adverse conditions.

PS tested six different models of handheld flares. These devices are intended to be held in the hand during their entire burn period, so the spattering of molten slag is a serious consideration, particularly if the flare is being deployed from a life raft. We tested two that meet SOLAS standards: the Pains-Wessex Red Mk 7 and Simpson Lawrence's SOLAS MK4; and four that meet USCG standards: Pains-Wessex Pinpoint, the Bristol Marine Hand Red Flare, the Orion Hand-held Red Signal Flare, and the Skyblazer Life-Star Red Flare.

In performance testing, the Pains-Wessex Mk 7 Handflare grabbed first place. Its only real disadvantage is its price—$19.95 each. The SOLAS MK4 performed almost as well and carries a somewhat lower price tag ($15.75), but in our opinion produced an undesirable degree of spatter. In terms of value, the Pains-Wessex Pinpoint was the clear winner. It did virtually everything its pricier sibling did, and while its minimum rated brightness is lower than that of the Mk 7—10,000 candela versus 15,000—it's still much brighter than the 500 candela typical of the other U.S. Coast Guard–approved flares. And the Pinpoint costs only about $1.50 more.

Of the three other USCG-only approved flares, the Bristol edged out the Skyblazer for a distant third. It was much less effective than either of the SOLAS-grade models. The Orion, due to its inability to stay lit in a heavy rain, is not recommended. Though all the flares lighted after they had become immersed in water, the Bristol, Orion, and Skyblazer flares were much more difficult to light than samples whose striking surfaces were dry. What's the lesson? Store flares in a dry place. This is a sound idea even for the SOLAS-grade flares and the Pinpoint, though those models were immune to this problem.

One piece of advice: savvy mariners will also carry a signal flag, like those from Orion or Skyblazer, as part of their signaling arsenal.

none of which we really like. A judicious choice of options, such as the tri-arch canopy, will fix the most significant drawbacks and give you nearly top-rated performance and features at a relative bargain price, though still not inexpensive.

And Winslow's survival equipment packs carry individually vacuum-packed items grouped by use with a list of what's inside, all packed into the SEP bag in logical order. The company has also upgraded to SOLAS handheld flares as standard throughout the product line, addressing one of the few weaknesses.

There is a lot to like in Switlik's Search and Rescue Mk II ($6,695). Its toroidal ballast is excellent and

CO DETECTORS

Carbon monoxide is a cumulative poison. A by-product of combustion and a major component of exhaust fumes, when inhaled, CO bonds with oxygen-carrying hemoglobin molecules in the blood, inhibiting your body's ability to absorb and circulate O_2. As the concentration of CO in your body increases, your body becomes less and less able to oxygenate tissue, and over time, even mild exposure to CO—concentrations below 100 parts per million (PPM)—can result in dizziness, disorientation, headache, and nausea. Prolonged heavy exposure will make you chemically hypoxic, leading to seizures, brain damage, and death, if left untreated.

Okay, so what's a boat owner to do? If you have a gasoline engine (diesel engines produce fewer PPM of CO than gas engines, but produce some nonetheless), or a gas-powered generator on board, and your boat has enclosed spaces, you should install a CO detector. Marine CO detectors aren't cheap. UL-certified marine devices can run from $45 to $190. Though the UL standards require that these products be more durable than their domestic counterparts, their sensors are perishable

The five CO detectors that *PS* tested included, from left, the CO Star, the Fireboy/Xintex CO Sentinels (these small rectangular units are identical except that the more expensive one on the right will interface with other units installed on a vessel), the Safe-T-Alert (bottom middle), and the Fireboy/Xintex 9Volt.

and need to be regularly recalibrated. Also, their sensors can be fouled by extreme temperatures and humidity as well as a number of chemical vapors. Of course, nuisance alarms have been the cause of much eye rolling and faintly muttered profanity. However, when CO builds to dangerous concentrations in your cabin, galley, engine compartment, or a cockpit enclosed with canvas, a properly functioning detector can save your life.

PS gathered five such devices and tested them in an airtight chamber fed by a steady stream of CO. Four of them are UL-approved marine devices: the Safe-T-Alert from Marine Technology Industries ($55); and three models from Fireboy-Xintex, the CO Sentinel ($157), the CO Sentinel with generator shutoff and multiple-detector interface capability ($190), and the 9-volt battery-powered, surface-mount model ($146). We also tested a 9-volt surface-mount detector from the Quantum Group called the CO Star Marine ($68), which is marketed as a marine detector. Although it does not have UL certification, it is endorsed by the Recreation Vehicle Industry Association.

---

goes a long way toward ameliorating the potential stability problem of a drogueless, boat-shaped raft. Its biggest drawback is weight—the trade-off for its robustness—and the fact that its tether is a mere 30 feet long.

West Marine's Offshore ($3,699 for the six-man version, which is built by Zodiac) has many well-thought-out features, including the spacious dual-arch canopy, boarding ramp, swivel for the drogue, and vacuum packing, among others. It's a good value for those on a budget and with less demanding requirements. But the occupants of this raft will need to bring along their own well-equipped abandon-ship bag.

Maker Model	Marine Technologies Safe-T-Alert	Fireboy/Xintex CMD-IMR-9V	Fireboy/Xintex CO Sentinel	Fireboy/Xintex CO Sentinel†	Quantum Group CO Star Marine
Price	$55	$146	$157	$190	$68
Dimensions	5.5" x 3" x 1.3"	4.75" (dia.) x 1.5"	3.5" x 2.4" x 1.3"	3.5" x 2.4" x 1.3"	4.75" (dia.) x 1.5"
Type of Sensor	solid-state	biomimetic	solid-state	solid-state	biomimetic
Sensitivity	60 ppm	70 ppm	70 ppm	70 ppm	70 ppm
Power Source	hardwired 12V DC	9V battery	hardwired 12V DC	hardwired 12V DC	9V battery
Amp Draw	6 mA	6 mA	16 mA	46 mA	6 mA
Slow Release to 550 ppm*	23:31	21:26	22:08	23:02	22:36
Slow Release to 750 ppm*	13:57	11:33	13:09	14:55	10:04
Slow Release to 1,000 ppm*	11:58	11:01	10:47	10:21	9:20
Rapid Release to 1,500 ppm*	2:43	1:37	1:52	2:08	1:49

*Figures indicate minutes and seconds required for the respective units to register the given amount of CO. The rate of release wasn't perfectly constant for each product, thus these times are more relative than definitive.
†This unit is identical to the other CO Sentinel, but it's equipped to shut down a generator and interface with other alarms.

Although they are not calibrated to give an immediate alarm when detecting low or moderate concentrations of CO, the marine detectors we tested will respond quickly to a rapid, lethal CO intrusion. We think that identifying a slow accumulation of CO is a very practical concern. Time-weighted sensors are a good innovation in that they may reduce the number of nuisance alarms by prioritizing the CO threat relative to time. But they also desensitize detectors in a way that we think may preclude them from warning against a less potent yet still significant concentration of CO.

Among the 9-volt surface-mount units we tested, the Fireboy-Xintex will offer more comfort in that its durability is backed up by UL approval, but the less expensive CO Star works just as well and may last just as long,

depending on how rigorously you use your boat. At just $68, the CO Star is certainly appealing.

Of the hardwired models, the CO Sentinels from Fireboy-Xintex ($157 and $190 for the interface and generator-shutoff capabilities) are the better value because of their warranty renewal plan, which will ensure that you have a properly functioning device for as long as you care to keep up with it. The product support offered by Fireboy-Xintex is the kind of thing that reinforces trust in CO detectors, and that's something that can save lives. The Safe-T-Alert was on par in terms of performance, and is much less expensive than its counterparts at $55. Because of that, and its additional features, we deem it a Best Buy; but keep in mind that you'll have to replace it at least every five years.

DBC's Swiftsure Global ($3,625 for six person in a valise) is a moderately capable offshore raft at a moderate price. We like that its fabric comes with a 10-year warrantee, but overall this product is a notch below those mentioned above because of its single-arch canopy. The remaining offshore rafts we tested had significant flaws and shortcomings.

Sea Anchors

When properly deployed, a well-designed and well-built sea anchor can be an excellent tool to control vessel drift under a variety of conditions. If things go badly, and your vessel is adrift without power or a rig, a sea anchor can hold the vessel's bow into a seaway, substantially improving the boat's ability to safely ride out the weather. And if the need arose, a sea anchor could even keep a vessel in distress off a lee shore for a while. For these reasons, many knowledgeable blue-water cruisers consider sea anchors mandatory safety gear.

PS took a group of six sea anchors out to sea and deployed three of them in 5- to 8-foot waves to examine their functionality. Among our test specimens were four from Fiorentino (the Coast 9, the FPA-9, the Coast 16, and the FPA 18), and two from Para-Tech (a 15-footer and a 9-footer).

The Fiorentino FPA-9, seen here fully deployed with its 16 shroud lines showing prominently, was *PS*'s top choice among 9-foot models. The theory behind more shroud lines (Para-Tech outfits its sea anchors with eight) is that this will make the canopy less prone to inversion when the waves really kick up. This sea anchor is rated by Fiorentino for boats under 40 feet and under 20,000 pounds.

We deployed them first on a short, 20-foot rode, and later on a longer 300-foot rode. In addition to our in-water testing, which we conducted only with the 9-foot sea anchors, all the products were reviewed regarding price, construction quality, and warranty.

All of the sea anchors we looked at are of good quality and should last for years considering how rarely they're used. There are also others on the market that we didn't test, including those from Dan Shewmon, Cal-June, and W. A. Coppins in New Zealand.

The 9-footers we tested performed properly. They are well constructed and carry substantial warranties. Fiorentino's FPA-9 ($677) uses 16 sections of 8-ounce nylon in the canopy construction, whereas

the Coast 9 ($396) uses only eight sections of the same cloth. It also has twice the number of shroud lines; again 16 for the FPA-9 and eight for the Coast 9. The Para-Ring and swivel are also a size larger on the offshore sea anchor, and the nylon panels have a higher thread count. And the FPA-9 weighs 19 pounds, whereas the Coast 9 weighs just 13 pounds.

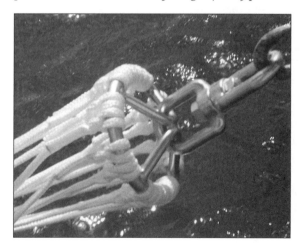

Fiorentino's Para-Ring, shown here, is a stainless steel fabrication that comes in different sizes depending upon the size of the sea anchor. It's intended to spread out the shroud lines, thus preventing chafe and enabling the swivel to work without restriction.

Maker	Fiorentino	Para-Tech	Fiorentino	Para-Tech	Fiorentino	Fiorentino
Model	Coast 9	Model 9	FPA-9	Model 15	Coast 16	FPA 18
Deployed Size (canopy diameter)	9 feet	9 feet	9 feet	15 feet	16 feet	18 feet
Weight (pounds)	13	9	19	20	22	38
Recommended Vessel LOA	under 40 feet	under 25 feet	under 40 feet	30 to 40 feet	under 50 feet	under 50 feet
Vessel Displacement (pounds)	20,000 or less	8,000 or less	20,000 or less	12,000 to 25,000	40,000 or less	46,000 or less
Material Weight Used in Panels	8 oz.	4 oz.	8 oz.	4 oz.	8 oz.	8 oz.
Number of Shroud Lines	8	8	16	16	12	28
Shroud Line Breaking Strength	2,500 lbs.	2,000 lbs.	2,500 lbs.	2,000 lbs.	2,500 lbs.	2,500 lbs.
Warranty Period (years)	5	5	5	5	5	5
Package Includes	Chute, Bag, Swivel, and Para-Ring	Chute, Bag, Shackle, Float Line	Chute, Bag, Swivel, and Para-Ring	Chute, Bag, Shackle, and Float Line	Chute, Bag, Swivel, and Para-Ring	Chute, Bag, Swivel, and Para-Ring
Price	$396	$349	$677	$859	$783	$1,521
Source	paraanchor.com	seaanchor.com	paraanchor.com	seaanchor.com	paraanchor.com	paraanchor.com

The 9-foot sea anchor from Para-Tech uses eight sections of 4-ounce nylon to form the canopy. The main shroud lines, made from $^9/_{16}$-inch tubular nylon webbing, are sewn onto the bottom 5 inches of the canopy at section seams. Additional webbing serves to connect the reinforced skirt to each of the eight shroud lines. And these sea anchors are "failure tolerant," meaning if the whole system is overstressed, the sea anchor is designed to blow a panel, but will still keep a boat's bow into the seas, though the rate of drift will increase slightly.

If not for the difference in the weight of the cloth used to fabricate each company's product, and the rated breaking strength of the shrouds, we'd be left with little but price to pick a winner. But that's not the case.

Yes, the 9-foot sea anchor from Para-Tech is less expensive than its counterparts from Fiorentino, particularly the FPA-9. However, Para-Tech doesn't include a swivel, which would add $40 to $60 to the price, and shipping isn't included either. But sea anchors are products intended for use in emergency situations, and at those times, we'd feel more comfortable relying on something that's overbuilt. Fiorentino builds top-of-the-line sea anchors using stainless-steel hardware. We'd gladly pay the additional money for Fiorentino's products because we feel their more rugged construction will enable them to endure Neptune's savage moods longer than those from Para-Tech.

Onboard Medical Kits

Medical kits are a little removed from our usual areas of expertise, so we sought the counsel of Dr. Paul Gill, who is not only a sailor, but an emergency room physician and author of *The Onboard Medical Handbook*. To paraphrase his basic advice on the topic: Keep a well-stocked medical kit on board, not because it might save someone's life (although it could), but because it can save you expensive and time-consuming trips to the hospital while you're daysailing or cruising.

Aboard his own boat, Dr. Gill relies on a home-made medical kit, comprised mostly of materials he purchased at a local drugstore. He recommends storing your medical supplies in an organized fashion, either in a waterproof bag, a fishing tackle box, or some other suitable container that is compact enough to store in an out-of-the-way yet easily accessible place on board.

We asked the good doctor to review some commercially available medical kits marketed to sailors. These kits, we stipulated, would be suitable for coastal cruising, which could be defined loosely as sailing or motoring for several days at a time within relatively easy reach of expert medical help—a matter of hours, not days, away. We expected these kits to be better stocked than rudimentary kits suitable for daysailing, but not quite as comprehensive as those that might be carried by offshore sailors who venture beyond or at the extreme range of rescue craft.

Dr. Gill examined the Medical Sea Pak Coastal Cruising Kit, which has since been replaced by the Coastal Cruising Pak ($380 in the soft foam bag, $449 in a hard Pelican case). He also looked at the Comprehensive Aquatic Kit from Adventure Medical Kits (since replaced by the Marine 500, which sells for around $100 and is intended for use aboard vessels that would remain within six hours of medical assistance). And, he evaluated the Master Mariner First Aid Kit from Orion ($99.99), which has since been discontinued and has been replaced by the Coastal Kit.

Dr. Gill gave the Coastal Cruising Kit high marks for the generous-sized, easily stowable bag that it comes in, for its easily accessible layout, and for its generally ample wound care and miscellaneous supplies. He felt, however, that the kit's major draw-back was its lack of medications, most of which could be had at a neighborhood pharmacy for $100 to $150. And though it comes with a *First Aid by Numbers* reference guide, he felt that booklet didn't offer sufficient information regarding some of the problems the kit's user might encounter. Ultimately, he thought the kit was grossly overpriced for what it contains. Those comments also apply to the Coastal Cruising Pak.

The Master Mariner First Aid Kit, Dr. Gill told us, would be of limited use to coastal cruisers and would be best suited for daysailing boats. He said you could treat sunburn, abrasions, minor sprains, and small cuts with this kit, but it would prove wholly inadequate for most significant injuries or illnesses at sea. Though it's the least expensive of the three kits, it's not an advantage that would count for much in a medical emergency. And those comments also apply to the Coastal Kit.

He did, however, recommend the Comprehensive Aquatic Kit from Adventure Medical Kits—without reservation. The Marine 500, which has replaced the Comprehensive Aquatic Kit, is nearly identical. He spoke highly of how the kit's contents were organized, and said it lacked only a cravat (which can be easily improvised), tongue blades, melatonin (for sleep), a 6-inch elastic bandage, a single-edged razor, and a magnifying lens. "It's compact yet amazingly comprehensive for its size," wrote Dr. Gill, "and Dr. Weiss's *A Comprehensive Guide to Wilderness and Travel Medicine*, which comes with the kit, is a gem. I doubt that you could buy the contents of this kit and an equivalent container for less than the asking price—better simply to buy this kit, study its contents, then stow it in an accessible place and hope you won't have to use it too often."

CHAPTER 9

Onboard Maintenance

The bane and the joy of every sailboat owner is maintenance. You—or someone—has to see to this important aspect, or your vessel will simply go to seed. And we're not talking mere cosmetics here. Sure, keeping the topsides waxed can prolong the life of a vessel's gelcoat, and it's always nice to see sparkling brightwork, but if you don't monitor the condition of things like seacocks, hoses, and anchor rodes, you may not have a vessel for very long. This chapter offers information on a broad spectrum of boat maintenance topics. We'll begin with tools and work our way to materials.

Tool Locker

MARINE TOOL KITS

When it comes to tool kits, functionality, quality, and reliability top the list of criteria, especially on the water where a good pair of pliers may be the only thing that can get you out of a jam. To get a handle on off-the-shelf tool kits for onboard use, we scanned the marine catalogs and the Web, and came up with a group of 11 pre-packaged sets of tools ranging from $25 to $100. West Marine's private label and Seafit kits are supplied by Allied Tools of Sylmar, CA, while BOAT/U.S. carries the Great Neck line. Two of the kits appeared to be nearly identical (our West Marine set and the Great Neck MS36), except for the color of their cases, their screwdriver handles, and the size of the adjustable wrench and pliers.

Pre-packaged kits like these offer two main advantages: rapid acquisition of a lot of new tools, and a low unit price compared to buying the tools individually or buying a high-quality tool set from a company like Snap-On or Mac. Another plus is the toolbox itself, which protects the tools and keeps them organized.

The big drawback of these sets is obvious: The tools are cheap. While they may do the same job as a higher-quality tool in many instances, their sub-par materials and finish will eventually lead to failure. One key difference between the average home or shop tool set and one used on a boat is operating in an environment that's more corrosive. Although various claims of rust resistance appear on several of the boxes our sets came in, only one told us how that extra resistance was gained: the stainless steel set

LINK TOOLS

Link Tools are generally regarded as spare-no-expense tools. They're made entirely of high-grade steel plated with nickel and highly polished chrome. (Don't scoff at chrome; if it's properly applied, say some metallurgists, it's the most enduring coating for metal you can find.) We think the company's 41-piece set is outstanding. Every piece is equipped with Link's patented locking mechanism, a case-hardened pin actuated by a spring-loaded collar. It simply will not let go, so the tip won't come off and drop in the bilge. When first introduced, the set was not cheap ($250 list), but we fully understand that sailors often want something they can depend on forever. (This set has a complete ¼-inch socket set and includes some screwdriver bits.)

Not long ago, Link put together a more modest tool set ($160 list). The 18-piece kit is basically a ¼-inch ratcheting screwdriver and T-bar set, with 14 screwdriver bits to fit any screw you may encounter—slotted, Phillips, square-drive, hex, Torx, or star. Included in the boxed kit are a T-bar, extender, and U-joint.

PS testers have long been impressed by the quality of Link Tools. This 18-piece set includes a ratcheting screwdriver and a T-bar, making it versatile, if somewhat expensive ($160) tool.

from West Marine. As we examined these tool kits, it became clear that the term "marine" really had to do with tool selection—not corrosion resistance. Some of the larger sets include tape measures, electrical fuses and continuity testers, ignition files, utility knives, wire, wire terminals, and battery terminal brushes.

Unless otherwise specified, the tools we tested are not made of stainless steel; alloy formulas are not provided, and given the price of the tools, we didn't attempt to determine alloy content. Suffice it to say that if they're not stainless, and you don't oil them (and maybe transfer them to a moisture-proof box), they'll begin to rust the minute you put them aboard.

The marketers behind these sets try to impress consumers with high tool counts. Don't pay too much attention to this, except in a relative sense, since marketers give the same weight to, say, a wrench and a tiny piece of wire. In many cases we found the actual count was less than the advertised quantity. For example, we counted only 30 pieces in the Great Neck 36-piece tool set.

PS examined the cases that house each tool set and checked the action of pliers, cutters, and ratchets, as well as the usefulness of small tools such as Allen wrenches and hex bits. And tools embodying novel approaches to traditional functions were tested for usefulness.

▷ **The Bottom Line** For sheer quality and projected durability, the $100 Sears Craftsman set is the clear winner. This general-purpose set weighs 9 pounds and includes a securely fastening plastic case

West Marine's tool kit being used here, is compact, yet it includes most of the basics, including a razor knife and electrical tape.

with carrying handle. These were the highest-quality tools in the evaluation, and although the 38-piece set costs as much as the 149-piece Seafit Deluxe Boatyard set, in this case quality counts for a lot. This would be a good starter set, augmented by others from that company's extensive line of tools. As a rule, higher quality is cheaper in the long run because it does the job better and lasts much longer than something bought on price tag alone. That's true up to the point when you drop a Craftsman-quality tool over the side. Thus, we also liked the Seafit 149-piece Deluxe Boatyard Set—because its tools are generally of a high quality, and you get a lot of them for a

decent price. We have no track record for Allied Tools, but West Marine does offer a "No Hassles Satisfaction Guaranteed" warranty with no time limit. All the rest of the tool sets appear to be of lower quality.

The fitted cases that contain these kits were generally disappointing and shouldn't weigh much in a buying decision. This is true especially for the larger cases, which are merely specialized shipping cartons. The tools themselves will likely end up in a more conventional toolbox. Also, we feel that any choice of tools will depend on what type of boat you have and what gear you have aboard. It will also depend on your skills, and on the amount of space you have to stow them. So, by far the best approach is to develop your kit after studying what you might need on your particular boat. That way you'll select only those tools you actually need. No harm in using one of these pre-packaged kits as the basis of a full set—just remember that no single one will do the job alone.

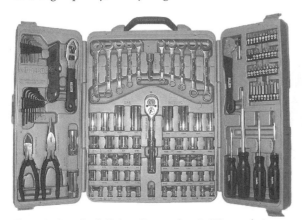

The 149-piece Seafit Deluxe Boatyard set is *PS*'s top choice for a pre-packaged marine tool kit. Its tools are of a higher quality than the others we tested, and its case does a better job of holding tools.

The Sears Craftsman 38-piece is a good starter set. *PS* testers opined that these tools make an appropriate foundation for a personalized on-board tool kit.

MULTITOOLS

The expense of a good multitool—a specialized apparatus containing small tools that most sailors already own individually—is justified by the increased convenience and efficiency this combo affords. With a good multitool, you have most of the tools you need, all in one place, and they can travel with you wherever you go—even in the water. We like that the weight and size of a multitool can often be less than a single, stand-alone hand tool, and the fact that some multitools can accommodate accessories or standard items like hex bits or sockets.

PS has attempted to stay on top of the ongoing developments in this realm because these tools truly are valuable for sailors, and we recommend that every serious sailor carry one when on board. In our most recent update regarding multitools, we examined a group of eight tools, most of which had finished high in a previous test of eighteen models. Among these eight are some newer items and one revamped model as well. They include: Gerber's MP800 Legend ($60), Kershaw's Multitool No. A100CX ($80), Leatherman's Charge Ti ($124), Crunch ($62), and Wave ($58), SOG Powerlock T60G TiNi ($87), Spyderco SpydeRench T01 ($82),

and the Victorinox Swisstool Plus ($72). Each comes with a belt pouch and a lanyard attachment, except the Kershaw tool has no lanyard attachment and the SpydeRench T01 has a clip instead of a pouch.

▷ **The Bottom Line** Certain tools are more appropriate for certain applications. If cutting wire and harder items is important, consider the mechanical advantage and overall smoothness of SOG Powerlock's compound leverage aided by one-handed opening/closing. If you must deal with some special fasteners like Torx, Allen, Posidriv, and Robertson (square) drive, the modular bits included with Leatherman's Charge and Wave should appeal. The two locking-jaw models—the Kershaw and the Crunch—are chiefly helper tools in our view, but are good at what they do. If you insist on trying to get by with one of these alone, we suggest the Leatherman Crunch, which comes closer to bridging the gap between Vise-Grips and pliers. If turning fasteners in larger, unpredictable sizes is a likely application, the SpydeRench by Spyderco allows you to turn and grip at the same time. If one-hand access to a maximum number of tools is key, consider the Gerber Legend, which also has tough, replaceable cutting inserts. The Swisstool will appeal to Victorinox knife

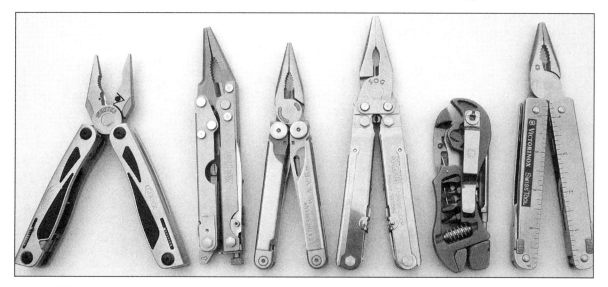

In one of *PS*'s most recent evaluations of multitools, we examined six items, from left: the Gerber MP 800, the Kershaw A 100CX, Leatherman's well established Wave, the SOG Powerlock, the Spyderco SpydeRench T01, and the Victrinox Swisstool Plus. Of these, our we felt the Leatherman Wave and the SOG Powerlock were the most versatile.

Among the sheath knives that *PS* examined were the following, clockwise from upper left: Benchmade's 100 SH20, a Myerchin marlinspike, Myerchin's A 508, Myerchin's Shark A 566, the SOG Seal Pup, Benchmade's 140H SSR, and the Mission MPK.

TOOL CORROSION

Readers often write to solicit advice on preventing or forestalling rust on their onboard tools. Usually, we advise them to obtain a good, sealed container or box for stowing the tools. The basic problem is the condensation of moisture inside a boat. (Moisture must be present to support the rusting process.) Of course, condensation results from temperature differences. If a boat is well ventilated, the interior temperature will change with the exterior temperature, and condensation will be virtually eliminated, thus minimizing the accumulation of moisture and holding at bay the dreaded reddish oxidation. For the purpose of ventilation, *PS* favors solar vents, in particular those from Nicro, which incorporate a solar-powered NiCad battery to provide 24-hour air movement.

fans, but there's not much additional here beyond the pliers.

Among these eight, the four that are designed for the most comprehensive applications are the Gerber Legend, Leatherman Wave, Leatherman Charge, and the SOG Powerlock. Any of these four would be our top choice, depending upon the features you choose to emphasize.

SAILOR'S KNIVES

There can be no overstating the importance of a good knife to a sailor. It does everything from routine maintenance to saving life and property. Not only should every sailor carry a knife on his belt or in his pocket, sharp knives should be strategically located around the boat to grab in emergencies. Whether you prefer the speed of a sheath knife, the convenience of a folding pocketknife, or the versatility of a multitool, don't leave the dock without your own blade.

Due to success in past tests, *PS* has favored the Boye Dendritic Cobalt knife for some time now. However, the knife industry continues to introduce new products with improvements in corrosion resistance, weight, and design making them more suitable

to marine applications. So, we try to stay abreast of these developments by orchestrating regular tests. In the most recent of those, we evaluated 18 knives.

After assessing the cutting capability (using $^7/_{16}$-inch polyester line and $^1/_2$-inch polypropylene rope), checking magnetic influence, evaluating corrosion resistance, and examining portability and deployment, we have to admit that a good deal of selecting the proper knife involves subjective criteria. We can only indicate what knife or knives we'd choose from this group and explain why.

The best cutters in both types of rope were the 140HSSR from Benchmade ($120), and the D'Allara ($55) and Salt I ($50) from Spyderco. If you don't use rope as difficult to cut as polypro, the following join this group: Benchmade 100SH20 ($70) and 806SD2 ($120), Emerson SARK ($110), Fällkniven U2 ($50), Mission MPK ($329), Myerchin A508

PS VALUE GUIDE | KNIFE ATTRIBUTES

Model	Type
Benchmade 100SH20	Fixed-blade w/sheath
Benchmade 140HSSR	Fixed-blade w/sheath
Benchmade 770BC1	Folder w/axis lock
Benchmade 806SD2	Folder w/axis lock
Benchmade 942SBT	Folder w/axis lock
Emerson SARK BTS	Folder w/liner lock
Fällkniven U2	Lockback folder
Mission MPK	Fixed blade w/sheath
Myerchin A508	Fixed-blade w/ spike & sheath
Myerchin A566P	Fixed-blade w/neck sheath
SOG Flash II	Folder w/assisted opening
SOG SEAL Pup	Fixed blade w/sheath
Spyderco Assist	Lockback folder
Spyderco D'Allara Rescue	Folder w/ball-bearing lock
Spyderco Dodo	Folder w/ball-bearing lock
Spyderco Rescue 79/93mm	Lockback folder
Spyderco Salt I	Lockback folder
West Marine Rigging	Folder w/liner-lock

Not long ago, the editors of *PS* examined 18 different sailor's knives, 13 of which were folding knives. Those included, top to bottom: the Fällkniven U2, the Spyderco Dodo, the Benchmade 770BC1, the Spyderco Salt I, Spyderco Rescue, West Marine Rigging Knife, Benchmade 942BST, the SOG Flash II, the Spyderco D'Allara Rescue Knife, a version of the Spyderco Rescue Knife that's no longer offered, the Emerson Sark, the Spyderco Assist, and the Benchmade 806SD2.

($72), and Spyderco Dodo ($78) and Rescue ($50) models. Among these, the tops in portability and deployment were the 100SH20, 806SD2, SARK, the Rescues, and the Salt I. To narrow the group further, the two that were the lowest in magnetic influence were the 100SH20 and the SARK—and both of these are in the medium–low price range.

Alternatively, you could select corrosion resistance as your prime criterion. The best here were the Mission MPK, Benchmade 100SH20, and Spyderco Salt I. But, for absence of magnetic influence, the MPK is the clear choice. And the fastest in deployment was the Emerson SARK, with its "wave" feature.

If price were your major criterion, consider the U2 and Salt I—both of which were among the top cutters. If you want an all-round model that rated "good" or better in every category except price, consider the 100SH20, the SARK, and the MPK. Factor in price, and you have the 100SH20.

LOA	Weight	Blade	Blade Shape/Edge	Blade Finish	Deploy	Origin	Street Price
7.5"	3.5 oz.	3.23"	Modified sheepfoot/Combo	Brush	One hand	USA	$70±5
9.45"	5.2 oz.	4.5"	Drop point/Combo	Black Teflon	One hand	USA	$120±15
6.5"	1.6 oz.	2.8"	Clip point/Plain	Boron-carbide	One hand	USA	$140±10
9.37"	4.78 oz.	3.94"	Clip point/Combo	Black Teflon	One hand	USA	$120±20
7.87"	2.9 oz.	3.4"	Modified reverse tanto/Combo	Black Teflon	One hand	USA	$125±25
8.3"	4.4 oz.	3.6"	Hawkbill, rounded tip/Combo	Black Teflon	One hand	USA	$110±15
5.75"	1.5 oz.	2.5"	Drop point/Plain	Satin	Two hands	Japan	$50±10
10.5"	8.5 oz	5.75"	Clip point/Combo	Non-reflective	One hand	USA	$325±25
8"	5.25 oz.	3.5"	Sheepfoot/Combo	Brush	Two hands	Japan	$72±8
5.5"	1.75 oz.	2.25"	Sheepfoot/Combo	Satin	One hand	Japan	$24±6
8"	3 oz.	3.5"	Drop point/Combo	Black titanium-nitride	One hand	USA	$70±10
9"	5 oz.	4.75"	Clip point/Combo	Gray powder	One hand	Japan	$56±4
8 3/8"	3.9 oz.	3 11/16"	Sheepfoot/Combo	Brush	One hand	Japan	$56±6
7 7/8"	5.75 oz.	3 1/2"	Modified sheepfoot/Serrated	Brush	One hand	Japan	$55±5
6 1/8"	2.6 oz.	2 1/6"	Reverse "S"/Serrated	Brush	One hand	Japan	$78±4
7 1/8"/ 8 3/16"	2.25 oz. / 2.6 oz.	3 1/8"/ 3 5/8"	Sheepfoot/Serrated	Brush	One hand	Japan	$43±5/ $53±10
7"	2 oz.	3"	Modified drop-point/Serrated	Brush	One hand	Japan	$46±4
7.5"	3 oz.	3"	Modified sheepfoot/Serrated	Satin	One hand	China	N/A

For the greatest number of top ratings, including cutting performance, and their low prices, we nominate as Best Buys the Spyderco Salt I and Benchmade 100SH20, in that order. The Salt I is Spyderco's first knife to feature the new H1 steel, a material which "doesn't rust." A similar claim is made for all the other steel parts of the knife. Whereas low carbon content typically leads to poor cutting performance, Myodo Foundry in Japan has apparently discovered how to achieve hardness with a small amount of nitrogen in the alloy. The Benchmade product uses the same H1 steel, but differs from the Spyderco in that it's a sheathed knife. It can be carried on the belt point-down, point-up, or sideways, or it can be lashed to one's arm, leg, or vest. A secure locking mechanism prevents loss. We found it comfortable to wear, especially in the conventional point-down manner, and convenient for drawing and replacing the knife with one hand.

Remember, dull knives are dangerous, especially to the user, and all knives, without exception, eventually need resharpening. If you don't know how to sharpen, don't hand your fine knife to the guy down the street with a grinding wheel. Return it to the manufacturer, who will probably charge only a nominal fee, plus return postage, to bring back that edge.

Specialized Tools

DIGITAL MULTIMETERS

When problems occur in your boat's electrical system, the first tool you should reach for is the multimeter. By definition, the multimeter is an electronic measuring instrument that combines several metering functions into a single case design. Thus a basic multimeter usually consists of an ammeter, voltmeter, and ohm-meter, with each "meter" being selectable from a dial on the front of the meter case

Model	Cutting, ⁷⁄₁₆" Sta-Set/ ½" Polypro	Portability	Deployability	Absence of Magnetic Influence	Price, by Quartile	Corrosion Resistance*
Benchmade 100SH20	Excellent/Good	Excellent	Excellent	Good	Medium Low	Excellent
Benchmade 140HSSR	Excellent/Excellent	Good	Good	Poor	Medium High	Fair
Benchmade 770BC1	Fair/Poor	Excellent	Good	Fair	Medium High	Good
Benchmade 806SD2	Excellent/Good	Excellent	Excellent	Fair	Medium High	Good
Benchmade 942SBT	Good/Fair	Excellent	Good	Poor	Medium High	Good
Emerson SARK BTS	Excellent/Fair	Excellent	Excellent	Fair/Good	Medium Low	Good
Fällkniven U2	Excellent/Good	Excellent	Poor	Fair/Good	Low	Good
Mission MPK	Excellent/Good	Good	Good	Excellent	High	Excellent
Myerchin A508	Excellent/Good	Good	Fair	Fair†	Medium Low	Good
Myerchin A566P	Good/Fair	Good	Good	Poor	Low	Good
SOG Flash II	Good/Good	Excellent	Good	Poor	Medium Low	Good
SOG SEAL Pup	Good/Good	Fair	Good	Fair	Medium Low	Good
Spyderco Assist	Good/Good	Fair	Good	Fair	Medium Low	Good
Spyderco D'Allara Rescue	Excellent/Excellent	Good	Excellent	Fair	Medium Low	Good
Spyderco Dodo	Excellent/Good	Excellent	Good	Fair	Medium Low	Good
Spyderco Rescue 79/93mm	Excellent/Good	Excellent	Excellent	Fair	Low/ Medium Low	Good
Spyderco Salt I	Excellent/Excellent	Excellent	Excellent	Fair	Low	Excellent
West Marine Rigging	Poor/Poor	Excellent	Fair	Fair	Low	Good

*Estimate based on relative alloy content, and coating if present. †Measured with included marlinspike.

and viewed on a common display. More advanced multimeters can measure parameters such as capacitance, inductance, temperature, and even include test sockets for checking the health of diodes and transistors. The very high-end multimeters are usually classified as industrial or scientific meters. These top-tier units will interface with a PC and can even display a graph of waveform shape, much like an oscilloscope, right on the meter's LCD.

You can purchase pocket-sized digital multimeters (DMM), which are smaller than a deck of cards, in colors that coordinate with your toolbox. But beware, there are scores of inexpensive private-label DMMs on the market that are downright junk. There's nothing more frustrating than trying to solve an onboard electrical problem when you can't rely on the readings that your DMM is displaying.

Selecting a test group of basic durable meters that would be worthy of the mariner's toolbox was a daunting task. We asked the pros at a number of top New England Boat Yards what their DMM preferences were. What we found was that the pro's meter of choice was as varied as the acronyms that they assigned to their meter. The marina mechanics and riggers tended to prefer products from Ideal Industries and Triplett, while the technicians opted for multimeters almost exclusively from Fluke. There was no single "popular" model used by either group surveyed—everyone had an affinity toward their own personal meter. The consensus was that once a quality meter was purchased, it was expected that the meter would remain in service for a good many years, and that the readings observed on the meter were absolute.

Here is a list of the features we feel are indispensable in a digital multimeter:

AUTO POWER OFF If a meter doesn't automatically turn itself off after a preset time, avoid it.

LOW-BATTERY INDICATOR It's important to know the health of your meter's battery to avoid questioning the validity of the readings you measure.

OVERLOAD PROTECTION This feature protects the meter from damage if the dial selector switch is set for the wrong parameter test. The best type of overload protection is one that provides protection on all ranges. Also, pay attention to what kind of protection the meter offers in the current measuring mode. Most quality meters are either fuse-protected or thermally protected in the current test at 10 amps. The majority of the low-cost DMMs do not provide any current overload protection.

CONTINUITY CHECK When this feature is selected, the meter emits an audible tone when the two meter probes are shorted together (continuity). Thus one is able to "ring" out a circuit and verify the presence or absence of continuity without having to view the meter.

DATA HOLD When working in a tight or dimly lit area (most of the work areas on a boat), the data hold feature will allow you to press a button on the meter to retain the reading on the meter until you can shed some light on the meter's LCD.

MAX/MIN HOLD This feature is very helpful when measuring voltage pull-down on a circuit when certain motors or appliances are first turned on. If the voltage reading on the circuit falls to a lower reading than when the motor was turned on, the meter automatically stores the lower reading.

AUTO-RANGING An auto-ranging DMM does not require you to set the range scale on the meter's dial. The DMM will automatically sample the input and choose the range scale that yields the best resolution. You will still have to select the correct mode (DC/AC Volts, Amps, etc.).

QUALITY ELECTRICAL TEST LEADS Many of the meters that we have omitted from this comparison simply did not come equipped with quality insulated test leads. Our choice for insulated test probes are ones manufactured with very flexible silicone leads of at least 24 inches in length. All too often, we found ourselves trying to untangle stiff lead sets on the less expensive models, only to have the leads disconnect from the meter and ultimately subject the meter prematurely to a drop test.

Pictured here are six of the eight digital multimeters that *PS* tested, along with an old Simpson analog meter (upper right-hand corner). They are, clockwise from bottom right: the Ancor 702073, the Ancor 702078, the Ancor 702072, Gardner Bender's GDT185A, Fluke's 111, and Radio Shack's RS22813. (Not shown is the Triplett 9025 and the Gardner Bender GDT200A.) These meters range in price from $30 to $130.

Also, look at the tips of the test lead set. Test lead sets with stainless steel tips make probing into electrical tie points more positive. With the stainless tips you are able to apply more pressure to the probe and press deep into a junction without fear of bending off the tip, as is often the case with a cheaper tin/steel-tipped set.

PS tested eight multimeters that range in price from $30 to $130: Radio Shack RS22813, Gardner Bender GDT185A, Gardner Bender GDT200A, Ancor's 702072, 702073 and 702078, Triplett 9025, and the Fluke 111. The $30 Radio Shack DMM holds its own on the entry-level side of the field, though it only carries a 90-day warranty. The $130 Fluke 111

INFRARED THERMOMETERS

Boat owners who do their own maintenance like to get as much help as possible diagnosing problems. One tool we've found helpful in this area is an infrared thermometer. These handy devices allow the user to measure the temperature of just about anything by simply pointing it at the object. You don't actually have to touch the item, which is a nice feature to have when working on hot engines or electrical components.

An IR (infrared) thermometer can be used to find a dead cylinder on an operating engine—it would be cooler than all the others—or to check a pump bearing for overheating, or an HVAC duct for proper outflow temperature. Anything that varies in temperature can be monitored with an IR thermometer.

Though both the Telatemp, seen here, and Raytek both work well, *PS* testers preferred the former. Here, the Telatemp assesses engine cylinder temperatures.

We looked at a pair of portable battery-powered units: one from Raytek, the MT4 Mini-Temp; and one from Telatemp, the High-Value IR Thermometer, model No. 42529. Both are trigger-activated, pistol-grip units. Features common to both units include backlit LCD displays, laser sighting, and a 6:1 field of view, and both run on a 9-volt battery.

Laser sighting helps the user point the temp probe in the exact direction of the object being measured. Keep in mind that with a 6:1 field of view, the actual area where the temperature is being sensed is far larger than the laser sight would indicate. At 6 inches from a test surface, the probe is gathering data from an area 1 inch in diameter. But, the farther the thermometer is moved away, the larger the sampling area becomes. For example, at 4 feet, the coverage area is 8 inches in diameter.

Both units will have trouble getting accurate readings from highly polished or very shiny objects. In this case it's best to apply a piece of electrical tape to the object, allow time for it to acclimate, and then measure the tape.

We like the compact size of the Raytek unit and its comfortable fit in the hand. However, we'd opt for the Telatemp unit because of its switchable laser, switchable backlighting, and slightly wider temperature-sensing range. Its lower price of $79 compared to the Raytek's $99 also factored into our decision.

gets top honors for best in class under $200. This is definitely a technician-grade meter. When we showed this meter to the marina pros, almost everyone guessed that the unit was two or three times more expensive than it really is. At first glance, the Fluke may seem a little excessive for the average do-it-yourselfer. However, when you factor in what it costs to have a technician visit your vessel for just one hour, the meter will pay for itself—provided, of course, that you're skilled or lucky enough to solve the problem.

PORTABLE OIL CHANGERS

Changing the oil on a typical diesel or gas-powered auxiliary engine is a royal pain in the neck, and if you have to hire someone else to come and do it, it's a pain in the wallet. Everything is more expensive when it comes to boats—we all know this. That's why gadgets like the portable oil changer can be so valuable, not only for larger auxiliary engines and gensets, but for the new crop of four-stroke outboards as well.

There are two types of portable oil changers—manually and electrically powered. To evaluate the market, *PS* collected five electricals: Jabsco Porta Quick, Jabsco 17850-0012, ShurFlo Flex Vane, Reverso OP-700, and, X-Change-R; and four manuals: Airpower Marina Pro, Airpower Topsider MVP, Tempo Oil Boy, and the West Marine Oil Vac. (In previous tests, the Jabsco Porta Quick was the top portable because it was easy to use, efficient, and reasonably priced. Fittingly, we included it in this test as well.) Most portable systems available provide closed containers for collecting and transporting of used oil, which is convenient and also lessens the like-lihood of a spill. The portable units also can be used to service your car and even your friends' boats (once they know you have one).

Two of the units in our test—the Reverso and the X-Change-R—did not come with a container. Nor did those two come with an extraction tube. Aside from using these products, we also evaluated their ease of assembly, clarity of instructions, and ease of use—which included the stability of the container—and ease of cleanup. Overall, we were looking for a pump that did the job quickly and cleanly from start to finish.

▷ **The Bottom Line** If you run your engine a lot, then an electric oil changer makes sense. In this category, we still prefer the Jabsco Porta Quick. It has all the ingredients we were looking for. It comes with an 8-foot-long power cord with alligator clips, 4 feet of neoprene hose, and a female garden hose connector for threaded dipstick tubes. The 7-amp pump is mounted to the bucket's lid, and the nitrile impeller is oil-resistant and self-priming. The bucket also has a carrying handle. In our tests, the Porta Quick lived up to its name, siphoning the oil in four minutes, which was the fastest of any pump tested. The runner-up is the smaller Jabsco (17850-0012).

The *PS* test group of portable oil changers included five electrically powered pumps and four manual ones. Here are, from left to right: the Airpower Topsider, the Jabsco Porta Quick, Shur-Flo Flex Vane, the Jabsco 178-50-0012, the Tempo Oil Boy, the West Marine Oil Vac, and the Airpower Marina Pro (foreground). Not pictured is the X-Change-R and the Reverso OP-700.

Model	Price	Source	Current Draw	Change Speed (5 quarts)	Instructions Rating	Ease of Use	Ease of Cleanup
ELECTRIC							
Jabsco 17850-0012	$108.86	boatfix.com	4 amps	7 minutes	Good	Excellent	Good (not reversible)
ShurFlo Flex Vane	$170.99	West Marine	7.5 amps	15 minutes	Good	Excellent	Good
Jabsco 17800-200 Porta Quick	$148.36	boatfix.com	7 amps	4 minutes	Good	Excellent	Good
Reverso OP-700	$299.99	foreandaftmarine.com	12 amps	7 minutes	Poor	Fair	Fair
Ray Zagar X-Change-R	$119.00	Manufacturer	8 amps	15 minutes	Excellent	Fair	Fair
MANUAL							
Airpower Marina Pro	$74.19	West Marine		10 minutes	Good	Good	Excellent
Airpower Topsider	$64.69	West Marine		18 minutes	Fair	Excellent	Fair
Tempo Oil Boy	$76.49	West Marine		10 minutes	Good	Excellent	Fair
West Marine Oil Vac	$51.79	West Marine		14 minutes	Good	Good	Excellent

We also think that Reverso makes good products, and the OP-700 is one of them. But at nearly $300, it's a bit too expensive for the boat owner who will change his oil only two or three times a year. However, it certainly would be worth sharing the cost—and the pump—with a few fellow boat owners.

Still better for the owner who only changes his engine's oil once or twice a year is a manual hand pump. In this category, it's a toss-up between the Tempo Oil Boy and the West Marine Oil Vac. The former is faster, but slightly more expensive. The latter is easier to use, but a little more messy. In the end, we'd save a few dollars and buy the Oil Vac. And,

if you want a manual model with a larger storage capacity, the Airpower Marina Pro is the choice.

Cleaners

GELCOAT RESTORERS

When we considered testing gelcoat care products, we contacted Nick Buchanan, proprietor of Scuba-Do Yacht Detailers in Sarasota, Florida. It was our intention to test only those products that claim to restore gelcoat surfaces, but he assured us that he could bring back the sheen on hull the old-fashioned way, with wax. So we decided to include a wax, too. Buchanan recommended Collinite #925 Fiberglass Boat Wax, a liquid wax. It would go up against three wipe-on products that have fared well in our past gelcoat tests: Poli Glow, Vertglas, and New Glass 2.

For a test boat we used a 21-foot runabout owned by our colleagues at *Powerboat Reports* magazine.

PS tested three leading gelcoat restorers, all of which are sold in kit form. They are, from left, Poli Glow, Vertglas, and New Glass 2. The mid-priced option—Poli Glow—had the best applicator and performed just as well as the others.

Holding Capacity	Comments
14 quart	Solid performer. Top heavy, not reversible.
14 quart	Top heavy, unprotected power switch, slow.
14 quart	Fastest electric, reversible. Easy clean-up.
No container	Fast. No siphon tube or container.
No container	Came with nothing for portable set up.
8 quarts	Fast. Need two hands to pump.
8 quarts	Sturdy, but slower. Messy pour. One-hand operation.
5 quarts	Best manual performer. Gulps when emptying.
5 quarts	Clean dumping. Insert tube drifts. Need two hands.

The boat, to our knowledge, had never been cleaned, inside or out. It was essentially the floating version of Oscar Madison's bedroom: Fish blood and rust stains, grease, grime, and dirt covered the cockpit from gunwale to gunwale. Scuffs and stains grubbed up the gelcoat, which was also chalking and fading.

Allegedly, the three wipe-on products consist of resins of higher molecular weight that provide a harder and more durable film than can be achieved with wax. The products we tested consist of water-based emulsions of acrylic or acrylic/urethane resins. The resins are in the form of tiny droplets that are suspended in water. When the products are applied, the water evaporates, and the droplets flow together to form clear films. These emulsions dry rapidly and require multiple coats. And each requires reapplication about every 12 months.

So, to test, we divided the boat into three sections, one for each restorer, with the wax being applied next to them. Each of the three products, which all come in kit form, was applied according to its directions. As for the wax, Buchanan wet-sanded, applied rubbing compound, and then waxed the top surface. To make our assessment, we considered not only the performance of each product, but the ease of applica-

tion, cost, and the amount of time it takes to apply each.

The makers of all three hull restorers make it clear that surface preparation is essential to their product's success, meaning that if you miss a streak or stain, that streak or stain will become embedded under the hull restorer. Not good. So, we were very careful to get rid of all stains, surface scratches, and abrasions.

▷ **The Bottom Line** At the end of our efforts, the test sections of the boat looked brand new. We can't really judge the longevity of the restorers at this juncture, so our initial conclusions come down to application and price. In this regard, Poli Glow ($55) surpasses the rest because of its variety of applicators, its more effective cleanser, and the product's clear directions. We felt that Vertglas ($70) could use additional applicators and the New Glass 2 ($48) needed a larger applicator. We also had little success with this product's stain remover.

The sections of the boat that were waxed with Collinite looked equally new, although the hull restorers achieved a higher gloss. The good news is that it's tough to botch a wax job. There's less room for error when working with hull restorers, and hull restorers are tougher to remove.

NONSKID CLEANERS

Nonskid—whether it's raised diamond, speckled, or some other form—plays a crucial role in keeping you safe while traversing the decks of your boat. And since boat manufacturers are sometimes stingy when it comes to handrails and handholds, an aggressive nonskid is all that more important.

Nonskid's bumpy surfaces, crevices, and contours are, alas, an ideal home for dirt, grime, and the like, and thus more difficult to clean than smooth surfaces. Talk about elbow grease. If you're not using the right cleaner, you'll never get the job done.

The marine industry has developed a number of products formulated specifically to clean nonskid. We rounded up a bunch of them for our test, and then threw in a couple of household cleaners for comparison's sake. Our group includes some familiar names in the boat-cleaning business: Star brite,

Aurora, Marykate, West Marine, 3M, and Meguiar's. An Internet search yielded a nonskid cleaner from Nautical Ease, a Saginaw, Michigan, company. We also found a cleaner from Sea Bowld. And, we threw in four household cleaners—Soft Scrub, Fantastik, Orange Clean, and 409. (We should note that West's cleaner is made by Star brite, and is an identical formulation.) All these products advertise that they're biodegradable. Some claim to leave behind a protective coating. Star brite covers the clean surface with Teflon, for instance, but only the 3M product listed its contents.

On board a boat, you don't just have to worry about grime, grease, and fish blood. These may be the most frequent substances dirtying your decks, but all kinds of other substances can make a mess. Think about it. It wouldn't be hard to find mustard, ketchup, cranberry juice, suntan oil, motor oil, or coffee stains on your deck. So, we incorporated most of those in our test, including the blood and guts of a recently caught kingfish.

To test, we segmented the cockpit aboard one of our boats into sections that measured roughly 2 feet by 2 feet. Within each square, we applied a 2-inch-wide strip of each staining element using a paintbrush. The kingfish was two days old and frozen, so most of the blood was congealed even after it thawed. Still, we were able to dig into the fish's innards with the paintbrush and obtain a fearsome mixture of blood and guts. After applying all the staining elements, our testers then allowed the surfaces to get good and dry before the cleaning commenced.

Working carefully to avoid having a cleaning agent contaminate the adjacent squares, our testers applied the cleaners, closely following the directions of each. We used either a small handheld scrub brush or a white cotton cloth to clean the surfaces, and we spent an equal amount of time cleaning with each product. A handful of the products require you to wait anywhere from 30 seconds to two to three minutes after application and before rubbing or scrubbing.

All of the marine cleaners did a good job of attacking the cranberry juice, beer, and other liquid stains. The grease and the fish blood/guts proved to be the toughest stains to remove. Even the best cleaners left faint stains from the fish blood/guts on our deck.

Only Soft Scrub completely removed the fish blood/guts. However, you really shouldn't use Soft Scrub on gelcoat because much of its cleaning prowess comes from abrasive particles. And, the manufacturer stipulates this on the bottle: "ATTENTION: To prevent scratching . . . fiberglass . . . surfaces, use sparingly and rub gently." Among the other household cleaners, Fantastik performed the best, leaving behind only some fish blood/guts and grease stains.

▷ **The Bottom Line** The products from Meguiar's and 3M performed the best, easily removing all of the substances and leaving only faint fish blood/guts stains. We used these two products to clean the rest of the boat's nonskid surfaces. Ranking right behind

PS's test group included these marine-specific products: They were (from left to right): West Marine Nonskid Deck Cleaner, Star brite Nonskid Deck Cleaner, Marykate Cleaning Detail, Sea Bowld Deck Cleaner, Nautical Ease Non-Skid Deck Cleaner & Black Streak Remover, 3M Non-Skid Cleaner, Aurora Boat Scrub, and Meguiar's Non-Skid Deck and Hull Cleaner.

The staining substances were applied to each of the taped-off sections of the cockpit sole aboard our test boat. We let them dry for a while, and then each nonskid cleaning product was put into action to clean a square.

Meguiar's and 3M in cleaning performance were the products from Nautical Ease, West Marine, and Star brite. The Aurora Boat Scrub worked well, too, but it left behind a slight coffee stain, along with some grease and blood/guts.

Now let's look at pricing—specifically, price per ounce. Of the top five performers, the West Marine and Star brite products are the cheapest by the ounce: 25 and 28 cents, respectively. Nautical Ease's cleaner is less expensive, but you almost certainly have to buy it online, which will add a couple of bucks in shipping. The Meguiar's and 3M products are the most expensive in our group. And Fantastik is very inexpensive when compared to the others (roughly 6 cents per ounce).

So, we recommend getting the Meguiar's or 3M cleaners for tough nonskid jobs. Boat owners who conduct their own maintenance—meaning occasional oil and grease stains on deck—would do well with either of these two more expensive cleaners. For the rest of these stains, we recommend the Star brite, West Marine, or Nautical Ease cleaners. They're effective and not that expensive. If your deck rarely sees stains like these, then Fantastik should do the job.

RUST REMOVERS

Most of us, at one time or another, have left the anchor chain on the bow or tools exposed to the elements—thus opening the door to an oxidation process that leaves us with that familiar nasty reddish stain on the deck or cockpit sole. These stains, which are among the toughest to remove because rust seeps into the gelcoat, often form around deck hardware like cleats, handrails, and stanchion bases.

PS recently rounded up nine products that claim to remove rust stains. Most are cleaners made expressly for fiberglass, but a few also can be used to clean chrome, tile, and porcelain. Most of the products we tested contain some sort of acid, like oxalic, or hydrogen chloride. Despite their acidic ingredients, some claim they won't hurt a boat's gelcoat. Marykate, one of the most popular brands of cleaning products in the marine industry, is one such product. Other recognizable marine names in our test include Star brite, Aurora, and FSR gels (Fiberglass Kreme Cleaner) from Davis. Five of the others are liquid and two are sprays.

The more expensive products are the "marine" cleaners. For instance, prices range from $2.39 for a bottle of muriatic acid bought at Ace Hardware to $12.69 for a can of Boeshield's Rust Free bought at West Marine.

To test these products, we taped off equal-sized sections of the cockpit sole aboard a test boat owned by the magazine and created some nasty rust stains in each by leaving tools, some chain, and several rusty fish hooks in place for several weeks. Then, we followed the directions of each product, using either a small handheld brush or a white cotton cloth to clean the surfaces. All of the cleaners instruct the user to let the product sit on the stain, some for as little as 30 to 60 seconds, some for as long as five minutes. Some call for just a rinsing with fresh water after application, others instruct you to do some scrubbing.

We learned that muriatic acid worked the best, leaving only a speck of a rust stain in its square. None of the other products completely cleaned the stains in their sections. But some of these products worked better than others. Four products—all sold

SELF-HOIST MAST CLIMBERS

When the time comes to ascend to the masthead to fix that cantankerous tri-color light, you'll want to make sure that you're using the safest, most reliable, functional equipment you can find and afford. *PS* has tested mast-climbing devices of various stripes in the past, including fixed mast steps. Most recently we had a close look at one industry standard—the ATN Topclimber—and a new player, the Mast Climber from On Rope 1.

Both of these products are essentially harnesses made of nylon webbing that are affixed to ascenders —or jumars, in mountain-climbing parlance. With both systems you strap on the harness, and then alternately slide one ascender up, and allow it to bear your full weight as you then slide up the next one. It's a climbing method that takes some practice, but even a less-skilled mariner can master it.

These two products differ principally in that the ATN Topclimber requires that you thread a dedicated climbing line through the ascenders, whereas the ascenders on the Mast Climber simply clamp on to any existing line of the right diameter. That makes it more versatile than the TopClimber, and there's less setup time. However, with the device from On Rope 1, you'll have to invest more time learning to use it and $115 more to own it.

The Mast Climber's components are more ergonomically engineered, and it also comes with a third ascender, which is intended to bear your weight while resting. Still, we prefer the simplicity of the Topclimber. You can learn to use it in a few minutes, and it lends itself to one-handed use more readily than the Mast Climber. It comes with a lifetime warranty and a durable case. However, one caveat here: It's vitally important to make sure that the shackles on the ascenders' arms are dogged down securely. More than one user has seen them back out due to having them inserted in the wrong direction. For more involved climbing, the Mast Climber is a good choice, but if you simply need to go aloft for routine maintenance and infrequent emergencies, the Topclimber should serve you well. Just be careful with those shackle pins.

On Rope 1's sophisticated Mast Climber (top) utilizes two harnesses and three jumar-type ascenders. It's more versatile than ATN's TopClimber (middle), but also more expensive. The TopClimber is a simple device, but it requires more set up time and must be used with a line that's secured to the deck. The third approach shown here (bottom) is a simple 2:1 purchase system coupled to a bosun's chair. It's less expensive, but also less secure than the other two, and it can easily tire the user on longer ascents.

as rust-stain removers for fiberglass—made the cut after the first round: Star brite's Rust Stain Remover (a spray), FSR stain remover (a gel), Power One Rust Stain Remover, and Fiberglass Kreme Cleaner. We tried these four again on a fresh set of stains. It became clear that the longer you let them soak into the affected areas, the better they work. So, to be fair, we applied the four finalists and gave them all five minutes before rinsing.

The Fiberglass Kreme Cleaner cleaned its section, but this blue gel also turned the deck light blue. The Star brite spray cleaned its entire stain, while the FSR and Power One left only trace amounts of stain. So, the question remains: Should you use muriatic acid—a product not sold specifically for cleaning fiberglass—on your boat?

No, says Mark Hollenback, technical director of the research group at Cook Composites, a major manufacturer of construction resins and gelcoats. "It can cause fading of certain pigments in gelcoat," he said. The safest way to go is to put the responsibility on the people who produce a product for boats, he said.

We have to agree. So we recommend that you go with one of the products intended for the job. The top fiberglass-specific brand—the Star brite—worked just as well as the muriatic acid when it was allowed to soak for five minutes, and it's our top pick. If the Star brite isn't available, we'd get the gel from FSR. The Power One cleaner is the cheapest per ounce, but it's only available online, so you'll have to pay for shipping.

BILGE ABSORBERS

If you spend any time working on your boat's engine, you'll know what we mean when we say that anyone who fools around with their engine while unprotected by oil absorbers is courting problems. Those who do so sooner or later regret their folly, because the second you drop a loaded oil filter into your bilge, you realize that the most important piece of gear on your boat is the bilge absorber. If you're prepared, you already have one strategically placed under the filter, or at least somewhere under the engine. Even then, any errant oil will very quickly turn all the surfaces of the bilge a slick gray-black. It

will foul the bilge pump, it will slosh up against the undersides of the floorboards, and it will coat every wire and connection.

An oil or fuel spill on board has to be cleaned up by hand—pumping it overboard is criminal, and carries steep fines—as much as $38,000 in some U.S. states. A bad spill, or a small spill that's left to slosh around, is a nightmare, and some bilges, particularly those with rough fiberglass or wood surfaces, never look the same again.

We took it upon ourselves to determine which of the oil-absorbent products on the marine market really work best, so we ordered a variety of them and put them in plastic bins filled with 6 gallons of water, a half a cup of antifreeze, and a quart of oil. We then let the bins sit for about two months in the back of the office, regularly jostling and jouncing them to keep things sloshing. A couple of the products worked quickly and very well. A couple worked slowly and fairly well. One didn't seem to work much at all.

There are two basic types of absorber. One absorbs "mechanically," by means of wicking and adsorption or absorption. ("Adsorption" means that a liquid is attracted and adheres only to the outside of a surface, while "absorption". . . well, you know what absorption means.) The other type absorbs the fluid and then reacts with it chemically or biologically, converting it into another state. In both cases, the products are intended to absorb only oil or fuel—not water.

The products come in three forms—thin sheets, pillows or packets, and rolls or socks (mini-booms). The sheets are intended to be used both during work projects and for long-term maintenance. The pillows and rolls are intended more for long-term absorption; they are typically left in the bilge for several months or one boating season. We tested 3M's Sheets, the MDR Engine Pad, the MDR Mini Boom, Petrol Rem's BioSok, Envirobond's Captain's Choice, and Imbiber Beads.

▷ **The Bottom Line** If you have oil or fuel in your bilge, you should remove it—immediately. Given this imperative, the products that must remain in your bilge for any length of time to work don't appeal to us much. Among those we tested, the BioSok, for instance, requires a year to completely biodegrade the oil it has taken in. This type of product may be

GASKET SOURCE

Like a lot of sailors, we abhor leaks down below. You can fashion temporary fixes for some leaks, but for others—like those on a hatch seal—you'll need to install a new gasket, and that presents problems of its own. Finding a properly sized and configured gasket isn't always easy, particularly for an older boat. That's why we were so pleased when we happened upon Jerry Belsha and his company A Glass Act out of Long Beach, California.

Belsha owns almost 5,000 custom dies for extruding rubber products, and roughly 4,000 of them are specifically for boats. He can extrude gaskets using an existing die from his vast catalog, or he can create a die to meet your gasketing needs. For the best reproduction accuracy, Belsha requests that you send him a slice of the original gasket. If he doesn't have that configuration in his collection, for $150 he'll fabricate a new die, and in a couple of weeks he'll send you sample of the newly extruded gasket.

If it fits your needs, you can order whatever length you need of the material for somewhere around $4.50 per foot.

Belsha extrudes gaskets from EPDM (ethylene propylene diene monomer, a rubber material whose principal components consist of the compounds ethylene and propylene). He recommends using 3M Super Weatherstrip Adhesive for installation. About 90 percent of the gaskets that Belsha sells are black, but the material can also be extruded in white or gray.

Yes, this approach is much more expensive than using some store-bought closed-cell-foam gasketing that you might find at hardware stores, but if you want that original-type seal and don't like the glue giving out on the store-bought weather-stripping, then custom gaskets from A Glass Act might be the answer—especially if your boat uses one of those 4,000 dies that Jerry Belsha has in stock.

---

useful for long-term light duty, but not when you need to mop up a significant spill.

The products that did this best in our evaluation were the Sheets from 3M. These are made of random fibers of polypropylene, or plastic, which attract fluid by wicking, a capillary action in which the surface of a liquid and the surface of a solid are drawn together. The polypropylene fibers contain millions of tiny air pockets that hold the oil or gas.

The 3M sheets can be stuffed, packed, laid flat, or turned into a trough or funnel. In our test they soaked up the oil fastest (most of it in a few minutes) and held it in what became otherwise fairly clean water for two months. The soaked pads could be lifted out of the bilge easily without falling apart. They were also the cheapest products we tested.

Of the five products we tested, only the MDR Engine Pad did as well soaking up the oil, but the 3M pad's excellent performance, combined with its low cost, make it our Best Buy.

BILGE CLEANERS

If you were to closely inspect your bilge and identify what ends up there, you'd surmise that what *PS* editors have referred to in past articles as a "noxious soup" contains varying amounts of water (salt/fresh), oil, grease, fuel, and other detritus including dirt, hair, and possibly soap from the boat's shower (if it drains to the bilge). Much of this can be cleaned with everyday detergents, but oil, grease, and fuel present the biggest problems. None of these three mix with water, and the first two tend to act as binders for dirt. They also tend to cling to surfaces in the bilge and float on top of the bilgewater, presenting a triple threat: They're messy, they can clog up a bilge pump, and they pose the potential of a fire hazard.

The usual approach to bilge cleaning has been to help these incompatible materials mix into an emulsified puree that can then be pumped or drained out of the bilge and disposed of properly. The instructions on most bilge cleaning products call for them to be added to the bilge, along with a sufficient amount of water so that mixing occurs. Most manufacturers suggest that a rocking boat is sufficient to mix these products, the water, and the offending matter so that the resulting slurry can be removed.

To find out which off-the-shelf bilge cleaners really do that job, we assembled 15 different products that advertise themselves as such and put them to the test. (Actually, one, Clean Water Solutions' Microbial Powder, only claims that it "eliminates oil contaminants on . . . porous surfaces," but always seeking environmentally sound options, we chose to try it anyway.) Of the other products, 12 are liquids and two are gelatinous.

The manufacturers of most bilge cleaners stipulate the amount of the product to be used, and often this is relative to boat size. Aurora Marine, for instance, recommends 7 ounces of its Bilge Bath for every 10 feet of boat length. The directions on Meguiar's Bilge Cleaner dictate "Use 32 ounces for a 25-foot boat and proportionally more or less on smaller or larger boats." And Bass Pro Shops' Heavy Duty Bilge Cleaner indicates 2 ounces of cleaner for every gallon of water in the bilge. These directions are typical of the 15 products we tested, though none take into account the widely varying volume in bilges of boats the same size.

To ensure that our test would evaluate each product in the same manner, we poured identical amounts of motor oil, gasoline, and water into 8-ounce jars and agitated the mixtures. Then we added one-eighth of a cup of each cleaner—one cleaner per jar—and agitated them again. After 10 minutes, we examined the jars to see how thoroughly the oily substance had emulsified. We then let the jars sit for 30 minutes and agitated them again. After that, we let the specimens sit for a week and then rechecked them.

We also sicced the cleaners on a 1-inch-long bead of unused axle grease to see how each would react with a tough task. We checked the jars at 48 hours

Among the 15 different bilge cleaning products that PS assembled for testing were (bottom row, left to right): Star brite's Power Pine, Sudbury's Bilge Cleaner, Aurora's Bilge Bath, Marykate's Big Bully Bilge Cleaner, West Marine's Bilge Cleaner, OR Bilge Bilge Cleaner, Star brite's Sea Safe, Meguiar's Bilge Cleaner, and West Marine's Heavy Duty Bilge Cleaner; (upper group, clockwise from bottom right) Bass Pro Shops' Heavy Duty Bilge Cleaner, Clean Water Solutions Microbial Powder, West Marine's Bilge Pro, Sea Bowld's Heavy Duty Bilge Cleaner (partially hidden), Heller Glanz's Marine Bilge Cleaner, and Star brite's Super Orange Bilge Cleaner (partially hidden), which was our top performer.

BARNACLE REMOVERS

PS and its sister publication *Powerboat Reports* co-own a 21-foot runabout that we regularly use for product testing. We realized at some juncture that we'd been pretty lax in maintaining this vessel's bottom. The boat, which resides in Florida, was recently discovered with several thick, healthy, and hard clusters of barnacles covering some bare areas on the bottom. Naturally, this was a great opportunity to test barnacle removers.

After scouring (an intentional pun) the marine catalogs and the Web, we came up with three products: Marsolve biodegradable marine solvent ($15 per gallon), Marykate On & Off Hull and Bottom Cleaner ($11.99/quart, $25.99/gallon), and Star brite Barnacle and Zebra Mussel Remover ($11.99/quart, $28.99/gallon). The Star brite product is also sold as West Marine EZ-On EZ-Off—and for a few dollars less. Marykate no longer sell its Barnacle and Zebra Mussel Remover, but the company told us its Hull and Bottom Cleaner could be used on barnacles.

Marsolve, which we reported on a few years back, is used primarily to remove water scale, rust, and marine growth from the cooling systems of marine engines, or from water heaters. It poses no waste disposal problem because it's biodegradable in any concentration. Marsolve also has no special ventilation or respiratory requirements—but eye protection and gloves are recommended. Use a 2:1 solution of water and Marsolve.

The makers of this product claim that it kills barnacles and mollusks and dissolves their shells and the glue that holds the shell to the boat or engine. It has a shelf life of about five years.

Marykate On & Off Hull and Bottom Cleaner utilizes three acids—hydrochloric, phosphoric, and oxalic. It causes burns on contact; its fumes are corrosive; and it should be used in a well-ventilated area. Rubber gloves, protective clothing, and eye protection are all necessary.

The Star brite product, which contains hydrochloric acid, is just as dangerous. The same precautions are recommended.

---

and then again at one week to see how much grease had been dissolved and whether a ring had formed on the sides of the jar.

▷ **The Bottom Line** It's our belief that bilge-cleaning products should be used in small amounts for final cleanup rather than for dealing with a large quantity of oil and water. If you have large amounts of water with some oil in your bilges, you might as well pump that into a suitable container for disposal and save the cost of the bilge cleaner. (If there's gasoline in the water, however, a bilge cleaner will help suppress vapor generation.) Then you can use small amounts of cleaner to remove what's left.

The best approach, however, is to avoid the mess from the start. To do this, keep your engine tuned and change oil filters often. Regularly check fuel and oil fittings, hydraulic lines, engine seals, and gaskets, and find and fix all fuel and oil leaks. If you do have

a leak, sop up as much oil or fuel as possible with absorbent pads.

In our test, all of the products were capable of emulsifying the oil to varying degrees, but some had trouble dissolving the grease. And some of these cleaners work faster than others. We were initially impressed by the performance of Aurora's Bilge Bath in our emulsification test, but after we shook its test jar 30 minutes later, it was clear that the emulsification didn't last long.

The best performer across all of these tests was Star brite's Super Orange Bilge Cleaner. In our grease test, it didn't completely dissolve the bead after 48 hours, but a week later the grease was gone and all that remained was a milky liquid with no ring on the jar. Super Orange also outperformed the others at every stage of the emulsification test. If Super Orange has a downside, it's that it comes in a very thick liquid form that prohibits squirting

To test these products, we hauled our test boat and allowed things to dry out for a good month or so. This allowed the barnacles to dry completely, so they would be harder to remove.

The Marykate product instructs the user to pour the product in a plastic bucket and apply it with a bristle brush. That just didn't work for us. It was like trying to put shaving cream on the beard of Grizzly Adams. So we sprayed it on instead.

The Star brite remover says a roller, brush, or plastic sprayer can be used. The key to using all three products is to really saturate the area with the remover. When working on the bottom of a boat, the liquid drips down, so care is required.

▷ **The Bottom Line** We would recommend you do anything you can to avoid allowing barnacle growth on your boat. Why? Because this was perhaps the nastiest job we've ever undertaken—even worse than testing bottom paint strippers some years back. And, it's not only nasty, but dangerous. You need goggles, a hat, a mask, and heavy-duty gloves. And you should be fully clothed. Also, using acid can damage the gelcoat, so don't use a scraper.

If the barnacles aren't too resistant, start out with the Marsolve cleaner. It's less toxic, and that's a good thing. If you can't get the barnacles off with that, then try one of the acid-based products—Star brite's cleaner was slightly better than the Marykate cleaner, in our estimation.

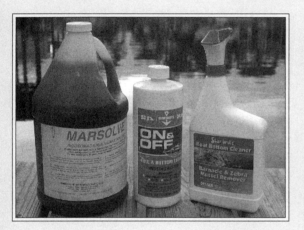

Marsolve (left) is an aqueous organic salt solution that is biodegradable, nontoxic, and noncorrosive. It's been around a long time and is primarily used to treat and clean steam boilers. Marykate On & Off (middle) contains hydrochloric, phosphoric, and oxalic acids. It's also sold under the West Marine name. Star brite Barnacle and Zebra Mussel Remover also contains acid.

and makes measuring more of a task. Among liquid cleaners, Star brite's Sea Safe Biodegradable Bilge Cleaner and Big Bully Natural Orange both earned our recommendation. The top gel was OR Bilge Cleaner. And if being kind to the environment is important to you, then the Clean Water Solutions Microbial Powder will do a good job keeping your bilge and your conscience clean.

Bottom Paint Strippers

Okay, right up front, we need to state that stripping bottom paint off a boat is simply a nasty job. Nothing fancy required. Just a paper suit, head gear, rubber gloves, a good scraper, a strong arm, and a high threshold for messy, occasionally painful work.

Over the years, the editors at *PS* have tried everything—chemical paint strippers, sanding (wet and dry), and sandblasting with conventional media and baking soda. None of these methods is ideal and none without risks. Strippers with methylene chloride are dangerous because the active ingredient is said to be carcinogenic. Even new "environmentally friendly" strippers contain some scary-sounding chemicals—methyl ethyl ketone, acetone, toluene, dimer acid, hydroxyethanoic acid, dibasic ester, and methyl-2-pyrrolidone. Some of these claim to be biodegradable but carry the skull and crossbones on the can and a warning, "Cannot be made non-poisonous." Ingest it or get it in your eye, and you go to the hospital, pronto. After all, this stuff's job is to eat bottom paint . . . lots of it.

Sanding with a good random-orbit tool or a buffing wheel with foam pad and sandpaper puts up a cloud of dust, which isn't much appreciated by your neighbors in the yard, and requires that you wear a respirator. It'll take the arms out of a good man, especially when working overhead on the hull bottom.

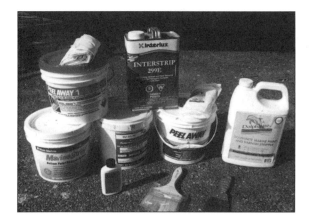

The seven bottom paint strippers that *PS* evaluated are, from left to right: West Marine's MarineStrip, Peel Away 1, Napier SV-35M, Interlux Interstrip 299E, Peel Away Marine Strip, Dolphinite, and (in the small sample bottle in front) Franmar Soy-Gel.

For several years we favored wet-sanding using 3M abrasive sheets (they look like waffle-patterned screens) wrapped over a stiff sponge. The bottom paint dribbles off with the water, so you don't need a respirator, but you do need rags tied around your wrists so the dirty water doesn't run down into your armpits. These sheets cut fairly quickly, but it's still a chore. And if your boatyard has been hassled by the environmental police about containing removed bottom paint, they might not like seeing rivers of blue, green, and black water coursing across the facility.

Shotblasting, for us, was a one-shot trial. We had professionals blast part of our old C&C 33's hull with Armex baking soda, and the results were quite good. But the company that was promoting the process to boatyards isn't actively pursuing it any longer. Developed as an industrial cleaning process for jobs such as removing grease from equipment, it requires a skilled operator. Theoretically, at the right pressure, he can remove the paint without harming the gelcoat, but a few pounds over the limit, and you end up blowing pin-sized holes in your gelcoat. Which is precisely what happened when we rented our own equipment and tried blasting with conventional media. We stopped quickly.

That brings us back around to chemical strippers . . . livin' and dyin', to paraphrase some country music singer, "with the choices we've made."

For several years now *PS* has tested so-called "safe strippers," that is, products without methylene chloride. Pretenders have come and gone, but Peel Away Marine Safety Strip, made by Dumond Chemicals, has always come out on top. Not too

long ago we tested it against Dolphinite, Interlux Interstrip 299E, Napier SV-35M, and West Marine MarineStrip. Peel Away won, followed by West Marine MarineStrip. Both require covering with paper or plastic and fairly long waiting periods—up to 24 hours—though we found both achieved most of their action in far less time—around four hours. After 24 hours, the West Marine stripper had started to harden, making scraping of the residue difficult. Dolphinite and Interstrip 299E were effective, and require just one to two hours. But in gelcoat damage tests, we found that they can dramatically crack and lift gelcoat from its substrate. This appears to happen not only on bare gelcoat, but even "inside" bottom paint left on the hull. Our conclusion then was that users of these products should not put off scraping after applying the stripper—get the paint off now and then neutralize with a liberal spray of water from a hose. The Napier product is intended for professional use only, and for spraying only, but it worked reasonably well.

We retested all five of those products as well as two recommended by readers—Peel Away #1 and Soy-Gel, made by Franmar Chemical, Inc. Peel Away # 1 contains calcium hydroxide, magnesium hydroxide, and sodium hydroxide. We were somewhat surprised to read in a Peel Away 1 handout at a store that in addition to removing "up to 30 coats of paint in one application" from "almost all surfaces, wood, brick, concrete, plaster, steel, cast iron," it also offers "safe removal of marine coatings with NO damage to the fiberglass." Hey, we thought this was for household use only! Aren't we supposed to use the Peel Away Marine for our boats? Maybe we're on to something here!

Soy-Gel does contain soybean oil; why, we're not sure. The Material Safety Data Sheet (MSDS) says, "The precise composition of this product is proprietary information." The active—and hazardous—ingredient is n-methyl-2-pyrrolidone. Nevertheless,

Franmar's literature says it "meets San Diego's toughest air quality requirements," "No ODC's, no HAP's, Low VOC," "Made from American grown soybeans," "land-fill friendly, biodegradability at 28 days."

We tested each of these products on a boat with multiple layers of black bottom paint over much older blue paint. Each of the strippers was applied as liberally as possible with a paintbrush. You learn quickly that the thicker the stripper can be laid onto the surface, the better it will work. On a vertical surface, like the keel, or an upside-down horizontal surface, like the bottom of the hull, the thicker the gel, the more will stick. This may be Peel Away's advantage, rather than the active chemicals used, because more of it stays on the hull than any of the others.

Following the instructions, we scraped away the Dolphinite after one hour, the Interstrip 299E after two hours, the Napier after six hours, and the other four—Peel Away 1 and Marine, West Marine MarineStrip and Soy-Gel—after 24 hours. (Franmar's instructions say it may start softening the paint after 30 minutes to two hours; after eight hours it may cause dulling, and over lengthy periods of 18 hours or more, damage to fiberglass may occur. Elsewhere it says if left on overnight, to cover it with plastic to keep it wet and active.)

Judging from the amount of black paint removed (the blue proved tenacious in most areas), Peel Away 1 and Marine Strip performed virtually the same, followed very closely by Soy-Gel. West Marine MarineStrip was next. Dolphinite and Interstrip 299E did very well, in much less time, but didn't remove quite as much as the top finishers (perhaps because they don't remain on the surface as long). Napier, we won't count, because it was watery and did not apply well.

▷ **The Bottom Line** When it comes to removing layers of old bottom paint, there is no free lunch. Having someone else do the job would be our first choice! However, for a do-it-yourself job, off-the-shelf chemical strippers seem to be the easiest. Remember that thickness is everything. If you can lay the gel on 1/8 to 1/4 inch thick, most of the paint will scrape off like skinned-over pudding. Then spray with water, sand lightly, and repaint.

We have to say that Peel Away works best. Peel Away 1 is considerably less expensive than the Peel Away Marine Strip and appears to work just as well, at least on the one boat bottom we used for testing. Soy-Gel and West Marine MarineStrip would be our next choices. As noted earlier, we'd start work early in the day and check results before day's end as leaving some of these gels on overnight seems too long a time, causing the gel to harden.

Dolphinite and Interstrip 299E work very well and much more quickly, so if you're in a rush and don't mind working with more volatile chemicals (like acetone, toluene, MEK, etc.), try them. We're inclined to use Peel Away for the total hull strip, then come back to problem spots with Dolphinite or Interstrip 299E.

Paints and Varnishes

BOTTOM PAINTS

Choosing bottom paint remains a tangled web for even the most experienced boat owner. Indicative of that, our most recent tests of antifouling paints have featured huge fields, in excess of 50 different paints. Aside from enabling us to determine what we believe are the best paints on the market, these tests give us the opportunity to home in on trends. One recent trend is paints with anti-slime additives. Twenty-four of the paints in our most recent test include some kind of slime fighter. These paints cost slightly more than similar paints that lack these additives, and so far, our tests indicate that having an anti-slime agent in your bottom paint is no guarantee of better antifouling protection. We'll see if these paints perform better over the long haul, as claimed by their manufacturers.

Another trend we're watching is the introduction of paints that tout a broader selection of colors, including white. The latest entry into this group is Blue Water Paints, which has come out with a line of colorful paints, called "Kolor," that includes green, red, yellow, white, black, and two types of blue—royal and bright. This follows the debut of Pettit's Vivid line, which includes a bright white paint and several bright colors. Like Pettit, Blue Water claims to have the whitest whites, the blackest blacks, the reddest reds, and so on. Interlux has long offered a

Testers inspect the painted panels after roughly six months in the water in Florida (left) and Connecticut (right). At this point, the paints are anonymous. Later, a code of drilled holes is used to identify the paints.

wide range of colors in its Trilux line. In this subsection, Vivid came out on top, but none of these paints produced particularly stellar results.

While color is certainly a consideration for bottom paint, what matters most is how well the paint repels growth. One key decision when choosing an antifouling paint is whether you want a "hard" or a "soft" paint. The difference between the two is fundamental, so we divided our results into these two groups. In the accompanying tables, we've also recommended paints in three other subgroups: water-based paints (which make for easier cleanup), white paints (examples of paints with broader palette choices), and less toxic eco-paints.

Traditionally, bottom paint consists of either metallic copper powder or copper oxide biocide mixed into a film-forming coating that also includes binding agents and pigmented solids. In a hard paint, this coating is not water soluble; the formulation allows the biocide to leach out at a fairly consistent rate. A soft paint is somewhat soluble in water, with its outer layer washing off in time to expose fresh paint. Also called ablative or self-polishing paints, soft paints typically fall into two subcategories: less expensive sloughing ablatives that simply wear away to expose fresh paint; and the more expensive co-polymer ablatives, which are formulated to better control the rate at which the biocide is released. As our tests show,

hard and soft paints can be equally effective in combating marine growth, so the choice between the two comes down to certain personal preferences and how your boat is used.

Bottom paint typically contains between 45 and 77 percent copper, and some manufacturers make a big deal about how much copper their products contain. Copper is a powerful biocide (though not as effective as the now-banned tributyltin), but the days that you could just grab the paint with highest copper content and be done are over. Our recent tests show no clear link between copper content and effectiveness. The paint with the highest copper content in our most recent test—SeaHawk Tropikote (76 percent copper)—finished near the bottom, while Interlux Optima (28 percent) was one of our top picks.

And three paints we tested don't use any copper; all are from E-Paint. Along with Kolor from Blue Water, the newest paints include Interlux's Super Ablative with Slime Fighter, Super KL with Slime Fighter, Fiberglass Bottomkote with Irgarol, and Fiberglass Bottomkote ACT with Irgarol. Pettit has

Name	Maker	Price (per gallon)	Source	RATING FL	CT	Copper %	Anti-Slime Additive	Seasons
Sea Bowld Coastal 45	Blue Water	$50	Boater's World	Good −	Fair −	45%	No	One
EP 2000 ✔	E-Paint	$232	epaint.net	Fair	Good	None	Zinc Pyrithione	One
Epoxyoap	Interlux	$50	shipstore.com	Good +	Fair +	41.20%	No	One
Fiberglass Bottomkote Aqua $	Interlux	$70	shipstore.com	Good +	Good	46.50%	No	One
Fiberglass Bottomkote	Interlux	$85	shipstore.com	Good −	Fair	42.75%	Irgarol	One
Micron 66 ✔	Interlux	$242	shipstore.com	Good +	Good −	40.41%	Zinc Pyrithione	Multiple
Regatta Baltoplate Racing ✔	Interlux	$180	Defender.com	Good	Good +	41.15%	No	One
Super KL	Interlux	$110–$115	yachtpaint.com	Fair +	Fair −	66%	Irgarol	One
Ultra	Interlux	$160	shipstore.com	Good −	Fair −	66.65%	Irgarol	One
Ultra-Kote	Interlux	$150	shipstore.com	Fair +	Fair +	66.50%	No	One
VC 17m (Canada only)	Interlux	$45–$49 (qt.)	yachtpaint.com	Poor	Fair +	20.35%	No	One
VC 17m Extra	Interlux	$45 (qt.)	West Marine	Poor	Fair	20.35%	Irgarol	One
VC Offshore	Interlux	$190	West Marine	Good	Fair	41.15%	No	One
SR-21	Pettit	$40 (qt.)	shipstore.com	Poor	Fair	21%	Irgarol	One
Super Premium	Pettit	$95	shipstore.com	Good	Fair	65.80%	No	One
Trinidad	Pettit	$150	shipstore.com	Good	Fair	65.80%	No	Multiple
Trinidad SR	Pettit	$180	West Marine	Good +	Fair	70%	Irgarol	Multiple
Unepoxy Plus	Pettit	$99	shipstore.com	Good −	Fair	55.60%	No	One
Unepoxy Standard	Pettit	$63	shipstore.com	Good −	Fair	45.70%	No	One
Vivid ✔	Pettit	$149	reddenmarinesupply.com	Good +	Fair −	25%	Zinc Omadine	Multiple
West Marine Bottom Pro Gold	Pettit	$140	West Marine	Good −	Fair +	70%	Irgarol	One
West Marine Bottomshield	Pettit	$70	West Marine	Excellent	Fair	45.70%	No	One
Tropikote	Sea Hawk	$130	refinishlinedirect.com	Fair +	Fair	75.80%	No	Multiple
Tropikote Biocide Plus	Sea Hawk	$175	refinishlinedirect.com	Good +	Fair	73.75%	*	Multiple
SeaLife 1000	SeaLife	$229	sealifemarine.com	Fair +	Fair +	39%	No	Multiple

$ Budget Buy ✔ Recommended *N-Cyclopropyl-N-(dimethylethyl)-6-(methylthio)1,3,5-triazine-2-diamine

one new paint in this test, SR-21, a paint for fresh and low-salt water. And for the first time, we also tested Sea Hawk's Tropikote Biocide Plus and Cukote Biocide Plus.

PS tests bottom paint in two locales: One set of panels was suspended in a saltwater canal in the Florida Keys, and the other was tied to the docks at a boatyard in eastern Long Island Sound in Connecticut. The panels took the plunge in July and were retrieved and rated in early January. Before rating the

paints, we look at the growth both before and after sluicing them with a bucket of water.

Only three paints in our test allowed hard growth—and that growth was sparse. There were no full-grown barnacles. So the final score usually came down to an evaluation of the amount of slime on each panel. The paints that were absolutely clean—they looked like they had just been painted—were given Excellent ratings. Those with any hard growth were given a Poor rating. We weeded out the Fair

Name	Maker	Price (per gallon)	Source	RATING FL	RATING CT	Copper %	Anti-Slime Additive	Seasons
Copper Pro 67 ✔	Blue Water	$130	bluewatermarinepaint.com	Good	Good	67%	No	Multiple
Copper Pro SCX 67	Blue Water	$150	bluewatermarinepaint.com	Good –	Fair +	67%	Irgarol	Multiple
Copper Shield 45	Blue Water	$90	bluewatermarinepaint.com	Good +	Fair +	45%	No	Multiple
Copper Shield SCX 45	Blue Water	$130	bluewatermarinepaint.com	Good	Fair +	45%	Irgarol	Multiple
Kolor	Blue Water	$150	bluewatermarinepaint.com	Good –	Fair +	45%	No	Multiple
Sea Bowld Ablative 56	Blue Water	$80	Boater's World	Good	Fair	56%	Irgarol	Multiple
Sea Bowld Ablative 67 Pro ✔	Blue Water	$130	Boater's World	Good +	Good –	67%	Irgarol	Multiple
EP-21	E-Paint	$125	epaint.net	Fair +	Fair –	None	None	One
ZO	E-Paint	$199	epaint.net	Fair	Fair –	None	Zinc Pyrithione	1–2
Aquagard	Flexdel	$95	aquagard-boatpaint.com	Excellent	Fair +	26.37%	No	Multiple
Bottomkote XXX	Interlux	$93	binnacle.com	Excellent	Fair	28%	No	One
Fiberglass Bottomkote ACT	Interlux	$100	shipstore.com	Good –	Fair +	42%	Irgarol	One
Micron CSC	Interlux	$165	shipstore.com	Fair +	Fair +	37.20%	No	Multiple
Micron Extra	Interlux	$172	shipstore.com	Good	Good –	38.62%	Irgarol	Multiple
Micron Optima ✔	Interlux	$198	boatersland.com	Excellent	Good –	28.45%†	Zinc Pyrithione	Multiple
Super Ablative	Interlux	$118	yachtpaint.com	Good	Fair	41.97%	Irgarol	One
Trilux 33	Interlux	$188	shipstore.com	Fair +	Fair –	16.95%	Zinc Pyrithione	One
Tri-Lux II (Canada only) ✔	Interlux	$235	yachtpaint.com	Good	Fair	22%	No	One
Tarr & Wonson Copper Paint	Interlux	$62	fisherissupply.com	Good	Fair +	25%	No	One
Horizons	Pettit	$114	shipstore.com	Good +	Fair	47.50%	No	Multiple
Hydrocoat	Pettit	$95	shipstore.com	Excellent	Fair +	40.30%	No	Multiple
Premium	Pettit	$126	shipstore.com	Good –	Fair	35.70%	No	Multiple
Ultima SR	Pettit	$180	shipstore.com	Good	Fair +	60%	Irgarol	Multiple
West Marine CPP ✔	Pettit	$90	West Marine	Good +	Good –	37.50%	No	Multiple
West Marine PCA $	Pettit	$80	West Marine	Good +	Good	29.73%	Irgarol	Multiple
Cukote	Sea Hawk	$140	refinishlinedirect.com	Good –	Fair +	47.57%	No	Multiple
Cukote Biocide Plus	Sea Hawk	$190	refinishlinedirect.com	Good	Fair	47.57%	*	Multiple
Monterey ★	Sea Hawk	$140	refinishlinedirect.com	Excellent	Good –	54.67%	No	Multiple

$ Budget Buy   ✔ Recommended   ★ Best Choice

*N-Cyclopropyl-N-(dimethylethyl)-6-(methylthio)1,3,5-triazine-2-diamine   †Controlled depletion polymer and Good paints by comparing the amount of slime on the panels.

For the second straight year, the Connecticut panels had more growth than the Florida panels. In fact, none of the paints could muster an Excellent rating in Long Island Sound. In the Keys, six paints earned scores of Excellent. Our top honors went to the two paints that earned Excellent ratings in Florida and Good-minuses in Connecticut: Micron Optima and Sea Hawk Monterey, both of which have done well in previous tests. Micron Optima is a two-part paint with a copper content of 28 percent. It uses zinc pyrithione to prevent slime. Sea Hawk calls its Monterey a "semi-hard ablative," and it has a 55-percent copper content and no anti-slime additive. Both Micron Optima and Monterey are water-based paints rated as multi-year, meaning they are meant to be used for more than one season.

Interlux Fiberglass Bottomkote Aqua, West Marine PCA, which is made by Pettit, and Interlux Regatta Baltoplate Racing also rated high overall. The Baltoplate was one of only five paints that fared better in Connecticut than in Florida.

Blue Water Paints had a strong showing for the second year in a row. Its Copper Pro 67 and Sea Bowld Ablative 67 Pro (available through Boater's World) looked very clean to our testers in both locales. So did Interlux Micron 66 (a previous overall winner), Micron Extra, and West Marine's CPP. In the category of water-based paints, Flexdel Aquagard and Pettit Hydrocoat stood out in Florida.

Only three paints scored Poor, all in Florida water: Interlux VC 17m and VC 17m Extra, and Pettit SR-21. The latter is a fresh and low-salt paint, so the result was tenable.

The effectiveness of white paints was spotty. In Florida, the Vivid earned a Good-plus, and Trilux II was awarded a Good. EP 2000 scored a Good in Connecticut. But no white paint did well in both places.

Did copper content make a difference this year? No. Only one paint with a copper content higher than the median 42 percent received an Excellent rating in Florida; and four with less copper were rated Excellent. And in Connecticut, the paints with lower copper content scored more Good ratings (seven) than those with higher copper (four).

▷ **The Bottom Line** The vast majority of the paints we tested performed very well. The ratings are based on the amount of soft growth. In most cases, a sponge or soft brush can be used to wipe the slime away (although scrubbing soft paints is banned in some waters), and if we'd taken the panels for a short cruise, that alone might have wiped them clean.

Overall, the Sea Hawk Monterey deserved top honors because it performed as well as the Interlux Micron Optima, and costs less. In addition, Micron Optima is an antifouling paint that requires mixing two parts, so application is a bit more involved than with the Sea Hawk.

Budget Buy rankings go to the Pettit's $80-per-gallon West Marine PCA and Interlux Bottomkote Aqua ($70). The "Value Guide" tables also indicate our Recommended paints, those that were among the top-performing hard paints, white paints, and eco-friendly paints in both locales.

TOPSIDE PAINTS

To garner a better understanding of how topside paints perform—and which ones endure—*Practical Sailor* initiated a massive test several years ago. We gathered up 39 different paints and applied them to the sheer of a small test boat we owned. The idea was to try out high-quality marine paints that could

Interlux Micron Optima (left) was completely foul-free in Florida, which earned it an excellent rating. Interlux VC 17M Extra (right) allowed some hard growth on the bottom section of its panel and was rated poor in Florida. Along with the Interlux paint, Seahawk's Monterrey—a reasonably priced ablative paint—also scored well in both locations.

Product	Price	Source	Type	Color	2004 Ratings	2006 Ratings/Comments
Interlux Toplac $	$38	jamestowndistributors.com	Alkyd	White	Excellent	Excellent; best white
Interlux Interthane Plus*	NA		Two-part polyurethane	Red	Excellent	Excellent starboard; port worn
Interlux Interthane Plus*	NA		Two-part polyurethane	White	Excellent	Excellent
Interlux Interthane Plus*	NA		Two-part polyurethane	Blue	Good	Excellent; best blue
Epifanes Mono-Urethane ✔	$33	jamestowndistributors.com	One-part urethane	Blue	Excellent	Excellent
Epifanes Poly-Urethane ✔	$51	jamestowndistributors.com	Two-part polyurethane	Red	Excellent	Good to Excellent; best red
Epifanes Poly-Urethane ✔	$51	jamestowndistributors.com	Two-part polyurethane	Blue	Excellent	Good
Epifanes Yacht Enamel	$31	jamestowndistributors.com	Alkyd	White	Good	Good
Epifanes Yacht Enamel	$31	jamestowndistributors.com	Alkyd	Blue	Good	Good
Epifanes Poly-Urethane	$51	jamestowndistributors.com	Two-part polyurethane	White	Good	Good
Rust-Oleum	$11	Contact manufacturer	Fish oil	Brown	Good	Good but somewhat drab
Rust-Oleum	$11	Contact manufacturer	Fish oil	Yellow	Good	Good; lost shine; still robust
U.S. Paint Awlgrip	$62	jamestowndistributors.com	Two-part polyurethane	Blue	Good	Good to Excellent starboard; worn port
Kop-Coat Z-Spar	$29	West Marine	Alkyd	Blue	Good	Good
Andek Corp. Polagard AG	NA		Two-part polyurethane	Red	Good	Good
Andek Corp. Polagard AG	NA		Two-part polyurethane	Blue	Good	Good

$ Budget Buy   ✔ Recommended
*Interlux has replaced this paint with Interlux Perfection; $62 (qt.)/West Marine.

be applied by an owner with a brush, so as to avoid the high cost of having a boatyard do a fabulous-looking but expensive job with Awlgrip, or one of its competitors, which need to be sprayed on in a controlled environment by really skilled professionals. The question was, could an owner do a good-looking job that would last for a reasonably long time for a lot less money?

The paints that were applied in swatch "bracelets" along each side of our 13-foot Boston Whaler included one- and two-part polyurethanes, alkyds, a water-soluble acrylic, fish-oil-based paints, and the proprietary Awlgrip as a sort of control. Identical bracelets were painted, numbered from 1 to 39 (with a few repeats to even things out), from the bow aft on one side and from the transom forward on the other. (In general, the port-side paints fared worse, since they bore the brunt of fendering, docking, and dings.) All were applied carefully, by brush, with one coat only. The single coat allowed us to make some observations about ease of application, paint viscosity and thickness of coverage, and initial gloss. It also accelerated the deterioration of the paints, so that we could draw some conclusions in two years instead of more. As we wrote in our initial report, the one-coat test couldn't help but favor coatings that "went on thicker," at least initially, but as time went on truer properties were revealed.

Two answers emerged. First, it's hard to beat Awlgrip as the best answer to a faded gelcoat. Although it went on thinner and more transparent than most of the rest, after two years it looked just about as hard and glossy as it did an hour after it dried. And it looked about the same after four years. Second, while you may not beat Awlgrip, you can at least give it a run for the money. It is possible to get good results from off-the-shelf paints, even excellent results if you're willing (and capable enough) to work with two-part polyurethanes. Although we tested some non-marine coatings—e.g., Pittsburgh's Pitt-Tech, Royal alkyd from Ace Hardware, and Rust-Oleum—we found that the best paints came from companies with long track records in the marine paint trade.

To quote from our last report: "(1) If you want your hull white and you prefer an easy-to-use one-part paint, buy Interlux's Toplac. (2) If you want a white hull and are willing to do the work needed with a longer-lasting, two-part urethane, use Interlux's Interthane. [Interlux has since replaced Interthane Plus with a similar paint it calls Perfection.] (3) If you want a blue hull and prefer the easier one-part urethane, the choice is Epifanes' Mono-Urethane. (4) If you want a blue hull with a two-part paint, Epifanes' Poly-Urethane is preferred. (5) If you want to do your hull red with a one-part paint, don't. Use Epifanes' two-part Poly-Urethane."

In our intial report, six of the 39 paints received Excellent overall ratings, and 10, including Awlgrip, received Good overall ratings. After more than four years, we made one final tour of the paints on that boat, noted any that still looked a cut above the rest, and put added some final comments pertaining to the 16 paints that did well in our initial report (see the Value Guide).

▷ **The Bottom Line** Your paint pick will depend upon color. For a one-part white, go with Interlux Toplac. For a two-part white, we could assume Interlux's new Perfection is at least as good as our earlier winner Interthane Plus, but can't vouch for it. For red, only a two-part paint will do. Use Epifanes Poly-Urethane.

The choice of blue, however, has grown tricky. Among the two-parters, all three of our inspectors this time thought the Interlux Interthane Plus looked best—slightly better than the Epifanes blue. And this paint was rated "Good" last time.

Also performing well in the home stretch was Andek's Polagard AG, an "aliphatic urethane" coating. It's not meant to be a pleasure-boat paint, though—more of an industrial coating that can be used on "brick, stucco, concrete, structural steel, industrial equipment, and other surfaces." The AG actually stands for anti-graffiti. Since it's normally a clear coating, and its colors are "custom," and since it's a bit off the beaten path and not much cheaper than pleasure-boat paints, we'd suggest sticking with Interlux or Epifanes. If you're painting a freighter, that's another matter.

VARNISHES

Several years back, the editors at *PS* initiated another large test of varnishes, something that's been going on at the magazine for most of its 30-plus years. We didn't get any truly useful feedback on these products

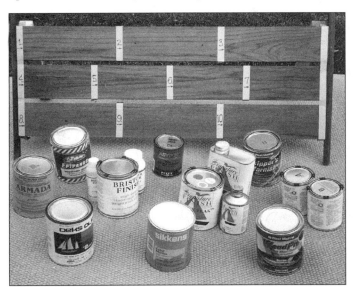

This photo was taken at the beginning of *PS*'s most recent test of teak protecting products. Our evaluation included varnishes, teak treatment systems, and oils that had been prequalified due to their superior performance in previous tests. After almost two years of exposure on *PS*'s test panel, our testers deemed Epifanes High Gloss as the top performing varnish, and Sikkens' Cetol as providing the best matte finish. Both products outperformed the two oils included in this test.

Make	Product	Color	Surface Prep	Min. # coats
VC Systems	Plus-5	Light	thinner	5–6
Interlux Yacht Finishes	Interthane +	Dark	thinner	2+
Interlux Yacht Finishes	Jet Speed	Light	thinner	5–7
Interlux Yacht Finishes	Schooner	Light	thinner	5–7
Interlux Yacht Finishes	Clipper	Light	thinner	5–7
Z Spar	Captain's	Medium	clean & sand	4
Z Spar	Flagship	Light	clean	4–5
West Marine	Skipper	Dark	clean & sand	4
West Marine	Wood Pro	Medium	clean	4
West Marine	Admiral's	Light	clean & sand	3–4
Epifanes	Clear	Dark	sand, spray thinner	7
Epifanes	Wood Finish	Dark	sand	6–7
Pettit Paint	Hi-Build 2056	Dark	sand	5
Pettit Paint	Old Salem	Medium	sand	5
Pettit Paint	Ultra Gold 2067	Dark	sand	5
US Paint	AwlSpar	Light	—	—
Target Enterprises	Oxford Hybrid Spar	Medium	alcohol	9–10
Sears, Roebuck & Co	Poly Outdoor Spar	Light	sand, tirpolene	3+
Cabot	Oil-based Poly	Light	clean & sand	3
Absolute Coatings	Last n' Last Marine Spar	Light	sand	2–3

until after two years of exposure. By then, however, the 20 kinds of varnish that were meticulously applied to matched teak boards, in two-, three-, five-, and seven-coat panels, were beginning to show some differences.

"The Rack," as our test panel became known, was placed outdoors to face sun, snow, sleet, fog, smog, rain, heat, cold, and the odd passing bird to test each brand's film integrity, gloss, and color retention. In plain language, we were seeking to determine which lasts the longest and looks the best. In our first thorough examination, six months down the road, three of the two-coat panels had failed and seven other brands were starting to fail. Only two things were learned: (1) two coats of varnish don't give teak very long-lasting protection; and (2) color and gloss changes occur rather quickly.

▷ **The Bottom Line** After 12 months, the results were fairly definitive. Except for West Marine's "breathable" Wood Pro (which probably doesn't meet the strict definition of "varnish"), all the two-coat segments had failed. Six three-coat sections also had failed. Only six brands still had "excellent" gloss. Color changes were all over the place, some fading, some getting darker. Summaries of pertinent 12-month data (Gloss and Film Integrity) are shown on the accompanying table.

After a full two years, we brought The Rack inside and removed the yardsticks that protected a portion of each of the 20 segments from exposure in order to compare the exposed portions with the original. Only seven of the three-coat segments were intact. Those varnishes whose three-coat segments were intact were also intact where they had more than

6-MONTH RESULTS 2 coats—Film Integrity	12-MONTH RESULTS Gloss	Film Integrity	24-MONTH RESULTS Gloss	Color	Film Integrity
Starting to fail	Good	2 & 3-coat failed	Poor	Bit lighter	Edge failure
Starting to fail	Excellent	2-coat failed. Rest OK	Good	Much darker	3-coat intact
Best	Poor	2-coat failed. Rest OK	Poor	Badly faded	2 & 3-coat failed
Best	Good	2-coat failed. Rest OK	Poor	Badly faded	3-coat intact
Failed	Poor	2 & 3-coat failed	Poor	Badly faded	2 & 3-coat failed
Best	Good	2-coat failed. Rest OK	Fair	No change	2 & 3-coat failed
Fair	Fair	2-coat failed. Rest OK	Poor	Medium fade	2 & 3-coat failed
Failed	Excellent	2-coat failed, 3-coat going	Good	Slightly darker	3-coat still going
Fair	Poor	2-coat beginning to fail	Poor	Lighter	Not applicable
Starting to fail	Good	2-coat failed. Rest OK	Fair	Bit faded	3-coat intact
Failed	Excellent	2 & 3-coat failed	Fair	Bit darker	2 & 3-coat failed
Starting to fail	Excellent	2-coat failed. Rest OK	Excellent	Bit darker	3-coat intact
Fair	Excellent	2-coat failed. 3-coat going	Good	No change	3-coat still going
Fair	Excellent	2 & 3-coat failed	Good	Medium fade	2 & 3-coat failed
Fair	Fair	2-coat failed. 3-coat going	Fair	No change	2 & 3-coat failed
Fair	Fair	2-coat failed. Rest OK	Poor	Bit faded	3-coat intact
Starting to fail	Fair	2-coat failed. Rest OK	Poor	Much darker	2 & 3-coat failed
Fair	Poor	2 & 3-coat failed	Poor	Bit faded	2 & 3-coat failed
Starting to fail	Poor	2-coat failed. Rest OK	Poor	No change	2 & 3-coat failed
Starting to fail	Good	2 & 3-coat failed	Good	Medium fade	2 & 3-coat failed

three coats. The seven survivors were Interlux Interthane (the only two-part finish), Interlux's Schooner, West Marine's Skipper, West Marine's Admiral's, Epifanes Wood Finish, Pettit's Hi-Build 2067, and U.S. Paint's AwlSpar.

Next, the gloss remaining on those seven survivors was examined; and the color was compared with the original (as protected throughout the exposure by those yardsticks). Melding the intact coats (which are, by far, the most important), the gloss, and the color produced three top performers in this test. First, with three or more coats unbroken, excellent gloss retention, and little color change was Epifanes Wood Finish. Second was Pettit's Hi-Build 2056. Its multiple coats starting with three were unbroken, the gloss was good, and the color sustained no change. Third was West Marine's Skipper, with three or more coats intact, good gloss, and only slight darkening of the color.

Of passing interest is the fact that the varnishes that clawed their way to the top in the testing all started out being among the darker varieties to begin with. The crystal-clear brands seemed to lose their gloss quicker and/or suffer more severe color loss.

This testing does not mean that one of these varnishes applied to a horizontal surface on a boat in Florida or the Caribbean would last for two years. In such locations, exposure to the sun, which does most of the damage, is more severe than in the New England locale where these tests were conducted.

So, the bottom line is, you can't do better than Epifanes Wood Finish, Pettit's Hi-Build 2056, and West Marine's Skipper.

Nonskid Compounds

Deck refurbishment is an important topic for many owners of used boats. When you evaluate the many nonskid paint additives and compounds, it's important to acknowledge that this topic area is fraught with hard-to-control variables including different shoe treads, changes in the posture of tester, differences in how the powders are applied and suspended in the paints, and subtleties in the sensations of slipping, creeping, or standing secure. We've found it's best to simply keep doing tests in order to develop reliable data over time.

It's also important to consider how difficult these compositions are to mix and apply, how they look, and how comfortable are they for sitting or kneeling. And perhaps most important is how the various additive/paint mixtures stand up to wear. Having to repaint the deck every couple of years lacks a certain appeal for most boat owners.

For our most recent investigation, we opted to use three different paints as a base and test four nonskid additives. The paints we selected are all one-part coatings because we think that using a two-part paint on a deck makes the job more difficult and might result in considerable waste and, thus, greater expense. The first paint we tested was West Marine's SeaGloss, a "plain Jane" polyurethane that costs $22 a quart. Next we selected an old reliable—Pettit's Easypoxy, which costs $29 a quart. It's a well-proven urethane,

The non-skid additives that *PS* tested included, left to right: SoftSand, Pettit 9900 Skidless Compound, Interlux Intergrip, and Awlgrip (US Paint) Griptex.

silicone, and alkyd blend, with an ultraviolet filter. The third was Interlux's Toplac, which is a silicone, copolymeric resin "system" that the company hopes will come close to behaving like a two-part paint. Being a premium paint (it also has UV filters), it costs about $40 a quart.

The four additives we selected (there are many others) are representative of the different kinds on the market. Three of the four are marine products: Interlux's Intergrip ($23 a quart), which consists of fine polymeric spheres that Interlux claims don't collect dirt as badly as some grits; Pettit's 9900, a "skidless compound" medium-grit silicon oxide that costs $17 a pint; and Awlgrip's Griptex, which is about $26 a quart. (It should be noted that Griptex is recommended only for professional applications.) The fourth additive we used was a commercial product called SoftSand, which is granulated rubber that comes in several "meshes" and many colors. To these 12 combinations (three paints and

Traction tests were done in several kinds of footwear (dinghy boots are shown here) with panels inclined at 45 degrees. An old pair of deck shoes with worn soles was used to consolidate the ratings.

Product	Price	Price Per Oz.	Price Source	Cleaning Rating	Comments
West Marine	$7.99		West Marine catalog	Very Good	Slight grease and blood/guts stains remaining
Meguiar's	$15.99	25 cents	West Marine catalog	Excellent	Faint blood/guts stains remaining
3M	$19.99	67 cents	West Marine catalog	Excellent	Faint blood/guts stains remaining
Star brite	$8.99	59 cents	West Marine catalog	Very Good	Slight grease and blood/guts stains remaining
Nautical Ease	$7.29	28 cents	yachtingessentials.com	Very Good	Traces of grease and blood/guts stains
Mary Kate	$8.99	23 cents		Good	Left a little grease, mustard, blood/guts, and oil stains
Sea Bowld	$6.99	28 cents	West Marine catalog	Good	Good job on grease; left coffee and blood/guts stains
Aurora Boat Scrub	$7.59	32 cents	Boater's World catalog	Good	Slight grease, blood/guts, and coffee stains
Soft Scrub	$2.97	47 cents	auroramarine.com	Excellent*	Cleaned all substances
Orange Clean	$1.97	9.3 cents	Wal-Mart	Fair	Left behind stains from most substances
Fantastik	$1.97	6.2 cents	Wal-Mart	Good	Left blood/guts, oil, suntan lotion, and grease stains
409	$1.89	6.2 cents	Wal-Mart	Fair	Left behind stains from most substances

*Scft Scrub is an abrasive cleaner and not recommended for use on fiberglass surfaces, particularly those with gelcoat.

four additives) we added one ready-mixed product from West Marine—Non-Skid Paint ($24/quart)—because it was deemed a Best Buy in a previous *PS* test, for a total of 13 test specimens.

One at a time, we mixed and applied the 12 combinations (and then the West Marine product) to a sheet of carefully prepared plywood, each on its own separate segment. After the panel had thoroughly dried, we noted the difference in texture of the samples. They varied from very comfortable to so abrasive that any significant contact with less-than-calloused skin could draw blood.

A word here about subjective preferences: Selecting a nonskid surface is a cake-or-eat-it dilemma. A rough surface is generally safer, but can be uncomfortable to bare skin. A smoother surface is more comfortable, but more slippery. Only the individual boat owner can decide how effective he or she wants the nonskid surface to be. An offshore singlehander might rarely sit or kneel on deck and thus want maximum nonskid. A cruiser-racer might prefer a smoother surface for his crew to sit on while hiking. And those with youngsters on board would likely choose an even smoother deck. If you want a surface that's less abrasive, the manufacturers all suggest using a brush rather than a roller when applying it.

The roller method produces a more aggressive nonskid, but it's more difficult to get an evenly coated surface using a brush.

There is little doubt that which additive you select is important. Most of these additives come in several choices of grit. Further, if the surface you end up with is too rough for your liking, you can apply additional coats of paint (which would be a good idea anyway) to tone down the final result.

The differences in mixing and applying the additives weren't pronounced. Some mixtures went on very smoothly and evenly. The best in this regard were the three mixtures containing Pettit 9900, which rolled on easily and spread very evenly, with not much more effort than applying West Marine's Non-Skid paint. Almost as easy were the batches containing Interlux's Intergrip. Only one of those, the Pettit Easypoxy/Interlux Intergrip combination, required a bit of practice to spread it evenly. And the three batches containing SoftSand were somewhat lumpy and took considerable rolling to even out the grit. All three batches using the Awlgrip Griptex required a bit of practice to get a smooth distribution.

Six of the mixtures took what seemed like too long a time to dry. After 24 hours, the following

Product	Type	Price	Price Source	Parts	Coats (recommended)	Original Finish
Epifanes High Gloss	Varnish	$17 (500ml)	West Marine catalog	1	4–5	Best Gloss
Pettit Hi-Build	Varnish	$26 (qt.)	Boat/US catalog	1	5	High Gloss
West Skipper [Admiral's]	Varnish	$20 (qt.)	West Marine catalog	1	4	High Gloss
Armada MC 2000*	Synthetic	$32 (qt.)	www.armadacoatings.com	1	3	Matte
Bristol Finish	Synthetic	$54.95 (qt.)	www.bristolfinish.com	2	6	High Gloss
Honey Teak	Synthetic	$1.94 (sq. ft.)	www.signaturefinish.com	2	3	High Gloss
Smith & Co. 5-Year	Synthetic	$2.50/$4.50 (sq. ft.)	www.fiveyearclear.com	2	4–5	High Gloss
Deks Olje	Oil	$21 (qt.)	West Marine catalog	1	3	Very Dull
Sikkens Cetol	Pigmented Stain	$30 (qt.)	West Marine catalog	1	3	Matte
West Wood Pro	Pigmented Stain	$25 (qt.)	West Marine catalog	1	3	Matte

*Armada Coatings ceased making MC 2000 after our test began; it is now marketed as Clear Wood Finish.

combinations remained sticky: Toplac/SoftSand, Pettit Easypoxy/Pettit 9900, Pettit Easypoxy/SoftSand, West SeaGloss/Pettit 9900, Pettit Easypoxy/Awlgrip Griptex, and Toplac/Interlux Intergrip. There's no obvious rhyme, reason, or pattern to why this happened.

▷ **The Bottom Line** The best nonskid surface was the Toplac/Pettit 9900 combination. It was excellent in terms of traction, and also in terms of smoothness and comfort. If you prefer a glossy look, this would also be the top choice. Toplac with Awlgrip Griptex also provided excellent traction, but was noticeably coarser. The combination of West Marine SeaGloss and Awlgrip Griptex provided the second-best non-skid surface (by a very slight margin), was comfortable on bare skin, and had a flat, non-glare appearance that we found pleasing to the eye. We acknowledge that this combination might be a bit more difficult to keep clean than the Toplac/Pettit 9900, but it was almost 20 percent less expensive.

Anyone undertaking the considerable job of over-hauling a deck should consider spending some extra money to experiment with different approaches on test surfaces, to account for preferences mentioned earlier—rougher, perhaps, for offshore work, and smoother for a rail-sitting crew on a racing boat, or for kids. The easiest compromise, of course, would be to use West Marine's Non-Skid paint—right out of the can.

Teak Treatments

Hardly a month goes by at the *Practical Sailor* offices without someone writing to the editors and inquiring, "What should I do to take care of the teak on my boat?" From time to time, we've orchestrated tests of teak treatment products in an effort to address those queries. Most recently, we launched a test of varnish versus teak oils versus "teak systems" to determine what products keep teak looking its best.

Original Comments	Comments at Six Months	Final Comments
A bit cloudy when liquid. More viscous than most varnishes. Fills grain quickly. Has a bit of color. Sand for last coat.	Film intact. Still very good gloss. Some darkening.	Intact, smooth. A bit darker. *PS*'s top pick for shiny finish.
A traditional varnish. Sealer recommended. Not quite as viscous as Epifanes; tackier to spread. Fills grain very well.	Film intact. Good gloss. Good light, natural color.	Intact. Faded slightly. Very good varnish.
Less expensive varnish, but it's thin, drippy, and harder to apply. Spreads easily, but builds up less rapidly.	Film intact. Fairly good gloss. A shade darker.	Intact, but a bit thinner, less smooth appearance.
Made in France. A brown liquid, it has an orangish hue when dry. Took several days to dry in 65° workshop.	Dull. Seems to have acquired slight purple hue.	Slight purple hue visible at six months inspection has faded away.
Good viscosity. Wet-on-wet means job takes but a day. Let dry and sand before last coat. Satin additive available.	Film compromised underneath ends of panel.	No comment because formulation changed.
Acrylic urethane with medium viscosity. Heavily pigmented. Renew with one coat a year; two in the tropics.	Film intact. Wood grain seems more obscured.	Two-part pigmented stain darkened considerable.
Darkens wood slightly. When it fails, it must be completely removed. Peculiarly, it's rubbery when excess dried in can.	Has several dozen scratch-like bleached streaks.	Streaks from 6-month exam still present.
Don't apply in sun. Thin and runny to handle. Penetrates best of all. It imparts a simple, wet look to the teak.	Oil is gone, leaving bleached natural teak.	Long gone Dean, from Bowling Green.
Don't work in sunlight. Medium viscosity, brown liquid. Scrub and renew annually. Can be gloss over-coated.	Surface unbroken. Has acquired a salmon color.	Has a salmon hue. *PS*'s choice of matte finishes.
Like Sikkens Cetol, but thinner to handle; don't use in sunlight. Butterscotch color when liquid.	Shows more grain than Sikkens; is a bit glossy.	Surface broken down. Blotchy appearance.

Varnish tests have been taking place at *PS* for almost 20 years. Teak oils have been tested exhaustively. Synthetic "systems," often presented by their makers as the "perfect solution," have also been put through their paces. Because such tests are long-term projects, no sooner is one completed than it's time to begin another. That's because manufacturers are constantly introducing new solutions to this old problem.

The basic overriding truth is that the teak on your boat is never, ever going to look as good as it did when it was new. The elements are working against you. Dirt, stains, and salt water do some damage, but UV rays from the sun account for 99 percent of the problem. The only way to recapture the original beauty of newly milled teak is to sand off a very thin layer of weathered teak, but how many times do you want to do that? Even though the weathered layer is very, very thin (try it on a piece of scrap), there's no escaping the fact that you're removing material, and there's only so much of that to begin with.

So, after years of testing varnish, teak oil, and "systems," we decided to combine the results and undertake a Teak Treatment All-Stars test. The intent was (1) to evaluate how the products handle in the application; (2) see how they look when first applied; and, most important, (3) subject all of them to exactly the same exposure and see how they fare over time.

Selecting from our most recent tests, the three best varnishes, the four best "systems," and the three best oils were gathered together for this "best-of-the-best" run-off. (We included one oil, the widely known Deks Olje, even through the maker concedes that its matte-finish variety is good for just one season, or about six months.) And one of the "systems," C Tech Marine's Bristol Finish, had its formulation changed while our test was underway. So we can't weigh in on the new formulation of that product.

That left eight products to soldier on. Mind you, all of them had ranked one, two, or three in previous tests of their own product type. The three varnishes are Epifanes, Pettit's Hi-Build, and West Marine's Skipper. The three synthetic "systems" are Armada MC 2000, Honey Teak, and Smith & Co. 5-Year. (We learned after the test began that Armada discontinued making the MC 2000.) The two oils (or stains) are Sikkens's Cetol and West Marine's West Wood Pro.

The products were applied, as directed, to ample-sized segments of well-seasoned teak boards. Small 1-inch covering strips were added to the bottom edge of each of the three boards to provide a comparison with the exposed areas.

The rack was placed outdoors in the winter, oriented to get full perpendicular sunrays, along with wind, rain, snow, blowing dirt, and a few deliberate dashes of saltwater fetched from the harbor. We checked it after six months, and published a report. In that article, we described all three varnishes as "the best by far," but the heavily pigmented Honey Teak and the two pigmented stains—Sikkens's Cetol and the West WoodPro—were still in the running. Then we put the rack back outdoors, and checked on it from time to time, making our final examination after almost two years.

▷ **The Bottom Line** For the meticulous boat owner who does his own work and is concerned with all facets of teak treatment, we recommend a review of all three published reports in *Practical Sailor*. If you want your teak varnished, any one of the three varnishes we included is excellent. In our test, all of them remained intact, with no breaks in the skin. The Epifanes has the smoothest skin, but appears to have darkened a bit. The Pettit seems to have faded slightly. The West Marine has a thin look to it, perhaps because it is very thin coming out of the can. Because it seems more substantial, the edge goes to Epifanes.

Among the three remaining synthetics, the matte-finish Armada MC 2000 is intact, but lacks the good color that Sikkens's Cetol has. And the gloss Honey Teak doesn't seem the equal of Epifanes varnish. (The gloss Smith & Co. 5-Year didn't do well in the six-month review; it had developed streaks.) Of the two pigmented oils (or stains), the West WoodPro has gone blotchy and discolored, leaving the Sikkens Cetol as the best choice for a matte finish.

PS VALUE GUIDE WAXES

Mfg./Supplier	Product	Type
Fibre Glass-Evercoat Co.	Boat Armor	Liquid
Collinite Corp.	Collinite #870	Liquid
Collinite Corp.	Collinite #885	Paste
Turtle Wax Inc.	Turtle Wax 2001	Paste
Namico	Trewax	Paste
Dolphinite Inc.	T-Wax	Liquid
Dolphinite Inc.	Fiberglass Spray Wax	Pressure Spray
Heller Glanz	Carnauba Cream	Liquid
Heller Glanz	Quick Gloss	Liquid
BoatLIFE	LifeWax	Paste
Meguiar's Inc.	Mirror Glaze	Paste
Meguiar's Inc.	Flagship	Liquid
Maguiar's Inc.	Quick Spray	Pump Spray
Poli Glow Products	Poli Glow	Liquid
T.R. Industries	Seapower	Liquid
Star brite	Spray Wax Pump	Spray
Star brite	Marine polish	Liquid
Star brite	Marine Polish w/Teflon	Liquid
Star brite	Marine Polish w/Teflon	Paste
Star brite	Pre-Softened	Paste
3M Marine	Marine Protective	Liquid
3M Marine	Finesse-It II	Liquid
3M Marine	Ultra Performance	Paste
West Marine	Teflon Boat Polish	Liquid
West Marine	Premium Polymer	Liquid
West Marine	Carnauba	Paste

Waxes

Among the many colossal, time-intensive tests that *Practical Sailor* has conducted is an ongoing series of wax tests. In the most recent of these, we placed outdoors a tired old fiberglass and gelcoat panel to which had been applied 26 kinds of waxes, along with one liquid plastic and one Teflon coating. We were seeking to determine which, if any, of the finishes—hand-applied to the weathered panel—would

Price	Price (per oz.)	Initial Gloss	Initial Comments	Final Comments
$6.24	45¢	Good	Mud color. Carnauba/Teflon/UV. Hard to get lid off.	No wax remains
$13.99	87¢	Good	Slightly abrasive cream-colored fairly thick liquid.	Down to bare fiberglass
$14.40	$1.20	Excellent	Very hard whitish paste. No mention of ingredients.	The best
$12.99	93¢	Good	Soft pink past that 'lasts a year.'	Bit of circle left
$14.99	$1.25	Good	Can was half full, space taken up by applicator sponge.	Little of circle left
$12.95	81¢	Good	Quite a claim: 'Lasts 6 times longer than any other'.	Better than #5
$12.25	87¢	Good	No mention of ingredients. Pressurized can wasteful?	Almost bare
$19.95	62¢	Good	Custard-colored liquefied carnauba wax. A bit thin.	Vanished
$15.99	50¢	Excellent	Strange stuff. Probably very liquefied pure carnauba.	Tiny bit of circle
$8.29	83¢	Good	Tan paste, fairly soft. Says, 'Contains a sun shield.'	Circle is thin
$13.99	$1.27	Fair	Medium hard blue paste. Says, 'Contains carnauba.'	Good, 2nd best
$16.99	$1.06	Good	Feels a bit abrasive. Medium thin, tan liquid.	Very little left
$7.99	50¢	Excellent	No ingredients stated on this pump spray sample.	About like 13
$34.95	$1.09	Excellent	Says, 'Not a wax; minimum of 4–6 coats.' It's plastic.	Good, but not a wax
$13.99	87¢	Fair	Very fancy claims, says it's a 'polymer, wax, cleaner.'	Gone with the wind
$10.99	50¢	Good	Spray on, wipe dry and buff immediately. Seems thin.	Likewise
$8.49	53¢	Fair	'For best results, apply 2nd coat.' Who'd do it?	Bit of ink left
$13.99	87¢	Good	UV and Teflon. But as above, 2nd coat recommended.	Better than #18
$13.99	$1.00	Good	Cream-color paste w/Teflon. Seems slightly abrasive.	Bit less than #19
$9.99	71¢	Fair	In a paste can. Surprise! It pours freely. Too thin.	Faint circle
$22.99	72¢	Fair	White liquid, good consistency. Slightly abrasive.	A little half circle
$21.99	$1.37	Good	Nice name, but nothing special. See the next one.	Another faint half
$21.99	$2.31	Good	3M's best. Very hard paste. Contains Montan wax.	Good, 3rd best
$11.99	75¢	Excellent	'Clean, shine, protect,' but 2nd coat recommended?	O.K. but it's Teflon
$11.99	75¢	Good	Brownish polymer. Too thick for flip-top bottle.	Not much here
$12.99	85¢	Good	Tan, no-nonsense paste in nice, new-type can.	Medium circle

restore some gloss and provide protection for the gelcoat for a full year.

The topsides of a fiberglass boat can remain new-looking for years, if kept clean and coated with something that resists weathering. New gelcoat may seem as impervious as glass, but it isn't; it's porous, and it gets worse as it ages. If left uncoated, bare gelcoat picks up stains that are very difficult to remove.

The test panel had been washed, scrubbed, rinsed repeatedly, and thoroughly dried. Each product was applied as directed (except for several that called for multiple coats) to small circles on the panel. Each circle was delineated by a black-inked line. After being hung outdoors, the panel was eyed often during its 365 days of exposure to New England's rain, snow, sun, and wind.

It was easy to spot the winners. Most inked circles were badly faded; some were barely discernible. However, on some the ink was more intact—meaning that the ink, as well as the gelcoat, had been protected by the coating, which we extended over the inked lines of each circle. Based on how well the inked rings were preserved, the best results came about with Collinite paste wax, Turtle paste, BoatLIFE's paste, Meguiar's Mirror Glaze, Star brite's paste, Star brite softened paste, 3M's paste, and West Marine's paste. Note that all of these are paste waxes.

Two non-wax coatings did well, too. They were the Poli Glow liquid plastic and West Marine's Teflon. Although many boat owners like these coatings because they're easy to apply and have a good initial shine, years of testing have caused *PS* to favor a good hard wax, which can be removed fairly easily in order to apply a new coating. (Some liquid plastics, we've learned, discolor and deteriorate in time and are difficult to remove.)

Next we evaluated beading, which was tested by spraying a fine mist on each circle. On most, the accumulated water simply ran off in small streams, with none remaining in place. However, six of our test specimens did very well. They included the aforementioned Poli Glow liquid plastic and West Marine's Teflon, but neither was as good as the best paste wax.

The other four—all paste waxes—were, starting with the best, the Collinite, Meguiar's Mirror Glaze, 3M's paste (which is called Ultra Performance), and West Marine's paste.

It's interesting to note that in the initial examination of the gloss, when the coatings were first applied, only five rated Excellent and all five were liq-uids. After 12 months' exposure, as indicated by both the ink protection and the beading test, no liquid was as good as the paste waxes. The conclusion has to be that the liquids lack legs.

Straight up, we favor wax. And paste wax is best, primarily because it goes on thicker. Over time, wax discolors, like anything else, but can be removed with a good household cleaner like Fantastik. We're aware that paste wax is hard to apply and polish out, but preserving that precious gelcoat as long as possible makes it worth the effort that you'll expend. If done once a year in the northern climes—or every six months in the tropics—a wax like Collinite can keep gelcoat looking like new for a dozen or more years. We think that's time, energy, and money well spent.

Caulks and Sealants

In olden days, landlubbers used tons of putty to caulk and seal. For ships, sailors used oakum, which was pine-tarred rope or cotton waste, and a caulking (or chancing) iron and mallet to drive the oakum into the seams and cracks. Modern oakum is made of jute impregnated with something called Bentonite, which makes the stuff expand 10 times in size. Though putty is still used ashore for window glazing, for marine applications, it's all polymers now.

Among the many variants of polymers, the ones called polyurethane and polysulfide—along with distant cousins silicone and multi-caulk—are what

PS's recent test of caulking and sealing products included 23 specimens. Because they are prominent in the marine field, the largest number of samples came from 3M, Sikaflex, and BoatLife, The rest are primarily hardware-store varieties, some from prominent companies like Elmer's Products, Inc., GE, RPM Inc., and West Marine. Some come in tubes, some in cartridges, along with a squeeze bottle and a couple of pressurized cans.

concern us when we want to mount or replace things on our boats—cleats, winches, keels, vangs, radar mounts, port lights, hatches, padeyes, and stanchion bases, etc.

Polysulfide, an organic compound made of two sulfur atoms and one of carbon, is not much used anymore in exposed applications because it suffers badly from ultraviolet degradation. Multi-caulk usually is a tough, hard adhesive that lacks the needed flexibility for some applications. Silicone and polyurethane (NHCOO) are more complicated and more versatile. Silicone, which while curing gives off acetic acid (smells like vinegar), skins quickly and is easy to handle. Polyurethane is much stickier and difficult to handle. Get a dab on the edge of your hand, and very soon it's everywhere; it pays to keep everything pristine, with lots of paper towels, tools, and rubber gloves, which you discard after using them. Polyurethane makes what is considered a "permanent" bond.

On a boat, the goal is to make everything absolutely impervious to leaks—which can cause rot and lead to the deterioration of most any material. Besides solid wood (even teak and cedar) and fiberglass, wood-cored decks (balsa or plywood) are particularly vulnerable. Salt water, one of nature's most complex solutions, is the chief culprit. It contains so many elements that scientists have trouble counting them all, and neutralizing all of them is virtually impossible.

To bolster our test, *PS* contacted a number of experts in the field, among them Steve Mishra, vice president of technology for Tremco Sealants. Tremco is one arm of RPM, Inc., a company with 7,900 employees, and 68 plants in 17 countries. RPM owns Rust-Oleum, Dap, Bondo, Watco, Pettit, Woolsey, Z-Spar, and sundry other enterprises. Another was Steve Paget, technical coordinator for Sikaflex, which claims to be the world's largest (6,000 employees) polyurethane caulk maker. At 3M, a company whose widely known "5200" has the aura of a benchmark in marine caulks and sealants, it was Alison Berka-Bennett, one of 3M's many savvy regional representatives.

All of the experts agreed that sealing a portlight, for instance, is much easier than sealing a cleat attached to a balsa-cored deck, even one with spot reinforcement in the deck layup. The portlight does not move, whereas the cleat, which will be subjected to heavy tugging from perhaps multiple directions, must have a more elastic sealant to cope with the forces applied and still remain waterproof.

Our test included 23 varieties of caulks and sealants (see the accompanying table). We attempted to evaluate the most important qualities of these products and answer, on a comparative basis, the following questions:

1. Are they really waterproof?
2. How long do they remain elastic?
3. How strong is the bond?

In addition to these three basic attributes, caulks and sealants sometimes are used to electrically isolate the parts joined. In these cases, a lot of pressure shouldn't be used so that you avoid squeezing the caulk out of a joint.

Another consideration: Above or below the waterline? Silicone is not for use underwater, nor is it paintable. Polysulfide and polyurethane are.

As explained by Steve Mishra, the strength and elasticity requirements of any caulk or sealant oppose each other. And further defining the purpose of caulks and sealants is the question of whether adhesiveness is more important than watertightness.

"We can create and produce caulks and sealants with amazing qualities," Mishra said, "but combining the various properties is what's difficult."

To test adhesiveness, strength, and elasticity, five "surfaces" were prepared: raw aluminum, anodized aluminum, teak, fiberglass, and stainless steel. Twenty-three globs of caulk about the size of walnuts were applied to each material. In the raw aluminum, stainless washers were embedded standing up. In the anodized aluminum, oak dowels were embedded. The remaining combinations were teak/stainless steel bolts, fiberglass gelcoat/stainless steel bolts, and stainless sheet/brass screws. All 115 globs of caulk were kept indoors for four months to fully cure. Because the globs have considerable bulk, they require much more time to cure than would a thin layer in a joint. As a general rule, 10 days' curing time is needed for each 1/8 inch of caulk, so our provisions were overkill, naturally.

Manufacturer/ Product Name	Type	Cure Time (Tack Free/Complete)	Price (Per Ounce)	Paintable	Clean Up	Elasticity
Ace Hardware/Clear Sealant	Not stated	10 mins/72+ hrs	$.81	Yes	Mineral spirits	Most
BoatLife/Life Seal	Polyurethane/Silicone	10 mins/24 hrs	$1.14	No	Acetone	Moderate
BoatLife/Teak Deck Sealant	Polysulfide	30 mins/24 hrs	$.93	Not Stated	Acetone	A little
BoatLife/Silicone Rubber	Silicone	30 mins/24 hrs	$.86	No	Acetone	Most
Elmer's/Squeeze N Caulk	Silicone/Acrylic Latex	2 hrs/Not Stated	$.63	Yes	Water	Most
GE/Marine Silicone Rapid Cure	Silicone	30 mins/12+ hrs	$.63	No	Acetone	Moderate
GE/Silicone II XST	Silicone	2 hrs/48 hrs	$2.08	Yes	Water	A little
Eclectic/Goop	'Contact Adhesive'	2–10 mins/24 hrs	$2.55	Yes	Acetone	None
Gloucester Co./Phenoseal	Vinyl Adhesive	1 hr/12–45 hrs	$.45	Yes	Water	Most
RPM Inc./Dap	Acrylic Latex/Silicone	30 mins/24 hrs	$.65	Yes	Water	None
RPM/Dap Kwik Seal	Acrylic Latex	2 hrs/24 hrs	$.75	Yes	Water	Moderate
Sashco/Lexel	Acrylic Latex	30 mins/1-2 weeks	$1.15	Latex only	Acetone	Moderate
Sika/291	Polyurethane	Not Stated/1 week	$.78	Yes	Mineral spirits	None
Sika/291 LOT	Polyurethane	Not Stated/1 week	$.79	Yes	Mineral spirits	A little
Sika/295 UV	Polyurethane	Not Stated/12 hrs	$1.11	Yes	Mineral spirits	None
3M/101	Polysulfide	5 hrs/2–3 weeks	$1.99	Yes	alcohol	None
3M/5200	Polyurethane	48 hrs/5–7 days	$1.59	Yes	Acetone	A little
3M/5200 Fast Cure	Polyurethane	1 hr/24 hrs.	$1.89	Yes	Acetone	None
3M/Silicone	Silicone	5–10 mins/24 hrs	$1.59	No	Acetone	Moderate
3M/4000 UV	Polyether	2 hrs/24+ hrs	$1.79	Yes	Alcohol	None
West Marine/Silicone	Silicone	1 hr/24 hrs	$1.29	No	Acetone	A little
West Marine/Quick Cure	Polyurethane	2 hrs/2–3 days	$1.39	Yes	Acetone	None
West Marine/Multi Caulk	Polyether	2 hrs/1 day	$1.49	Yes	Acetone	A little

Then the panel was placed outdoors in open sunlight, exposed to all weather—winter and summer. Because the globs of caulk are more exposed to sun and weather than might occur in, for instance, a thinner layer used to bed a cleat or toerail, the "aging" should be accelerated.

To test waterproofness, 25 (two without caulked tops were to serve as controls) small, tall, very clean bottles were carefully scribed with an abrasive tool and filled with water to that half-full mark. The bottle lids were smeared liberally inside with caulk and caulk was "tooled" at 45 degrees against the inside lip of the lids. The lids were snugged down without much force, in order to assure that the caulk was not squeezed out.

The 25 bottles, numbered on their sides and bottom, were placed in a wooden rack made expressly to assure that each bottle was equally exposed to sun, shade, hot, and cold (including freezing). The bottle rack was placed outdoors, always on its side, not only to assure that the caulked tops had both air and water contact, but to permit the water to freeze without breaking the bottles. Constant expansion and contraction, along with some sunlight to work

Waterproofness (loss of water)	Comments
None	Looks, smells, and feels like ordinary silicone.
None	Apparently a blend. Claims to stick to anything.
None	Not very sticky. Made primarily for teak decks.
Slight	Standard silicone; trims neatly when cured.
None	A blend; too thin and runny, with difficult cure time.
Slight	Not for gaps or joints greater than ½" x ½".
Slight	Very stiff. Could barely squeeze from the tube.
Gone	Much too runny. Website doesn't seem to exist.
Slight	Very stiff to handle. Does not adhere well.
None	Nice container, but much too thin and runny.
None	Another nice container, but too thin and runny.
None	Easy to handle, but looks and feels like silicone.
None	Trouble with cartridge, but finally broke loose.
None	As above, nice 'body' and easy to put in place.
None	Sika's very best caulk; so far worth every penny.
Slight	Handles well, but not equal to a polyurethane.
None	Much runnier than above. Too long to form skin.
None	Seems superior to 3M's highly-regarded 5200.
None	Like other silicones, useful above the waterline.
None	3M's best. Same formulation as 4200 Fast Cure.
Slight	West Marine's name brand for standard silicone.
None	Probably made by 3M or Sika for West Marine.
None	Same as comment immediately above.

Shown here is the finished test panel with globs of the 23 products applied to five different surfaces and with various washers, bolts, dowels, and screws embedded in the globs. The surfaces are (from right to left) raw aluminum with stainless washers; anodized aluminum with oak dowels; teak with stainless steel bolts; fiberglass with stainless steel bolts; and stainless steel plate with brass screws. The panel resided outdoors for the better part of a year in coastal New England.

on whatever thin layer of caulk it could reach, will test the caulk's integrity. If a caulk is not waterproof, water loss would be plainly revealed by the waterline.

▷ **The Bottom Line** Elasticity in a caulk is desirable if great force is to be exerted on whatever equipment is involved. For instance, a cleat used to belay a sheet is better mounted with a caulk that has long-term elasticity. By contrast, a portlight or hatch should be mounted with a caulk that has great adhesiveness and is very waterproof.

Even after being cured for four months, three products were so flexible that within a month the stainless bolts sagged and dropped free, two from the teak, one from the fiberglass. The products involved were Elmer's Squeeze N Caulk and the Gloucester Company's Phenoseal. The bolts, screws, and washers set in the other products drooped but kept their grip.

These first comparative measurements all proved to be consistent, meaning that the percentage differences between fiberglass, wood, aluminum, etc., were the same. After that was established, fine measurements were done on the ¼-inch stainless bolts—primarily because the bolts were the easiest to scale accurately. Subjected to equal pressure from the side, the range of deflection on the stainless bolts was considerable—from zero to ⅝ inch. The ranges were broken into four groups, which are labeled on the chart as "Most," "Moderate," "A Little," and "None."

The only notable surprise in this elasticity test is that not all silicones were equally elastic, although they are more flexible than the polyurethanes, which were generally the least elastic. The greatest anomaly involved two silicone/acrylic caulks—Elmer's

Squeeze N Caulk and RPM's Dap. The Elmer's was among the most elastic—so elastic that, as noted above, it lost its grip on the stainless bolt. The Dap cured very hard.

In the waterproof testing, only a few bottles lost water. The bottle sealed with Eclectic Goop lost all of its water in slightly less than two weeks. It may be, then, that the silicone, which is not recommended for use underwater, dissolved and allowed the water to leak out. A few other bottles leaked very slightly (less than 10 percent), and four of those were sealed with products the maker identified as silicones. (Yet, four other bottles sealed with silicones lost no water.) The other "leakers" were sealed, one each, with polysulfide, vinyl, and acrylic latex. It is curious that the water turned milky in three of the four bottles sealed with what the manufacturers call acrylic latex; we take that to mean that something is dissolving.

The accompanying table indicates the results for each of these products in elasticity, and waterproofness.

Self-Bonding Tape

Self-bonding tape is very handy, and in the past couple of years we have become mildly addicted to the stuff. Known more formally as elastomeric, self-amalgamating tape, it's usually just silicone containing tiny bubbles of a chemical plasticizer. When you stretch this non-sticky tape (and it really likes stretching), the bubbles break and the gas contained therein permeates the silicone and morphs it into a ductile solid. Out of the sun, it lasts for years; in sunlight, it tends to dry, harden, and tear.

Self-amalgamating tape is much better, for most purposes, than duct tape or electrical tape (either plastic or cloth), all of which get brittle, crack, leak, or go gummy. With this watertight silicone tape, you can seal electrical connections, do emergency fuel or water hose repairs, insulate, make pressure bandages (even splints), whip rope ends, stop leaks, reduce vibration, pad wear points, wrap tool grips—anything on which you can get a couple of wraps. It has an amazing temperature tolerance (-60° to 500°F) and a dielectric rating up past 10,000.

Here in a pre-joust photo are samples of X-treme tape and Tommy Tape. The latter has prevailed in every test of these types of tapes that *PS* has conducted.

In previous *PS* tests (we've examined seven tapes of this sort—Navtec's Rig-Rap, Simpson Lawrence Rubbaweld, Tommy Tape, West Marine Rigging Tape, and three from Mariner's Choice, called Mast Boot, Rigging Tape, and Safety Wrap), only Tommy Tape and West Marine's Rigging Tape survived a full year of outdoor exposure. The rest lasted from three to eleven months.

We've subsequently reported on two other tapes, X-treme Tape and Atomic Tape. We've yet to render judgment on the latter, but we put the former up against Tommy Tape in a head-to-head contest, and learned that Tommy Tape is still the endurance champion, and still the most economical at roughly 31 cents per foot.

Corrosion Inhibitors

Dozens of spray products found on chandlery and hardware store shelves promise to inhibit rust, fight corrosion, and generally protect metals from attack. If that weren't overwhelming enough, the labels on these products are confusing at best. They all claim to be formulated of secret ingredients that enable them to beat out the competition when it comes to preserving your expensive hardware and electronics. And all claim to burrow under moisture and bond to the target metals. As it turns out, most of these products, at least those we tested, perform reasonably so long as you take the time to read the small print and select a product appropriate to the job.

The products we selected for our comparison come from four families of protectants—waxy barrier coatings, active fluid thin films, penetrating oils, and PTFE (generic Teflon) dry lubricants. Ultimately we narrowed the group to 17 products based mainly on availability in the major marine discount stores and recommendations from boaters we know. While several of the formulations we tested are available in bulk liquids and grease bases, we chose to limit our survey to spray products.

We tested the products side-by-side outdoors, but it's important to understand that intended uses vary widely among the product groups. Just because the label says the product "inhibits corrosion" doesn't mean that it does so in every environment. Nor, for that matter, will it be equally effective on every metal. Waxy barrier coats, for example, are tough and long-lasting, and especially suitable for use in areas that are repeatedly wetted or submerged. However, they can trap existing moisture on the surface of the target metal, allowing corrosion to take place under the barrier coat.

Fluid thin films, on the other hand, work their way under surface moisture, but can be washed away relatively easily; therefore, they do their best work in protected environments—inside a relay box, for instance, or in the engineroom.

Corrosion is an electrochemical process. It can occur at the molecular level causing micro-pitting, or on a macro scale, eating away large chunks of metal. At any scale, the corrosion process requires an anode, a cathode, and an electrolyte. Remove any one of the three elements, and you inhibit corrosion.

Some corrosion inhibitors, such as the CorrosionX and Corrosion Block, employ passivating agents—chemicals that work at the molecular level to make the target metal less vulnerable to the electrolytic process. The molecules of these passivating agents tend to burrow through existing moisture and corrosion to the target metal's surface, where they spread out like ball bearings on a tabletop. Often many of these ingredients are included in a product, one for each metal the product attempts to protect.

The waxy barrier coats work by preventing the electrolyte (water) from gaining contact with the target metal. Typically the wax components are dissolved in a solvent for delivery. Once the coating contacts the metal it's intended to protect, the solvent evaporates, leaving the wax behind. (Pure water actually is a poor electrolyte, but marine equipment rarely sees pure water. Water in the marine environment is full of salt and dissolved minerals and is a very efficient conductor of electric charges—a great electrolyte.)

Penetrating oils are thin and flow easily. The more sophisticated penetrating oils are formulated with proprietary passivating agents.

Using clean, mild steel test panels guaranteed to be metallurgically identical to each other and free of contamination, we treated each plate (except one) with a different product (according to the label instructions) being careful not to contaminate adjacent plates. The plates were labeled alphabetically so our judges couldn't associate a plate with a product (until the end of the test). We mounted our rust farm outdoors where it would be subjected to the vagaries of a New England winter. To make matters more interesting, we filled a spray bottle with a salt solution and sprayed all the plates once a week. We inspected the plates at 10 and 20 days into the test and finally at 82 days. Grading the results was a simple (though subjective) task—we estimated the percent of surface area that had rusted.

Within a few days, the untreated plate began to scale (rust), as did both of the PTFE-treated plates and two of the penetrating-oil treated plates. (The PTFE products were SailKote and Sea Spray; the penetrating oils that folded early were CRC 6-56 and PB Blaster.) By day 20, 3M's 4-Way Lubricant and ProLong SPL100, both penetrating oils, started to permit significant scaling. At the same time, traces of rust began to appear on plates protected by Corrosion X-HD, LanoCote, LPS-3, Corrosion Block, and Lube-It-All.

On the last day of the test, only two panels remained entirely scale free, those protected by CorrosionX Max Wax and CRC HD Corrosion Inhibitor. Both are flexible waxy barrier coatings. Two other waxy barrier coatings—LanoCote and Boeshield T-9—also performed well.

CorrosionX and Corrosion Block (two popular passivating thin films widely used on electrical and electronic components) fared very well, especially considering that they are formulated for use in rela-

Product	Manufacturer	Test Description	Price Can	Street Per Oz.	Price
CorrosionX Max Wax	Corrosion Technologies	flexible waxy barrier coat	11 oz.	$1.36	$14.95
CRC HD Corrosion Inhibitor	CRC Industries, Inc.	flexible waxy barrier coat	10 oz.	$0.70	$6.95
Corrosion X-HD	Corrosion Technologies	viscous film coating	12 oz.	$1.04	$12.49
LanoCote	Lanocote	flexible waxy barrier coat	7 oz.	$1.18	$8.25
Boeshield T-9	PMS Products	flexible waxy film	12 oz.	$1.07	$12.79
LPS-3*	LPS Laboratories	flexible waxy barrier coat	11 oz.	$.071	$7.84
CorrosionX	Corrosion Technologies	fluid thin film coating	16 oz.	$0.78	$12.49
Corrosion Block	Lear Chemical Research	fluid thin film coating	12 oz.	$1.12	$13.48
3M 4-Way Spray Lubricant	3M	multipurpose lubricant	12 oz.	$0.42	$5.09
WD-40	WD-40 Company	penetrating oil	11 oz.	$0.36	$3.99
LPS-2*	LPS Laboratories	non-drying oily film	11 oz.	$0.59	$6.46
LPS 1*	LPS Laboratories	penetrating oil	11 oz.	$0.55	$6.03
Lube-It-All	Federal Process Corp.	penetrating oil	6 oz.	$0.65	$3.89
ProLong SPL 100	Prolong Super Lubricants	penetrating oil	12 oz.	$0.75	$8.95
CRC 6-56	CRC Industries, Inc.	penetrating oil	9 oz.	$0.44	$3.99
PB Blaster	B'Laster/B.C.C.I.	penetrating oil	12 oz.	$0.42	$4.99
SailKote†	Team McLube	PTFE†	16 oz.	$0.87	$13.95
Sea Spray	Mariner's Choice	PTFE†	11 oz.	$0.72	$7.95

*LPS product results available only for 10- and 20-day tests. Positions in the table, therefore, are estimates and approximate. We'll report on the results at 82 days in a later issue of the magazine.   †polytetrafluroethylene = generic Teflon.   ‡According to the label or product sheets.

tively protected areas. The 3M product showed early signs of distress but hung in well for the long term, giving up only 50 percent of its test plate to rust at the end of the test period. WD-40 and Lube-It-All, both popular with mechanics as all-around penetrants, hung on in the early stages but suffered washout at the end.

▷ **The Bottom Line** It's clear that reading the label is vital on these products. No single one holds the solution for all corrosion-protection projects. We learned that the waxy barrier coats perform better and longer in soaked environments than do the thin films. So the waxy coats might be ideal for engine mounts, brackets, steering system supports, and other bilge hardware. None is cosmetically attrac-

tive—typically they leave a dry amber/yellow film—so you have to be careful when using them topside. Of the waxy barrier coats we tested, only LanoCote left a tacky film when dry. The others felt smooth and probably will accumulate less dirt.

Waxes are fine for large electrical components such as battery terminals (after the connection has been made) but aren't so good for switch contacts or PC boards. Waxy coatings must be allowed to dry when applied, and can be removed with a solvent, typically mineral spirits or other degreasers. All of the wax coats performed well in our tests. If you operate in thermally harsh environments, consider CorrosionX Max Wax. It stays flexible in temperatures well below zero and will resist flow at temperatures up to 398°F.

Electrical Connections‡	Electronic Components‡	Percentage of Rust		
		10 Days	20 Days	82 Days
Yes	No	0	0	0
Yes	No	0	0	0
Yes	No	2	2	5
Yes	No	5	5	5
Yes	No	0	0	10
Yes	No	0	0	NA*
Yes	Yes	0	0	50
Yes	Yes	0	5	50
Yes	No	2	20	50
No	No	0	0	80
Yes	No	0	0	NA*
Yes	No	0	0	NA*
Yes	No	2	5	80
No	No	5	20	90
Yes	Yes	50	80	100
Yes	No	80	80	100
No	No	80	80	100
No	No	80	90	100

LPS 3 is especially heavy-duty stuff designed for offshore drilling equipment, outdoor electrical components, underground installations, air brake release springs, and similar applications. It meets several mil specs.

The active fluid thin films—those products designed specifically for corrosion protection—are widely used on all metal surfaces and electrical components in and around boats. One of our technical correspondents has used CorrosionX and Corrosion Block for years in marine, aviation, and firearms applications, and reports that neither product has ever failed to protect a treated surface when used as recommended. The companies that make these products—Corrosion Technologies and Lear Laboratories—offer their formulations in many varieties including greases and bulk liquids. They're both used by military naval and air services to protect machinery and electronics working in the world's harshest environments.

The penetrating oils all claim to penetrate (thus to free stuck parts), lubricate moving parts, clean surfaces, displace moisture, and protect against rust and corrosion. In terms of protection, all seemed to do okay to the 20-day point, but rapidly lost effectiveness as they were washed off by repeated applications of salt spray and the winter rains. We suspect that if we had reapplied them every 10 to 15 days, they would have done fine. They would also have done well, we think, in enclosed spaces, and they are certainly less expensive than the top-end active thin films from Corrosion Technologies and Lear Labs.

The PTFE products have unique properties. As an example, SailKote, as its name implies, was originally formulated for application to sails. It reduces wear and friction in sail systems and tends to repel water, salt, and grime. To the extent that it repels water, it acts as an anticorrosive agent. We included SailKote in our test of corrosion inhibitors only because a number of sailors we know said they use it for that purpose. Our guess is that as a corrosion inhibitor, it's a fine dry lubricant. The same can be said, probably, for Mariner's Choice Dry PFD Sea Spray.

For long-lasting corrosion protection in very wet areas, we can give a thumbs-up to CorrosionX Max Wax and CRC Heavy Duty Corrosion Inhibitor. Both of these products leave a flexible waxy barrier coating on the protected metal surface that stands up to wet conditions.

For lighter-duty work, especially protecting electrical and electronic components in enclosed spaces, we like CorrosionX and Corrosion Block. These fluid thin films contain passivating agents that are safe for use on electronics and precision machined parts. They are especially effective belowdecks where they will not wash off.

For general-purpose rust-busting and short-term protection, the old standards turn out to be solid, cost-effective performers. WD-40 and Lube-It-All are especially good.

For engine mounts, brackets, steering system supports, and other bilge hardware, use products that seal with a waxy coat, such as CRC's Heavy Duty Corrosion Inhibitor, shown here. In our testing, this product, along with CorrosionX Max Wax, performed best in the long term.

Subsequent to that test, *PS* evaluated a newer product called Strike Hold, which was developed to protect small weapons from moisture intrusion. The manufacturers of this product make many claims: that it will cut through "dirt, rust, carbon, scale," leaving "a shield-like film" that won't wash off. We performed a few basic tests with it, and it does appear to work in the short term. Because it sells for essentially the same price as Boeshield T-9 and WD-40, we think it, too, is worth a try.

CHAPTER 10

Creature Comforts

Sailboat dealers are often fond of quoting sail-away prices. Yes, you can upgrade from a base boat and get your new vessel with the sails, some electronics, and maybe even a dockline or two, etc., as part of the package. But, if you want the kind of amenities that customize a boat to suit your own needs and tastes regarding comfort, that will require aftermarket additions in most cases. We've corralled those sorts of items in this chapter and given them a generic label—creature comforts—since these run the gamut from personal gear like sunglasses to larger, permanently installed items like refrigeration units. Let's begin by examining some products for the cockpit.

Deck Gear

PEDESTAL-MOUNT COCKPIT TABLES

Time was when yachtsmen and their ladies—if the boat was splendid—tripped below, after aperitifs on deck, to dine at a polished table, sometimes even gimbaled. These days, even mid-sized sailboats are fitted with some form of cockpit table. Those mounted on pedestal guards are what concern us here.

To assess the products in this realm, we gathered up a dozen or so cockpit tables from the following companies (listed alphabetically): Edson, Garelick, Lewmar, Magma, Marinco/AFI, SnapIt, and Teak-Flex. Of course, there are other table makers—like Tracy International and Todd (both of which make pedestals), Nemo (which makes Hideaway tables),

and Arneson (which makes side-mount tables)—but these specimens make for a good representation of the market.

To try these tables straight out of the box, each was affixed, if possible, to a standard Edson pedestal steering platform. (There are other pedestal steerers—like Goiot from France and the extensive Lewmar-owned Whitlock systems from England—but most table makers have adapters to fit any of the pedestal guards used.) The tables that did not fit on the Edson guard were assembled and disassembled (to determine the degree of difficulty) and closely examined.

▷ **The Bottom Line** If you're in the market for a pedestal-mount table, you would likely have to grapple with the following questions:

1. Do I want the table to be permanently in place (suggesting that it'll be used frequently), or stowed away to protect its finish or hardware?
2. Do I prefer a small table, for use by two (or for buffets), or a larger table for eating full meals?
3. Is sanding, finishing, and varnishing my cup of tea? Or do I want a carefree table that can stand up to the elements for years?
4. Is beauty and "setting a fine table" important to me?

There are many options available, but here are our general assessments. Garelick's tables are inexpensive assemblies of aluminum and poly, but their sharp corners and edges are intimidating. And, they're not at all pretty, either.

Lewmar tables are top-ranked for their gorgeous woodwork, but the support system requires drilling holes in the pedestal itself, so it's not as good as, nor as easily installed, as the tables from Edson.

Marinco/AFI makes good teak products at very reasonable prices (despite leaving exposed a lot of end-grain). However, again, the support system, which depends on two clamp-on poly blocks and a

Edson's 'luncheon table,' shown here, lists for $295 and easily doubles its 13.5-inch by 24-inch size with the optional add-on leaves available from the company. In the view of *PS's* testers, Edson builds the best cockpit tables for the money.

vertical wood leg that easily can be bent and damaged, is not the equal of Edson's.

Ken Clift, at TeakFlex, is the man you need for any seemingly impossible custom table design or installation. He's a genuine "wood guy," who can produce tables and other teak amenities that would be fit for even the finest yacht.

Cockpits can become much more functional with an aftermarket addition like the teak pedestal-mount table aboard this Beneteau 373.

BLUE PERFORMANCE BAGS

When we first spied Blue Performance Bags at a boat show, we were excited. Here was a handsomely designed, seemingly well-built product that would provide for a number of specific needs on board. The company (Blue Performance Bags is part of Holland-based Interfield Sports) makes bags for stowing sheets, halyards, winch handles, charts, and other on-deck gear. They come in a number of sizes and models. In fact, Blue Performance manufactures over 30 products. Apart from the bulkhead-mountable halyard and sheet bags and combo bags (the latter have winch handle pockets and mesh outer pockets for smaller items), there are also sunshades, awnings, hatch covers, elastic sail stops, see-through chart covers, mast-mount halyard bags, lifeline bags, winch covers, outboard motor covers, and other specialty storage bags.

Blue Performance makes three sizes of bags that strap onto the mast to hold and protect halyard tails or other control lines (the smallest one is shown here—$45—hung on the mast of a Santa Cruz 70). The one we tested sat in the sun for eight months before the nylon webbing on its straps deteriorated, but the company assures us that this problem has now been addressed.

Almost all Blue Performance products come with mounting hardware, which includes countersunk stainless steel screws that recess into the bases of hard plastic hooks to affix them to a boat's outer surfaces (or inner surfaces in the case of cabin bags). The designer has cleverly sewn durable line onto the products to fit over the upper hook attachments and elastic bungee cord to slip over the lower hook attachments on most products so that once attached, the bags are kept in tension and can't fall off. This system is more secure and reliable than the simple snap buttons, suction cups, and twist-lock fasteners utilized by most other cockpit bags.

Additionally, the bags are reinforced with stiff plastic inserts so that they don't bunch up and become less usable. And most of Blue Performance's products come packaged with diagrammed instructions for mounting, including easy-to-use templates.

PS examined five of the products from Blue Performance, including a mast-mount halyard bag, and presented the products in the Chandlery section of our July 1, 2005 issue. In that, we wrote: "They seem well built, and particularly well conceived. Will they hold up over time? We expect they will, but we can't say for sure until we put them in service for a goodly amount of time." We subsequently discovered—after eight months of exposure in the sun aboard one of our test boats—that the nylon webbing on that mast-mount bag had deteriorated entirely. We sent a sample back to the manufacturer, who tested it. This, company officials told us, was an isolated incident not common with their products. Nonetheless, we were assured that the webbing would be upgraded with better-performing UV protection.

We think the Blue Performance Bags have good potential for keeping boats organized, but we'll wait until we've tested further samples before endorsing these products.

Maker and Model	Price	Type	Table Top Material	Table Top Size	Weight	Table Top Finish	Table Support Type
Edson #761TK	$295	luncheon	solid teak	13½" x 24"	9.5 lbs.	Good	diagonal rod
Edson #737TK	$595	double-leaf	solid teak	26" x 27"	18.5 lbs.	Good	diagonal rod
Edson #849TK	$345	slide-on	solid teak	13½" x 24"	9 lbs.	Good	finger brackets
Garelick #75349	$198	side-mount	white poly	15" x 28"	16.5 lbs.	Good	base plate & tube
Garelick #75400	$187	deck-mount	melamine	18" x 30"	16 lbs.	Poor	side bracket
Garelick #75339	$143	deck-mount	melamine	20" (diagonal)	13 lbs.	Fair	base plate & tube
Lewmar #89400283	$803	double-leaf	solid teak	26" x 27½"	14 lbs.	Excellent	alum casting
Magma #T10-306	$70	rail-mount	white poly	12" x 24"	7 lbs.	Good	rail clamp
Marinco/AFI #60392	$319	double-leaf	joined teak	25" x 32"	21 lbs.	Fair	folding leg
SnapIt #M0011	$175	all polymer	white poly	17½" x 24"	18 lbs.	Excellent	polymer beams
Teak-Flex	$350	sliding leaves	solid teak	24" x 24"	16 lbs.	Good	telescoping leg

Still, in our view, the top tables in this evaluation are made by Edson. This company makes three kinds of tables, and we include all three in this judgment. The line begins with No. 849, the simple slip-on model that sells for $345 (teak version) or $272 (white poly version); continues with No. 761, "the luncheon table" ($295 in teak, $207 in white poly); and culminates with Edson's full-sized folding teak table, No. 737. This beauty has a mounting and support system that competitors should simply copy. It uses just four stainless steel split collars for mounting, each of which is attached to the guard with two Allen screws. It all makes for an extraordinary but lightweight system; the most rigid and convenient of all those *PS* tested. Yes, these tables are expensive, definitely, but we feel that the quality of the design and the work make them worth every penny.

For a more economical alternative—if you don't mind a bunch of white plastic hanging on your pedestal guard—we recommend the SnapIt table for $175. It's not unattractive, and it's essentially carefree because it can remain in place nearly forever.

COCKPIT SEATS

Ever a mystery is why most places to sit on a boat appear to have been designed by disciples of Frank Lloyd Wright. America's most famous architect never saw a right angle he didn't like—one leg perfectly horizontal; the other absolutely vertical. There are a few European boats with properly cocked seats, maybe even curved, with slanting backrests. But the majority of cockpits are as cruel as Wright's austere dining room chairs.

Due to that outlook, *PS* editors have since been on the lookout for remedies of any sort. To that end, some time ago we reported on a bean-bag-style product—a 20-by-40-inch Sunbrella rectangle that opened up double-width, made a float, and had a mesh panel for drainage and drying called the Aqua Lounge. Invented by Roger Olson, it sold for $99.

We also reviewed other cockpit seats. One of them, a pipe-framed, foam-sleeved, two-position seat called the Backjack, is still made and sold for $49.75 by a company called B. J. Industries. It's sold through various online retailers. The Backjack is comfortable, and we've seen it in use on boats, but it has only a couple of positions and is a bit bulky and difficult to stow.

Then there was the Howda Seat, a canvas frame with hardwood slats that conforms to the shape of the horizontals and verticals you use during sitting. It also rolls up for easy stowage. It's available from Howda Designz of Newburyport, Massachusetts.

We also looked at the Ridge Rest-R, made by a very active outdoor sport equipment company called

Support Material	Fiddles?	Support Fit	Cover Available?	Installation	Overall Sturdiness	Assemble and Stow	Comments
stainless steel	Yes	Excellent	Yes	Easy	Excellent	Easy	Small and demounts easily
stainless steel	Yes	Excellent	Yes	Easy	Excellent	Easy	Big version of above
cast aluminum	Yes	Excellent	No	Very Easy	Excellent	Very Easy	Excellent concept, versatile
anodized alum.	No	Good	No	Difficult	Fair	Fairly Easy	Okay if space permits
anodized alum.	No	Fair	No	Difficult	Good	Not Easy	Too many sharp edges
anodized alum.	No	Good	No	Difficult	Fair	Fairly Easy	Demounts to stow
stainless steel	Yes	Excellent	Yes	Not Easy	Excellent	Very Easy	Available in poly for $437
extruded alum.	No	Poor	No	Difficult	Poor	NA	The price is right
poly/teak	No	Fair	No	Care Required	Fair	Easy	OK for laminated teak
all poly	Yes	Good	No	Very Easy	Good	Easiest of All	Best-Buy by a mile
all teak	No	Good	No	Not Easy	Good	Not Easy	Good solid teak work

Cascade Designs, in Seattle, Washington. It's no longer made, but Cascade now makes several other seats, including a lightly padded camp chair and a stadium chair with closed-cell-foam cushions sewn into ripstop nylon. Back support is adjusted by side straps. The large camp chair sells for $40; the medium for $36.

And the seat that we once felt was the best is the Sport-a-Seat made by the Paradise Co. of Herndon, Virginia. This is a well-padded, six-position, ratchet-hinged seat with Sunbrella-covered foam. The retail price, sometimes bested by boat show sale prices, is serious: $95.

In this niche of the outdoor market, there are about 20 companies known to be making seats, but few of them met the *PS* criteria: padded; self-supporting backrest; foldable; stowable, and reasonably weatherproof.

One new company is HelmSense Products. Marc Cohen, the owner and founder, has spent too many hours at the helm of boats without a backrest of any kind. (He sails a Cal 33.) So Cohen, an engineer out of Tufts University, invented something different. He calls it a Helmsman's Backrest. Basically, it's an 18-by-36-inch cushion attached with hook-and-loop to a thick backing plate (made of high-density polyethylene like Starboard) that accommodates (in various positions) a pair of standard powerboat radio antenna mounts, thus giving the backrest adjustability. The antenna mounts join, via two PVC thick-wall pipes, to small universal mounting brackets clamped to the stern rails. It appears that with a bit of tinkering, the brackets could be deck-mounted. All the parts are shown in one of the accompanying photos.

For stowage, the rig comes off quickly via two Fast-pins, leaving only the two (relatively) inconspicuous stainless steel brackets in place. It's not inexpensive at $219 for the kit.

Marc Cohen's Helmsman's Backrest is an ingenious and proper solution for a support problem that exists on many boats. It unhooks quickly, but costs a pretty penny and won't stow well.

And finally, the Crazy Creek fold-up chair is a sort of space-age cousin to the Howda Seat, which is an old New England design originated for circus-goers. While the Howda uses hardwood slats, the Crazy Creek seat (billed for use in the stadium, campsite, and cockpit) is built of light, high-quality fabric and closed-cell foam over padded internal struts. The sewing is first-class. Except for the struts, the Crazy Creek seat is mighty reminiscent of the Cascade Designs chairs.

Crazy Creek's standard chair costs $38.50; the large one is $41.75. If your cockpit seats are narrow, Crazy Creek's stadium chairs (with shallower seats) might be the ticket. All of them fold and stow beautifully.

▷ **The Bottom Line** Simple as they are, each of these seats is luxurious, at least when measured against a barbarous slab of cold, flat fiberglass with a low (or no) backrest. To make the helmsman happy, Marc Cohen's backrest, mounted with its lower edge resting on a cockpit seat cushion, would make the hours while away wondrously. It well might be left in position for a season, but demounts easily and stows fairly well. The $219 price might make you think twice, and it's only for the helmsman, so it's not overly versatile.

Crazy Creek's very light, fold-up seat is fine, too. It can be used anywhere, stows very quickly (just fold and roll), and the padding, while skinny, is still pretty comfortable. The same comments would probably apply to the new Cascade Designs chairs.

The seat that, year after year, hangs in there in the marine catalogs is that nice, thick, six-position, ratchet-hinged Sport-a-Seat, which sells for $95, in six colors, no less. It's a bit difficult to store, of course, and is pricey—but for sheer comfort and adaptability, it has yet to meet a peer.

Galley Amenities

BARBECUE GRILLS

To grill or not to grill, that is the question. Whether 'tis better to pack a picnic lunch or to buy a stainless propane barbecue—and in doing so assume the initial cost, the work of setting it up and keeping it clean and free from corrosion—rests on just how

Everything tastes better off the grill, but marine gas barbecues—like this old-model Magma kettle—have a downside too: They get dirty quickly, they rust, and they require propane, which can be a storage hazard. However, at $200, this Magma grill is *PS*'s choice for a kettle-style grill.

important grilling is to you. While the benefits of marine grills are largely existential, the pitfalls tend to be concrete, like layers of baked-on grease. These things get dirty, they rust, and they require bottled propane, which can be a storage hazard on boats.

To get a sense of what you can expect from marine-grill ownership, we tested six propane-fired, stainless steel models; four are rectangular grills with hinged, fold-back hoods, and two are kettles.

PS testers used a slab of pizza dough and a digital thermocouple to evaluate the heat distribution of gas grills on one recent test.

Make	Magma ★	Sport Barbeques	Dickinson	Force 10 $	Magma ★	Tasco
Model	Marine Kettle 2	Sport Extreme	Sea-B-Que	Sea Grill 180	Catalina Gourmet Series	Seacooker
Price	$200	$180	$260	$240	$300	$236
Source	defender.com	bartswatersports.com	Dickinson Marine	westmarine.com	defender.com	Taunton Stove Co.
Cooking Area	226 sq. in.	153 sq. in.	148 sq. in.	180 sq. in.	306 sq. in.	166 sq. in.
Dimensions (L x H x D)	17" x 17" x 12"	14" x 14" x 9"	16.5" x 9.5" x 10"	20" x 16" x 13"	18.5" x 15" x 13"	18" x 10" x 12"
Weight	10 lbs.	8.5 lbs.	15 lbs.	26 lbs.	25 lbs.	15 lbs.
Lid Type	Hinged	Hinged	Roll-up	Roll-up	Roll-up	Roll-up
Burner Rating	11,000 BTUs	7,000 BTUs	12,000 BTUs	14,000 BTUs	13,000 BTUs	12,000 BTUs
Mounts	Rail, rod; shore stand	Rail; shore stand	Rail; rod; shore stand	Rail; rod; shore stand	Rail; rod; shore stand	Rail; rod
Removable Grease Tray	No	Yes	Yes	Yes	Yes	Yes
Other Features	Tripod stand	Carry-case	Temp gauge	Hood locks; temp gauge	Hood lock; temp gauge; warming rack	
Construction Quality	Excellent	Poor	Good	Excellent	Excellent	Fair
Ease of Assembly	Good	Good	Fair	Excellent	Good	Good
Ease of Cleanup	Good	Fair	Good	Good	Good	Fair
Cooking Rating	Good	Good	Good	Good	Good	Fair
Materials	Polished; 18-9 stainless steel	Brushed stainless steel	Porcelain; brushed stainless steel	Polished stainless steel	Polished 18-9 stainless steel	Brushed stainless steel
Warranty	Limited, covers mnf. defects	1 yr. limited	1 yr. limited	1 yr. limited	Limited, covers mnf. defects	1 yr. limited

$ Budget Buy   ★ Best Choice

We looked at barbecues from Magma, Force 10, Tasco, Dickinson, and Sport Barbecues, and found that the price range was not as varied as the range in quality, from the metalwork to the mounting hardware. *PS* testers evaluated each grill for heat distribution, mount stability in a swell, ease of cleaning, and quality of construction.

▷ **The Bottom Line** In the marine grills race, it comes down to quality. If you're going to spend $200 or $300 on a marine grill, you want one that will last. Of the big rectangular units, the Force 10 Sea Grill 180 ($240) and the Magma Catalina ($300) are equally well made. Do the Catalina's warming rack, fractional grill, and easy-to-install propane fitting make it worth $60 more than the Force 10, with its

numeric thermometer, simple latches, and convenient thumbscrews? That depends on how you plan to use the grill.

The gas regulators used on the Catalina and Magma's kettle-style grill use the same "bayonet" system as the other grills, but they allow the regulators to be rotated while in use. Most of the test grills have fixed regulators, but the Magmas' are detachable. This makes it easier to screw on propane bottles and allows quick access to the propane jet for cleaning.

The final ratings came down to the pizza dough test. Our top choice, the Catalina, showed fairly even heat distribution, while our Budget Buy, the Force 10, had some hot spots. We'd need to see the prices of the smaller, brushed stainless rectangular grills drop before we'd consider picking one up. Mirror-polished stainless steel, while requiring more fuss to keep it shiny, does a better job at resisting rust. *PS* found the bodies of the Sea-B-Que and Tasco more prone to rust stains and more difficult to clean. The Magma's mounting hardware was also affected.

If you want a smaller grill than the Catalina or the Force 10, opt instead for the Magma kettle, our Best Choice in the kettles category. At $200, the Magma kettle is $20 more expensive than the Sport Extreme, but this difference boils down to the quality of materials. Magma's stainless steel construction is certainly worth it if you want a grill for the long haul. The Sport Extreme's corrosion was much more pronounced, and unless you need it for just one season, we would not recommend buying the Sport Extreme.

SINGLE-BURNER STOVES

Any boat with a cabin ought to have some sort of stove to heat food and boil water. Sailing is, after all, a civilized pastime, is it not? While larger boats seem to have increasingly complicated galley systems—dedicated freezers, watermakers, icemakers, microwaves, broilers—there's much to be said for simplicity. And single-burner stoves are, if nothing else, simple.

For this report, we examined five stoves, with discount prices ranging from $40 to about $150: the Forespar Mini-Galley, the Force 10 Seacook, the

Origo 1500, the Glomate GM 1600, and the Kenyon Express. Three different fuels are used by the five stoves: denatured alcohol (CH_3CH_2OH), propane or LPG (C_3H8), and butane (C_4H10). A standard test is time to boil a quart of water (see the Value Guide). Results are a function of the Btu (British thermal unit) rating of the fuel and burner size. Alcohol is rated at 2,500–3,000 Btu output, and LPG at twice that—5,000–6,000.

Most marine and camping butane stoves use a standard 8-ounce canister. These must conform to Department of Transportation regulations. The two cans we bought, one with the Glomate label and the other with the Kenyon label, were both made in Korea, by the Daeryuk Can Co. and the Tae Yang Industrial Co.

In our previous evaluation of stoves, we noted that the American Boat & Yacht Council (ABYC) approves of the use of these 8-ounce butane canisters in the living areas of boats. However, only one canister at a time is allowed; spare canisters are supposed to be stored outside, in a compartment ventilated overboard, perhaps where you keep the outboard motor gas tank.

ABYC standard A-30 allows only the 8-ounce butane canister, and not the heavier 16.4-ounce propane bottle commonly used for camp and some marine stoves. This is unfortunate because propane is a commonly accepted fuel; both the Seacook and Mini-Galley use the canisters, and the extra amount

The stoves that *PS* tested in one test included (left to right, front row): the Kenyon Express, the Origo 1500, and Glomate's GM 1600. In the back are the Forespar Mini-Galley at left and the Force 10 Seacook.

Make	Glomate	Kenyon	Force 10	Forespar	Origo
Model	GM 1600	Express	Seacook	Mini-Galley	1500
Price	$39.99	$49.95	$89.99	$99.95	$141.29
Source	BoatUS	Defender	BoatUS	Defender	BoatUS
Fuel	Butane	Butane	Propane	Propane	Alcohol
Width	$13\frac{1}{2}$"	$13\frac{1}{2}$"	$10\frac{5}{8}$"	$7\frac{9}{16}$"	$9\frac{5}{16}$"
Depth	$10\frac{3}{16}$"	$10\frac{7}{16}$"	$12\frac{1}{4}$"	$7\frac{3}{4}$"	$10\frac{5}{16}$"
Height	$3\frac{3}{16}$"	$3\frac{1}{2}$"	$8\frac{3}{16}$"	$7\frac{1}{2}$"	$5\frac{3}{8}$"
Weight (empty)	$4\frac{1}{4}$ lbs.	4 lbs.	$4\frac{1}{2}$ lbs.	$1\frac{1}{2}$ lbs.	7 lbs.
Feet	Plastic	Plastic	NA	NA	None
Gimbal?	No	No	Yes	Yes	Optional $84.99
Time to Boil 1 qt. water	$5\frac{1}{2}$ min.	$5\frac{1}{2}$ min.	10 min.	$5\frac{1}{2}$ min. (Pan provided does not quite hold 1 qt.)	$11\frac{1}{2}$ min.
Options	Potholder $9.99	Sea Leg Suction cups $10.99 Permanent mount kit $11.99 Potholder $29.99		Teapot $20.79 Nine-cup percolator $19.95	Potholder $94.99

wouldn't seem to pose much additional danger. While we suppose ABYC had to draw the line somewhere, why not at 16 ounces? We point out ABYC's position in case this is of interest to you or your insurance company.

Several stoves carry warnings about CO (carbon monoxide) and oxygen deprivation. Forespar's regulator, for example, is a lantern model made by the Century Tool Co. of Cherry Valley, Illinois. It carries the warning (that could apply to all of the stoves in this evaluation) that the device can produce CO, "a colorless, odorless gas which can kill you."

Combustible fuels also consume oxygen, which can lead to asphyxiation. Therefore, Century warns not to use the burner in "tents, campers, pickup toppers, cars, vans, etc." One could easily add boats. But the same applies to any combustible fuel-burning device, including auxiliary engines, conventional stoves, and cabin heaters. On boats, you can't always move them outside. To be safe, good installation is paramount, as are safe operating practices.

As in the past, each stove was operated at full throttle to see how fast it boiled a quart of water. Results are similar except for the Origo alcohol stove

and, surprisingly, the Seacook LPG stove. Beyond this one empirical test, each stove was examined for quality of materials and workmanship, and safety features.

▷ **The Bottom Line** Though all five stoves tested are single-burner units, they can be divided into two categories twice: those that gimbal and those that don't; and those that gimbal in all axes and those that don't. For rough weather, the Seacook and Forespar Mini-Galley are the obvious choices—even if you have a larger boat with a stove/oven. The Mini-Galley is nicely made, well designed, and should last a long time. It's lightweight and comes with a nylon storage bag for the pot, and a larger nylon bag for the entire unit. We only wish it held larger pots; when compared to the Seacook, that's where it comes up short. At $99.95, it's just $10 more, but we don't see any reason to fork over a sawbuck.

The Seacook won't double as a camp stove because it has to be suspended, but it's the one you want on board for rough weather. At $90, it's twice the price of the butane stoves, but it is marine-grade and should last for many years. We also like that it holds larger pots than the Mini-Galley, but we remain annoyed at how long it took to boil water.

Stoves that can't be made to gimbal, like the Glo-mate GM 1600 and Kenyon Express, must be used with care on boats. Securing them to a countertop improves safety, but if the boat rolls too hard a pot could spill or be thrown off, even with the recommended pot holder. Therefore, we view these two butane stoves as less desirable. At the same time, their low prices and reliable operation make them easy choices for, say, use on a trailer-sailer where, often as not, you might be cooking on the hard. For use on board, consider limiting cooking to the cockpit.

If you just can't get past the explosive nature of butane or propane, there's no doubt that the Swedish-built Origo is a quality stove, well made and simple. Alcohol, for all its shortcomings, is not explosive, and many boat owners would trade the longer cooking times for that measure of safety any day. The cost of the Origo, however, seems out of proportion with the others. With the optional gimbals and pot holder, you're talking $300. Yikes!

COOLERS

Portable coolers are a staple of American outdoor life, from camping trips to backyard barbecues. Certainly they are familiar, if not essential, to nearly every boat owner. Some smaller boats are actually designed with the cooler in mind, with space allocated under a seat, or elsewhere in the cockpit. Even if the boat is big enough to have a built-in icebox and/or refrigeration system below, some owners find it useful to carry pre-chilled drinks and food to the boat in a cooler for transfer once aboard. Then there's the cooler for keeping caught fish cold, carrying frozen food to the boat . . . the possibilities are without limit.

There are essentially three types of portable coolers: 12-volt thermoelectric ones, which do not require ice, and two that do—hard and soft-sided coolers. The most important quality of any cooler is the ability to

The Seacook from Force 10 is ruggedly made and a solid choice for heating meals in rough conditions.

keep its contents cold, which means preventing the ice inside from melting too quickly. Igloo claims its coolers can keep ice for five days in 90°F heat. *PS* tested that for this report. But considering that nearly all contemporary portable coolers are of similar construction (thermoformed polyester or polyethylene plastic shells with foam inside), one might expect similar performance— again, we tested that, too. In that case, other features might drive the purchase decision—rust-resistant and sturdy hinges and latches, and convenient carrying handles. Some models have wheels, drink holders in the lid, sliding trays, and other compartments.

Coolers come in all sizes, mostly rectangular boxes. We settled on nine models in the 60-quart range. Five makers were represented: Coleman, Igloo, Rubbermaid, Frigid Rigid, and Icey-Tek. Some have wheels, some do not. We came to prefer wheeled models for their ease of transport; it's a heck of a lot easier wheeling one of these babies down the dock than carrying it by the handles. Stocked full with food, drinks, and ice, a 60-quart cooler can easily weigh 40 to 50 pounds.

Several of the manufacturers we checked with provide tips on how to get the best performance from a specific cooler. They all agree that you should:

- Pre-cool drinks and food before putting them in the box.
- Do not keep the cooler in sunlight.
- Open the lid as infrequently as possible to keep cold from escaping.
- Don't drain water; more energy is required to cool air than to maintain the colder temperature of the water.
- Place drinks and food in first, then fill to the top with ice.
- Icey-Tek even suggests pre-cooling the box for three hours with several bags of sacrificial ice, the water from which is drained before refilling the box with more ice.

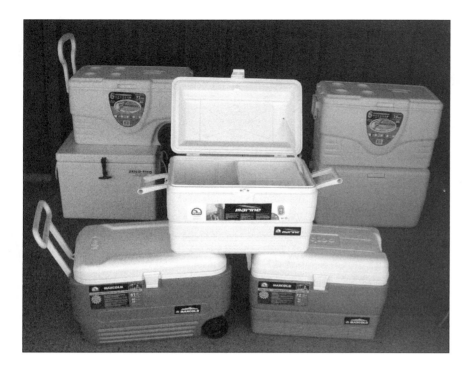

The three coolers in the foreground are all from Igloo. In *PS*'s ice-melt test, these models exhibited moderately good performance, but the best keeper of the cold was Coleman's Ultimate Extreme Marine (background, far right). That cooler sells for around $68. Finishing a close second was the much more expensive and more sophisticated fiberglass Frigid Rigid (bottom left, rear) cooler ($445).

- If there is room, consider using a combination of block and cube; the former lasts longer, but reduces storage flexibility in the cooler.

To learn which coolers retain cold the best, we placed a room-temperature six-pack of soda in the bottom of each cooler, and then covered that with two 8-pound bags of cube ice. The bags were weighed and found to be very consistent, varying at the most by ¼ pound. Using the same scale, ice was added or subtracted until each cooler contained almost exactly 16½ pounds of ice, give or take a few cubes.

Once each day, the coolers were drained of meltwater and the amount measured in a graduated container, rounded off to the nearest ounce. We didn't open the coolers, which would have more accurately simulated real-life usage. Again, our purpose was only to compare the ability of each cooler to keep ice. Outdoor ambient temperatures ranged from 80°F during the day to 60°F at night.

The performance results of the nine coolers fell into two groupings, with the two Coleman Extreme Marine models and Frigid Rigid faring the best. Total meltwater over five days for these three ranged from a low of 167 ounces to 177 ounces. The second group included two Igloo models (MaxCold wheeled and Marine), Rubbermaid, and Icey-Tek, with total melt ranging from 203 ounces to 220 ounces. The Igloo MaxCold, with 196 ounces melted over five days, ranked between the two groups.

Because differences in volume can affect cooling performance, *PS* also calculated the ratio of meltwater drained from each cooler per quart of capacity. The results here were no different for our winners, but the largest cooler—Coleman's Marine 68-Quart—did perform better when capacity was factored in.

▷ **The Bottom Line** Unless you have reasons not to want a wheeled model (if short transport distances apply, and the extra capacity of non-wheeled models is critical), we'd look at the wheeled models before buying. The Rubbermaid cooler ($90) totes beautifully, but its cooling performance lagged. The non-wheeled Frigid Rigid ($445) keeps its cool, but is heavy and quite expensive. That leaves us with the two Coleman Ultimate Extreme Marine coolers, one with wheels, one without. The wheeled one, at $64, has a short handle (just 13 inches long), which makes pulling it somewhat awkward. And "marine" evidently means

THERMOELECTRIC COOLERS

Most *PS* readers are aware that compressor-driven refrigeration isn't about adding cold air to the space, but about continually removing heat from it. Similarly, coolers remove heat from their insulated spaces by driving an electric current through those dissimilar metal partnerships (called thermocouples) set up in a series (called a thermopile), and pulling the warmth away from the thermopile and outside the cooler with a fan. It's simple, quiet, and has one moving part—the fan. It's also lightweight and portable—a cooler with a thermopile and fan weighs only marginally more than an empty cooler, and of course everything except the power cord is contained in the box itself.

One very nice thing about these coolers is that they're cheap, particularly when compared with the cost of a new compressor-driven refrigeration system.

Of course, there are drawbacks to thermoelectric coolers, too. First, they're quite power-hungry, most needing about 4.5 amps continuously. That'll draw your house battery down fast if you're not generating power to it. Second, they're not very well insulated, simply because their makers expect that you'll be supplying ample amounts of power to them. Third, they generally cannot cool their innards lower than about 40°F degrees below the ambient temperature. This means (obviously) that they won't make ice if the outside termperature is warmer than 72°F. If it is chillier than that, they can make ice,

PS tested four thermoelectric coolers from four different manufacturers. The prices for these units ranged from $99 to $120. They are, from left to right: the Coleman Power Chill 5640B, the Adler/Barbour Tropicool Classic TC-32, the Igloo KoolMate 3392, and the Koolatron P-65. We favor the Tropicool for all-around marine use.

but very gradually. It's better to think of them as ice-preservers, not icemakers. Fourth, they're stand-alone boxes, and big ones at that. So if you intend to use one on your boat, you'll need to think carefully about where you're going to put it and secure it, especially considering that you'll need to plug it in to a cigarette lighter adapter or wire it directly to a circuit breaker.

PS tested various models recently and concluded that they're much the same. The Igloo KoolMate 32 had the best cooling performance, but only by a slight margin. The Koolatron demanded the least of our batteries, though it was a bit slower in the cooling department. The Coleman Power Chill 40 was large, but well priced. But our top choice was the Adler/Barbour Tropicool. It's a bit smaller to stuff with food, but also a bit easier to stow on board, and we liked the sliding temperature adjustment. We think that would be handy for folks sailing in climates with wide variations in temperature.

For most sailors, the most important shopping points will be outside dimensions and power requirements. Given the fact that all of these boxes draw lots of power and have poor insulation, we can't see that anyone with a well-insulated icebox and a working refrigeration system would want to trade it in for one of these. On the other hand, if you have no compressor-driven system, or need to replace a broken one, a box like these might make sense.

The $150 Icey-Tek finished sixth in our melt test. It has two screw-in drainage plugs (each equipped with O-rings), a hasp for a padlock, and built-in skids molded into the bottom to protect it from abrasive surfaces.

that it has a scale for measuring fish length, a plastic interior divider, and some nautical-looking rope handles. The non-wheeled version, at $68, is almost identical except for its 58-quart capacity and the lack of wheels, but it did the best job of retaining ice.

These last two from Coleman were our top picks. That information surprised the maker of the Frigid Rigid, and he subsequently conducted his own tests. He claims his product holds ice significantly longer than the Coleman coolers. Whichever results you believe, the less expensive Coleman remains a better buy by far in our estimation.

Cabin Comfort

MARINE AIR-CONDITIONING

The demand for marine air-conditioning (A/C) continues to increase. Once found primarily on medium to large boats, systems suitable for even the smallest cabins are now available. While A/C equipment is connected to shore power whenever possible, or gensets, some of the small systems can be powered from portable, on-deck, gasoline generators or from a 12-volt DC power source. Air-conditioned comfort can be enjoyed on virtually any size boat.

Virtually all marine air conditioners use electric motor-driven refrigeration compressors, and unlike land-based A/C systems that usually transfer heat into the atmosphere, marine air conditioners deposit the heat in water. Marine A/C equipment may be classified in three groups: self-contained direct expansion, split direct expansion, and chilled water.

Although there are no hard and fast rules, most boats less than about 50–60 feet loa use self-contained direct-expansion equipment. Larger vessels usually use either split direct-expansion or chilled-water systems.

For all types, note that as the temperature of the air is reduced, the relative humidity of the cooled air increases. Therefore, the cooling capacity and airflow system must be properly chosen to ensure adequate removal of excess water vapor from the cooled air.

A wide range of variables must be considered when determining the amount of cooling capacity required for a given installation. Among these are the size and shape of the space to be cooled, the prevalent external ambient conditions, and the degree of exposure of the external surfaces of the cooled volume to solar radiation. The manufacturers of marine A/C systems have prepared tables that are useful guides. The tables are based on maintenance of interior temperatures about 10°F less than exterior ambient temperatures, up to outside temperatures of about 90°F. One major marine A/C manufacturer recommends 60 Btu per square foot of belowdeck cabin area, with 90 and 120 Btu per square foot for mid-deck and above-deck spaces. Cooling capacity for tropical locations increases to 90, 120, and 150 Btu per square foot.

And, keep in mind that the number of people in the cabin increases the heat load on the A/C system by between 500 Btu/hour for inactive persons and 800 Btu/hour for active people.

Energy consumption is often an important consideration in A/C systems where the required electrical power is supplied from an onboard generator set. A comparison of two 120-volt, 60-hertz, one-ton (12,000 Btu) self-contained systems, one using a rotary compressor, the other a piston compressor, is illustrative. The full load demand of the rotary compressor-equipped system is 11.5 amps, compared to 14.9 amps for the piston compressor-equipped unit, a 22-percent advantage. Further, the rated starting current for the rotary compressor unit is 26 amps, while the piston compressor-equipped system may demand 33 amps. Total system power consumption for either system will be increased by the 1 to 2 amperes consumed by the seawater pump.

Manufacturer	Model	BTU Cool	Heat Type	Size (L"xW"xH")	Weight (lbs.)	Run Amps (115AC)
Aqua Air	MC-05	5,000	none	15 x 10.32 x 9.88	49	6.2
	AQSC-07	7,000	R/C	21.6 x 13.2 x 11.6	58	8.5
	AQSC-10	10,000	R/C	21.6 x 13.2 x 14	72	11.5
	ASQC-16	16,000	R/C	24.6 x 15.2 x 13.25	80	14.4
AquaCal	Krusin Kool	7,000	None	26 x 21.5 x 9	65.5	5.5
		7,000	R/C	18.5 x 9.63 x 15.75	40	7.4
		10,000	R/C	20.25 x 10.63 x 15.75	52	10.3
		12,000	R/C	22.75 x 10.63 x 16.5	56	10.8
		16,000	R/C	22.75 x 12 x 16.63	59	14.5
Cruisair	CO 5000	5,000	None	30.5 x 15.75 x 13.75	60	6
	SHF5/SXF5	5,000	R/C	16.5 x 9 x 11.8	42	6.3
	SHF7/SXF7	7,000	R/C	18 x 9.6 x 12.3	49	7.8
	SHF10/SXF10	10,000	R/C	20.3 x 10.6 x 13.6	59	10.3
	SHF12/SXF12	12,000	R/C	20.3 x 10.6 x 13.6	63	11
	SHF16/SXF16	16,000	R/C	20.3 x 12 x 13.6	65	14.7
	SXR7/SHR7	7,000	R/C	20.5 x 12.5 x 13	58	8
	SXR10/SHR10	10,000	R/C	22.5 x 13 x 13.25	68	10.5
	SXR12/SHR12	12,000	R/C	22.5 x 13 x 13.25	70	11.5
	SXR16/SHR16	16,000	R/C	23.5 x 14.5 x 14.75	76	15
	SX7/SH7	7,000	R/C	20.5 x 12.5 x 13	56	10.6
	SX10/SH10	10,000	R/C	22.5 x 13 x 13.25	73	14.3
	SX12/SH12	12,000	R/C	22.5 x 13 x 13.25	75	14.9
	SX16/SH16	16,000	R/C	23.5 x 14.5 x 14.75	84	17.3
HFL	HSD6012	6,500	None	17.5 x 14 x 11.5	70	40@12VDC
	HSD7024	7,000	None	18 x 14 x 11.5	77	24@24VDC
Marine Air	VC"5K	5,000	R/C	16.5 x 12.75 x 11.75	42	6.3
	VC"7K	7,000	R/C	18 x 12.88 x 12	49	7.8
	VC"10K	10,000	R/C	20.25 x 14.38 x 12.25	59	10.3
	VC"12K	12,000	R/C	20.25 x 14.38 x 13.63	63	11
	VC"16K	16,000	R/C	20.25 x 16 x 16	65	14.7
Mermaid	M-5C-U	5,200	None	15 x 11 x 11	35	4.4
	M-5CHPU	5,200	R/C	"	35	4.4/5.5
	M-6EH-R	6,500	Electric	16 x 11 x 11.5	45	7.5/12.5
	M-6C-R	6,500	None	"	45	7.5
	M-12C-R	12,000	None	19.5 x 13 x 12.5	68	10.5
	M-12CEH-R	12,000	Electric	"	68	10.5/12.5
	M-23CHP-R	12,000	R/C	"	68	10.5/12.5
	M-16C-R	16,000	None	19.5 x 14 x 13	70	13.5
	M-16CHP-R	16,000	R/C	"	70	13.5/14.5
Ocean Breeze	OB6CH	6,000	Electric	17.5 x 11.75 x 11	51	5.2
	OB9CH	9,000	"	17.5 x 11.75 x 11	55	7.7
	OB12CH	12,000	"	20 x 13 x 12	68	10.3
	OB16CH	16,000	"	21.75 x 13.25 x 13.25	72	11.3
	WA12C1	12,000	"	22 x 16 x 18	108	14.2
	WA16C1	16,000	"	22 x 16 x 18	112	16.8
Westerbeke	50528	10,000	R/C	20.5 x 13.75 x 13.25	55	8.0 Cool
Rotary Aire	50530	17,000	R/C	21.25 x 16.5 x 13.5	63	12.0 Cool

*List prices shown are generally for self-contained A/C units, less controls, ducts, grills etc. †Cruisair package prices shown include A/C Unit, SMX Digital Control, Sea Water Pump, Return Grill and Discharge Grill, no ducting. ‡These units use a high velocity blower to distribute air from the A/C unit mounted in the engine room or other similar space; see text.

Compressor Type	Warranty	List Price* A/C Unit Only	
P	1 year		
P	1 year w/mech	$1,263	
P	control, 2 years	$1,439	
P	w/electronic control	$1,662	
R	1 year		
R	1 year	$1,535	
R	1 year	$1,785	
R	1 year	$1,890	
R	1 year	$1,990	
R	all Cruisair		
R	2 years main	$1,245	
R	3 years digital	$1,390	
R	2 years mech.	$1,605	
R	1 year remove/	$1,670	
R	reinstall	$1,785	
R		$1,730	$2,147†
R		$1,995	$2,407†
R		$2,060	$2,478†
R		$2,175	$2,651†
P		$1,730	
P		$1,995	
P		$2,060	
P		$2,175	
R	1 year	$3,995	
R	1 year		
R	all MarineAir	$1,245	
R	2 years main	$1,390	
R	3 years digital	$1,605	
R	2 years mech.	$1,670	
R	1 year remove/ reinstall	$1,785	
R	5 years parts	$895	
R	& labor except	$995	
R	pump 1 year	$995	
R	thermostat	$895	
R	2 years	$1,195	
R		$1,295	
R		$1,345	
R		$1,395	
R		$1,545	
R	5 years for	$1,099	
R	compressor,	$1,299	
R	evaporator,	$1,399	
R	condenser	$1,539‡	
R	fan motor	$2,130‡	
R		$2,315‡	
R	2 years	$2,686	
R	2 years	$2,805	

Portable, air-cooled marine A/C systems are on occasion the only practical means for air-conditioning the smallest boats. Portables are designed to be used when the boat is at a dock where 120-volt AC power is available.

The most familiar portable A/C unit is the 5,000 Btu/hour Cruisair Carry-On. It is designed to be placed over a deck hatch, from which it extracts heated air, passes it through the evaporator, and reinjects the cooled air into the boat. The Carry-On is 13.75 by 15.75 by 30.5 inches and weighs 59 pounds. The running power demand of this unit is only 6 amps at 115 volts, low enough to tempt some boat owners to power the unit from a small (less than 1 kilowatt) on-deck, gasoline-powered generator. Unfortunately, the starting current requirement, as for all A/C compressors, is about three times the running current, in this case, 18 amps. For this reason, Cruisair recommends that the Carry-On be powered from a genset of at least 1,800-watt capacity.

The KomfortKool 7 is a suitcase-style, 7,000-Btu air-conditioner that can be used as a portable or if desired, removed from its case and built into the boat. The KomfortKool is water-cooled, eliminating the need to place it over a deck hatch. It can be positioned anywhere in the cabin, with its submersible cooling water pump, intake hose, and water-discharge hose led over the side through a port or hatch. Alternatively, permanent water intake and discharge connections can be installed, making setup even simpler. The 26-by-15-by-9-inch suitcase-housed unit weighs 56 pounds; the pump set and hoses weigh an additional 9.5 pounds. Power consumption is 5.5 amps of 120-volt, 60-hertz AC power. Starting current is approximately 17 amps.

Air-conditioning operating directly from a 12-volt DC source can be an ideal solution for boats where installation of a conventional genset is impractical. In most cases, however, operating a conventional AC-powered air conditioner from a DC/AC inverter is unacceptably inefficient. For example, powering a 6,500-Btu A/C from an inverter will require about 75 amps from the battery. HFL, well known for its AC and small DC power gensets, offers two specially designed, 12-volt-DC-input air conditioners. The 12-volt unit provides 6,500 Btu of cooling capacity with

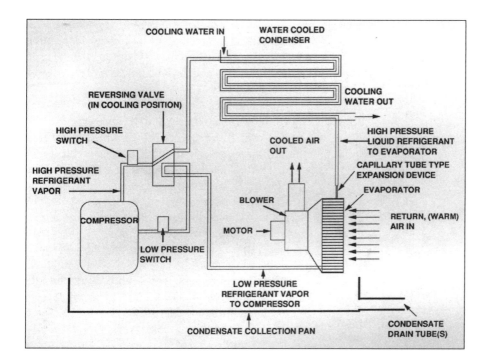

COOLING WATER IN — WATER COOLED CONDENSER

REVERSING VALVE (IN COOLING POSITION)

HIGH PRESSURE SWITCH

HIGH PRESSURE REFRIGERANT VAPOR

COMPRESSOR

LOW PRESSURE SWITCH

COOLING WATER OUT

COOLED AIR OUT

HIGH PRESSURE LIQUID REFRIGERANT TO EVAPORATOR

CAPILLARY TUBE TYPE EXPANSION DEVICE

EVAPORATOR

BLOWER

MOTOR →

RETURN, (WARM) AIR IN

LOW PRESSURE REFRIGERANT VAPOR TO COMPRESSOR

CONDENSATE COLLECTION PAN

CONDENSATE DRAIN TUBE(S)

Virtually all marine air conditioners use electric motor-driven refrigeration compressors. Unlike land-based A/C systems that usually transfer heat into the atmosphere, marine air conditioners deposit heat into the surrounding water.

a running current demand of 40 amps. A 24-volt version yields 7,000 Btu while drawing 24 amps.

The HFL systems use a special hermetically sealed refrigeration compressor powered by a low-voltage, three-phase AC motor. The AC power provided from the integral inverter varies in frequency in accordance with the starting and running requirements of the motor. The still considerable 40-amp current demand may be supplied from a fairly large battery bank.

Glacier Bay, best known for its electric motor–powered holding-plate refrigeration systems, offers a system that uses the refrigeration compressor to operate the A/C evaporator at times when refrigeration cooling is not required. A 12-volt-powered 1-horsepower compressor, the "Whisper Jet," provides 5,900 Btu of air-conditioning capacity while consuming an average of 55 amps. Glacier also offers larger-capacity systems. Installation of these systems is similar to the conventional split A/C systems, requiring field installation of refrigerant lines, evacuation, and charging.

Ocean Breeze offers an interesting alternative approach to self-contained A/C units called the Whisperaire series. These systems are designed to be

installed in a space remote from the accommodation, including an engineroom. The unit is completely enclosed, isolating it from the surrounding air. A high-velocity (and higher-than-normal power consumption) blower forces cooled air through small-diameter PVC pipes to air distribution outlets in the cabin. The manufacturer claims that a couple of 2-inch-diameter pipes are sufficient for air delivery, with a 6-inch-diameter pipe used to return air to the A/C unit.

▷ **The Bottom Line** Because virtually all of today's marine A/C systems use common refrigeration system components, there is not a great deal of material difference on which to base the selection of one unit versus others offering equal features. The buying decision can, of course, be based on the price of the basic chassis and the control panel. However, unless you plan to install the system yourself, you will want to obtain a detailed quote for the total installation. It is important to consider the reputation of the installing company as well as the reputation of the manufacturer.

Be sure to obtain, carefully read, and compare the written warranty that applies to the systems you are

COOL CURRENTS

The Cruisair Carry-On is a popular air-cooled model powered by shore power or a genset.

With so many boats spending so much time in marinas, the demand for onboard A/C has grown rapidly, and manufacturers have responded with a number of systems, the most common of which are self-contained units that sit in hatches. Their major drawback is that they draw lots of AC power. This either limits them to marina use only, or demands an onboard genset.

The Cool Currents machine is intended to be an alternative to all that. It should be noted that it is not marketed as a head-to-head competitor against AC-powered systems for sheer cooling power. In that case it would surely lose. In a bang-for-the-watt competition, though, it has several advantages, some of which are constant (it's light, simple, low-powered, and less expensive), and some variable according to conditions.

Unlike standard marine-use A/C machines, which use electric motor-driven refrigeration compressors, Cool Currents operates on the simple principle of heat exchange. It uses hoses to pull cool water up from below the surface and through a heat exchanger (a radiator) in the unit. Two simple muffin fans pull the warm cabin air through the radiator and pump the cooler air out the other side. That's that. The efficiency of the machine depends entirely on sub-surface water temperatures and on the cabin temperature it's working with.

On a hot day in early September we took the Cool Currents machine to a nearby marina and tried it out on a friend's boat, which was locked up tight in the sun. It was quick to set up—the dual hoses are taken out of the base of the plastic case and uncoiled. The deep-water hose, which has a strainer at the bottom, is attached via a plastic quick-connector below the submersible pump, and let down as far as possible into the cooler water layers, but not all the way to the bottom. The pump is submerged nearer the surface; it should have a depth of at least a couple of feet to compensate for the boat's rolling, and has a maximum head depth of 9 feet. In shallow water the strainer can be attached directly below the pump, but there are various combinations of hose lengths that will allow the suction to go down as far as about 20 feet. In general, the deeper the water, the better the machine will perform.

While setup was quick, it did involve a bit of wrestling with the hoses, which tend to retain their coiled shape, and a lot of wrestling with the plastic housing, whose halves tended to come apart and not fit back together without a lot of TLC. The hoses needed to be lashed in a couple of places to keep them from infesting the cockpit, and to keep them secure at the toerail. It would be relatively easy for a boat owner to develop a system with markings on the hoses and preinstalled lashings to improve setup and reduce clutter.

If Cool Currents had been billed as a full-on A/C unit, we would have been disappointed; as it was, we'd call it a modest success: It was a lot better than a fan if you stood right in front of it. It drew little power. It was very nearly silent. And it cooled the cabin a few degrees while pulling water from the bottom that wasn't markedly colder than the surface water.

The current price of Cool Currents is $695—about half what a typical self-contained AC-powered marine air conditioner costs.

HATCH VENTILATORS

Though they can't really be used while your vessel is underway, hood-shaped fabric air scoops can be a godsend when moored or at anchor. There's no secret to their effectiveness. They're just big. They grab a lot of breeze and funnel it down below. Sailmakers have been known to cut and stitch custom versions of these devices. However, there are apparently only three "ready-mades" on the market. Here's a quick overview:

The Windscoop from Davis Instruments ($33) is made of nylon cloth in China and presents more than 10 square feet of area to the wind. It's a one-size-fits-all product that's easy to rig, can accommodate most hatch designs, and uses a wooden dowel and tie lines to remain in place. West Marine's Down-the-Hatch ($39) is described as 4 by 6 feet. Actually, its frontal area measures about 31 by 50 inches, nearly identical to the Windscoop, but it lacks the dowel. Instead, the four bottom corners of the Down-the-Hatch must be secured by long ties with adjustable cords with plastic snaphooks. If there's nothing to which the ties can be secured,

West suggests that you install screw-eyes or small eye-straps. We prefer the Windscoop.

Then there's the Breeze Booster ($65 to $90, depending upon size), also from West Marine. This product slips over the hatch and makes a hood shaped by flexible plastic inserts bent into shape by a pair of ties led below and secured to a wooden stick. For different types of hatches, the lower back edge's width can be adjusted with metal snaps, which are properly made of stainless and brass. Although not as large as the others, the Breeze Booster's principal advantages are that it can be oriented in any direction, remains open in any breeze, and requires no overhead support. It can, of course, come loose and tumble off the boat, so a lanyard is a good idea. It also can be purchased with optional insect screens.

We tested all three. The Breeze Booster collected and concentrated air a bit better even than the Windscoop. The Windscoop remains a best buy, but if you want better performance, cough up the extra dough for the Breeze Booster.

considering. For example, Cruisair and Marine Air warrant their direct expansion units and mechanical controls for two years, their electronic controls for three years, and will pay for removal and reinstallation during the first year. Some other manufacturers warrant the compressor for up to five years, excluding coverage for items such as the water pump or control. Ocean Breeze quotes a five-year warranty for the compressor, evaporator, condenser, and fan motor. Mermaid states their warranty is five years for parts and labor, except for one year for the water pump and two years for the thermostat. We believe that equipment such as direct expansion marine A/C

systems are, to a degree, subject to "infant mortality," an increased risk of failure during the first few months of use, after which a long period of trouble-free operation can be expected. For this reason, the remove-and-reinstall warranty coverage offered by Cruisair and Marine Air can be very attractive.

Use care when comparing manufacturers' specifications. Systems using electric heat will usually be less costly than those offering a reverse-cycle heating mode. Even when heating is not a major requirement, as in Florida, the presence of the reversing valve, operated by an electronic, microprocessor control, will be valuable in ensuring that internal refrigerant system pressure is reduced to zero before each start. This feature will be best appreciated when a momentary power interruption occurs. A system without the ability to bleed off trapped pressure will likely trip its power circuit breaker, either the one in the boat or the one on shore. Resetting it at 0200 will be no joy.

When comparing unit cooling capacity, check the manufacturer's claimed cooling Btu ratings versus the running current, including the power required for the air blower. Because compressors of the same type are largely identical, claims of lower power drain per Btu should be viewed with suspicion.

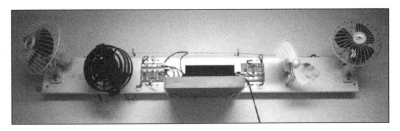

PS tested 12 different cabin fans and ultimately winnowed the competitors down to four units (two oscillating and two conventional). The two oscillating fans failed early: the Seafit (far right) after 21 hours of continuous operation, and the Guest (far left) after 123 hours. They didn't blow their fuses, they just stopped running. However, the Hella (near left) and Caframo (near right) were still spinning after 1,540 hours (more than two months) of continual operation.

CABIN FANS

There are lots of things that can make being aboard a boat unpleasant. Among them: Too little wind, seasickness, crowded waterways, rain, too much wind, bugs, a Wagnerian mother-in-law, lack of ice—the list is so long that it makes you wonder, occasionally.

Allied with too little wind is too much heat, especially when anchored, at a dock or in a following breeze that exactly matches your speed. That's when the wee word "fan" looms large. The word has special meaning for those who do their sailing in tropical climes, where fans are de rigueur. (Air conditioning? *Tres bien!*) Whether trying to do chart work, prepare a meal, grab a nap or read a while, the need to move air is particularly acute below in the cabin.

Static devices (like Dorades and fabric scoops) to direct air through the cabin are useless if there is no air movement to direct. That's when one can fall in love with anything that makes a breeze.

So, we collected almost a dozen fans—just about everything on the marine market at the time—and put them through their paces. Most of the fans are meant to be bulkhead mounted, plus one to place in a portlight. Included are fixed, oscillating, and directionally adjustable fans, most with caged blades, but one with open "soft" blades. And most are 12-volt models, but several are for dual or even triple power sources. The names are familiar—Guest, Hella, Caframo, BOAT/U.S., West Marine—but some of the fans are Far East knockoffs which invite a look askance.

We even included a fan which we—and a lot of readers—hold in high regard. It is Caframo's Model 737, which runs on four D-cells, or with 6 volts supplied by a 110-volt or 12-volt adapter. It can perhaps serve as a general benchmark to airflow. In putting the fans through their paces, it must be noted that the volume of air moved, the noise caused, and the power consumed are inextricably linked. So, which product offers the best blend of these three?

▷ **The Bottom Line** One way of ranking these fans is to place them in order according to the air velocity produced per milliamperes consumed. The range is not insignificant. The best fan produces a velocity more than four times that of the poorest. If considered that way, Caframo's 737 portable (the four-D-cell or 12-volt model, run on low) is best. Next in order would be the Hella Turbo (run on high), the Caframo 747 open blade (run on low), and the single-speed Hella Jet.

In considering noise created, there are remarkable differences. But for pure, flat-out wind velocity, the products can be segmented into three ranges, with the best figures generally recorded by the oscillating fans from Guest and Carlyn. We do not know why the West Marine fan, which appears to be identical

DECK-MOUNT VENTS

In the golden years of sail, all a crew could do to get some fresh air below was open the hatches or portlights if the vessel was fitted with them. Then, along came cowl vents, those odd-looking devices that present their broad round and oval openings to the wind to funnel some breeze down below while discarding any errant water through a simple diversion system. Often, these cowls were mounted atop Dorade boxes for that purpose.

In the contemporary era of sailing, much more common are low-profile vents designed to admit air but not water to the interior of a vessel, or to withdraw air. These can either be passive, like Beckson's Vent-o-Mate ($23 in plastic, $45 in stainless), which relies on air passing over it to create a vacuum and thereby exhaust air from the interior. Or they can be active, like Nicro's popular solar-powered Powervent 3000 ($193), which uses fans to introduce fresh air to and exhaust stale air from the cabin. Deck vents are manufactured in stainless steel like those from Nicro ($149 to $173, depending upon size), bronze (also from Mariner's Hardware $200), carbon fiber (Mariner's Hardware, $300 to $400), and plastic, like those from Beckson or Nicro.

In the past, *PS* has been impressed by the vent products from Nicro. We've had particularly positive experiences with the solar powered units. Nicro also makes a 12-volt/solar-powered Combo Vent that allegedly moves 110 cubic feet of air per hour. We like that kind of versatility when it comes to boat hardware, and the price isn't bad either ($164 for white plastic, $185 for stainless steel).

to the Carlyn, produced different numbers. If you want an oscillating fan and can tolerate the noise, the Guest is the clear choice over the two Chinese knockoffs.

In our view, the Hella and Caframo fans are superior. The Hella models draw less current, but lack the power of the Caframo fans, which are Best Buys—unless you want an oscillating fan. But we haven't yet found an oscillating model that lasts long enough to recommend.

However, what we cannot do is ascertain just how long each fan will last before breaking down. And break down they will . . . if you use them month after month, for years, piling thousands of hours on the brushes and bearings.

So, following our bench tests for air speed and noise, we mounted two oscillating fans and two regular fans on a board a test boat—the Guest, Hella Turbo, Caframo and Seafit—and let them run continuously. It was anticipated that after they were securely mounted, wired through proper fuses to a good transformer, and turned on, there'd be nothing to report for months, perhaps even a couple of years. Not so.

The Seafit failed after running only 21 hours. It started making a grinding noise. When turned off and back on, it did not turn the blades. Attempts to "kick-start" the fan by twirling the blades did not work—with or without the oscillator.

The other oscillating fan—the Guest—quit running after 123 hours, a little more than five days. When the oscillator mechanism was turned off, the fan blade started turning again. It ran for another 82 hours, stopped, and could not be induced back to life.

Neither the Seafit nor the Guest blew their fuses. They just stopped running. However, the Hella and Caframo fans, after 1,540 hours (more than two months of continual operation), were still spinning. That's pretty strong testimony.

CABIN LIGHTS

Among all the energy demands aboard a modern boat—electronics, pressure-water systems, watermakers, autopilots, refrigeration, and so on—it's simple DC cabin lighting that's often the largest factor in overwhelming the storage batteries. Turn on three measly 20-watt incandescent lamps and leave them on from dusk until bedtime—say, four hours—and you'll take 20 amp-hours out of your system (3 x 20 watts = 60 watts; 60 watts / 12 volts = 5 amps; 5 amps x 4 hours = 20 amp-hours). That's comparable to running an anchor windlass, under a working load of 40 amps, continuously for half an hour. If the battery switch has been left on "Both," or there's only one battery for all duties, including engine-starting, that carelessness can spoil your day.

The power demands of lights are so important aboard boats that for this article we initially intended to cut to the chase and review only LED-based cabin lights. We had in mind a scenario in which a boat owner wanted to use LEDs to replace reading lights in the forward and main cabins, and dome lights in the main cabin and galley. We think of dome lights as spreading a wide angle of illumination, and bulkhead reading lights as more directional, although these, too, are often used for general illumination, and aren't as strictly directional as a chart light in the nav station.

Would such a wholesale move be possible for both area and spot lighting? Yes. Would it be advisable? Not yet. In any case, LED lights really need to be compared directly with the other types of lights on the market, especially since most of the makers and purveyors of LEDs tell us that the technology is changing rapidly and markedly, and that what might be a decent cabin light now will be much better, and

cost less, in a matter of months. So we decided to expand our scope and survey a wide sampling of cabin lights on the market, including LEDs.

Some basic concepts and definitions are in order, so that we can make reasonable comparisons. A lumen is the measurement unit for luminous flux, the quantity of lamplight cast in all directions. A lux is the measurement unit for illuminance, the quantity or density of light cast on a surface. One lux equals one lumen per square meter. (Illuminance can also be expressed in foot-candles, which measure light on a square foot of surface, but the foot-candle measurement is becoming obsolete.)

These definitions are intertwined with those of candelas, luminance, luminous intensity, and several more that help people get a grip on artificial light. For this evaluation, we'll be speaking in terms of lumens, and measuring in lux units. Of particular concern is the relationship of lumens and watts. For example, a 60-watt incandescent household light bulb rated at 840 lumens produces 14 lumens per watt. On a boat, a 10-watt xenon bulb might typically perform about the same, while a fluorescent bulb would produce a much higher ratio of lumens per watt.

The apparent "warmth" of a lamp's color can be expressed through its color temperature in degrees Kelvin (K). The lower the color temperature, the warmer-looking the glow of the light. A candle flame has a color temperature of about 1,800 K. Sunlight at dawn or dusk is around 2,000 K. A 100-watt standard incandescent (tungsten) lamp is about 2,800 K. A standard "warm white" fluorescent would be about 3,000–3,300 K. Direct sunlight at noontime is around 5,000–6,000 K, and "daylight" fluorescents are in that range or somewhat cooler. And so on—up to the high numbers represented by various levels of sun/cloud combinations and cool blue northern skies.

Among the area lights that *PS* tested were the following products (top row, left to right): Perko incandescent; Guest halogen dome; Alpenglow fluorescent. Second row: West/ABI xenon 2x10 watt; West/ABI xenon 20-watt; Thin-Lite 2x7-watt fluorescent. Third row: West/ABI stainless LED dome light; Imtra/Cantalupi halogen "Chip"; Perko LED utility light; Imtra/Cantalupi LED utility light; D. R. Smith LED cluster "Montserrat."

	Source	Model	Name	Bulb	Watts	Warranty
AREA LIGHTS	West Marine (ABI)	Model 298168	White Aluminum Interior Dome Light	Xenon	2 x 10	1 year
	West Marine (ABI)	Model 260786	Brass/Mahogany Dome Light	Xenon	20	1 year
	Guest (via West)	West Model 398190; Guest Model 8218-5	Halogen Dome Light	Halogen	10	2 years
	Perko (via West)	West Model 281584; Perko Model 0300DP1CHR	Surface-Mount Dome Light	Incandescent	12	5 years
	Thin-Lite (via West)	West Model 3669215	800 Series Dual CF7 Dome Light	Fluorescent	2 x 7	2 years
	West Marine (ABI)	West Model 5007463	LED Dome Light stainless 7" dome	LED, 18 white	3.0	1 year
	Perko (via West)	West Model 3732906 Perko Model 1156DP112V	Utility LED Light, Ceiling Mount (flush)	LED, 12 white	2.5	5 years
	Imtra/Cantalupi	LED Utility Light, white, flush-mount	"Bob/L"	LED, 10 white	0.4	1 year
	Weems & Plath	Model 600	Mini Yacht Lamp (paraffin/oil fueled)	Wick & fuel	0	2 years
	Alpenglow	7-watt. dual West Model 3402443;	Aplenglow	Fluorescent	7	2 years
	Imtra/Cantalupi (via West)	Imtra Model CN20401R	Surface Mount Interior Light (stainless), "Chip"	Halogen	10	1 year
	Daniel R. Smith	12-LED cluster w. prismatic lens	"Montserrat" stainless steel area light	LED, 12 white	2.4	Lifetime
DIRECTIONAL LIGHTS	Gator Lights (via West)	West Model 2662971; Gator Model 8000-WH	Opal Bulkhead Light	Xenon	10	1 year
	West Marine (ABI)	Model 2660900	Xenon Swivel Berth Light Surface Mount	Xenon	10	1 year
	West Marine (ABI)	Model 129421	Xenon Swivel Cabin Light Surface Mount	Xenon	10	1 year
	Imtra/Cantalupi (via West)	West Model 3406469; Imtra Model CN40701R	Multi-Directional Reading spotlight (chrome), "Patty"	Halogen	10	1 year
	Taylorbrite (via West)	West Model 3731858; Taylor Model R1DM001B	CCF Marine Fluorescent, "Euro Brass"	Cold Cathode Fluorescent	6.6	1 year
	Aqua Signal (via West)	West Model 381913 (white) Aqua Sig. Model 15061-7	Halogen Mini-Spot	Halogen	5	1 year
	Hella Marine (via West)	West 373985 (black) Hella 2AB004532-101	Halogen Reading Light/ Chart Light	Halogen	5	1 year
	Imtra/Frensch	F1 White Recessed " Reading Light (prototype)	"Warm White"	LED, 8 warm white	0.8	3 years
	Imtra/Frensch	Fl Black Surface Mount Reading Light	ILF1-4456	LED, 8 white	0.8	3 years
	Imtra/Frensch	Touch LED, Shiny Chrome, w/Touch Red	IL-4500	LED, 16 white	1.6	3 years
	Daniel R. Smith	12-LED cluster w. prismatic lens	"Little Inagua" chrome reading light	LED, 12 white	2.4	Lifetime
LED CLUSTERS	Imtra	LED Cluster Bulb #1142-trade number	IL-B15D	LED, 12 white	1.5	3 years
	Sailor's Solutions	LED 19	Cabin Light Replacement Bulb	LED, 19 white	2.0	1 year
	SeaFit (West Marine)	Model 4811022	LEDCluster Lamp (replaces Davis 3351)	LED, 7 white	0.8	1 year

List	Brightness Rating	Light Circle @ 12"	Heat @ 6"	Current	Comments	Overall Rating
$22.39	Intense (hi) Medium (lo)	44" 38"	80°	1.72 A 0.87 A	Somewhat uneven light direction and spread w. 2 bulbs. '50s kitchen style white aluminum. Heat vents. Good price.	Good
$32.99	Intense	44"	86°	1.78 A	Nice mahogany base, warm light. Really bright, with even spread. Would be good with a dimmer.	Excellent
$47.09	Bright	20"	79°	0.87 A	Basic, white plastic. Warmish light, somewhat uneven through lens but pleasant. Not a great value.	Fair
$36.49	Medium	64"	80°	1.01 A	Pleasant, medium-warm light, even spread through lens. Retro-look chrome trim, quite warm to touch. Good warranty.	Good
$70.59	Intense	60"	77°	1.18 A	Quite bright and widespread. Cool temp but also cool light, typical fluorescent. Slight RF interference @ 12". Spare lens.	Good
$94.19	Medium	6" w. separated beams to 30"	77°	0.25 A	Well made; quite bright, but directional. Lens seems to add some yellow warmth to light, but it's still pretty icy. Decent price.	Good
$169.99	Dim	32"	77°	0.21 A	Billed as a utility light, not a dome light. Wide, nice and even spread of cool, dim light. Very high price.	Fair
$172.00	Dim	12"	75°	0.03 A	Good-looking, well-made flush-mount light, billed as utility. Low power. Brighter, narrower beam than Perko. Pricey.	Fair
$110.24	Dim	16"	80°	0	Good-looking, sturdy brass lamp, swings happily in a seaway, but strictly for some warm ambient light.	Fair
$114.00	Bright (hi) Medium (lo)	62" (hi) 48" (lo)	76° (hi) 76° (lo)	0.54 A (hi) 0.51 A (lo)	Two white setting, two red LED settings. Nice warm color, even spread. Slight RF interference at 18". Good value.	Excellent
$88.29	Low	52"	79°	1.00 A	Well-made, even, warm light w. 10W G4 bulb. Bright stainless trim, smooth lens. The quality is costly.	Excellent
$72.96	Low	16"	76°	0.02 A	Comparatively wide spread of even, cool, white light. Good combination of spot and small-area light.	Good
$38.89	Low	38"	79°	0.89 A	Warm, even, wide light, w. white-frosted glass shade; good combination of area and spot. Full swivel. Good price.	Excellent
$58.89	Bright	30"	80°	0.89 A	Attractive brass fixture; wide, fairly even spread of bright light. Good swiveling. Non-tarnish plating. Nice price.	Good
$35.29	Low	10"	82°	0.86 A	Utilitarian white metal. Somewhat uneven light pattern, quite directional. Good swiveling. Decent price.	Fair
$147.99	Low	22"	81°	0.91 A	Small-size w. shiny chrome finish, smooth lens, reflector inside. Well-made. Full swiveling. Bright, warm, even spread.	Excellent
$94.19	Low	26"	76°	0.56 A	Medium-bright/warm light w. even pattern. Attractive design. Long life an durability at fair price. No RF noise detected.	Excellent
$47.09	Low	10"	82°	0.36 A	White plastic fixture. Swivels sideways, but no up and down. Clear, smooth lens makes whiter, brighter light than Hella.	Fair
$44.69	Dim	14"	77°	0.38 A	Black plastic task light, nice design. Swivels up/down, not sideways. Comes w. red lens. Directional; best for chartwork.	Fair
$94.00	Low	6"	75°	0.07 A	Low power and warm, yellow cast for an LED light. Dim; best for bunk reading and accent light. Swivels down only.	Good
$94.00	Low	6"	75°	0.07 A	Same basic design as previous, but vertical, w. normal white LEDs showing brighter, cooler directional light.	Good
$199.00	Bright	7"	75°	0.13 A	Clever cluster in chrome gooseneck fixture. Touch LEDs to turn on one red or 16 white diodes. Cool-colored, spot only. Pricey.	Good
$89.96	Low	20"	75°	0.20 A	Attractive chrome fixture. Cool, white light, cast evenly and comparatively wide. Best dedicated LED bunk light.	Excellent
$19.51	Intense	6"	76°	0.13 A	Bright, highly directional cluster. As with other clusters below, question is "What if the socket is sideways?"	Good
$19.95	Intense	6"	76°	0.17 A	Biggest bang for the price. Maker advises not to leave on for more than 8 hrs. at a time to avoid dimming diodes.	Good
$42.99	Dim	8"	76°	0.07 A	Slightly wider spread of dimmer light than previous two. Low power use, but high-priced. OK for reading light socket.	Fair

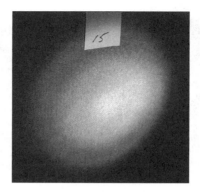

Three widely different spreads of light from a distance of 12 inches. Left, the wide, even coverage of the Alpenglow fluorescent. In the center is the contained, directional light from the West/ABI Xenon Swivel Cabin Light. At right is the intense spot beam from Sailor's Solutions' LED19.

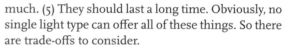

We'll make the assumption that all of us are seeking pretty much the same ideals in cabin lights aboard sailboats: (1) They should provide a large number of lumens per watt. (2) The light they cast should be warm and welcoming. (3) They should produce little heat. (There are, of course, people who sail in colder weather who often prefer a bit of extra heat when they can get it.) (4) They shouldn't cost much. (5) They should last a long time. Obviously, no single light type can offer all of these things. So there are trade-offs to consider.

LEDs are narrow-beamed and directional. They don't spread light, so if you want to use them as area lights, you have to arrange them in a cluster so that individual LEDs shine outward in a pattern. LEDs deliver long life (forever, for most practical purposes), hardiness (no fragile glass or filaments to break), very low power consumption per diode, and low heat per diode. On the downside, they're still quite expensive, and while red LEDs are good as night-vision lights in the nav station and cockpit, white LEDs emit a cool, bluish light, which few would say makes for pleasant company. Individual LEDs

The reading/spot lights that *PS* tested included (top row, left to right): West/ABI xenon cabin light; West/ABI xenon brass berth light; Gator Opal bulkhead light; Aqua Signal halogen mini-spot. Second row: Imtra Touch LED reading light; Taylorbrite CCF fluorescent; Imtra/Cantalupi halogen "Patty"; Hella halogen reading light. Third row: Weems & Plath Mini Yacht Lamp; LED clusters for bulb replacement; D. R. Smith LED reading light "Little Inagua"; Imtra surface mount LED reading light; Imtra recessed reading light with "warm white" LEDs (prototype).

vary in quality, and are culled and graded by manufacturers before they leave the factory.

If this sounds like faint praise, it isn't. The long life spans of LEDs eventually justify their cost. They're extremely versatile and hardy, and with the technology developing almost hour-by-hour, they're becoming both warmer and less expensive.

Fluorescent bulbs come in several varieties, such as standard, compact, and cold cathode. Color temperatures vary from about 2,700 K all the way to 5,000 K and above, depending on whether the tubes are standard, "warm-white," "daylight," and so on. The advantages of fluorescent bulbs are long life, excellent lumens-to-watt ratio, low heat, and reasonable cost. The downside of the typical fluorescent lamp is a color temperature that's too blue and cool; however, some fluorescents are quite warm, as we shall see. Also, all fluorescents run on AC power, which means that they must be adapted to DC power systems by means of a built-in inverter. Sometimes this can cause radio frequency interference, so be careful if you mount a fluorescent light near sensitive electronics and communications equipment.

Incandescent lights of the familiar tungsten-filament variety cost less than any other type, and offer a warm glow. Bulbs are readily available. The downsides are that they burn out relatively quickly, offer the lowest lumens-per-watt ratio, and produce heat. Interestingly, it's getting harder to find standard incandescent-bulb lamps in marine stores these days. (Replacement bulbs are available, but new lamps are scarcer.) Most light makers are now going with halogen and xenon bulbs.

Halogen and xenon bulbs are closely related to the standard incandescent. The difference is that the inert gas inside the bulb contains halogen, which helps return tungsten particles to the filament, slowing the burnout process as well as enabling the filament to be heated to a brighter temperature. In order for the process to work, the bulb has to be very hot. This, in turn, means that the bulb needs to be made of thick, heat-resistant glass or a quartz-based crystal.

Some bulbs contain high-quality xenon as the inert gas. This enables a more efficient process of returning tungsten to the filament, increasing brightness and bulb life still further.

Aside from cost, the downside to all this is—you guessed it—more heat, which can not only make it uncomfortable for people inside the boat in warm weather, but cause fire if a light is thoughtlessly installed. Even so, halogen bulbs are an excellent balance of cost with effective light. They typically show a whiter, higher color temperature than standard incandescents; about 3,200 K versus 2,800 K. This can be harsh in some situations, but makes great task lighting. And they have a good lumens-per-watt ratio of about 15.

Despite the overwhelming scientific concepts that underlie an evaluation of lights, it's not so difficult to define what kind of light serves what purpose best. Like the majority of sailors, we lean toward warmer lights for area lighting (like halogen lamps in the main cabin areas for reading lights) and fluorescent for galley, head, and engineroom areas. When we can substitute LEDs without sacrificing too much warmth or dramatically increasing cost, we will.

So, we went shopping at West Marine and ordered a pretty fair sampling of what's on their shelves. We also solicited lights from several of the big light purveyors and talked to experts about the state of the art in DC cabin lighting. Generally, the lights we evaluated were in two categories—overhead dome-type lights with wide light spread for area illumination, and bulkhead-mounted reading lights. Also included are a few LED lights that could go either way, and LED replacement clusters for incandescent bulbs.

We powered the lights with a 12-volt power supply, dimmed the office to an ambient light of 2 lux, and turned on the lights one by one. We measured the spread of each light from 12 inches away, and took photos for comparison. We took a multitude of light meter readings for each light from different angles and distances, using a Meterman LM631. Then, because handheld light meter readings can fluctuate so much, we took into account the spread of readings, did some averaging, added some Kentucky windage, and came up with the rather simple ratings—Dim, Low, Medium, Bright, and Intense. To measure heat produced by the lights, we used a Raytek Mini-Temp infrared temperature

Two basic requirements for mattresses on board boats are that they offer a comfortable platform and they can allow air to circulate beneath and around them to minimize mildew. Such a simple premise is surprisingly difficult to meet in practice. For that reason, when we discovered the Froli Sleep System, we were very encouraged about the nights we'd be spending on board from then on.

Resembling a child's plastic puzzle, the Froli Sleep System has numerous parts that fit together to create an adjustable spring system for berths of any size and almost any configuration. This product's existence in the U.S. came about because Elke Nickle and her husband Wolfgang enjoyed spending time on board their boat, but didn't like the bunks they had. They discovered the Froli Sleep System at a boat show in Germany, and after buying it, decided to become the U.S. distributors.

The Froli Sleep System is a user-assembled spring base that, when made up, fits under a foam rubber mattress or bunk cushion. It provides both flexibility (a quality sorely needed with most platform-type beds), adjustability (depending on a user's body weight and personal preference from very firm to soft), and ventilation.

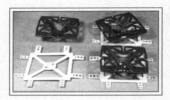

The components of the Froli Sleep System fit together in different ways as well as in different configurations to make the spring system adjustable as well as versatile.

Shown here with a small section of four-inch foam, the Froli Sleep System is ideal for promoting ventilation beneath a mattress.

A tribute to injection molding, the Froli spring base can be assembled and adjusted to be very firm or very soft, with each of five adjustments possible in any area. For instance, the base needs to be much softer in the leg area, firm in the torso areas, perhaps medium under the shoulders, and light under the head. The adjustments can be made and unmade, until the user finds it just right. Even more adjustability is provided by tension rings, shaped like four-leaf clovers, which are snapped on the top of the spring elements.

When assembled, the lightweight "spring" is less than 1.5 inches thick and fits easily under any boat bunk cushion. No fasteners and no tools are needed, other that the press-on one supplied. The entire base can be disassembled and done over again, if need be. To provide for non-rectangular shapes, the spring elements swivel, and half-size elements are available.

Although there are numerous models of the Froli system, we tested the "Travel" version, which makes a bunk spring about 27.5 by 79 inches and the "Star," which is 31.5 by 79 inches. Both sell for $169.95. The warranty is five years, but it would appear that the Froli spring system should last for many more than that.

sensor to report the surface temperature of a piece of brown particle board held 6 inches from the front of the lens for 10 minutes. (In each case, the ambient office temperature was kept at 75°F.) And we measured current draw using a Radio Shack digital multimeter.

▷ **The Bottom Line** The Alpenglow compact fluorescent light is warm and adjustable in four levels (two for the red LED light, two for the white fluorescent), the light it casts will pleasantly fill the typical saloon aboard a big variety of boats, and it's fairly priced (see chart).

The cold-cathode fluorescent lights from Taylor Made Products have an impressive design and cast a warm, even light. The one we examined—the self-contained bulkhead-mounted reading light—is expensive, and you would have to replace the whole fixture, but it should have a very long life span. Con-

sider these if you're thinking of replacing reading lights in the master cabin.

Among the incandescent dome lights, we'd buy the mahogany-based West/ABI 20-watt xenon model No. 260786, and put it on a dimmer, or the Imtra/Cantalupi halogen "Chip." For an incandescent bulkhead light, we'd go with the Catalupi "Patty" model.

As for LED lights, in our view they're still a bit too cool-colored and directional to be used where a warm mood is a must, but if you can use a coolish, medium-widespread LED for reading in the bunk, Daniel R. Smith's "Little Inagua" would be a good bet. Another strong contender for that job would be Imtra's F1 "warm white" cluster, which at this writing is just going to market. The former is more of a whole-bunk light, the latter more for directing right at a book. Imtra's Touch LED would do very well on its gooseneck over a nav table.

Appendix
Contacts and Useful Websites

3M Scotch Brand, 888/364-3577, www.3m.com

A Glass Act, 888/432-4312

Absolute Coatings, 914/636-0700, www.lastnlast.com

Acco Chain & Lifting, 800/967-7222, www.accochain.com

Accon Marine, 727/572-9202, www.acconmarine.com

Ace Hardware, 866/290-5334, www.acehardware.com

Achilles, 201/438-6400, www.achillesusa.com

ACR Electronics, 800/432-0227, www.acrelectronics.com

Adventure Medical Kits, 800/324-3517, www.adventuremedicalkits.com

Airforce Sails, 866/255-6100, www.airforceails.com

Airpower America, 800/225-2224, www.airpoweramerica.com

Alexander Roberts, 949/250-4571

Allied Tools, 818/364-2333, www.alliedtools.com

ALS Association, 888/949-2577, www.alsa.org

Ancor Products, 800/424WIRE, www.ancorproducts.com

Andek Corp., 856/786-6900, www.andek.com

Andersen (Scandvik), 800/535-6009, www.andersenwinches.com

Antal (Euro Marine Trading), 800/272-7712, www.euromarinetrading.com

Antenex, 361/855-0250, www.antennex.com

Aqua Force Future Products, 706/776-6072, www.aquaforce.com

Aqua-Buff 2000, 802/824-3954, www.aqua-buff.com

Aqualarm, 888/298-6206, www.aqualarm.net

Aramid Rigging (Southern Spars), 401/683-6966, www.southernspars.com

Armada, Blue Water Paints, 800/432-4333, www.armadacoatings.com

Armex & Accustrip, 978/988-8034

Atkins & Hoyle, 877/415-5167, www.atkinshoyle.com

Atlantic Sail Traders, 800/946-3800, www.usedsails.com

ATN, 800/874-3671, www.atninc.com

Attwood, 616/897-9241, www.attwoodmarine.com

Aurora Marine Industries, 866/214-3444, www.auroramarine.com

AutoProp, 401/847-7960, www.autoprop.com

Bacon & Associates, 410/263-4880, www.baconsails.com

Barnacle, 800/295-2766, www.barnacleanchors.com

Barton (Imtra), 508/995-7000, www.imtra.com

Barton Marine Equipment, Ltd., 800/343-8294, www.bartonmarine.com

Bass Pro Shops, 800/976-6344, www.probass.com

Beckson, 203/333-1412, www.beckson.com

Benchmade, 800/800-7427, www.benchmade.com

BEP Marine, 877/730-3700, www.bepmarineinc.com

Big Bully Natural Orange, 800/556-5074, www.crcindustries.com

BioBands Distributors, Inc., 800-BIO-BANDS, www.biobands.com

BioSok, Petrol Rem Inc., 800/246-2275, www.petrolrem.com/biosok

Blaster Chemical Co., 216/901-5800, www.????

Blue Sea Systems, 800/222-7617, www.bluesea.com

Blue Water Marine Paint, 800/628-8422, www.bluewatermarinepaint.com

Boat Armor, 513/489-7600, www.evercoat.com

BOAT/U.S., 703/461-4666, www.boatus.com

BOAT/U.S., 800/395-2628, www.boatus.com

BoatLife, 800/382-9706, www.boatlife.com

Boeshield, 800/962-1732, www.boeshield.com

Bogart Engineering (TriMetric), 831/338-0616, www.bogartengineering.com

Bosworth, 888/438-1110, www.thebosworthco.com

Box, Slide Anchor, 888/445-4869, www.slideanchor.com

Boye Knives, 800/853-1617, www.boyeknives.com

BP Solar, 410/981-0240, www.bpsolar.com

Briggs & Stratton, 800/743-4115, www.briggsandstratton.com

Brinkmann, 800/468-5252, www.Brinkmanncorp.com

Bristol Finish (C Tech Marine), 321/752-7533, www.bristolfinish.com

Bristol Flare Corp. 800/788-3008, www.orionsignals.com.

Bruce, Lofrans, Muir (Imtra Corp.), 800/989-2580, www.imtra.com

Brunton (Nexus/Silva), 888/284-2667, www.brunton.com

Bucket Potty Seat, 401/467-2750, www.toddusa.com

Bulwagga, 888/674-4465, www.noteco.com/bulwagga

Bushnell, 800/423-3537, www.bushnell.com

Cabot, 617/345-0100, www.cabot-corp.com

Cal-June Jim-Buoy, 818/761-3516, www.jimbuoy.com

Cameron Group, 360/650-0047

Campbell Chain, 919/781-7200, www.cooperhandtools.com

Captain Al's, 860/232-9065, www.boatus.com

Captain's Choice, Enviro-bond, Petroleum Environmental Tech, Inc., 616/258-0400, www.enviro-bond.com

Carborundum & Norton, 800/268-2262, www.carborundumabrasives.com

Casio, Inc., 973/252-7570, www.casio.com

Castlok (Loos & Co.), 860/928-7981, www.loosco.com

CDI, 607/ 749-4599, www.sailcdi.com

Celestron, 310/328-9560, www.celestron.com

Charles Industries, 800/830-5623, www.charlesindustries.com

Chutescoop (V. F. Shaw Co.), 800/367-9046, www.chutescoop.com

Citizen USA, 800/321-1023, www.citizenwatch.com

Clean Water Solutions' Microbial Powder, 401/846-4141, www.cleanwatersolutionsinc.com

Clipmount, 877/998-8646, www.good2goproducts.com

C-Map, 800/424-2627, www.c-map.com

Cobra, 773/622-2269, www.cobra.com

Cole Hersee Co., 617/268-2100, www.colehersee.com

Coleman Powermate, 800/445-1805, www.colemanpowermate.com

Collinite, 315/732-2282, www.collinite.com

Columbian Rope, 800/821-4391, www.columbianrope.com

Corrosion Technologies (CorrosionX), 800/638-7361, www.corrosionx.com

C-Plath, 800/638-0428, www.weems-plath.com

CQR, Claw, and Delta (Lewmar), 203/458-6200, www.lewmar.com

CRC Industries, 800/556-5074, www.crcindustries.com

Crewsaver, 619/239-9700, www.crewsaver.co.uk

Cruising Direct, 888/424-7388, www.cruisingdirect.com

CruzPro, 64-9-838-3331, www.cruzpro.com

Current Inc. (Silent Running), 877/436-6542, www.silentrunning.us

DaNard Marine Products, 805/983-8285, www.danardmarine.com

Danforth, 978/281-0440, www.danforthcompass.com

Danforth, Tie Down Engineering, 800/241-1806, www.danforthanchors.com

Davis Anchors, 800/328-4770, www.davisanchor.com

Davis Instruments, 510/732-9229, www.davisnet.com

DBC Marine Safety Systems, 800/931-3221, www.dbcmarine.com

Defender Industries, 800/628-8225, www.defender.com

Deka/East Penn Mfg., 610/682-6361, www.eastpenn-deka.com

Deks Olje, 800/321-3444, www.floodco.com

Del Mar (Emtech La Costa), 727/447-5919

Digital Antenna, 954/747-7022. www.digitalantenna.com

Dolphinite, 978/356-9834, www.dolphinite.com

Dometic/Sealand, 800/321-9886, www.dometicsanitation.com

Douglas, 800/368-4527, www.douglasbattery.com

Doyle Sails, 800/541-7601,
www.doylesails.com

Drip-Free Packing,
727/345-3354

Dumond Chemicals (Peel Away 1
and Marine Safety Strip),
212/869-6350,
www.peelaway.com

Duramax Marine, 440/633-1616,
www.duramax-marine.com

Easylock (Scandvik Marine),
800/535-6009,
www.scandvik.com

Eclectic Products, 800/767-4667,
http://eclecticproducts.com

Edson Marine, 508/995-9711,
www.edsonmarine.com

Elmer's, 800/848-9400,
www.elmers.com

Emerson, 310/212-7455,
www.emersonknives.com

Energy1, 757/673-7200,
www.energy1batterines.com

EOS Design, LLC (Air Head),
740/392-3642,
www.airheadtoilet.com

E-Paint Co., 800/258-5998,
www.epaint.net

Epifanes, 800/269-0961,
www.epifanes.com

Euro Marine Trading,
401/849-0060,
www.euromarinetrading.com

Eveready, 800/742-8377,
www.E-FLASH.com

Evergreen Pacfic,
425/493-1451,
www.evergreenpacific.com

Extrasport, 305/633-2945,
www.extrasport.com

Facnor, 704/597-1502,
www.facnor.com

Falcon Safety Products,
Inc.908/707-4900,
www.falconsafety.com

Fällkniven, 46-921-544-22,
www.fallkniven.com

Far East Sails, 206/339-3618,
www.fareastsails.com

Fastrac, 905/763-8711,
www.fastrac.globalserve.net

Federal Process Corp. (Lube-It-All),
800/846-7325,
www.federalprocess.com

Felco SA Mélèzes, 41 32 858 14 66,
www.felco.ch/en/monde.asp

Fiberglass Kreme Cleaner,
800/382-9706,
www.boatlife.com

Filter Wiz, 703/791-2921

Fiorentino, 800/777-0732,
www.paraanchor.com

Fireboy-Xintex, 866/350-9500,
www.fireboy-xintex.com

Flexdel Corp., 888/353-9335,
www.aquagard-boatpaint.com

Flexiteek Americas, Inc., 954/973-4335, www.flexiteekusa.com

Flojet, 949/859-4945,
www.flojet.com

Fluke Corporation, 800/44FLUKE,
www.fluke.com

Forespar Products (Passagemaker),
949/858-8820,
www.forespar.com

Forespar, 800/266-8820,
www.forespar.com

Fortress, 800/825-6289,
www.fortressanchors.com

Fox 40 Whistle, 888/663-6940,
www.fox40whistle.com

Franmar Chemical, Inc. (Soy-Gel),
800/538-5069,
www.soysolvents.com

Frederiksen, 727/545-1911,
www.ronstan.com

FSR, Davis Instruments,
510/732-9229,
www.davisnet.com

Fujinon, 973/633-5600,
www.fujinon.co.jp

Fulton Industries, 800/537-5012,
www.fultonindoh.com

Furlboom (Yachting Systems),
949/642-9530,
www.furlboom.com

Furuno, 360/834-9300,
www.furuno.com

FX Sails, 877/237-2457,
www.fxsails.com

Fynspray (Imtra), 508/995-7000,
www.imtra.com

Galley Maid, 561/848-8696,
www.galleymaid.com

GAM Electronics, 603/627-1010,
www.gamelectronicsinc.com

Gardner Bender, 800/822-9220,
www.gardnerbender.com

Garhauer, 909/985-9993,
www.garhauermarine.com

Garmin, 913/397-8200,
www.garmin.com

Garrity, 203/245-8383,
www.garritylites.com

GE/Marine, 800/626-2000,
www.gesealants.com

Gerber Knives, 800/950-6161,
www.gerberblades.com

Gibb (Navtec), 203/458-3163,
www.navtec.net

Gil Marine, 440/891-0999,
www.gilmarine.com

Gill North America, 800/822-6504,
www.gillna.com

Givens Marine Survival Co.,
401/624-7900,
www.givensliferafts.com

Glomex (Imtra) 508/995-7000,
www.glomex.it

Gloucester Co., 800/343-4963,
www.dap.com

Great Neck, 516/746-5352,
www.greatnecksaw.com

Greenwood Forest Products,
800/333-3898

Groco, 410/712-4242,
www.groco.com

Guest/Marinco, 800/767-8541,
www.marinco2.com

Hall Spars & Rigging, 401/253-4858,
www.hallspars.com

Hans-C, 800/728-4645,
www.hansanchor.com

Harken, 262/691-3320,
www.harken.com

Hayn Marine, 800/346-4296,
www.haynmarine.com

Healer Products, Inc., 800/223-5765, www.healerprod.com

Hella, 800/247-5924,
www.hellausa.com

Heller Glänz, 800/414-3466,
www.hellerglanz.com

Helly-Hansen, 425/883-8823, www.hellyhansen.com

Henderson Whale, 978/531-0021, www.whalepumps.com

Henkel Consumer Adhesives, 800/321-0253, www.duckproducts.com

Henri-Lloyd, 770/753-9887, www.henri-lloyd.com

Holland Yacht Equipment, 650/595-2009, www.hye.nl

Holt Allen, 888/390-3242, www.holtallen.com

Honda, 770/497-6400, www.hondapowerequipment.com

Honey Teak, 772/287-6077, www.signaturefinish.com

Hood Sailmakers, 800/888-4106, www.hoodsailmakers.com

Hood Yacht Systems (Pompanette), 813/ 885-2182, www.pompanette.com

Hotwire Enterprises, 727/217-9809, www.svhotwire.com

Hough Marine and Machine Co., Inc., 800/423-3509

HRO Systems, 800/366-4476, www.hrosystems.com

Huskie Tools, Inc. 630/893-7755, www.huskietools.com

HydroBubble, 919/404-0409, www.anchorconcepts.com

Ibsen Company (Norscot Shaft Seal), 206/364-2284

Icom, 425/454-7619, www.icomamerica.com

ICP Global Technologies, 514/270-5770, www.icpglobal.com

Imbiber Beads, Imbibitive Technologies, 888/843-2323, www.imbiberbeads.com

Imray-Iolaire, 44-0-1480 462114, www.imray.com

Indasa, 800/326-5909, www.indasausa.com

Innovative Lighting, 800/949-4888, www.innovativelight.com

Instant Rust Out, 800/654-0791, www.ironout.com

Interlux Yacht Finishes (Interstrip), 800/INTERLUX, www.interlux.com

Interlux, 800/468-7589, www.yachtpaint.com

Interstate, 800/541-8419, www.interstatebattery.com

Intertape Polymer, Inc., 800/474-8273, www.intertapepolymer.com

Island Marine Products, 727/698-3938, www.islandmarineproducts.com

ITT Industries (Rule), 978/281-0440, www.rule-industries.com,

Jabsco (ITT Industries), 949/859-4945, www.jabsco.com

Jack Rabbit Marine, 203/961-8133, www.jackrabbitmarine.com

Jim-Buoy, 818/761-3516, www.jimbuoy.com

John Mast, 45-43-90-5600, www.johnmast.dk/uk/hi-low

Johnson & Johnson, 800/526-3967, www.jnj.com

Johnson Marine, 860/873-8697, www.csjohnson.com

Johnson, 847/671-7867, www.johnson-pump.com

Johnson, 847/689-7090, www.johnson.com

JRC, 206/654-5644, www.jrcamerica.com

Katadyn North America, Inc., 800/755-6701, www.katadyn.com

Kato Marine, 410/269-1218, www.katomarine.com

Kel, 800/3342130

Kent Sporting Goods, 419/929-7021, www.kentwatersports.com

Kershaw Knives, 800/325-2891, www.kershawknives.com

Kidde, 800/880-6788, www.kiddeus.com

Kingston Anchors, 613/549-2718, www.kingstonanchors.com

Kiwi Anchor Rider, 321/385-1469, www.cruisingoutfitters.com

Kop-Coat (Pettit), 800/221-4466, www.pettitpaint.com

Kracor, 800/255-6335, www.kracor.com

KVH, 401/849-0045, www.kvh.com

Kyocera Solar Inc., 800/223-9580, www.kyocerasolar.com

Lakeland Boating, 312/276-0610, www.lakelandboating.com

Landfall Navigation, 800/941-2219, www.landfallnavigation.com

Lanocote Inc., 949/858-8820, www.forespar.com

Lear Chemical (Corrosion Block), 800/256-2548, www.learchem.com

LeathermanTool Group, 800/847-8665, www.leatherman.com

Leisure Furl (Forespar), 714/858-8820, www.leisurefurl.com

Lemar, 203/458-6200, www.lewmarusa.com

Lewmar, 203/458-6200, www.lewmar.com

Lifeline Battery, 626/969-6886, www.lifelinebatteries.com,

Lifeline PFDs, 714/893-1920, www.lifelinejackets.com

Lightwave, 800/305-3902, www.lightwave-USA.com

Link Tools, 773/248-5853, www.link-tools.com.

Lirakis Safety Harness, 800/USA-SFTY, www.landfallnavigation.com

Lopolight (Euromarine Trading), 401/849-0060, www.euromarinetrading.com

Lovett, 800/673-5976, www.lovettmarine.com

Lowrance, 800/324-1356, www.lowrance.com

LPS Laboratories, 800/241-8334; www.lpslabs.com

Luminox, 800/858-5215, www.luminox.com

Maffioli, 39 0321-692032, www.gottifredimaffioli.com

Magellan, 800/707-9971, www.magellangps.com

Maptech, 978/792-1197, www.maptech.com

Marine Development & Research Corp. (MDR), 516/546-1162, www.mdramazon.com

Marine Products Engineering, 310/831-2877, www.vangmaster.com

Marine Products International, 800/845-5255, www.marinehose.com

MarineDeck 2000 (STAZO Marine Equipment), 207/354-0914, www.stazo.nl, www.marquipt.com

Mariner's Choice (Sea Spray), 800/966-9974, www.multchoice.com

Mariner's Choice Sea Spray, 562/598-5861

Marsolve, 203/359-1000, www.marsolve.com

Martec, 562/435-4494, www.martec-props.com

Marykate, 631/244-8550, www.crcindustries.com

Mastervolt, 207/354-0618, www.mastervoltusa.com

Max Prop, 800/523-7558, www.max-prop.com

Maxwell, 714/689-2900, www.maxwellmarine.com

Mayfair (Johnson), 847/671-7867, www.johnson-pump.com

Medical Sea Pak, 800/832-6045, www.firstaidpak.com

Meguiar's, 800/347-5700, www.meguiars.com

Mercury Marine, 920/929-5040, www.mercurymarine.com

Mercury, 920/929-5040, www.mercurymarine.com

Micrologic, 450/664-2664, www.micromediaplus.com

Millworks Specialties International, 916/961-7378, www.underwaterglue.com

Minn Kota, 800/227-6433, www.minnkotamotors.com

Minney's Yacht Surplus, 949/548-4192, www.minneysyachtsurplus.com

Mission, 714/777-7881 www.missionknives.com

Moonlite Marine, 949/645-0130, www.moonlitemarine.com

MotorGuide, 920/929-5040, www.motorguide.com

MPH System Specialities, Inc., 866/331-0572, www.strike-hold.com

MPS (Swobbit Perfect Pole), 800/362-9873, www.swobbit.com

Mr. Funnel (Smart Tech LLC), 907/688-1550, www.mrfunnel.com

MTI Industries, 800/383-0269, www.mtiindustries.com

Mustang Survival, 800/526-0532, www.mustangsurvival.com

Musto, 800/553-0497, www.musto.com

Myerchin, 909/463-6741, www.myerchin.com

Napier International Technologies, 800/564-9929

National Sail Supply, 239/693-1896, www.nationalsail.com

Nauta (Imtra), 800/989-2580, www.imtra.com

Nautical Ease (Nautical Technologies), 800/783-7507, www.nauticalease.com

Nautical Engineering, 248/349-1034

Nautical Specialties Inc. (Lasdrop), 800/940 7325, www.lasdrop.com

Navionics, 800/48-5896, www.navionics.com

Navman, 866/628-6261, www.navman.com

Navtec Norseman Gibb, 203/458-3163, www.navtec.net

Neil Pryde Sails, 203/375-2626, www.neilprydesails.com

New England Ropes, 508/678-8200, www.neropes.com

New Glass-2, 904/829-3807, www.newglass2.com

New Nautical Coatings, 800/528-0997, www.seahawkpaints.com

Newmar, 714/751-0488, www.newmarpower.com

Nikon Americas, 800/247-3464, www.nikonusa.com

Nissan, 972/323-6003, www.nissanmarine.com

Norcross, 407/370-3600, www.norcrossmarine.com

Norseman (Navtec), 203/458-3163, www.navtec.com

North Sails, 203/877-7621, www.northsails.com

Northstar, 978/897-6000, www.northstargps.com

NRS, 800/635-5202, www.nrsweb.com

On Rope 1, 866/441-7673, www.onrope1.com

Optima, 888/867-8462, www.optimabatteries.com

Orca Green Marine, 866/535-5777, www.orcagreen.com

Orion Safety Products, 800/851-5260, www.orionsignals.com

Outdoor Research, 800/421-2421, www.orgear.com

Oxen, 41-32-842-6159, www.oxenblocks.com

Pains Wessex Australia 561/883-1201, www.painswessex.com

Par (Jabsco), 800/235-6538, www.jabsco.com

Para-Tech, 800/594-0011, www.seaanchor.com

Pelican Rope Works, 800/860-7673, pelicanrope.com

Pelican, 800/473-5422, www.pelican.com

Perkins Engines Company, Ltd., 44 (0) 1733 583000, www.perkins.com

Perko, Inc., 305/621-7525, www.perko.com

Pettit & Kop-Coat, 800/221-4466, www.kop-coat.com

Pettit Paint, 800/221-4466, www.pettitpaint.com

PlasTEAK, 800/320-1841, www.plasteak.com

Plastimo USA, 866/383.1888, www.plastimousa.com

Plastimo, 866/383-1888, www.plastimousa.com

PMS Products (Boeshield),
800/962-1732,
www.boeshield.com
Poli Glow 800/922-5013,
www.poliglowproducts.com,
www.myboatstore.com
Polymeric Systems Inc., 610/935-1170, www.polymerics.com
Porta-Bote International, 800/227-8882, www.porteboat.com
Power One, 315/486-9027,
www.fountainofyouthrestore.com
Powerwinch, 888/699-4624,
www.powerwinch.com
Princeton Tec, 609/298-9331,
www.princetontec.com
Professional Mariner, 603/433-4440,
www.pmariner.com
Pro-Furl (Wichard), 800/852-7084,
www.profurl.com
Progressive Epoxy Polymers, Inc.,
603/435-7199,
www.epoxyproducts.com
Prolong International, 949/587-2700, www.prolong.com
PYI Inc., 425/355-3669,
www.pyiinc.com
Quantum Sailmakers, 410/268-1161,
www.quantumsails.com
Radio Shack, 800/THESHACK,
www.radioshack.com
Ram Mounting Systems, 206/763-8361, www.ram-mount.com
Raritan, 856/825-4900,
www.raritaneng.com
Raske & van der Meyde BV,
31-0-299-371100,
www.rm69.com
Raudaschl Sails, 416/255-3431,
www.raudaschl.co.at
Raymarine, 800/539-5539,
www.raymarine.com
Rayovac, 608/275-3340,
www.rayovac.com
Raytek, 800/866-5478,
www.raytek.com
Reef Rite (Kiwi Sail Slides),
916/489-5431, www.anzam.com
REI, 800/426-4840, www.rei.com
Revere Supply, 973/575-8811,
www.reveresupply.com

Reverso, 800/225-2224,
www.reversopumps.com
Richardsons, 800/873-4057,
www.richardsonscharts.com
Ritchie, 781/826-5131,
www.ritchienavigation.com
Robertson (Simrad), 425/778-8821,
www.simradusa.net
Rode Rider, 800/688-3217,
www.roderider.com
Rolls, 800/681-9914,
www.rollsbattery.com
Ronco, 714/259-1385,
www.ronco-plastics.com
Ronstan Marine, 401/293-0539,
www.ronstanmarine.com
Ronstan, 727/545-1911,
www.ronstan.com
RPM, Inc., 330273-5090,
www.rpminc.com
Rust Free, 800/962-1732,
www.boeshield.com
Rust-Oleum, 800/553-8444,
www.rustoleum.com
Rutgerson (Challenge Sailcloth),
860/871-8030,
www.rutgerson.com
RWO, 401/845-9700,
www.rwo-marine.com
Sailing Services, 305/758-1074,
www.sailingservices.com
SailKote, 888/832-6625,
www.888teammclube.com
Sailkote, 899/262-5823,
www.mclube.com
Sailman (Bainbridge International),
781/821-2600,
www.bainbridgeint.com
Sailtec, 920/233-4242,
www.sailtec.com
Samson, 800/227-7673,
www.samsonrope.com
Sanitation Equipment (Visa Potty),
905/738-0055
Sascot Plough 30,
800/262-8464, www.
westmarine.com
Sashco, 800/289-7290,
www.sashcosealants.com
Schaefer, 508/995-9511,
www.schaefermarine.com

Scuba-Do Yacht Detailers, Sarasota,
FL, 941/587-0060,
www.boatdetail.net
Sea Bowld, 800/327-8583,
www.boatersworld.com
Sea Dog Marine, 425-259-0194,
www.seadogmarine.com
Sea Marshall Rescue Systems USA,
800/313-9714,
www.seamarshallrescue.com
Sea Recovery, 800/354-2000,
www.searecovery.com
Sea-Band, 401/841-5900,
www.sea-band.com,
Seachoice Products, 954/581-1188,
www.seachoice.com
Sea-Fire, 800/445-7680,
www.sea-fire.com
SeaLife Corp., 310/338-9757,
www.sealife1000.com
Seapower, 562/923-0838,
www.seapowerproducts.com
Seapro, 732/830-4802,
www.seapromarine.com
Sears, Roebuck & Co. (Craftsman),
800/9PAINTS, www.sears.com
Seattle Sports Co., 800/632-6163,
www.seattlesportsco.com
See Water, Inc., 888/733-9283,
www.seewaterinc.com
Seiko USA, 201/539-5730,
www.seikousa.com
Selden, Inc., 843/760-6278,
www.seldenmast.com
Seoladair, 800/437-7654,
www.boomkicker.com
SERPE-IESM (Kannad),
011 33 (0) 2 97 02 49 49,
www.serpe-iesm.com
SES Flexcharge USA, 231/547-9430,
www.flexcharge.com
Setamar, 44-0-20 8409 1582
Seven Seas Marine, 314/436-3332,
www.???
Shakespeare, 803/276-5504,
www.shakespeare-ce.com
Shell Solar Industries (Siemens),
805/482-6800,
www.shell.com/solar
Shields Rubber Corp.,
416/263-4600

Shurflo, 800/854-3218,
www.shurflo.com

Shurflo, 800/854-3218,
www.shurflo.com

Shurhold, 800/962-6241,
www.shurhold.com

Signaltone, 231/775-1373,
www.fiamm.com

Sika Corp, 201/933 8800,
www.sikacorp.com

Sikkens Cetol, 011-31 10 5033 54,
www.sikkensyachtpaints.com

Simpson Lawrence, 800/946-3527,
www.lewmar.com

Simrad, 425/712 1136,
www.simrad.com

Simrad, Inc., 425/778-8821,
www.simradusa.com

SK Watermakers, 800/489-0852,
www.skwatermakers.com

Skyblazer, Inc., 800/631-7269,
www.skyblazer.com

Smith & Co., 800/234-0330,
www.fiveyearclear.com

Snap & Zipper, 800/327-8583,
www.starbrite.com

SoftSand (Softpoint Industries),
508/754-5810,
www.softsandrubber.com

SOG Specialty Knives, 888/SOG-
BEST, www.sogknives.com

SOS Inc., 800/585-5876,
www.sospenders.com

Soundcoat Co., Inc., 949/955-9202,
www.soundcoat.com

Soundown Corp., 800/359-1036,
www.soundown.com

Spade, 216/71 869 099,
www.spade-anchor.com

Sparcraft, 704/597-1502,
www.charlestonspar.com

Spectra Watermakers, 415/526-2780,
www.spectrawatermakers.com

Speed Seal, 800/675-1105,
www.speedseal.com

Speedtech, 703/430-8055,
www.speedtech.com

Spinlock, 802/363-5258,
www.spinlock.co.uk

Spyderco, 800/828-1925,
www.spyderco.com

St. Brendan's Isle, Inc. (Lavac),
800/544-2136, www.lavac.com

St. Croix Marine, 952/858-8393,
www.davit.com

Standard Horizon, 714/827-7600,
www.standardhorizon.com

Star brite, 800/327-8583,
www.starbrite.com

Stay-Lok, 44 0-1206-391509,
www.stalok.com

Stearns, 800/333-1179,
www.stearnsinc.com

Steiner (Pioneer Research),
856/866-9191,
www.steiner-binoculars.com

Stormy Seas, 800/323-7327,
www.stormyseas.com

Streamlight, 800/523-7488,
www.streamlight.com

Strong, Tides Marine Inc.,
800/470-0949,
www.tidesmarine.com

SudBury's Bilge Cleaner, 978/281-
0440, www.rule-industries.com

Suncor, 508/732-9191,
www.suncorstainless.com

Sunmar (Ecolet), 888/341-0782,
www.sun-mar.com

Super Max, 800/824-0355,
www.creativemarine.com

Superior Polymer Products,
906/337-3355,
www.superiorpolymer.com

Superlube, 800/253-5823,
www.super-lube.com

Survival Products, 954/966-7329,
www.survivalproductsinc.com

Survival Technologies Group,
800/525-2747, www.switlik.com

Suunto, 800/543-9124,
www.suunto.com

Suzuki, 714/996-7040,
www.suzukimarine.com

Swift Instruments, 800/446-1116,
www.swift-optics.com

T&H Marine, 256/772-0164

Target Coatings, 800/752-9922,
www.targetcoatings.com

Tasco, 800/423-3537, www.tasco.com

Taylor Made, 518/725-0681,
www.taylormadegroup.com

Tek-Dek International,
604/880-3737,
www.tek-dek-international.com

Telatemp, 800/321-5160,
www.telatemp.com

Teleflex, 941/907-1000,
www.teleflexmarine.com

Tempo Products Company,
800/321-6301,
www.tempoproducts.com

The Dutchman, 203/838-0375,
www.mvpinfo.com

The PETT, 406/467-2750,
www.thepett.com

The Quantum Group, 800/432-
5599, www.qginc.com

The Sail Exchange, 800/628-8152,
www.sailexchange.com

The Sail Warehouse, 831/646-5346,
www.thesailwarehouse.com

The Sailing Foundation,
888/892-7245,
www.thesailingfoundation.org

Thetford, 800/521-3032,
www.thetford.com

Tides Marine, 800/420-0949,
www.tidesmarine.com

Titan (Lewmar), 203-458-6200,
www.lewmarusa.com

Todd Enterprises, 401/467-2750,
www.toddusa.com

Tohatsu, 972/323-6003,
www.tohatsu.com

Tommy Tape, 860/378-0111,
www.tommytape.com

Toon-brite, 800/280-3933,
www.melleemarine.com

Touchsensor Technologies, 630/221-
9000, www.touchsensor.com

TrellCom (Svelda Industries Inc.),
800/553-7036

Trewax, 800/527-5722,
www.trewax.com

Trident Marine, 800/414-2628,
www.tridentmarine.com

Triplett Corp., 800/TRIPLET,
www.triplett.com

Trojan, 800/423-6569,
www.trojanbattery.com

Turtle Wax, 800/227-9291,
www.turtlewax.com

Tylaska, 860) 572-8440,
www.tylaska.com

U.S. Battery, 888/398-7871,
www.usbattery.com

U.S. Paint, 314/621-0525,
www.uspaint.com

UK Halsey Sailmakers, 800/992-9422, www.ukhalsey.com

Ultra Safety Systems,
800/433-2628,
www.ultrasafetysystems.com

Uniden, 800/586-0409,
www.uniden.com

Unified Marine, 800/282-8725,
www.unifiedmarine.com

United Solar Systems (Uni-Solar),
800/843-3892,
www.uni-solar.com

V. F. Shaw co. (Chutescoop),
301/262-5266,
www.chutescoop.com

Valiant Technologies Inc., 877/825-4268, www.val-tech.com

Vertglas (Lovett Marine), 800/673-5976, www.lovettmarine.com

Vetus, 410/712-0740,
www.vetus.com

Victorinox, 203/929-6391,
www.swissarmy.com

Viking Life-Saving Equipment, Inc.,
305/374-5115,
www.viking-life.com

Village Marine Tec, 800/421-4503,
www.villagemarine.com

Vion (Pioneer Research),
800/257-7742,
www.pioneerresearch.com

Volvo Penta, 757/436-2800,
www.dieselnet.com

Walker Bay Boats, 888/449-2553,
www.walkerbay.com

Wal-Mart, 800/966-6546,
www.walmart.com

Wasi, 888/800-9574,
www.swiss-tech.com

Water Witch, 800/654-4783,
www.waterwitchinc.com

WD-40 Company, 619/296–0605,
www.wd40.com

Weems & Plath, 800/638-0428,
www.weems-plath.com

Wellington, 800/221-5054,
www.wellingtoninc.com

West Marine, 800/262-8464,
www.westmarine.com

Westerbeke Corp, 508/588-7700,
www.westerbeke.com

Wichard, 401/683-5055,
www.profurl.com

Wichard, 800/852-7084,
www.wichard.com

Wilcox-Crittenden, 860/447-1077,
www.wilcoxcrittenden.com

Winslow LifeRaft Co., 800/838-3012,
www.winslowliferaft.com

Wireless Concepts Inc.,
805/582-9000,
www.wireless-concepts.com

Woodworker's Supply (Mirka)
800/645-9292,
www.beta.woodworker.com

Woody Wax, 800/619-4363,
www.woody-wax.com

Woolsey/Z-Spar, 800/221-4466,
www.pettitpaint.com

Xantrex, 800/670-0707,
www.xantrex.com

X-Change-R, 800/922-4804,
www.x-change-r.com

X-Treme Tape, 866/652-9462,
www.x-tremetape.com

XYZ (DI Research & Design),
212/486-3912,
didesign@nyc.rr.com

Y-10, 203/637-9515

Yale Cordage, 207/282-3396,
www.yalecordage.com

Yale Cordage, 207/282-3396,
www.yalecordage.com

Yamaha Marine, 800/962-7926,
www.yamaha-motor.com

Yamaha, 800/962-7926,
www.yamaha-motor.com

Yanmar Marine, 770/877-9894,
www.yanmarmarine.com

Zipper Rescue Kits, 800/735-4620,
www.zipperrescue.com

Zodiac of North America, Inc.,
410/643-4141, www.zodiac.com

Index

A

Abandon-ship bags, 190
Acco Chain & Lifting, 153, 279
Air-conditioning units, 263–69
 Cool Currents, 267
AirForce Sails, 65–66, 67, 279
Air Head Environmental Toilet,
 81, 82
Airpower oil changers, 215,
 216–17, 279
Alexander Roberts turnbuckles,
 68, 69, 279
Alpenglow lights, 272–73, 277
Altitude Electric Barometer,
 113, 114
Anchoring (Bamford), 154
Anchors, 154–65
 chafing gear for, 162,
  164–65
 chain for permanent
  mooring, 151–54
 rode kellets, 159, 161
 rodes, 161–62
 sea anchors, 201–3

shackles, 160
and windlasses, 165–69
Andersen (Scandvik) winches/
 handles, 18, 19, 20, 21,
 22, 23, 279
Anderson, Don, 176
Annapolis Book of Seamanship
 (Rousmaniere), 154
Antal (Euro Marine
 Trading), 279
 blocks, 2, 4, 5
 clutches, 9–10, 11, 12
 mainsail control systems, 27
 traveler systems, 16, 17, 18
 winches/handles, 18, 20, 21,
  22, 23
Aqualarm bilge pump switches,
 75, 76, 279
Aramid Rigging, 37, 279
 high-tech shackles, 41–42
Arco-Hutton winches, 18, 19,
 20, 21
Atkins & Hoyle gear lifts, 44,
 45, 279

Atlantic Sail Traders, 62–63,
 67, 279
ATN, Inc. (Spinnaker Sleeve),
 42, 43, 44, 279
Attwood bilge pumps, 72, 73,
 74, 75, 76, 279
Autohelm Personal Compass,
 107
Autopilots, 149
 for tillers, 145–47
Avon Open Ocean raft, 195

B

Backstay adjusters, 24
Bacon & Associates sails,
 65, 279
Bamford, Don, 154
Barbecue grills, 256–58
Barnacle anchors, 156, 158, 279
Barnacle removers, 224–25
Barometers, 113–14
Barton Marine Equipment,
 Ltd., 279
 blocks, 2, 4, 5

cam cleats, 6, 7
shackles, 12
Battens, 26, 27
   Doyle Sails' rigid batten, 57
Batteries, 83–95
   boxes and trays, 93–95
   chargers, 88–91
   deep cycle AGM/gel
      batteries, 85–88
   selector switches, 91–93
   12-volt boosters, 98–99
   12-volt wet cells, 83–85
Belsha, Jerry, 222
Benchmade knives, 210–11,
   212, 279
BEP Marine, Inc., 279
   battery switches, 92
   electrical distribution
      panels, 96, 97
Berka-Bennett, Alison, 243
Bilge pumps, 71–77
   absorbers/cleaners for,
      221–25
   electric, 72–74
   manual, 71–72
   switches for, 74–77
Blake heads, 78, 79
Blocks, 1–6
   and friction, 2–3
   ratchet, 5–6
   safe working load of, 3
   snatch, 3–5
Blue Performance Bags, 253
Blue Sea Systems
   battery boxes, 94, 95
   battery switches, 92
   electrical distribution
      panels, 96, 97–98
Blue Water Paints, 229, 230,
   231, 280
Boat poles, 169–70
Booms
   in-boom furling, 31–33

rigid vangs for, 14–16
Bosworth (Gizzlers) bilge
   pumps, 71, 72, 280
Bow chocks, 162
Box anchors, 156, 280
Brehm, Bob, 24
Briggs & Stratton generator,
   104, 105, 106, 280
Brown, Eddie, 30
Bruce anchors, 155, 156, 157,
   158–59
Brunton, 280
   compasses, 108, 109, 110,
      111, 112
   GPS units, 115, 116
Buchanan, Nick, 216, 217

C
Cabin accessories
   air-conditioning units,
      263–69
   fans, 269–70
   Froli Sleep System, 276
   lights, 270–75, 277
Cal-June Jim-Buoy, 280, 282
   personal flotation devices,
      176, 177, 178, 183
   safety harnesses, 173–74
Calore, Dan, 61
Cam cleats, 6–8
Cams, 9
Carbon monoxide. *See* CO
   detectors
Castlok wire terminals, 70, 280
Caulks, 242–46
Chapman's Piloting, 154
Chargers. *See* Batteries
Charles Industries, 280
batteries, 89, 90, 92, 93
power inverter, 100, 101
Charts, electronic, 126–28
   big screen chartplotters,
      116–18

Chutescoop. *See* V. F. Shaw Co.
Cleaners, 216–19, 221–27
   gelcoat restorers, 216–17
   nonskid cleaners, 217–19, 237
   rust removers, 219, 221
Cleats. *See* Cam cleats
Cleverly, Brian, 60
Clift, Ken, 252
Clutches. *See* Rope clutches
C-Map charts, 126, 128, 280
Cobra GPS units, 114, 116, 280
Cockpit
   seats, 254–56
   tables, 251–52
CO detectors, 200–201
Cohen, Marc, 255
Cole-Hersee Co. battery
   switches, 92, 280
Coleman Powermate generator,
   104, 105, 106, 280
Collinite Corp. waxes, 240–41,
   242, 280
Colvin, Tom, 131
Compasses, 107–13
   hand-bearing, 107–10
   steering, 110–13
Complete Book of Anchoring &
   Mooring (Hinz), 154, 159
Contacts, 279–86
Cook, Fred, 3
Coolers, 260–63
   thermoelectric, 262
Corlett, Ted, 163
Corrosion, preventing, 209,
   246–50
Cotter pins, 64
C-Plath compasses, 110, 111,
   112, 280
Crewsaver inflatable PFDs,
   179, 181, 182
Cropley, Geoff, 22
Cruisair air-conditioning units,
   264–65, 267, 268

Cruising Design Inc. furling
    unit, 27, 28
Cruising Direct sails, 61,
    67, 280
Cruising guides, 127
Cummins, Clessie, 129
Curchod, Don, 41

D

Danforth, 280
    anchors, 155, 156, 157,
        158, 159
    compasses, 110, 111, 112–13
Daniel R. Smith lights,
    272–73, 277
Dashew, Steve, 25, 154
Davis Instruments, 280
    compasses/barometers, 108,
        109, 113
    hatch ventilators, 268
DBC rafts, 194, 197, 198,
    201, 280
Deadeyes. *See also* Blocks, 2
Deck hardware & accessories
    backstay adjusters, 24
    blocks, 1–6
    cam cleats, 6–8
    cockpit tables/seats, 251–52,
        254–56
    deck-mount vents, 270
    gear lifts, 44–46
    nonskid paint additives,
        236–38
    rope clutches, 8–12
    winches, 18–24
Deka batteries, 83, 84, 85,
    86–87, 280
Depthsounders, 125–26
Diesel, Rudolf Christian
    Karl, 129
Diesel engines, 129–32
    fuel funnels, 143
    horsepower needed, 131

inspecting oil filters, 141
soundproofing for,
    139–40, 142
Distribution panels, electrical,
    95–98
Docking, 151
    fenders for, 163
Doyle Sails, 56–58, 281
Dumond Chemicals (Peel
    Away), 226, 227, 281

E

Easylock (Scandvik Marine)
    clutches, 10, 12, 281
Ecolet (composting toilet),
    81–82
Edson, 281
    bilge pumps, 71, 72
    cockpit tables, 252, 254–55
Electrical systems, 83–106
    batteries, 83–88
    battery chargers, 88–91
    battery selector switches,
        91–93
    digital multimeters for,
        211–15
    distribution panels, 95–98
    portable generators, 103–6
    power inverters, 99–102
    solar panels, 102–3
    12-volt power boosters,
        98–99
Engines
    diesel, 129–32
    four-stroke outboards,
        142–44
    oil filter inspections, 141
    portable oil changers, 215–16
    soundproofing, 139–40, 142
    trolling motors, 144–45
Epifanes paints/varnishes,
    232, 233, 234–35, 238–39,
    240, 281

EPIRB (emergency position
    indicating radio beacon),
    189–91
EquipLites, 41

F

Fagan, Brian, 154
Fahrer, Betty, 63
Fans, cabin, 269–70
Far East Sails, 61, 67, 281
Fenders, 163
    fender boards, 170
Fiorentino sea anchors, 202,
    203, 281
Fireboy-Xintex, 281
    CO detectors, 200, 201
    fire extinguishers, 186,
        187, 188
Fire extinguishers, 186–89
Fisher, Brian, 41
Flares, 199
Flashlights, 182
Flotation devices. *See* Personal
    flotation devices
Flynn, Dave, 50, 51
Force 10 Seacook stove, 258,
    259–60
Forespar Products, 281
    gear lifts, 44, 45
    stoves, 258, 259
    throwable PFDs, 176,
        177, 178
    tiller extensions, 148,
        149, 150
    vangs, 14, 15, 16
Fortress anchors, 155, 156,
    158, 281
Franmar Chemical Inc. (Soy-
    Gel), 226–27, 281
Fredebaugh, Doug, 29
Frederiksen, 281
    blocks, 2, 3, 5
    mainsail control systems, 27

Freedom Marine power
    inverter, 101, 102
Fretwell, John, 30
Froli Sleep System, 276
Funnels, fuel, 143
Furlbloom, 32, 33, 281
Furling units, 27–33
    in-boom, 31–33
    roller units, 29–31
Furuno, 281
    chartplotters, 117, 118
    radar units, 119, 120, 121
    radios, 123
FXSails, 66–67, 281

G

Galley amenities
    barbecue grills, 256–58
    coolers, 260–63
    stoves, 258–60
Garelick cockpit tables, 252,
    254–55
Garhauer Marine, 281
    blocks, 2, 3, 4, 5
    gear lifts, 44, 45, 46
    vangs, 14, 15–16
Garland, Phil, 68
Garmin, 281
    chartplotters, 117, 118
    electronic charts, 126, 128
    GPS units, 114–15, 116
    radar units, 119, 120, 121
Gaskets, 222
Gear lifts, 44–46
Generators, portable, 103–6
Genoas
    discount options for, 59, 61,
        65, 66
    Doyle Sails, 57
    Neil Pryde Sails, 56
    price ranges for, 58
    UK Halsey, 52, 53
Gibb snapshackles, 12, 13

Gill, Paul, 203, 204
Gil Marine battery boxes, 94,
    95, 281
GPS units, 114–16
    in EPIRBs, 189
    holders for, 115
Great Neck tool kits, 205,
    206, 281
Grills. *See* Barbecue grills
Groco heads, 77–78, 79, 281
Guest/Marinco batteries, 89,
    90, 92, 93, 281
Gunther, Brad, 61

H

Hall Spars & Rigging vangs, 15,
    16, 281
Halyard, rigging for, 36–40
Handles, winches, 21–24
Hans-C anchors, 156, 281
Harken Yacht Equipment, 281
    blocks, 2, 5–6
    cam cleats, 6, 7
    furling units, 28, 31
    mainsail control systems, 27
    shackles, 12, 40
    traveler system, 16, 17, 18
    winches/handles, 18–19, 20,
        21, 22–3
Harnesses, tethers/safety
    harnesses, 172–74
Hatch ventilators, 268
Hayn Marine turnbuckles,
    68–69, 281
Heads. *See* Toilets
Headsails
    attaching to forestay, 60
    discount options for, 61–62,
        63, 65, 66–67
    Doyle Sails, 57–58
    furling units for, 27–33
    Hood Sailmakers, 55
    North Sails, 49, 50

Quantum Sailmakers, 51
    rigging for, 36–40
Helmsman's Backrest, 255, 256
HFL air-conditioning units,
    264–65, 265–66
Hildebrand, Dick, 41
Hinz, Earl, 154, 159
Holland, Ron, 131
Hollenback, Mark, 221
Holt Allen, 282
    blocks, 4, 6
    cam cleats, 6, 7
    winch handles, 22, 23
Honda generators, 104, 105–6,
    282
Hood, Ted, 27
Hood Sailmakers, 54–55, 282
Hood Yacht Systems furling
    units, 28, 31, 282
Hotwire Enterprises, 103, 282

I

Icom radios, 122, 123–24,
    125, 282
Impellers, 138
Imtra lights, 272–73, 277
Infrared thermometers, 214
Interlux, 282
    paints, 229, 230, 231, 232
    varnishes, 233, 234–35,
        236, 237
Interstate batteries, 84, 85, 282
Inverters. *See* Power inverters
Island Marine Products gear
    lifts, 45, 46, 282

J

Jabsco (ITT Industries), 282
    Compact head, 77
    Porta Quick oil changer, 215,
        216–17
Jacklines, 171–72, 173
Jack Rabbit Marine, 103, 282

Jim-Buoy. *See* Cal-June Jim-Buoy

John Mast in-boom furling, 32–33

Johnson Marine Hardware, 282
 bilge pump switches, 75, 76
 turnbuckles, 68, 69
 Wrap Pins, 64

JRC radar units, 119, 120, 121, 282

K

Kato Marine gear lifts, 45–46, 282

Kellets, 159, 161

Kidde fire extinguishers, 186–87, 188, 189, 282

Kingston Anchors, 155, 156, 157, 282

Kiwi Slides, 60, 282

Knives, 209–11, 212

KomfortKool air-conditioning units, 265

KVH compasses, 108, 109, 110, 282

Kwik Tek Life-line, 180

L

Lavac heads, 78

Leisure Furl, 32, 33, 282

Lewmar, 282
 anchors, 155, 156, 157, 159
 blocks, 2, 3, 4, 5, 6
 cam cleats, 6–7
 clutches, 11, 12, 12
 cockpit tables, 252, 254–55
 power windlasses, 165, 166, 167, 168–69
 shackles, 12
 traveler system, 16, 17, 18
 winches/handles, 19, 20, 21, 22, 23

Lifeline PFDs, 176, 177, 178, 282

Lifelines, 174–75

Life rafts, 192–201

Lights, cabin, 270–75, 277

Linehan, Collin, 29

Lines, 33–36
 bags for holding, 253
 high-tech & shackles for, 40–42
 nylon anchor rodes, 161–62
 for running rigging, 33, 36–40

Link Tools, 206, 282

Locator beacons, personal, 191–92

Lofrans power windlasses, 165, 166, 168

Loory, Adam, 51–52, 53

Lovett bilge pumps, 72, 74, 282

Lowrance depthsounder, 126, 282

LVJ winches, 19, 20, 21

M

Magellan GPS units, 115, 116

Mainsails
 attachment systems, 60
 control systems for, 24–27
 discount options for, 59, 61, 62, 63, 65, 66, 67
 Doyle Sails, 57, 58
 Hood Sailmakers, 54, 55
 in-boom furling, 31–33
 Neil Pryde Sails, 56
 North Sails, 49, 50
 price ranges for, 58
 Quantum Sailmakers, 50, 51
 UK Halsey, 52–53, 53–54

Mainsheets, travelers for, 16–18

Maintenance gear, 205–50
 barnacle removers, 224–25
 caulks and sealants, 242–46
 cleaners, 216–19, 221–27
 corrosion inhibitors, 246–50

digital multimeters, 211–15
gaskets, 222
infrared thermometers, 214
knives, 209–11, 212
mast climbers, 220
multitools, 208–9
nonskid paint additives, 236–38
paints and strippers, 225–33
portable oil changers, 215–16
self-bonding tape, 246
teak treatments, 238–40
tool kits, 205–7
varnishes, 233–35
waxes, 240–42

Marina guides, 127

Marinco/AFI cockpit tables, 252, 254–55

Marine Air air-conditioning units, 264–65, 268

Marine Products Engineering vangs, 14, 15, 16, 283

Marine Products International bilge pump switches, 75, 283

Marine Technology Industries CO detectors, 200, 201

Marshall Design gear lifts, 44–45

Marsolve solvent, 224, 225, 283

Marykate cleaners, 224, 225, 237, 283

Mastervolt batteries/chargers, 86–87, 87–88, 89, 90, 91, 93, 283

Mattresses. *See* Froli Sleep System

Maxwell windlasses, 165, 166, 167, 168, 283

Mayfair bilge pumps, 72, 73, 283

Medical kits, 203–4, 283

Meguiar's, 283

cleaners, 218, 219, 223, 237
waxes, 240–41, 242
Meissner winches, 19, 20, 21
Mercury engines, 142, 143, 144, 283
Mermaid air-conditioning units, 264–65, 268
Micron paints, 229, 230, 231
Minney, Ernie, 64
Minney's Yacht Surplus, 64–65, 283
Minn Kota trolling motors, 144, 145, 283
Mishra, Steve, 243
Moorings, permanent. *See also* Anchors, 151
MotorGuide trolling motors, 144, 145, 283
MPS Swobbitt Perfect Pole, 169, 170, 283
Muessel, Mike, 134
Muir power windlasses, 165, 168, 169
Multimeters, digital, 211–15
Murphy, Gordon, 130, 131
Mustang PFDs, 179, 181, 183, 283

N
Nash, G. P. B., 1
National Sail Supply, 59, 61, 67, 283
Nautical Ease cleaners, 219, 237, 283
Navigation aids, 107–28
barometers, 113–14
big-screen chartplotters, 116–18
compasses, 107–13
cruising/marina guides, 127
depthsounders, 125–26
electronic charts, 126–28
handheld GPS units, 114–16

radar systems, 118–21
radios, 121–25
steering devices, 145–50
Navionics charts, 126–27, 128, 283
Navman radios, 122–23, 283
Navtec Rigging Supplies turnbuckles, 68, 69
Neil Pryde Sails, 55–56, 283
Neri, Dan, 48–50
New England Ropes (NER), 35, 36, 37, 38, 283
Newmar, 283
batteries, 89, 90–91, 93
electrical distribution panels, 96, 97
power inverter, 101
Nexus compasses, 108, 109, 110
Nicholson, Nick, 22–23, 134, 135, 189
Norcross depthsounder, 126, 283
Norseman wire terminals, 70, 283
North Sails, 48–50, 283
spinnaker sleeves, 42, 43–44
Northstar radar units, 119, 120, 283

O
Ocean Breeze air-conditioning units, 264–65, 266, 268
Offshore Cruising Encyclopedia (Dashew), 154
Oil changers, portable, 215–17
Oil filters, inspecting, 141
Optima batteries, 86–87, 88
Outback (compass), 108

P
Paasch's Illustrated Marine Dictionary (Paasch), 1

Packing glands. *See* Stuffing boxes
Paget, Steve, 243
Paint, 227–33
bottom, 227–31
non-skid additives, 236–38
strippers for, 225–27
topside, 231–33
Para-Tech sea anchors, 202, 203, 283
Pelican hooks, 175
Perkins engines, 130, 283
Perko, 283
battery switches, 92–93
lights, 272–73
Personal flotation devices (PFDs), 176–85
belt-style, 178–79
for children, 182–85
throwable, 176–78
vest-style inflatable, 179, 181–82
Pettit Paint, 283
paint, 229, 230, 231
varnishes, 234–35, 236, 237, 238–39, 240
Plastimo, 283
compasses, 108, 109, 110, 111, 112
rafts, 193, 197, 198
shackles, 12
throw bags, 180
PLBs. *See* Locator beacons
Ploch, Mark, 56–57, 57–58
Plumbing, 71–82
bilge pumps, 71–77
toilets, 77–82
Poles. *See* Boat poles
Poli Glow Products, 284
gelcoats, 216, 217
waxes, 240–41, 242
Power inverters, 99–102
Powerwinch windlasses, 284

ProFurl, 283
    furling units, 28, 30
    in-boom furling, 32, 33
ProMariner batteries, 89,
        90, 93
Propellors, 132–35
    adjusting pitch of, 134–35
    for sail-drive units, 135
    shaft seals, 136–37, 139
    on trolling motors, 145
Propulsion devices
    diesel engines, 129–32
    four-stroke outboards, 142–44
    propellors, 132–35
    sail-drives, 134–36
    trolling motors, 144–45
Prosine power inverter,
        101, 102
Pulleys. See Blocks
Pumps
    bilge pumps, 71–77
    impellers, 138

Q
Quantum Group CO detectors,
        200, 201
Quantum Sailmakers,
        50–51, 284
Quick power windlasses,
        165, 167
Quick Rig wire terminals, 70

R
Race-Lite, 12
Radar systems, 118–21
Radios, 121–25
    EPIRBs (emergency position
        indicating radio beacon),
        189–91
    handheld, 124–25
Rafts. See Life rafts
Ram National Products, Inc.
    holders, 115

Raritan heads, 78, 284
Ratchet blocks. See also Blocks,
        5–6
Raymarine, 284
    chartplotters, 117, 118
    depthsounder, 126
    radar units, 119, 120, 121
    radios, 122, 123, 124, 125
Raytheon tiller pilots,
        145–46, 147
Resources. See Contacts
Reverso oil changer, 215,
        216–17, 284
Richardson, Fritz, 29
Rickard, Todd, 29
Ricthie compasses, 108, 109,
        110, 111, 112, 113, 284
Rigging
    cutters for, 196
    replacing standing, 66
    rods for standing, 63
    running, 33–42
    terminals, 68–70
    turnbuckles, 67–69
Ritter, Doug, 190
Robertson autopilot, 149, 284
Rodes, 161–62
Rondeau, Dan, 5
Ronstan, 284
    blocks (Cam Locks), 4, 5
    cam cleats, 6, 7
    shackles, 12, 13, 14
    tiller extensions, 148–49
    traveler system, 16, 17
    winches, 19
Ronstan Marine turnbuckles,
        68, 69, 284
Rope clutches, 8–12
Ropes. See Lines
Rousmaniere, John, 154, 180,
        182, 188
Rule bilge pumps, 71, 72, 73,
        74, 75, 76

Running rigging, 33–42
Rust removers, 219, 221
RWO, 284
    blocks, 2
    cam cleats, 6, 8
    shackles, 12
    tiller extensions, 148, 149

S
Safety gear, 171–204
    abandon-ship bags, 190
    CO detectors, 200–201
    emergency flares, 199
    fire extinguishers, 186–89
    for getting noticed, 182
    harness tethers, 172–73
    jacklines, 171–72
    lifelines, 174–75
    life rafts, 192–201
    medical kits, 203–4
    406-MHz EPIRBs, 189–91
    personal flotation devices,
        176–85
    personal locator beacons,
        191–92
    personal strobe lights,
        185–86
    safety harnesses, 173–74
    sea anchors, 201–3
    throw bags, 180
    whistles, 184
Sail-drive units, 134–36
Sail Exchange, 65, 67
Sail-handling equipment
    attachment system, 60
    blocks, 1–6
    furling units, 27–33
    mainsail control systems,
        24–27
    mainsheet travelers, 16–18
    rigid boom vangs, 14–16
    running rigging, 33–40
    shackles, 12–14, 40–42

spinnaker sleeves, 42–44

Sails. *See also* specific sails;
Sail-handling equipment,
47–67
attachment system of, 60
construction of, 47–48
discount options for, 59,
61–67
Doyle Sails, 56–58
Hood Sailmakers, 54–55
Neil Pryde Sails, 55–56
North Sails, 48–50
Quantum Sailmakers, 50–51
UK Halsey Sailmakers,
51–54

Sailtec backstay adjusters, 24,
284

Sail Warehouse, 62, 67

Samson Ropes, 35, 36, 37, 38,
284

Sascot anchors, 156, 158, 284

Schaefer Marine, 284
blocks, 2, 3
cleats, 6, 7, 8–9
furling units, 28, 31
in-boom furling, 32, 33
mainsail control systems, 27
shackles, 12, 13, 14
traveler system, 16, 17
winches/handles, 19, 22

Sea anchors, 201–3

Sea-Dog Marine, 284
turnbuckles, 68
winch handles, 22, 23

Sea-Fire Marine fire
extinguishers, 186, 187,
188, 284

Seafit tool kits, 205, 207

Sea Hawk paints, 229, 230, 231

SeaLand toilets, 79, 80

Sealants, 242–46

Sears Craftsman tool kit,
205–6, 284

Seats. *See* Cockpit

SeeWater bilge pump switches,
76–77

Selden Inc., 284
furling units, 28, 31
mainsail control systems, 27
vangs, 14, 15

Seoladair vangs, 14, 15, 284

Shackles, 12–14
on anchors, 160
for high-tech line, 40–42
Wrap Pins for, 64

Shakespeare radios, 124, 284

Sharland, Dirk, 59, 61

Sheller, Scott, 65

Shotwell, Gary, 29

Shurflo, 285
bilge pumps, 72, 73–74, 75
bilge pump switches, 75–76
portable oil changers, 215, 216

Signal flags, 199

Simas, Ken, 130

Simrad, 285
chartplotters, 117, 118
radar units, 119, 120, 121
tiller autopilots, 145–47

Small-Boat Seamanship Manual
(International Marine), 154

Smith, Robert A., 154

SnapIt cockpit tables, 254

Snapshackles. *See also*
Shackles, 4, 12–13

Snatch blocks. *See also* Blocks,
3–5

Solar panels, 102–3

SOS Inc. (SOSpenders), 285
PFDs, 177, 179, 181, 183
safety harnesses, 174

Soundproofing materials,
139–40, 142

Spade anchors, 155, 156, 157,
158, 285

Sparcraft, 285

snapshackles by, 13
vangs, 14, 15

Speedtech WeatherMate
Electronic Barometer, 113,
114, 285

Spinlock, 285
clutches, 9, 10–11, 12
Powercleat, 7–8, 10
tiller extensions, 148,
149–50

Spinnakers, sleeves for, 42–44

Spyderco, 285
knives, 210–11, 212
multitools, 208

St. Croix Marine gear lifts, 44,
45, 46, 285

Sta-Lok Terminals, Ltd., 285
turnbuckles, 68, 69
wire terminals, 70

Standard Horizon
depthsounder, 126
radios, 122, 123, 124, 125

Standing rigging
replacing, 66
rod for, 63
terminals, 68, 69–70
turnbuckles, 67–69

Star brite, 285
cleaners, 218, 219, 221,
224–25, 237
poles, 170
waxes, 240–41, 242

Staying Put (Fagan), 154

Stearns PFDs, 179, 181, 183, 285

Steering devices
Robertson autopilot, 149
tiller autopilots, 145–47
tiller extensions, 147–50

Stoves, 258–60

Strippers. *See* Paint

Strobe lights, personal, 185–86

Stuffing boxes. *See also*
Propellors, 136, 137

Suncor, 285
    blocks, 4
    shackles, 12, 13
Suunto compasses, 108, 109,
    110, 285
Suzuki engines, 142, 143–44, 285
Switlik rafts, 195, 197, 198,
    199–200

T

Tables. *See* Cockpit
Tackles, 1–2
Tape, self-bonding, 246
Teak, treatments for, 238–40
Teleflex depthsounder, 126
Tempo Products, 285
    battery boxes, 94, 95
    oil changer, 215, 216–17
Terminals, rigging, 68, 69–70
Tethers, harness, 172–73
Thermometers. *See* Infrared
    thermometers
Thetford toilets, 79, 80, 285
T & H Marine battery boxes,
    94, 95, 285
3M Scotch Brand, 279
    abrasive sheets, 226
    caulks & sealants, 244–45
    cleaners/absorbers, 218,
        222, 237
    corrosion inhibitors,
        248–49
    waxes, 240–41, 242
Throw bags, 180
Tillers
    autopilots for, 145–47
    extensions for, 147–50
Titan handles, 22, 23, 285
Todd Enterprises battery boxes,
    94–95, 285
Toilets, 77–82
    composting, 80–81
    portable, 79–80

Tools
    corrosion of, 209
    knives, 209–11, 212
    multitools, 208–9
    tool kits, 205–7
Toss, Brion, 37, 38, 40
TouchSensor Technologies bilge
    pump switches, 76, 285
Travelers, mainsheet, 16–18
Trojan batteries, 86–87,
    87–88, 285
Trolling motors, 144–45
Trunnion, 4
Turnbuckles, 67–69
    Wrap Pins for, 64
Tylaska shackles, 13, 14, 286

U

U.S. Paint, 286
    Awlgrip, 232, 233, 237, 238
    AwlSpar, 234–35
UK Halsey Sailmakers,
    51–54, 286
Ultra Safety Systems bilge
    switches, 75, 76, 286
Uniden, 286
    depthsounder, 126
    radios, 122, 123, 124
Universal engines, 130

V

V. F. Shaw Co. (Chutescoop),
    42, 43, 44, 286
Vangs, rigid boom, 14–16
Varnishes, 233–35
    teak treatments, 238–40
Veenstra, Alan, 29–30
Vents, deck-mount, 270
Viking RescYou raft, 195,
    197, 286
Villiers, Alan, 1
Vion compasses, 107, 108,
    109, 286

Visa heads, 79, 80
*Visual Encyclopedia of Nautical
    Terms Under Sail, The,* 1
Volvo engines, 130–31

W

Wadson, Alex, 37
Wal-Mart power booster, 98,
    99, 286
Walters, Neil, 46
Water Witch bilge pump
    switches, 77, 78, 286
Waxes, 240–42
Way, Jim, 176
Websites, 279–86
Weems & Plath, 286
    barometers, 113–14
    compasses, 108, 109
    lights, 272–73
Westerbeke Corp., 286
    air-conditioning units,
        264–65
    engines, 130
West Marine, 286
    abandon-ship bags, 190
    anchors, 156, 159
    batteries, 83, 84, 86–87
    battery boxes, 94, 95
    battery switches, 92
    bilge pumps, 72, 74, 75, 76
    boat poles, 170
    caulks & sealants, 244–45
    cleaners, 218, 219, 237
    electrical distribution
        panels, 96, 97, 98
    fuel funnels, 143
    hatch ventilators, 268
    knives, 210–11
    oil changers, 215, 216–17
    paint stripper, 226, 227
    paints/varnishes, 229, 230,
        231, 234–35, 236, 237,
        238–39, 240

power booster, 98, 99
radios, 122, 123, 124
rafts, 193, 194, 195, 197,
    198, 200
tethers, 172
throwable PFDs, 177
throw bags, 180
tool kits, 205–6, 207
waxes, 240–41, 242
Whale bilge pumps, 71, 72, 73
Whistles, 182, 184
Wichard, 286
    blocks, 2, 4
    cam cleats, 7
    shackles, 12, 13–14, 160
    tethers, 172
    tiller extensions, 148, 149

Wilcox-Crittenden heads, 77,
    78, 79, 286
Winches, 18–24
    handles, 21–24
    power windlasses, 165–69
Windlasses. *See* Winches
Wind vanes, 149
Winslow LifeRaft Co., 193, 194,
    197, 198–99, 286
Woodhouse, Tim, 54–55, 58

X
Xantrex Technologies, Inc., 286
    batteries/chargers, 89, 90,
        91, 93
    power booster, 98, 99
    power inverter, 101, 102

Y
Yale, Tom, 41
Yale Cordage, 35, 36, 37–38,
    39, 286
    Yale Loups (shackles), 40–41
Yamaha Marine, 286
    engines, 142, 143, 144
    generators, 104, 105, 106
Yanmar engines, 130,
    131–32, 286
Yourieff, Tim, 55–56

Z
Zodiac rafts, 195, 197, 286